Collective emotions and political violence

Manchester University Press

New Approaches to Conflict Analysis

Series editors: Peter Lawler (School of Social Sciences, University of Manchester) and Emmanuel-Pierre Guittet (Centre for Conflict, Liberty and Security, CCLS, Paris)

Until recently, the study of conflict and conflict resolution remained comparatively immune to broad developments in social and political theory. When the changing nature and locus of large-scale conflict in the post-Cold War era is also taken into account, the case for a reconsideration of the fundamentals of conflict analysis and conflict resolution becomes all the more stark.

New Approaches to Conflict Analysis promotes the development of new theoretical insights and their application to concrete cases of large-scale conflict, broadly defined. The series intends not to ignore established approaches to conflict analysis and conflict resolution, but to contribute to the reconstruction of the field through a dialogue between orthodoxy and its contemporary critics. Equally, the series reflects the contemporary porosity of intellectual borderlines rather than simply perpetuating rigid boundaries around the study of conflict and peace. *New Approaches to Conflict Analysis* seeks to uphold the normative commitment of the field's founders yet also recognises that the moral impulse to research is properly part of its subject matter. To these ends, the series is comprised of the highest quality work of scholars drawn from throughout the international academic community, and from a wide range of disciplines within the social sciences.

PUBLISHED

Christine Agius *Neutrality, sovereignty and identity: the social construction of Swedish neutrality*

Tim Aistrope *Conspiracy theory and American foreign policy: American foreign policy and the politics of legitimacy*

Eşref Aksu *The United Nations, intra-state peacekeeping and normative change*

Michelle Bentley *Syria and the chemical weapons taboo: exploiting the forbidden*

M. Anne Brown *Human rights and the borders of suffering: the promotion of human rights in international politics*

Anthony Burke and Matt McDonald (eds) *Critical security in the Asia-Pacific*

Ilan Danjoux *Political cartoons and the Israeli–Palestinian conflict*

Lorraine Elliott and Graeme Cheeseman (eds) *Forces for good: cosmopolitan militaries in the twenty-first century*

Clara Eroukhmanoff *The securitisation of Islam: covert racism and affect in the United States post-9/11*

Greg Fry and Tarcisius Kabutaulaka (eds) *Intervention and state-building in the Pacific: the legitimacy of 'cooperative intervention'*

Anna Geis, Maéva Clément and Hanna Pfeifer (eds) *Armed non-state actors and the politics of recognition*

Emmanuel-Pierre Guittet *Counter-terror by proxy: the Spanish State's illicit war with ETA*

Sophie Haspeslagh *Proscribing peace: how listing armed groups as terrorists hurts negotiations*

Naomi Head *Justifying violence: communicative ethics and the use of force in Kosovo*

Charlotte Heath-Kelly *Death and security: memory and mortality at the bombsite*

Richard Jackson *Writing the war on terrorism: language, politics and counter-terrorism*

Tami Amanda Jacoby and Brent Sasley (eds) *Redefining security in the Middle East*

Matt Killingsworth, Matthew Sussex and Jan Pakulski (eds) *Violence and the state*

Jan Koehler and Christoph Zürcher (eds) *Potentials of disorder*

Matthias Leese and Stef Wittendorp (eds) *Security/Mobility: politics and movement*

David Bruce MacDonald *Balkan holocausts? Serbian and Croatian victim-centred propaganda and the war in Yugoslavia*

Adrian Millar *Socio-ideological fantasy and the Northern Ireland conflict: the other side*

Jennifer Milliken *The social construction of the Korean War*

Ami Pedahzur *The Israeli response to Jewish extremism and violence: defending democracy*

Johanna Söderström *Living politics after war: ex-combatants and veterans coming home*

Maria Stern *Naming insecurity – constructing identity: 'Mayan-women' in Guatemala on the eve of 'peace'*

Virginia Tilley *The one state solution: a breakthrough for peace in the Israeli–Palestinian deadlock*

Collective emotions and political violence

Narratives of Islamist organisations in Western Europe

Maéva Clément

MANCHESTER UNIVERSITY PRESS

Published by Manchester University Press
Oxford Road, Manchester M13 9PL

www.manchesteruniversitypress.co.uk

British Library Cataloguing-in-Publication Data
A catalogue record for this book is available from the British
Library

ISBN 978 1 5261 6769 9 hardback

First published 2023

Typeset
by Cheshire Typesetting Ltd, Cuddington, Cheshire

Contents

Figures

Tables

Abbreviations

AM	*al-Muhajiroun*
DWR	*Die Wahre Religion*
EZP	*Einladung zum Paradies e.V.*
GIMF	*Global Islamic Media Front*
HT	Hizb ut-Tahrir
HTB	*Hizb ut-Tahrir Britain*
IS	Islamic State
ISIL	Islamic State of Iraq and the Levant
ISIS	Islamic State of Iraq and Syria
MAB	*Muslim Association of Britain*
MI	*Millatu Ibrahim*
OBM	Omar Bakri Mohammed

Acknowledgements

This book is about the collective emotions that bind political actors to specific understandings of (world) politics. The motivation to study political activism and violence under the prism of emotions rose from a place of curiosity and an observation. The discourse on organised political violence in the early and mid-2010s was still dominated by hyper-subjectivist accounts of 'radicalisation' and operated on a narrow understanding of rationality to account for individual motivations. I was curious about other motivations, experiences, and ways to make sense of changes in beliefs and attitudes – at the collective level. Conversely, the discourses and images produced by organised political actors involved in such processes were largely imagined under the prism of 'propaganda', 'terrorist messaging', and 'strategic narratives'. It seemed to me that, much as other political actors, non-state actors engaging in (the justification of) political violence would talk and write about themselves and others in complex ways that cannot be reduced to ideological precepts or strategic discourses.

Working at the time on the meaning of social recognition for Islamist organisations in a Western European context, I was inspired by the idea found across theories of recognition that being recognised by others fulfils a basic *emotional* need. This holds true for individuals and collectives. This project thus began as an endeavour to study emotional needs as expressed by organised actors turning to political violence. While the book focuses on non-state agency in the context of Islamist activism in Western Europe in recent decades, its argument is by no means restricted to non-state (Islamist) actors. Socio-political discourses and practices of all kinds draw on the politics of emotions and this calls for an epistemic shift in the way we approach (world) politics.

This book would not have been possible without the intellectual environments from which the first idea emerged, later took form, received feedback, matured, and was ultimately couched into a book. I wish to thank the Political Science community of the Sorbonne University, Sciences Po Paris, the Goethe University Frankfurt and Cluster of Excellence 'The Formation of Normative Orders', my former colleagues and other faculty members at the Helmut Schmidt University Hamburg, and the team at the Chair of International Relations and Peace and Conflict Studies at Osnabrück University.

I am deeply grateful to Anna Geis, Thomas Lindemann, Hanna Pfeifer, Katarina Ristić, Eric Sangar, Gabi Schlag, Ulrich Schneckener, and Reinhard Wolf for their helpful feedback and sound advice on various parts of the book.

I wish to thank Janusz Biene, Claudia Dantschke, Patrick Möller, and Nina Wiedl for their generous insights into the German Islamist scene. Special thanks go to Patrick for generously granting me access to some of the audio and video material for this book.

The research presented in this book has benefited from the many talks, workshops, conferences, working group meetings, and more informal conversations with colleagues in the broader academic community: Thierry Balzacq, Timm Beichelt, Martha Crenshaw, Christopher Daase, Donatella della Porta, Véronique Dudouet, Raquel da Silva, Clara Eroukhmanoff, Luca Falciola, Maik Fielitz, Karin Fierke, Tuomas Forsberg, Caterina Froio, Carolin Goerzig, Petra Guasti, Hendrik Hegemann, Aida Hozic, Simon Koschut, Alice Martini, Matthias Quent, Frédéric Ramel, Sybille Reinke de Buitrago, Alex Spencer, Harmonie Toros, Yuri van Hoef, and Claire Yorke.

I also wish to thank the Politics and International Relations editor for Manchester University Press, Rob Byron, and the co-editor of the New Approaches to Conflict Analysis series, Emmanuel-Pierre Guittet, for their enthusiasm for the book, as well as the reviewers for their insightful comments. The publication of the book in open access was funded by the German Research Foundation (Deutsche Forschungsgemeinschaft – DFG project number 507194873).

Finally, I am deeply grateful for the emotional support from my family and friends. I deeply thank my mother and my grandmother, Françoise and Fernande, for giving me the opportunities that have brought me here today. Special thanks go to the dear friends who have encouraged me at various times during this project, especially Aline, Anne-Cécile, Aurore, Eric, Janne, Jean-François, and Solène. I also wish to thank Jutta and Martin for their thoughtful enquiries about the project's progress. Finally, I am deeply grateful to Janusz, my partner, for his emotional and intellectual support, patience, and unwavering confidence in this project.

Note on the text

In Part I of the book, quotes from the data are referenced by organisation and date (e.g. HTB, 21.10.2002). After the reconstruction of phases of activism in Chapter 2 and subsequent delineation of *cases* (see summarising table 2.4, p. 75), quotes from the data are thereupon referenced by *case* and *date*. Each case refers to an organisation and a phase of activism. For example, *Hizb ut-Tahrir Britain*'s first phase of activism over the period of study is shortened to 1-HTB.

Please note that the publishing dates of the texts by UK-based organisations are predominantly complete. The German-based organisations present a small number of texts, audios, and videos for which the publishing *day* could not be reconstructed; they are referenced per month and year.

Quotes from the data in German were translated by the author into English. For further information about transcription and translation, as well as the system for representing and quoting the data, please see Appendix D (pp. 238–240).

Introduction

On 21 May 2004, the UK-based organisation *al-Muhajiroun* (AM) published an article on its official website entitled 'Why have Muslims turned their backs on Palestine?' The article discusses the challenges of mobilising a transnational Muslim community against injustice and occupation. Taking the Palestinian issue as a case in point, the organisation denounces a lack of continued solidarity from Muslims worldwide and points to two explanations. For one thing, Palestinian nationalist calls would blur the conflict roots and divert attention away from it being a Muslim issue; for another, media depictions of suffering would produce fewer effects. Centrally, AM worries that UK Muslims will become deaf to the plight of fellow Muslims:

> The media show the killings in Palestine, in Iraq etc ... every day, after a while you will begin to become immune to it all [sic]. In the past people were upset about just one man being killed, now the enemies are able to kill thousands with minimal reaction. The numbers have begun to mean nothing and Muslims have become used to it. The feelings and emotions will become dead after a while (www.muhajiroun.com, 21 May 2004).

Here, AM raises exemplarily the issue of compassion fatigue – the gradual lessening of compassion over time, in societies in which news and social media are saturated with visual and textual depictions of suffering. It sees a direct link between caring less and disengaging from the cause of the Muslim *ummah* (transnational community), thereby alluding to an essential link between individual/collective action and emotions. The article goes on to offer solutions to counter this development and sustain transnational armed resistance.

This book argues that to engage in political violence, individuals and organisations alike need to *feel moved*. Violent extremism is not a simple issue of ideological beliefs nor primarily a question of individual commitment, and neither is it a mere question of strategic opportunity. Political violence has to feel right, as a collective, for an organisation and its followers to move from moderate activism to extremism and violent action. This is not to attract emotionally disturbed followers. Nor is it primarily about presenting one's struggle as rightful to a world audience. Rather, organisations need to legitimate such a change in orientation towards members and followers to keep them committed and to incentivise (violent) collective action. In radicalising into extremism, non-state organisations face high risks of repression and implosion, as well as considerable difficulties maintaining a high level of activism over time, as the example above illustrates. The central proposition of this book is that organisations radicalising into extremism couch this change in narrative productions, through which group-appropriate emotions are performed and gradually institutionalised.

Islamist activism in Western Europe in the 2000s and 2010s evolved in ways deeply connected to the politics of emotions. To unpack this topic, the book explores the forms of political activism of three organisations active in the UK in the 2000s and two organisations active in Germany in the late 2000s–early 2010s: *al-Muhajiroun* (AM), *Hizb ut-Tahrir Britain* (HTB), the *Muslim Association of Britain* (MAB), *Die Wahre Religion* (DWR), and *Millatu Ibrahim* (MI). Islamist organisations represent a pertinent research case, not least because the experience of repression by public authorities would play a part in the politics of emotions.

To question the extent to which a common Islamist narrative spanning organisations and national borders was (re)produced during this period, I study organisations evolving in two different countries. Over the period ranging from the 2000s to the early 2010s, a distinctly European Islamist scene developed, especially in the UK, Germany, France, Belgium, and the Netherlands. Islamist groups were increasingly called to take a position on international events and stood in greater competition with one another. The UK Islamist scene was the first to emerge and served as an example for the development of others across continental Europe. In Germany, the local Islamist scene developed later and borrowed features from UK organisations. Much like the UK organisations in the early 2000s, the German organisations came to play a large role at the turn of the 2010s and constitute an important node of the European Islamist scene. A comparison between German and UK organisations thus appears particularly interesting.

Arguably, right-wing extremism heightened in Western Europe over the same period (Klandermans & Mayer, 2006; Koehler, 2016; Köttig et al., 2017; Staemmler, 2017). While this book cannot cover all forms of non-state activism in one stride, it should not convey the impression that far-right actors would politicise emotions less. There are good reasons to believe that far-right organisations draw extensively on collective emotions when turning to political violence. Admittedly, they do so in ways partly different from the organisations studied in this book, not primarily because of their ideological orientation, but rather because they entertain a different relationship to state and society than Islamist organisations in a Western European context.

The analytical focus lies with Western Europe for several reasons. Compared to North America and Eastern Europe, the region has seen an increase in local Islamist activism from the 2000s onwards.[1] The small strand of research comparing North American and Western European local Islamist activism contends that the latter has seen 'a larger number of home-grown jihadist networks' (Vidino, 2009, p. 2). While the number of US citizens charged with terrorism temporarily increased around 2009–2010, the phenomenon of violent activism by local Islamist groups has remained very limited. Similarly, successive surveys showed that support for 'Islamic extremism' in the US is 'negligible' (PEW, 2009, 2011).

Over the period, public perceptions of 'Islamic extremism' in Western Europe led to growing concerns over its impact on social, political, and security issues. The comparison with North America and Eastern Europe is again telling. Surveys showed that European publics, especially German and Spanish publics, 'worried' about 'Islamic extremism' much more significantly than US, Canadian, and Polish publics (PEW, 2005). The comparison across publics, that is, the general population compared to Muslim minorities, further revealed that, except in France, a large majority of the general population in Western Europe held that 'there is a conflict between being a devout Muslim and living in a modern society'. In contrast, the majority of European Muslims disagreed with this proposition (PEW, 2005). The heightened Islamist activism that the region experienced over the period, and the conflicting perceptions among publics over its meaning, make Western Europe a particularly interesting region on which to focus.

Radicalisation and extremism: conceptual-theoretical impasse and ways forward

Scholars and practitioners have argued that it has become increasingly difficult, since the 2000s, to differentiate empirically between Islamist actors rejecting violence absolutely and Islamist actors expressing flexibility towards the question of political violence (Malthaner, 2011; Wiedl, 2014a). In a 2017 report, the UK Institute for Global Change contends that from the early 1980s to the Syrian civil war, '77% of British jihadis [had] moved towards jihadism after exposure to non-violent Islamist ideologies' (Bryson, 2017, p. 29). Based on the public profiles of prominent UK militants, the report implies that Islamist organisations which are not condoning or engaging in violence would nevertheless act as a steppingstone towards violent forms of activism and/or extreme ideologies. Beyond the fact that non-violence (and extremism) remains unspecified in the study, this statistic hides two central developments since the 2000s. First, the number of Islamist organisations in Western Europe has increased, and so has the competition for members, resources, and prestige. With more choices, followers have changed organisations more readily if they felt that political change was not happening fast enough.

Second, several Islamist organisations *have changed* over the period and moved away from moderate politics. This second development is of central interest in this book. If some organisations moved away from moderate politics over the period, how did they mediate such a profound change to members and followers? Methodologically, it poses the challenge of breaking down organisations' phases of activism: How to reconstruct empirically how once-moderate organisations move discursively away from moderate politics and towards (violent) extremism?

In a European context, 'extremism' has been discussed in politics, media, and academia in starkly different ways. Scholars in various European academic contexts associate different national and community experiences with extremism, focusing on academia only. In the Anglo-Saxon scholarship on political violence, some have been loath to use the term extremism. Not merely because the concept risks being too subjective, as this could be mitigated with conceptual efforts, but more importantly because it has been used in political, policy, and media discourses 'selectively and inconsistently to construct Muslims as a suspect community and to discourage the expression of radical opinions' (Kundnani, 2015, p. 26; see also Martini et al., 2020). Further, some models of terrorist mobilisation and many policy actors still work on the assumption that holding extremist beliefs would ultimately lead to terrorist activity (Crone, 2016; Schuurman & Taylor, 2018). Combined, these developments have led to massive shifts in security policies, infringements on personal freedoms (e.g. criminalisation of freedom of expression), and the marginalisation of entire sections of the population defined along racial or religious attributes (Kundnani, 2015).

While similar developments can be observed in other European countries, this research has been mostly concerned with the UK political context and, specifically, the consequences of the UK government's Prevent and Channel strategies. In other political and academic contexts, 'extremism' is also contested but roots in partly different knowledge and power dynamics. In countries that have experienced Nazism and fascism full force, extremism is used as a category to differentiate, on one side, from 'radicalism' and the expression of 'radical opinions', and, on the other side, from the use of physical violence implied in militancy and terrorism (Quent, 2016). The term has been used to grasp those attitudes and discourses that exclude, reify, and work to exert symbolic violence on others, chiefly ethnic, religious, and sexual minorities. This book uses the term extremism in the latter understanding and with regards to *organised groups* (organisations and networks), not individuals.

In this book, extremism refers to collective actors aiming to bring about a profound change in the socio-political makeup of society in striving towards a *homogeneous social collective* and 'suppressing all opposition and subjugating minorities' (drawing on Schmid, 2013, p. 8). Extremist organisations do not merely hold anti-pluralistic beliefs; they envision and pursue political projects resting on the structural superiority of their group over others. Extremism is to be differentiated from *radicalism*. While both are regarded to be about 'sweeping political change' and 'the conviction that the status quo is unacceptable' (Schmid, 2013, p. 8), radicalism means, at a basic level, going to the root of a problem and is contingent on a society's positioning at a given moment in history. Scholars studying the history of political ideas stress that radical political actors 'accept diversity and believe in the power of reason rather than dogma', unlike extremist actors who reject diversity, give collective goals the primacy over individual freedoms, and encourage the use of force over persuasion (Schmid, 2013, pp. 9–10; Quent, 2016). Conceptualised as such, extremism qualifies organisations whose activism denigrates other ways of being, feeling, and thinking in society as wrong, inferior, and deserving to be suppressed.

Regrettably, the scholarship relies overwhelmingly on the concept of *radicalisation* to describe the processes of moving into (violent) extremism (Malthaner, 2017). The alternative term, 'extremisation', might have been a closer fit, yet it did not establish itself in the scholarship (Kundnani, 2012; Biene & Marcks, 2014; Pisoiu, 2015). Moreover, while radicalisation would not necessarily be associated with violence – if it had been understood as the process of becoming *radical* – it has come to connote just that. This ubiquitous practice rendered the term 'extremisation' superfluous. To clarify that they refer to the issue of *extremism*, some employ the expression 'radicalisation into extremism' (Schmid, 2013; Quent, 2016). This terminology[2] is more specific and implies, among other things, that attitudes towards violent means of action and/or behaviour are changing and becoming positive. At the level of organisations, group radicalisation is hereby a process, and extremism a temporary outcome (collective attitudes and behaviour).

The processes of group radicalisation into extremism are not linear; radicalisation and terrorist violence should not be imagined as a continuum. Radicalising organisations do not necessarily act on the attitudinal preference for violent means. Radicalisation is about the combination of attitudes and actions, formulated and taken at a moment in time, within a specific framework of interactions (Alimi et al., 2015). That said, the literature on radicalisation, extremism, and violent political activism[3] has evolved in directions that have impeded, paradoxically, from explaining *changes* in attitudes and forms of action. To underline this, I carve out three central research desiderata. First, the over-emphasis on ideology has led to the neglect of group dynamics and reduced the capacity to account for change. Second, extremist organisations' relationship to violence has remained conceptually unclear, underspecified, and static. Third, the dominant assumption that extremist organisations' preference for violence is strategically rational has led to overlooking alternative explanations at the group level.

(1) In routinely explaining the turn to political violence by ideological factors, radicalisation research has been overly ideology-centric. For a long time, it has carried the belief that individuals and collectives would start engaging in violent extremism because they come to believe in a violent ideology. Faced with the overwhelming counterfactual evidence that most people who subscribe to a violent ideology do not act upon it, radicalisation research has scaled down and centred on explaining *individual* processes of radicalisation. Where political scientific inquiry generally aspires to study meso- and macro-level processes, scholars now focus on *individuals'* particular experiences of radicalisation. As important a subject of inquiry as it may be in micro-sociology, social psychology, and anthropology, political-scientific research is surely more pertinent when studying group radicalisation processes.

In extremism research, too, much emphasis has lain on the role played by ideology. Schmid contends, for instance, that extremists' strong emphasis on ideology is a key distinguishing characteristic (2011, 2013). Contrary to radicalisation research's focus on individual trajectories, extremism research in a Western European context has focused on how extremist groups operate and interact with mainstream society. This strand of research views such interactions as grounded in ideologically determined collective attitudes and beliefs. It thus tends to describe outcomes – groups' specific brand of extremism – without accounting for entry *into* extremism and change *within* extremism.

Consequently, both research strands' narrow focus on ideology brings us no closer to understanding how organisations and their members *move* from moderate activism to extremism. A conceptualisation of radicalisation in which groups have a fixed and stable relationship with ideology, and where belief in ideology mechanically translates into behaviour, is reductive and misleading. In between, something crucial comes up short: how do we account for organisations radicalising *into* and *within* extremism? To act, individuals and collectives alike need to feel moved, or better put, be 'moved to move'.[4] This at once implies affective movement (kinetic) and emotion

(Sheets-Johnstone, 1999). Consider a computer machine: it could register 'injustice', designate culprits, and even how they could be chastised, but 'injustice' would not *move* it to take action. This book focuses on studying performances of emotions in discourse and the moral-volitional movement involved in speaking for and acting on political violence. Without attending to emotion/affect,[5] it is hardly possible to understand collective behaviour, and *changes* in collective behaviour even less. Social science researchers can interrogate the dynamics and ambiguities of group radicalisation only if they explore collective emotions and the degree of their institutionalisation in group discourses and practices.

Furthermore, conceptualising extremism as a temporary state instead of an outcome opens the possibility of theorising change *within* extremism. Fairly recently, alternative conceptualisations of radicalisation and extremism have emerged, addressing processes towards 'further' radicalisation. Conceived as radicalisation *within* extremism, this refers not to the entry into extremism but the later intensification of an organisation's extremist agenda and/or the escalation of the violent means it advocates and/or uses to pursue this agenda.[6]

Conversely, conceptualisations of processes of *moderation* within extremism are still largely missing. It would describe the equally important empirical phenomenon of an organisation entering a phase in which it narrows its political agenda and/or the scope of violent activism. While such a phase of moderation within extremism would not equate to de-radicalisation, it would call attention to the process by which an organisation recants parts of its agenda and/or relents in its use of violence, and thus interrogate potential 'internal brakes' in Islamist militancy (Holbrook, 2020) and other contexts (Busher & Bjørgo, 2020). Studying change *within* extremism in this way is important. It reminds us that radicalisation is not deterministic, and neither individuals nor groups 'tip and fall' into extremism. Our concepts and theories need to reflect such a complex, dynamic, and ambiguous phenomenon.

(2) Closely linked to the previous issue, research on radicalisation and extremism maintains an ambivalent conceptual relationship to violence. In the literature, radicalisation tends to be reduced to a process by which an individual or a group comes to view the use of physical violence as inevitable to further one's political goals. Yet, violence is but one aspect of such comprehensive change. The definition by Schmid discussed earlier – *radicalisation into extremism is the process by which individuals or organisations come to see change towards a homogeneous social collective as necessary and aim to suppress all opposition and subjugate minorities* – makes clear that radicalisation has only partly to do with the use of physical violence. When a group's beliefs, attitudes, and everyday practices are

anti-pluralistic, supremacist, and dehumanising, physical violence may be the most visible manifestation but not necessarily the most telling. In short, physical violence is not *per se* a sufficient criterion to qualify group extremism. It is as much about the kind of socio-political project that reifies and denies agency to 'Others', a dimension arguably much more difficult to study. Empirically exploring processes of radicalisation into extremism calls for studying both action-based *and* discourse-based dimensions of extremism.

Further, such an empirical exploration necessitates specifying forms of extremism *qualitatively*. Extremism comes in many shades, yet studies on radicalisation processes often describe a given organisation as 'extremist' without further characterisation. This is important though, not least to compare organisations and trace changes in practices. When considering Jihadism, for instance, different positions are found empirically. Some organisations see the use of violence as one type of action within a repertoire, while others consider it the *only* form of action capable of resulting in socio-political change. Within the latter attitude – qualitatively more extreme – organisations again display a wide range of positions, for example, towards the scope of violence. Some argue for killing enemy combatants only, others for killing 'treacherous' Muslim leaders as well, others still for killing all non-Muslims who are not currently under the 'protection' of a caliphate. The relationship of an organisation to violence in a given phase of activism needs to be specified to characterise group extremism more dynamically, appreciate changes in activism, and recognise differences among organisations.

(3) Closely related to this, the dominant assumption that organisations' (newly found) preference for violence is strategically rational is equally problematic. Orthodox and part of the more critical work in terrorism studies explains that some organisations set moderate activism aside and engage in political violence through narrow concepts of rationality.

Despite the high risks to members, a high probability that the organisation disappears in the process, and very low chances of success, organisations' choice for violence is depicted as strategically rational. Indeed, while terrorist activity bears low efficacy (Cronin, 2006; Weinberg & Perliger, 2010), paradoxically, some of the most cited scholars see 'rational radicalization'[7] as what occurs when organisations opt for terrorism as a strategic choice (for instance in Crenshaw, 1990; Bloom, 2005; Kydd & Walter, 2006; Pape, 2006; Sprinzak, 2009). Since organisations with a small base of support cannot engage in guerrilla tactics, they would consider terrorism as the course of action most likely to attain their goals. Some have contested such a perspective and argued that organisations also turn to political violence to satisfy short-term desires such as revenge or renown

(Richardson, 2006; Fattah & Fierke, 2009; Lindemann, 2012). Others point out that most terrorist organisations behave as 'social solidarity maximizers', attaching more importance to social bonds and benefits than political success (Abrahms, 2006, 2008). Yet, as Tsintsadze-Maass and Maass stress, 'the conventional wisdom regarding terrorist radicalization views it as a rational process' (2014, p. 737; also Abrahms 2012).

Similarly, in social movement theory (SMT), conventional explanations of why groups turn to violent extremism rely almost exclusively on a restrictive conception of rationality as *strategic*. In studies on contentious politics and social movements, groups and larger movements are said to turn to violence either when state authorities exert strong repression (Lindekilde, 2014), when other means have failed (i.e. lack of political opportunity), or in cases where interactions between movements and security agencies lead to escalation (Demetriou et al., 2014; Alimi et al., 2015; Bosi et al., 2019). All three explanations draw on 'rationalist approaches' (Bosi, 2016, p. 192).

While coming from different disciplinary traditions,[8] much of the scholarship in SMT and terrorism studies offer strikingly similar explanations, conceiving the preference for violence only when couched as strategically rational. Even SMT research focusing more on 'how' movements change than 'why' they do so provides accounts of mobilisation which restrict change to narrow concepts of rational agency, for example, material structures, strategic agenda-setting, and framing processes. Arguments emphasising alternative explanations have had a hard time piercing through. In 2001, social movement theorists Goodwin and Pfaff hailed fellow SMT researchers to 'bring emotions back in':

> It is impossible to grasp the general causal mechanisms that are implicated in processes of popular mobilization and historical change without attending to the emotional dynamics on which many if not most such mechanisms are dependent. (2001, p. 301)

Since then, scholars working on non-violent social movements have shown a growing interest in the sociology and politics of emotions (Jasper, 1998; Calhoun, 2001; Goodwin & Jasper, 2004; Ost, 2004; Flam & King, 2005; Traïni, 2009). However, in comparison, there is little work on organisations and movements moving beyond moderate politics (Wright-Neville & Smith, 2009; Johnston, 2016; van Stekelenburg, 2017; Clément, 2020). Research on radicalisation and political extremism resists bringing emotions in. By decoupling 'rationality' from 'logical' or 'strategic' to account for the large normative change implied in radicalisation into extremism, the scholarship would acknowledge the existence of other ways of thinking and attributing 'reasons' for thoughts and actions, not least emotional ones (Clément, 2021).

The research presented in this book addresses these research desiderata. It anchors the analysis at the group level and focuses on understanding how organisations' forms of activism shift temporally. It develops an interpretative methodology to study stability and change in discourse and practice qualitatively. Finally, it explores organisations' narrative understandings of (world) politics and respective performance of collective emotions in-depth.

Research aims and methodological approach

This book aims to provide an alternative, nuanced understanding of group radicalisation into extremism. Subordinately, it provides insights into radicalisation *within* extremism and moderation *within* extremism. By delving into Islamist organisations' narrative performances of emotions, it offers an alternative account of how organisations *move* from moderate politics to extremism. Specifically, two questions are central. How do organisations legitimise the turn towards extremism, in general, and political violence, in particular? How do organisations incentivise members and followers to engage in political violence? The core argument is that collectives and individuals alike need to *feel moved* in order to take action. Without a focus on emotions, we cannot explain collective behaviour, and changes in collective behaviour even less. The analysis in this book centres on how and to what extent Islamist organisations moving towards (violent) extremism engage, through narrative activity, in the management of emotions.[9]

Interpretative research fits well with the aim of analysing changes in narrative and emotion practices as it is about understanding rather than explaining social phenomena. I focus on language as a site of inquiry in the production of social meaning. Social meaning about concepts, ideas, events, and practices is in flux. It varies over time, space, and groups; it is temporarily dominating, contested, and (re)negotiated. Interpretative research calls for an effort to understand how social meanings can represent something different to different people in different socio-political contexts. However, interpretation is but 'a temporary resting point' (Wibben, 2011, pp. 27–28). Notions such as 'love' (Luhmann, 1986; Belli & Harré, 2010) or 'security' (Constantinou, 2000; Wibben, 2011, p. 100) have evolved hugely from their original social meanings.

Interpretation as a methodological position means challenging the content of social meanings *and* the very processes through which they are constructed. I ask not only 'Which contents do Islamist groups focus on to justify political violence', but 'How are these contents mediated, represented, performed, and to what extent do they become actionable forms of collective knowledge?' The research interrogates the processes of knowledge production and mobilisation within Islamist organisations. My attempts at understanding such processes also impact knowledge production. I probably highlight stories that another researcher might have deemed of lesser importance or interpreted from a different perspective – and vice versa. In this regard, the research presented here may, at most, provide an interpretation that is convincing for a time in a given scientific discourse.

Two UK-based organisations, *Hizb ut-Tahrir Britain* (HTB) and *al-Muhajiroun* (AM), have been selected and two German-based, *Die Wahre Religion* (DWR) and *Millatu Ibrahim* (MI). To contrast their practices with the larger Islamist spectrum, I further selected one organisation known for its moderate discourse and rejection of violence, the *Muslim Association of Britain* (MAB). These organisations, including networks,[10] present a clear leadership – individual or collegial (the latter being obvious in the case of a network) – and a relatively top-down relationship between leaders and members (be it based on charisma or the organisation's formal structure). They are comparable in size and political relevance. Some have been the object of much scholarly attention, such as the UK-based AM. Others have played an important role in their country of activity and beyond but have been little studied, such as the German MI.

The five organisations share several other characteristics. Importantly, they have been created for a local (Western) audience and established across the territory of one country – none has been a purely local organisation. All have conducted outreach activities in the respective local language. They have positioned themselves towards the international order and the state in which they operate. However, they purport different visions of Sunni Islam: MAB and HTB can be described as representing the 'classical' Islamist spectrum, whereas AM, DWR, and MI represent the Salafi spectrum.

In an interpretative methodology, the self-reports of social actors are considered valuable material because they are 'expressions of how things are to the subject' (Harré & Gillett, 1994, p. 21). In this book, the data gathered for interpretation consists of the organisations' discursive productions, ranging from press statements, communiqués, policy-like papers, audio and video seminars and sermons (*khutbah*), magazine issues, leaflets, official blog posts, commented translations of Arabic texts written by major Salafi clerics, to media interviews. The various data types are considered equal in the process of interpreting how organisations talk about themselves and others and how their emotional worlds evolve across discursive productions.

Textual, audio, and video data were selected along four criteria: i. they were produced by the organisation itself, the leaders, or the spokespersons;[11]

ii. they were produced during the organisation's lifetime, or study period when shorter; iii. they referred to international politics and/or local and national politics in the UK or Germany;[12] and iv. they had a certain length, that is, enough text or speech to explore narratively. Further, to study the diverse narrative deployments of an organisation, variety as to the where (diverse geographical spaces, when possible), by whom (diverse leaders), and to whom (the audience at talks, seminars, public events, interviews) was important in selecting data. Audio-visual material was included from various event formats, speakers, location, and periods.[13] The audios and videos in the corpus share two further features: the public character of the recording or filming and the public character of the diffusion, ensuring a large reception, for example through its upload on a sharing platform (e.g. YouTube, Dailymotion, Vimeo). Overall, the corpus comprises 134 documents[14] and amounts to 211,819 words. The list of primary data can be consulted in Appendix A. Further information about data preparation (i.e. transcription and translation) and the system for representing and quoting the data can be found in Appendix D.

The research methodology is qualitative. Overall, three analyses are conducted throughout the book. First, I reconstruct organisations' discursive articulations on a continuum between moderation and extremism over the period of study. The interpretation of stability and change in such articulations enables temporal phases of activism to be delineated, for example, moderation, radicalisation into extremism, or (moderation within) extremism. The second analysis interrogates the organisations' narrative constructions of the international order and the relationship between Muslim communities and larger political communities. In a literary-critical approach, I explore whether an identifiable romantic narrative unfolds across all phases of activism or in specific phases only. The third analysis zooms in on the performance of emotions within this narrative. Building on the concept of narrative emotionalisation, I develop a hermeneutic approach to explore its processes in phases of radicalisation and extremism, and interpret how it participates in incentivising violent collective action. Overall, the comparison between organisations plays a central role in both challenging and supporting the interpretative work.

The concrete methods and approaches mobilised in this research are thus inspired by methodological insights from several (sub)disciplines. In critical terrorism studies, scholars have long criticised the methodological exceptionalism that characterises research into radicalisation, extremism, and terrorism (Gunning, 2007; Jackson et al., 2009; Guibet-Lafaye & Rapin, 2017). For example, Egerton underlines terrorism studies' 'self-imposed separation' from the rest of the social sciences (2011, p. 143). Such exceptionalism draws on the belief that political violence cannot be researched with the same tools used to study other social phenomena, thereby precluding, among other things, the possibility of comparative research. However, much is to be gained from opening to various disciplines' methodological tools, especially those that routinely gather and analyse linguistic and visual data.

Methods stemming from the humanities are increasingly used to study the emotional dimension of politically motivated violence (Bleiker & Hutchison, 2008; Åhäll & Gregory, 2015; Clément & Sangar, 2018). Similarly, literary-critical approaches are enjoying renewed interest in the study of militant narratives (Glazzard, 2017; Copeland, 2019; Pfeifer & Spencer, 2019). Further, such research would benefit from drawing more widely on insights from international relations and conflict (transformation) research to enrich theorising (Sjoberg, 2009; Egerton, 2011, p. 163; Tellidis & Toros, 2015). The research methodology presented in this book fits in with this perspective. It breaks methodological exceptionalism and draws on insights from world politics, peace and conflict studies, critical terrorism research, literary studies, and transdisciplinary emotion research.

Research practical implications and relevance to society

The insights presented in this book contribute to the conflict theoretical study of group radicalisation and extremism. As such, the book has implications for critical research on terrorism and counter-terrorism. Beyond, it contributes more generally to peace and conflict research and the scholarship studying emotions in socio-political discourse and practice. At a research-practical level, the book offers conceptual and theoretical foundations to study collective processes of radicalisation into extremism from an emotion research perspective.

In a research field where scholars have deplored the over-reliance on formal modelling methods, the lack of data, and empirically grounded research, this book builds on original primary data and offers a theoretical, methodological, and empirical contribution. It problematises current theoretical approaches to political violence and contributes to innovative theory-building on the relationship between collective emotions and knowledge/power. Furthermore, by drawing on insights at the intersection of research on political violence and transdisciplinary emotion research, the book shares in the effort to de-exceptionalise the study of group radicalisation into extremism. Seen as a phenomenon of political violence among others – counter-radicalisation and counter-terrorism included – it can be researched from a comparative perspective. Finally, the book puts methodological plurality into practice and exemplifies the productive exploration of diverse empirical material and the use of a combination of qualitative methods. The result is a methodology flexible enough to explore processes of group radicalisation (and moderation) and the mediating role of collective emotions couched in group narrative.

Insights into group processes towards violent extremism and the politics of emotions at play are of socio-political relevance in several respects. At a basic level, this impacts how we talk about radicalisation and political violence. By systematically re-contextualising radicalisation into extremism as a socio-political phenomenon, the book contributes – along with other works in the literature – to disqualify public discourses and practices referring to 'indoctrinated individuals', 'fanatics praying on weak minds', or 'cold-blooded individuals'. Although the analysis in this book focuses on Islamist mobilisation, it indirectly interrogates further forms of emotional governance by non-state and state actors alike.

This leads to a more general point: an epistemic shift is needed to acknowledge collective emotions as standard phenomena in the public sphere. Emotions are not exceptional, as the liberal, rational imperative would have it, but commonplace in politics and social discourse. While people are expected in modern societies to suppress their emotions routinely, increasingly large parts of society seem to reject this and turn towards populist parties, engage in extreme activism, or disengage from socio-political life altogether. Acknowledging that collectives routinely engage in the management and governance of emotions is essential. To give just one example, many US voters during the run for the US presidential election in 2016 stressed how 'free' candidate Donald Trump was and how thrilled they were about his unfiltered expressions of emotion. This illustrates the extent to which the modern imperative to suppress emotions in the public space and the conduct of politics has been undermined. Breaking the taboo of collective emotions opens the possibility of making their effects in politics and the public space *visible*. This, in turn, enables interrogating their assumed 'collectiveness', uncovering the diverse conflicting emotions circulating in the public space, and highlighting attempts by social actors to resist conforming to dominant emotion rules. Incidentally, it questions unequal emotion work in society (based on gender, class, minority status, ethnicity, etc.). In short, this book adds to the critical scholarship aiming to further our understanding of emotions and political agency.

At a community level, the insights developed here question the routine way policy-makers address the political and social issues linked to radicalisation into extremism. For instance, contemporary 'de-radicalisation programmes' have been, in their overwhelming majority, conceived on ideology-centric premises, emphasising the need to 'combat the ideology'

(Madriaza & Ponsot, 2015). Beyond the obvious ethical and political issues raised by such programmes, practices centred around the de-radicalisation of *beliefs* are symptomatic of the far-reaching impact of ideology-centric notions in the field of preventing and countering violent extremism. However, if organisations mediate the turn to extremism through narratives because of their *emotional power*, then civil society prevention and disengagement initiatives should not be primarily concerned with ideology. The book initiates alternative ways of thinking about prevention in the larger context of political education. Civil society organisations might engage diverse publics with offers of a different kind, strengthening individual and collective capacity to question and resist attempts made by non-state and state actors alike at governing emotions.

Book chapters

The book consists of two parts. Part I is dedicated to locating changes in political activism empirically. It does so by highlighting the ambiguous and dynamic character of Islamist organisations' political activism (Chapter 1) and reconstructing their respective phases of activism empirically (Chapter 2). Part II turns to the central ambition of the book: exploring the narrative performance of collective emotions in the organisations' respective phases of activism. Chapter 3 presents the theoretical approach underpinning the subsequent analyses of organisations' narrative deployments (Chapter 4) and performances of emotions therein (Chapter 5). While the methodological approach proposed here is fundamentally interpretative, the two parts of the book draw on (partly) different concrete methods adapted to the specific focus of each empirical chapter. Chapters 2, 4, and 5 thus begin purposely with a discussion of the methodological approach.

Chapter 1 serves as an entry point into the dense empirical material. Therein, the complex borders between radicalisation, extremism, and violence, on one side and Islamism, Salafism, and Jihadism, on the other are problematised empirically. The chapter then situates the five organisations – HTB, AM, DWR, MI, and MAB – by discussing critically their respective organisational structure, membership policy, political goals, online and offline activities, and interaction with public authorities. The chapter stresses some preliminary differences and common patterns between the five organisations. In contrast to some empirical approaches to the more well-known organisations discussed here, it problematises previous categorisations of Islamist activism. By highlighting the ephemeral character of some activities and the ambiguity maintained by most of the organisations towards political violence, this chapter offers a nuanced approach to fluctuations between moderation and extremism. In doing so, it paves the way for the next chapter, which delineates phases of activism.

Chapter 2 turns to the empirical reconstruction of the five organisations' phases of activism over their respective period of study. As group radicalisation is an emergent and partly contradictory process, the chapter argues that a more accurate characterisation of changes in activism would draw on the data-driven, empirical reconstruction of (alternate) phases of moderation and/or radicalisation and/or extremism. To this end, the chapter studies the organisations' textual, audio, and video data and focuses on how they articulate changes in activism discursively. It draws on a qualitative content analysis to interpret the large textual corpus and compare discursive articulations temporally. The chapter discusses the merits of reconstructing longer-term phases of activism and ends with the temporal delineation of phases of moderation, radicalisation (if any), and/or extremism (if any) for each of the organisations. These phases of activism are the *cases* studied in the remainder of the book.

Part II addresses the central ambition of the book: exploring the narrative performance of collective emotions in the organisations' respective phases of activism. Chapter 3 starts with conceptualising emotions/affect, collective emotions, and their social functions, thereby problematising how collectives engage in the politics of emotion. In a second step, it turns to the politics of their representation in language and, more specifically, in narrative form. It argues in favour of approaching collective emotions via their performance *in* and *through* narratives. It shows how different narratives create different meanings about one's collective in a political context, orders and (de)legitimise social actors in dissimilar ways, and provide different collective and individual orientations for political action. While all narratives draw on emotions/affect, some do so more intensely than others. Bridging the scholarship on narrative and emotions, the chapter then introduces the original concept of *narrative emotionalisation* to grasp the process by which a body of stories becomes increasingly emotionalised. Through emotionalisation, a romantic narrative *demands* decisive collective action. The chapter expounds on the four combined sub-processes that participate in an organisation's fully emotionalised narrative, their characteristics, and functions.

Chapter 4 turns to the analysis of the organisations' narrative activity in their respective phases of activism. It explores the extent to which organisations reproduce a similar romantic narrative. After explaining the narrative approach, the chapter presents the main insights from the narrative analysis by contrasting the phases of moderation with the other phases of activism. It offers an in-depth interpretation of the meanings attributed by organisations to narrative categories, zooming in on the phases of radicalisation and phases of extremism. While the analysis points to some differences in creedal beliefs and the prioritisation of goals, the central insight is that organisations are, narratively speaking, *identical* in phases of radicalisation and extremism. The chapter ends with a preliminary conclusion on the narrative changes accompanying an organisation's move away from moderate politics.

Chapter 5 zooms in on *narrative emotionalisation*. To do so, it starts by discussing how the four sub-processes of emotionalisation theorised in Chapter 3 can be approached hermeneutically. The chapter then traces the four sub-processes successively and offers an interpretation of how extensively they unfold within the cases. Key differences emerge by comparing the phases of radicalisation with the phases of extremism. The strong and consistent performance of collective emotions in phases of extremism stands out. By contrast, in phases of radicalisation, the sub-processes do not unfold as consistently nor as comprehensively – organisations' narrative occurrences are only partially emotionalised. The comparison across phases highlights that the strong incentivisation to take violent action hinges on the consistency and intensity of narrative emotionalisation.

The concluding chapter discusses the book's central insights and contribution to the research gaps carved out in this introduction. It stresses the theoretical, methodological, and empirical significance of the book for the scholarship on radicalisation and extremism and its contribution to the study of emotions in (world) politics. Finally, the chapter presents some critical implications for political practice and prevention. Far from being a side story, interpreting (changing) performances of collective emotions helps us understand better the collective turn to political violence. Organisations move towards extremism when political violence feels right.

Notes

1 In terms of terrorism-related deaths, violent extremism is much more prevalent in other regions of the world, primarily the Middle East, South-Asia, and Southeast-Asia; see Global Terrorism Database (START, University of Maryland) and the Global Terrorism Index (Institute for Economics and Peace).

2 To lighten the prose, I will sometimes use the shortened term 'radicalisation', thereby meaning radicalisation into extremism.

3 Other literatures, such as social anthropology, explore political activism and extremism – albeit with other concepts – in more dynamic ways. For instance, Schiffauer's ethnographic work on the organisation Milli Görüş in Germany shows how the organisation's 'second generation' moved towards a 'post-Islamist' project in the 2000s (2010, pp. 19–21), thereby representing a process of moderation.

4 This expression, borrowed from Sheets-Johnstone (1999) stresses the intrinsic connection between emotion and motion/movement.

5 These concepts are elaborated upon in Chapter 3, 'A theory of emotionalisation in narrative form'. For now, it is important to note that the book focuses on performances of emotions in language and not on bodily movements.

6 Abay Gaspar et al. (2018) propose a similar concept – 'Radikalisierung in der Gewalt' ('radicalisation into violence') – although solely in relation to violent means.

7 Term used by Tsintsadze-Maass and Maass to criticise this position (2014, p. 737).

8 SMT comes from sociology and focuses on why and how social mobilisation occurs, whereas terrorism studies refer to a transdisciplinary research field originated from the larger field of security studies.

9 Term used by Goodwin and Pfaff (2001), drawing on Hochschild (1983) who introduced the concept of 'emotion work' into sociology. They extend Hochschild's concept to encompass the collective (not only individual) and unconscious (not only self-conscious) work performed to 'induce or suppress' emotions in social interactions (2001, p. 284). This work is further built upon in Chapter 3.

10 I define an organisation as a group of people who organise over time towards a collective goal (i.e. non-ephemeral). From there, the diversity of organisations is infinite: some are centralised, others decentralised; some are highly hierarchical, others display flat hierarchies, and so on. A network is a form of organisation characterised by informality and decentralisation.

11 Forum discussions of textual, audio, and/or video material produced by an organisation were not included in the data, but provided context on the reception of such material.

12 I did not select data that contained only theological discussions without any reference to contemporary political events.

13 The material includes videos ranging from an official seminar in the premises of a mosque, a demonstration, a festival with public conversion ceremony, to the more casual large barbecue party with guest speakers. Regarding speakers and locations, I selected videos from all the main centres of activity of DWR and MI and the main speakers. I included a relatively comparable number of videos for each year of the study period, although some periods are more represented than others due to increased group activity.

14 I stopped adding new texts, audios, and videos to the corpus when no substantially new content emerged, as is often practised in discourse analytical research.

Part I

Characterising changes in political activism

1

Contextualising Islamist organisations in Western Europe (2001–2013)

This chapter picks up the introductory discussion of the desiderata in radicalisation and extremism research and extends it to the specific actors discussed in this book. Thereby it zooms in on the ambivalences of scholarly conceptual and theoretical tools and the fluidity of the phenomena under study. The first part of the chapter problematises the relationship between radicalisation, extremism, and violence. Then it introduces conceptual and phenomenological distinctions between Islamism, Salafism, and Jihadism. The chapter zooms in on the various political projects that different Islamist actors may support and the differing relationships to violence they may entertain. The second part of the chapter introduces the organisations studied in the book (looking at organisational structure, followership, type of activities, etc.) and discusses existing scholarly work on their forms of activism. The chapter concludes with a critical summary of similarities and differences among the organisations so far.

Problematising the relationship between radicalisation, extremism, and violence

The dynamic evolution of Islamist organisations in Europe over the 2000s led to aporic comments on the relationship between radicalisation and violence. Too often, analyses have tended to reify radicalisation by using categories that already classify organisations as 'extremist' or 'radical but non-violent' before presenting empirical evidence of a process. Such conceptualisations cannot characterise group radicalisation in any other way than as a moment when a group 'tips and falls' into violence – a misleading image. Group radicalisation is characterised by meanderings, fluctuations in meanings, and political ambiguity. It calls for conceiving its processes as non-linear and partly contradictory, and delineating *phases* instead of tipping points.

All five organisations studied in this book have been depicted, at one point or another, in media, political and, to some extent, scholarly discourses as 'radical' – even the *Muslim Association of Britain*. Beyond the problematic politics of labelling organisations, such depictions eschew characterising what would make them 'radical'. Similarly, few empirical studies engage in defining criteria for 'extremism'. At times, a group's extremism is equated with holding extremist political views; at other times, it is equated with being violent based on political motives. If radicalisation merely corresponded to increasingly being violent, researchers would only need to look for those specific *actions* that qualify as violent.

And yet, the empirics do not seem to fit the equation 'extremist = (politically) violent'. Let me take the example of Hizb ut-Tahrir (HT). Scholarly work on HT has qualified the organisation as 'radical but non-violent' (Baran, 2004; Karagiannis & McCauley, 2006; Whine, 2006a; Ahmed & Stuart, 2009, 2010). However, HT's 'non-violence' remains unspecified. Does it reject violence as a legitimate political means? Or does it merely abstain from perpetrating violence itself? Or does it relate to legal categories, that is, whether HT can or cannot be held accountable for 'preparing terrorist acts' under national laws? In HT's case, scholarship oscillates between all three, thus leading to a conceptual stalemate in which non-violence becomes the vague opposite of terrorist activity. Under such a volatile conceptualisation, arguing that a group is 'radical but non-violent' leads to an aporia: the 'radical' (in our terminology, *extremist*) character of an organisation is assessed based on *violent actions*, yet the organisation does not engage in such actions.

Conversely, the book argues, first, that non-violence is more than just *not using* violence; it is the rejection of violence as a legitimate political means. This implies, for instance, that an organisation contributing funds knowingly to a group engaging in armed violence could not be considered *non-violent*. Second, 'extremism' cannot be conceptualised as action-based only. Justifying attacks on civilians and the killing of differently minded communities *is* a form of violence, if not physical, then at the very least symbolic. Third, I contend that a clear-cut delineation between the use of violent or non-violent means only helps minimally. Jihadi organisations such as al-Qaeda have advocated – and used – non-violent and violent actions concomitantly. This, in turn, tells us something about radicalisation processes: radicalising groups are increasingly departing from believing in, advocating for, and engaging in the political process and non-violent collective action. In short, radicalising groups move away from moderation in discourse and practice. In this regard, it is more helpful to introduce differentiations according to the scope of the political project and the relationship towards violence. Islamist actors in Western Europe display in this regard great diversity.

Islamist activism in Western Europe: conceptual and phenomenological distinctions

Islamist activism in a Western European context refers both to a wide range of social phenomena *and* contested political and scholarly concepts such as Islamism, Salafism, and Jihadism. By problematising the boundaries between these concepts and socio-political phenomena, this section provides context for the ensuing presentation of the organisations studied in the book and their forms of activism.

Islamic studies, comparative religious studies, sociology, and political science, to mention only a few, hold partly different understandings of Islamism, Salafism, and Jihadism. As a term, Islamism appeared in the 1970s, whereas the phenomenon it depicts would have started much earlier, namely in the 1920s with the creation of the Muslim Brotherhood[1] (Mandaville, 2007). A relatively recent concept, it gained traction in the wake of the Iranian Revolution in 1979, then experienced a renewal in the late 1990s with the rise of Hamas in the Palestinian territories and the activities of proponents of the Islamic jihad, such as the *Groupe islamique armé* (Schneiders, 2014, p. 11). After the attacks of the late 1990s in France and against US embassies in Kenya and Tanzania, and later the 9/11 attacks, the term Islamism became commonplace in political discourse.

Islamism remains a contested concept (Martin & Barzegar, 2010) that has been used in European media and political discourse to brand and lump together very diverse actors. This has led to the stigmatisation and profiling of minority faith communities (Lambert, 2008) and delegitimisation of Muslim civil society organisations (Hafez, 2019). However, for all its imperfections, the term allows for distinguishing between *political* and *non-political* Islamic activism: most individuals engaging in society as Muslims do not carry a political agenda linked to 'political Islam'. This seems rather obvious, yet often gets lost in the debate, not least because Islamist actors contend that Islam is not merely a faith but the very way to organise society. As such, for Islamist actors, Muslim activism could not be *but* political. Defining Islamism as activism referring to political Islam still means considering a wide range of phenomena: 'classical' Islamism (i.e. the Muslim Brotherhood), revolutionary Islamism, political Salafism, jihadi Salafism. Mandaville's definition of Islamism encompasses this varied empirical reality:

> [They are] forms of political theory and practice that have as their goal the establishment of an Islamic political order in the sense of a state[2] whose governmental principles, institutions, and legal system derive directly from the shariah. In the eyes of those who advocate Islamist solutions, religion is generally viewed as a holistic, totalizing system whose prescriptions permeate every aspect of daily life. (2007, p. 57)

Islamism may thus take many forms, both in terms of political outlook *and* practices. This results in a diversity of actors, displaying varying degrees of organisation and capacity for action, depending on their geographical, social, and cultural inscription. It is important to specify that Islam *per se* does not guide such a transformation towards a holistic system but, as Seidensticker puts it, 'values and norms that are *considered* Islamic' (2014, p. 9; emphasis added). This highlights the phenomenon's intersubjective character, the intimate links between (alleged) knowledge of Islam and political power struggles, and the many discourses that may be qualified as Islamist.

Much as Islamism, *Salafism* is a term derived from academic discourse (Wagemakers, 2012, p. 8). The term builds on the Arabic *al-salaf al-salih* (i.e. the pious predecessors), referring to the first three generations of believers in Islam, which Salafis aim to emulate. Individuals supporting this belief rarely talk about themselves as Salafis but rather as 'Muslims' or 'Sunni Muslims' (Wiedl, 2014a, p. 29). The term Salafism was not in vogue in the scholarly community before the 2000s. Previously, researchers studied 'Islamic fundamentalism' (Choueiri, 1990), Islamism (Kepel, 2000), and political Islam (Roy, 1996; Esposito, 1997). It came into the political spotlight much later, in the early 2010s, following a series of attacks,[3] whose perpetrators claimed to belong to a global Salafi movement. Security agencies started monitoring the activities of the Salafi scenes, especially in the UK, the Netherlands, France, and Germany. In parallel, the term entered academia through the prism of security studies (Meijer, 2009, p. 2).

As a social phenomenon, Salafism originated in the Muslim world in the 1960s and 1970s and can be described as 'a religious-political movement that emerged from Wahhabism and other Islamic currents' (Malthaner, 2014, p. 652). In Europe, it has been in use since the 1990s. Salafism is simultaneously *fundamentalist* as it takes the holy texts literally (i.e. they are infallible), thereby rejecting religious tradition, and *modern* insofar as it calls for the revival of the early practices of Islam, thereby 'disposing of most of existing Muslim culture, belief and practice' (Horst, 2013, p. 3). Such a revival has far-reaching cultural, social, and political consequences, often made opaque by the complexity of the theological debate. Concretely, it means that actions, behaviours, and beliefs which are not sanctioned in the original sources of Islam are considered 'deviations from the straight path of Islam' (Wiktorowicz, 2005, pp. 184–185). Salafis claim that there is only one correct way to live Islam and be in society – theirs.

Still, the *salafiyya* – the global Salafi movement – is divided along ideological and methodological lines. Salafi groups follow partly diverging political goals and recommend starkly contrasting forms of action. Salafism can be typified in two currents: quietist and political (Dantschke, 2014).

Quietist Salafis strive to replicate the example of the Prophet in their daily lives devoutly, yet they do not engage in political activism (Wagemakers, 2012; Wiedl, 2014b). In contrast, political Salafis are missionaries: they see it as their obligation to call to their understanding of Islam both non-Muslims *and* Muslims who believe differently. They engage in political activism and strive to remodel society to fit their conceptions of a rightful political order. Political Salafism is thereby one of the forms that Islamism may take.

Although it has drawn much public attention in the recent decades, it is a minority phenomenon in Western Europe (Boubekeur, 2007; Roex, 2014; Said & Fouad, 2014; Biene et al., 2016; Hamid, 2016). Among political Salafis, some are content with classical forms of political activism (e.g. advocacy, political education, forums, demonstrations), while others aim explicitly to change the present socio-political order(s) through the use of violence. In the literature, the latter are referred to as 'Salafi jihadis' (Schneiders, 2014; Wiedl, 2014a) or 'jihadi Salafis' (Wiktorowicz, 2006).

Though recent historical events have led to a focus on jihadis of Salafi creed – due to the identification of most present-day jihadi organisations with Salafism (al-Qaeda, Boko Haram, al-Shabab, the Islamic State) – other Islamist actors have advocated and/or practised jihad. Seidensticker notes that 'Jihadism has been historically advocated both by a fringe of the political Salafis, but also by a fringe of the more "classical" Islamist actors' (2014, p. 9). For instance, the foreign fighters who went to Afghanistan in the 1980s to join the insurgency and wage jihad against the Soviet army were not predominantly Salafis.

Ashour defines modern-day Jihadism as 'a radical ideology within Islamism that stresses the use of violence as a legitimate, and in some versions, *the* legitimate method of political and social change' (2009, p. 8). This tells us, first, that a large variety of Islamist actors using physical violence can be called jihadi, despite large differences in the scope of their political goals. Second, for some, the use of violence is one type of action within a repertoire, while for others, it is the *only* action that can result in socio-political change. This indicates varying degrees of extremism: arguing organised violence as the only legitimate method for change is qualitatively more extreme than considering violence as one option among others.

Bridging this discussion with the above problematisation of the relationship between radicalisation, extremism, and violence, organised Islamist actors in Western Europe can be approached along two dimensions: the scope of the political project they purport and the position they express towards violent action. Regarding the first dimension, we can discern three ideal-typical Islamist actors: i. nationalists, such as Hamas, Hezbollah, and the Taliban, which are least likely in a Western European context; ii. pan-Islamists, who long for a caliphate spanning Muslim lands, such as most of the Muslim Brothers and Hizb ut-Tahrir; and iii. globalists, who strive towards a *world* caliphate to the exclusion of all other systems, such as al-Qaeda, ISIS (Islamic State of Iraq and Syria), Boko Haram, and most other Salafi jihadi groups. Striving for a global caliphate strongly implies the use of force. In contrast, nationalists do not reject the possibility of being elected to a position from where they would implement their vision of sharia law. The pan-Islamists consider that the unification of Muslim lands within a caliphate necessarily means fighting the current rulers and bringing them down through military coups or popular revolutions. The globalists argue in a similar way regarding toppling the current Muslim state leaders. Further, they believe that the extension of a future caliphate to the rest of the world necessitates propagating the faith (through missioning and/or forced conversion) and/or waging wars of conquest.

Concerning the second dimension, expressed positions towards violent action may vary considerably among Islamist organisations in Western Europe. Positions range from i. the absolute rejection of violence as a political means ('under no circumstances is it allowed'); ii. the strategic rejection of violence in Western societies ('it is not allowed to use violence *here*'); iii. the legitimation of violence ('it is understandable that one reacts and defends oneself'); iv. the legitimation *and* incitation of violence ('you have to contribute to the armed struggle'); to v. the legitimation, incitation, and direct use of violence. Assuredly, an organisation's position on the (il)legitimacy of violence depends on the scope of the political project. Nevertheless, several combinations are imaginable. Shifts in the combination of the political project and the relationship towards violence point to changes in activism towards moderation or radicalisation.

In light of this, the next section introduces the organisations studied in this book. Thereby it critically discusses existing empirical work around several characteristics, which allow for situating the organisations within their broader socio-political context and stressing the ambivalences surrounding their activism. This lays the groundwork for the empirical reconstruction and analysis of *phases* of activism in the next chapter.

Introducing the organisations: structure, followership, aims, activities, and relationship to public authorities

This section contextualises the organisations around the following elements: i. structure (creation, leaders, geographical outreach); ii. followers and funding; iii. political aims; iv. politico-religious ideology, v. activities online/offline; and vi. relationship to public authorities and evidence of terrorist activities (when applicable). Doing so provides first insights into each organisation's political project and relationship to political violence over the years.

Hizb ut-Tahrir Britain *(UK)*

Hizb ut-Tahrir Britain (HTB) was officially created in 1986 by Omar Bakri Mohammed (OBM) and Farid Kasim, both Syrian-born and reputed 'most vocal [and] visible' Islamist activists in the UK at the time (Whine, 2003, p. 3). HTB was created as a relatively autonomous branch of the transnational Islamist organisation Hizb ut-Tahrir (HT). 'The Liberation Party'[4] (meaning of HT in Arabic) was created in 1953 in Palestine by Taqi-ud-deen Al-Nabhani, an Islamic court judge in former East Jerusalem. Initially, the core membership was based in Palestine, Jordan, Lebanon, and Syria. After its members became increasingly targeted by authorities, the 'Party' went underground. By the 1970s, it had expanded to all corners of the Muslim world except Iran.

HTB was originally built following similar goals as other HT branches, but its structure differed somewhat. OBM revealed in an interview that the Emir of HT in Germany had visited him in 1986 in Britain and asked him to work for the Islamist cause as a 'member' of HT but with more leeway. In the interview, he claimed that, at the time, the Emir allowed him and his small group to 'operate independently from the party's global leadership', unofficially under the HT umbrella (Abedin, 2005). Yet, over the years, HT's central leadership viewed him increasingly askance. His focus on the UK was perceived as a distraction from the wider goal of establishing a caliphate across the Middle East. OBM stressed tactical grounds for his frictions with HT: 'the real dispute was over the methodology to establish the Khilafah [i.e. caliphate], they did not like me attacking man-made laws here in the UK' (Abedin, 2005). The fundamental disagreement between OBM and HT's central leadership revolved around the issue of where the line should be drawn regarding the party's activities and objectives outside (Arab) Muslim-majority countries. OBM was ultimately compelled to leave the party in 1996 (Taji-Farouki, 2000, p. 30), which prompted him to turn his energy towards growing *al-Muhajiroun* (AM) in the UK.

After OBM's departure, HTB was headed by Fuad Husayn and later by Jalaluddin Patel (2000–2007). Further leaders over this period included: Abdul Wahid (HTB executive Chairman), Farid Kasim (HTB spokesperson), and Imran Wahid (HTB chief media advisor). The organisation exists to this day. HTB leaders are elected every two years to form an executive committee composed of nine members. All HTB members can take part in the elections. As Patel highlighted in an interview with the Jamestown

Foundation, HTB is 'a branch entrusted with its own administrative affairs' (Abedin, 2004), which underlines its relative independence from HT central. Over the years, HTB established itself across the UK and became particularly active on university campuses. Each HT branch controls networks of local committees. HTB has maintained strong links to HT structures in Germany,[5] Denmark, the Netherlands, France, and Ukraine (Taji-Farouki, 2000; Ahmed & Stuart, 2010; Sinclair, 2010).

Both HTB and HT central refuse to give membership figures (Sinclair, 2010). Gaining full membership in HTB is a tenuous process. New members spend about two years studying party literature, under the guidance of mentors, before they take the *Qasam*, the party oath (Patel in an interview with Abedin, 2004). A parallel, separate structure exists for women, who are encouraged to become fully active members (Malik, 2004). When Omar Bakri Mohammed left in 1996, the majority of HTB members followed him and joined *al-Muhajiroun* (Ahmed & Stuart, 2009, p. 66). The ensuing loss of members, combined with the efforts by Jewish associations and some Members of Parliaments to have HTB banned,[6] resulted in the group adopting a low public profile at the beginning of 1996 up until 2001. In the early 2000s, HTB started organising public events, which attracted large numbers of supporters and sympathisers. For instance, the conferences of 2002 and 2003 were attended on average by 7,000 participants (Ahmed & Stuart, 2009, p. 67). HTB's 2003 conference in Birmingham entitled 'British or Muslim?' attracted 10,000 sympathisers, making it the UK's biggest Muslim event at the time (Malik, 2004). While the number of sympathisers fluctuated between 7,000 and 10,000 until the mid-2000s, the number of core members would amount to a few hundred.

Much like the other organisations presented below, HTB funds itself by way of membership revenue and private donations (Ahmed & Stuart, 2009, p. 72). From the mid-2000s onwards, it started generating complementary revenue from its newly gained publishing role. HTB's responsibility and status increased when several administrative and publishing functions were transferred from HT central in the Palestinian territories to London (Whine, 2006a, p. 8).

HTB's political aim follows HT central's, namely the re-establishment of a caliphate over Muslim lands. Over its decades of existence, HT central formulated and successively amended a constitution of 187 articles for an Islamic state. Toward this end, HT's work targets two audiences: Muslims living in Muslim-majority countries, and Muslim communities and non-Muslim intellectuals in Western societies. HT sees itself doing political-educational work in Muslim-majority countries to bring civil society to recognise the advantages of establishing an Islamic state over Muslim lands. HT members and sympathisers in Muslim-majority countries are advised to '"fight their rulers" by challenging the existing government and fomenting a revolution' (Ahmed & Stuart, 2009, p. 63, quoting HT material). In the words of former HTB leader Jalaluddin Patel, 'the manner by which we can achieve this is by removing the rulers of the Muslim world' (Abedin, 2004). In Western societies, HT members and sympathisers strive to create support for its political goal and suggested course of action, both within Muslim communities and non-Muslim intellectual milieus, thereby creating a suitable environment for HT's revolution to come.

HTB understands its mission as 'intellectual and political' work (Imran Wahid, cited in Ahmed & Stuart, 2009, p. 112). Concretely, HTB asks for British Muslims to resist British values and tentative integration and expects them to identify with what it sees as the transnational community of Muslims (*ummah*). Ahmed and Stuart contend that HTB asks its members to individually and/or collectively subvert the society they live in and take 'Islam as the "only criterion" for "concepts about life, practical and actual"' (2009, p. 62; quoting from Hizb ut-Tahrir, 2000, pp. 72–73). Though it does not plan to establish an Islamist state in the UK, HTB preaches that working to establish the caliphate is a religious obligation for all Muslims.

In this regard, the organisation's specific activities in the UK over the years oscillate between increased activity within Muslim communities (i.e. explain the duty to work towards the caliphate) and increased outreach towards a wider audience (i.e. articulate the cause of the Muslim world and present the caliphate as a valid political and intellectual model based on Islam). From 1993 onwards, HTB began targeting second-generation British Muslims on UK campuses and mosques, distributing, for instance, leaflets condemning local imams who advocated tolerance and integration. This soon resulted in efforts to ban the organisation in 1994 and later in 2005. Both attempts failed. However, Ahmed and Stuart (2009) believe the group temporarily practised self-censure as a result. It became known to the general public by organising protests aimed at Middle Eastern and Central Asian regimes in front of the latter's UK embassies.

After 2001, HTB increasingly engaged with Muslim communities to appear more representative of the UK's Muslim population. For instance, it joined other groups to protest the war in Iraq. It also started fostering a dialogue with Western intellectuals, journalists, and politicians by staging large conferences in 2002 and 2003 discussing Islamism as a non-threatening and viable alternative ideology to Western capitalism (Ahmed & Stuart, 2010, p. 156). Some commentators believe that HTB's activities across the 2000s inherently carried a dual message to suit different audiences (Whine, 2003; Ahmed & Stuart, 2009, 2010). The persistence of covert practices, such as cover names for booking venues, propaganda leaflets without author name(s), and closed meetings (Malik, 2004; Whine, 2006a, p. 4) would lend some support to this claim. Ahmed and Stuart write about a '"keep your ideology in your heart" policy', which the group would enforce from 2005 onwards to mainstream its public appearance (2009, p. 4). They argue that controversial material was suddenly deleted from the group's *Khilafah. com* website after the 7/7 London bombings and the Blair government's proposed proscription against HTB in August 2005. On the other hand, the data gathered for this book shows that much controversial material remained accessible on the group's official English websites.[7]

To this day, HTB has remained a legal organisation in the UK, despite public authorities having tried or threatened to proscribe it on three occasions (1994, 2005, and 2010). Before the 7/7 bombings in 2005, the UK Home Office described HTB as a 'radical, but to date non-violent Islamist group', which 'holds anti-Semitic, anti-Western and homophobic views' (*Guardian*, 2005). After the attacks, the Blair government proposed its proscription. For some, its failure to ban the group rests on HTB's successful 'use [of] euphemistic language to disguise its ideology', as a defensive reaction to increased scrutiny from public authorities (Ahmed & Stuart, 2009, p. 110; see also Whine, 2006a, p. 2).

Others have looked at this issue from a different angle, focusing on individuals who committed attacks and/or were charged for having engaged in terrorist activities and who had been HT members at some point in their lives (Whine, 2003; Vidino, 2015; Bryson, 2017), thereby attributing to the group a role in terrorist mobilisation. Whine argues that while HTB's 'leadership decreed members should not participate in terrorist activity prior to the establishment of the Islamic State, [...] party members were, however, given leave to carry out jihad in *defense* of themselves or the party' (Whine, 2006a, p. 5). HTB has consistently denied allegations of violence and terrorism and systematically refuted publications by scholars and experts who argued to the contrary.[8]

Al-Muhajiroun *(UK)*

Al-Muhajiroun (AM) was officially created on 16 February 1996 in the UK by Omar Bakri Mohammed (OBM). The organisation's name means 'The Emigrants'[9] in Arabic, which depicts well its founder's journey. Syrian-born OBM first left Syria for Lebanon because of his anti-Baath party and pro-Muslim Brotherhood sensibilities. In Beirut, he joined HT, later left Lebanon to study in Egypt, then moved to Saudi Arabia where he tried to set up an HT branch, despite the organisation being banned there. Following a dispute with another HT branch in Kuwait, OBM launched a separate organisation with a few 'brothers' and called it *al-Muhajiroun* (March 1983). After being arrested in 1984 and briefly detained by the Saudi government, he finally fled to the UK in January 1986, where he was granted asylum. He started working towards the establishment of a British branch of HT. AM was 'revived'[10] ten years later after Bakri's breakaway from HTB, the organisation he and Farid Kasim had set up in 1986.

During its existence, AM was mostly based in England, with a head office in East London and several local chapters. It also had a Scottish branch, an Irish branch, a Pakistani branch with a safe house based in Lahore, and, briefly, a US branch. In terms of leadership, OBM was the organisation's self-proclaimed 'spiritual leader' using the title of *sheikh*. Anjem Choudary was the organisation's operational leader and executive director. The organisation had several spokespersons: Hassan Butt (in Lahore), Abdul Rahman Saleem 'Abu Yahya' (in London), Irfan Rasool (Scottish branch), and Adeel Shahid (Luton branch). Further leaders included Iftikhar Ali (in charge of physical training courses) and Simon 'Sulayman' Keeler (in charge of the National Dawa Committee of AM).

The group was organised around selective membership, meaning that members were chosen based on their adequacy with regard to the group's values, aims, and means. AM distinguished between 'activists' (comprising 'full members' and 'students') and 'contacts' (Wiktorowicz, 2005), that is, sympathisers. Becoming a full member was a long process. It started with being a student of OBM, learning about theology, and then attending every important AM event. This learning – one could say vetting – process could go on for up to two years (Wiktorowicz & Kaltenthaler, 2006). As a result, the number of AM full members in the UK before the organisation disbanded would range between 100 and 200. Adding to these the 'students', AM's 'activists' did not exceed 1,000 individuals at any given time, while the group's sympathisers ('contacts') came up to 7,000 individuals (Wiktorowicz & Kaltenthaler, 2006).

AM was self-financed. In an interview conducted by Mahan Abedin in May 2005, OBM details the organisation's three sources of income: 'Firstly, every member has to contribute a third of his salary if he is working. [...] Secondly, we sell audio cassettes, videos, CD's, and thirdly, we receive donations from Muslim businessmen here and abroad', the latter representing the organisation's biggest source of income (Abedin, 2005).

AM's religious-political message built on a Salafi understanding of Islam, for which only those Muslims following the example of *as-salaf as-salih* (the 'pious predecessors') are on the right path. It aimed to bring this 'true Islam' to non-Muslims *and* Muslims. Drawing on a political Salafi worldview, in which the world is clearly separated in *dar al-Harb* (lands of conflict) and *dar al-Islam* (Muslim lands), AM believed that the latter should be united under an Islamic caliphate ruled by sharia law.

AM conducted activities both online and offline. Online, AM leaders published content relating to the organisation's religious stance, political ideas, and goals. The content was broadcast almost exclusively in English and circulated predominantly through the group's websites. AM maintained two official websites, www.almuhajiroun.com and www.muhajiroun.com, where the group published internal news, issued statements, decrypted British and international news for its followers, wrote policy-like briefs, translated key theological and political thinkers into e-book publications, and announced calls for demonstrations and events. In addition, two websites were dedicated explicitly to OBM, www.obm.clara.net and www.turn.to/Khilafah. These displayed his preaching videos and talks, although important statements published on AM's websites were to be found on these platforms as well.

Offline, AM leaders organised 'Islamic seminars' for new 'students' in their London office and local chapters. Members distributed leaflets and conducted *dawa* work (i.e. calling to Islam) on university campuses. They also organised demonstrations, rallies, and protests against the introduction of specific public policies, for instance, against the new Terrorism Law passed after 9/11 in the UK, the introduction of the 2004 French law forbidding 'ostentatious religious symbols' in schools, and UK foreign policy in the Middle East in the wake of the wars in Afghanistan and Iraq. AM's leadership organised conferences for large audiences, inviting prominent figures of the political Salafi scene, and at times jihadi scene, such as Yasser al-Siri, an Egyptian-born dissident who had been sentenced to death *in absentia* in Egypt for a bombing in the 1990s that killed a 12-year-old girl. More controversially, AM is said to have helped organise physical training courses for members.[11] Finally, it may have logistically and financially supported followers wanting to join theatres of war, notably through its office in Lahore, Pakistan. Hassan Butt, spokesperson of AM in Lahore, said as much in an interview with the press in November 2001 (Bassey, 2001). Subsequently, OBM repudiated Butt and denied this adamantly as a media campaign to smear his name, maintaining that AM merely sent money to Muslim charity organisations abroad (Abedin, 2005).

The relationship of the organisation to public authorities varied over its period of activity. Similarly to HTB, it enjoyed a wide berth from British authorities in the late 1990s. Though the group gained more scrutiny after the 9/11 attacks, it still enjoyed large freedom of expression up until its dissolution. The informal understanding – at least on AM's side – was that British authorities would tolerate the group as long as it did not enjoin its British members to commit violence on British territory. This 'covenant of security' (*A'qed Al-Aman*) with British society extended as long as AM leaders enjoyed British papers (i.e. visa/residency) and were free to conduct their political activities. Yet, a few organisations and companies used as fronts were investigated over the years, and some were closed by authorities. Similarly, the British National Union of Students banned AM members from university campuses in March 2001, after having received several complaints, which reported that the group was putting up posters and distributing leaflets on campuses calling for 'killing Jews' (Wendling, 2001).

Some scholars see clear links between AM and terrorist attacks in the UK and abroad. For one, the group's office in Lahore, Pakistan, seems to have been used from 2002 onwards to help members make their way to training camps run by insurgent groups in Afghanistan and, beyond that, to the frontlines of global jihad (Whine, 2006b). Neumann asks whether AM should still be considered a 'gateway organisation' or a terrorist group (2008, p. 34). A study conducted by Simcox et al. (2011) argues that 18% of UK terrorism-related convictions between 1999 and 2009 were linked to AM. Examples among the most prominent convictions include British 'shoe bomber' Richard Reid, seen at several AM meetings in Ilford in the months before his failed attempt to bomb American Airlines Flight 63 over Miami (Wazir, 2002), the 2003 Tel Aviv suicide bombers Asif Mohammad Hanif and Omar Khan Sharif, both Britons, who had been AM students (BBC, 2003), and some of the 2005 London bombers (Vidino, 2015). Pantucci (2015) contends that approximately half of the terrorist attacks carried out by Britons at home or abroad had links to AM.

The group was disbanded on 8 October 2004, in an official declaration by OBM, published on the organisation's websites. However, the group's internet presence kept on, months after the group had dissolved. Officially, OBM stated that he disbanded the group to unite Muslims beyond organisations' cleavages: 'this requires a brave decision and the moulding together of all the Islamic movements and groups and the propagation of the jihadi notion of the Ummah'.[12] Considering the increasing pressure on the group's members over 2004 (police raids, arrests, home searches) and talks of a ban by public authorities, it can be argued that AM leaders preferred to avoid an official ban and chose instead to disband and build anew.

Two successor organisations appeared almost immediately thereafter, with much of the same personnel in command: *al-Ghurabaa* ('The Strangers') and *The Saved Sect* (sometimes found under the name: *The Saviour Sect*). Both organisations merged in November 2005 under the name *Ahlus Sunna wal Jamaah* ('The people of the Sunnah and the community'). *Al-Ghurabaa* and *The Saved Sect* were later (17 July 2006) proscribed under the Terrorism Act 2004. In 2008, Anjem Choudary and activists of the former AM founded the organisation *Islam4UK*, which was ultimately banned in January 2010. Choudary's *Islam4UK* model was imported by several Islamist groups across Europe in 2010.[13] Over the years, former AM personnel and members have maintained activism in the UK under several organisations and names.

Die Wahre Religion *(Germany)*

Die Wahre Religion (DWR) emerged in 2005 as an association between several self-proclaimed preachers from the Cologne-Bonn area. *Die Wahre Religion* translates as 'The True Religion' in reference to Salafis' claim to hold the right version of Islam. Ibrahim Abou Nagie, a German of Palestinian origin, was instrumental in the creation of DWR, as were the German converts Kai Lühr and Pierre Vogel. DWR was a registered association from 2005 until 15 November 2016, when it was dissolved, along with the affiliated association 'LIES! Stiftung', by the German Minister of the Interior, Thomas de Maizière.

DWR's history, development, and protagonists are at times hard to follow because of rifts between leaders participating in the network. In the beginning, Abou Nagie and Vogel worked hand in hand, producing a great number of German textual and video material relating to the Quran and practical aspects of leading a life as a (Salafi) Muslim. Their publications enjoyed a lot of publicity at a time when there was close to no other online outlet offering Islamic preaching in German. Most of their lectures and preaching material was then accessible as DVDs, sold on DWR's website. At its inception, DWR is best understood as an informal network of preachers cooperating voluntarily. Most of the network's activities and many of its sympathisers centred around four metropolitan areas: The North Rhine region (Dortmund, Cologne, Bonn, Monchengladbach), Hamburg, Frankfurt, and Berlin. Important preachers in the network further included Ibrahim Belkaid (aka Abu Abdullah), Said el Emrani (aka Abu Dujana), and Sven Lau (aka Abu Adam).

The collaboration between Abou Nagie and Vogel temporarily ended in 2008 after Abou Nagie took a stand on *takfir* – the practice of ex-communication – which ran contrary to Vogel's interpretation and, more generally, to the Salafi exegesis that the network had supported so far. In a contentious video, Abou Nagie declared that the political leaders of the Muslim world, who have not established sharia in its entirety in their countries, should not be seen as Muslims any longer but as *infidels*. If the fallout started on theological grounds, it soon became personal: Abou Nagie and Vogel answered each other through battle-like videos posted by their respective fans on YouTube up until 2010. Vogel created a concurrent platform with Mohammed Ciftci in 2008: the association *Einladung zum Paradies e.V.* (EZP), translating as 'Invitation to Paradise'. Most of the

Salafi movement was swayed away from DWR to EZP by Vogel, who was considered the better speaker and had built quite a reputation thanks to his open-air conversion ceremonies across Germany. According to Wiedl, EZP became the most visited Salafi website in Germany around 2010, only two years after the fallout. At the time, EZP's website ranged in the 8,000 daily views, whereas DWR's amounted to less than 2,800 on average (Wiedl, 2014a).

The rift between Abou Nagie and Vogel ended in April 2011, when the two men publicly reconciled and walked together at a mass rally in Frankfurt (Möller, 2016, p. 41). The reunification of Vogel with the DWR network was officially announced on 20 June 2011 in a video message shot together with DWR preacher, Said el Emrani (Abou Taam et al., 2016, p. 6). In the summer of 2011, EZP was subsequently dissolved because of the association's financial issues, the growing differences of opinion between Ciftci and Vogel as to the future location of its mosque and Islamic school, and the increasing surveillance by the German Office for the Protection of the Constitution (*Bundesamt für Verfassungsschutz*, BfV). The reconciliation between Abou Nagie and Vogel in April and the dissolution of EZP over the summer of 2011[14] brought most Salafi sympathisers back to DWR. The network's leading preachers strove to reinforce unity instead of stressing differences. In this regard, the *LIES!* campaign (German for 'READ!') provided solid common ground. The proselytism campaign launched at the end of 2011 was conceived of as 'street *dawa*' and revolved around distributing free Qurans at stands installed in every large city centre and encouraging public conversions. This project, started by Abou Nagie, was very positively welcomed in the larger German Salafi scene. So much so that several non-affiliated Salafi preachers joined the effort at *dawa* stands. Mohamed Mahmoud and Denis Cuspert, the leaders of *Millatu Ibrahim*, also supported the project[15] and made appearances at *dawa* seminars organised by DWR (see next section).

As a network, DWR's number of sympathisers over the period is difficult to estimate. As Wiedl shows, although DWR was officially an association, the number of its members does not reflect its large popularity in Germany, especially in the wake of the *LIES!* campaign. According to the German security authorities, the number of political and jihadi Salafis in Germany at the end of 2011 would have amounted to 3,800 individuals (BfV, 2012, p. 251). Based on this number and the fact that EZP got the most attention from the scene at the time, illustrated by the number of its daily website views, DWR probably had fewer than a thousand sympathisers. This changed with the dissolution of EZP and the start of the *LIES!* campaign. By April 2012, only a few months after the start of the campaign, about 300,000 free Qurans had been distributed throughout Germany, mostly in Lower Saxony and Hesse.[16] According to the German security authorities, in 2015, four years after the beginning of the campaign, *LIES!* had 60 local initiatives, managed by eight leaders and a hundred local managers. Over the period of study, DWR's active supporters ranged from approximately 500 to 1,500+. Through the *LIES!* campaign, it further succeeded in gaining a large followership beyond the Salafi scene.[17]

Much like the other organisations studied here, DWR mostly self-financed over the years, relying on German sympathisers' donations and the sale of preaching DVDs and Islamic material (Wiedl, 2014a, pp. 50–51). The scale of the *LIES!* campaign prompted questions about whether bigger interests were helping finance Salafi missionary work in Germany. Abou Nagie repeatedly denied receiving funds from Saudi Arabia and Bahrain, arguing that he had been a rich businessman in the past and was funding the project philanthropically. Further, the *LIES! dawa* stands would have compensated giving out free Qurans by offering higher value Quran editions for purchase.

DWR was, from the beginning, committed to a Salafi creed. The network and its leaders understood their core goal as *dawa* work, the propagation of the faith. For DWR, this meant bringing both German non-Muslims *and* Muslims to the authentic Islam lived by Salafis. Wiedl (2014a, 2017) shows that Salafis primarily address the Muslim 'hypocrites' (the *munafiqun*), meaning all those who do not live in the Salafi way, from Muslims of other creeds to secular Muslims. One of the typical tenets conveyed in Salafi missionary work towards Muslims is that all non-Muslims are *kuffar* (literally 'polytheists'), those who have not (yet) recognised that there is only one God, Allah, and thus will end up in hell. DWR reproduced this tenet online and offline as commonplace knowledge. Although DWR may not have initially followed a specific political goal, its activities had, from the outset, a political dimension. Minimally, its members would have to be at liberty to live and propagate their faith without interference from German authorities. Maximally, the Salafi creed propagated by DWR implied the condemnation of differently minded individuals, the rejection of laws created by man (as opposed to those made by God), and the effort to convert all people living in Germany to Salafism.

DWR conducted its activities online and offline in German. Online, leading DWR preachers published (Salafi) interpretation of Quranic passages of practical interest to Muslims living in non-Muslim countries and provided news from the global Salafi movement. Additionally, each preacher had a favourite issue area. For instance, Abu Dujana specialised in discussing relationships between men and women, Abu Abdullah focused on local and international *dawa* work, and Abou Nagie mainly discussed the incompatibility of Islam with democracy and issues relating to the afterlife. The content put online was mostly video-based: from filming public conversions to Islam to advertisement-like shoots of *dawa* stands and the announcement of public talks, and private videos of seminars held in mosques and rented venues. This video material was circulated through the group's website (www. diewahrereligion.de) created in 2006 and, later, the YouTube channels of the preachers and fans, as well as DWR's Facebook pages.

Offline, besides the large public *LIES!* campaign from the end of 2011 onwards, DWR's leading preachers held regular seminars in the west and north of Germany. These were held in German and addressed a young audience of mixed origins – converts, Muslims of Turkish, North-African, and Southeast-European descent – a niche when considering that Islamic religious institutions in Germany were preaching almost exclusively in Turkish. Mostly held behind closed doors, such seminars and talks were announced on YouTube and Facebook with great publicity, and sympathisers would come from afar to hear a speaker give a talk.

DWR cooperated with several organisations across Germany, respectively inviting preachers to speak at events, organising workshops and conferences jointly, and providing public support for preachers who came under the scrutiny of the German public authorities. For instance, it maintained relationships with Abdellatif Rouali's *DawaFFM*, a group based in Frankfurt and banned by German authorities on 13 March 2013. Similarly, DWR preachers cooperated for a time with the newly founded *Millatu Ibrahim* (MI). At the end of 2011, DWR's website presented contents from the new organisation, and preachers Abu Abdullah and Abu Dujana regularly invited MI leaders to participate in *LIES!* actions. DWR also entertained ties to organisations abroad. At the end of 2009, some DWR activists established contact with Abu Waleed and Anjem Choudary, the leaders of the British *Need4Khilafah*, one of the spin-off organisations of the late *al-Muhajiroun* (Wiedl, 2014a, p. 76). DWR and *Need4Khilafah* started cooperating in 2010, with DWR setting up an affiliated German website to *Need4Khilafah*'s, linking and translating content to/from its British partner.[18]

Public authorities monitored key preachers of the DWR network across the period. Abou Nagie was investigated at least four times between summer 2011 and winter 2013, once on charges of 'disturbing the religious peace' after legitimising violence against people of other faiths, once as part of a large investigation in seven federal provinces with the goal to ban DWR, *Millatu Ibrahim*, *DawaFFM*, and smaller groups, once on charges of inciting the murder of an Islam critic, and once on charges of fraud regarding welfare benefits. Most of these investigations failed until DWR members were arrested after a police crackdown and public authorities ultimately banned the organisation in November 2016. In the charges brought to justify a ban, German authorities linked participation in DWR's activities and terrorist mobilisation for the Islamic State. The Ministry of the Interior stated that it knew in 2015 of 'over 140 individuals, who after participating in *LIES!* activities [had] travelled to Syria or Iraq to join the IS organisation' (Abdi-Herrle et al., 2016), which would make up 20% of all departures from Germany to Syria and Iraq between 2011 and 2015 (BKA/BfV/HKE, 2015, pp. 3–4). The network's leaders went underground after the ban.

Millatu Ibrahim *(Germany)*

Millatu Ibrahim (MI) started as a project when German-Ghanaian Ex-Rapper Denis Cuspert and Austrian activist Mohamed Mahmoud met in Berlin in October 2011. On this occasion, they decided to bring together fellow Muslims dedicated to 'Abraham's faith' – the meaning of *Millatu Ibrahim* in Arabic[19] – who wanted to become more active. A dedicated website was launched a month later, in November 2011. Shortly after, Mohamed Mahmoud moved from Berlin to the city of Solingen (in North-Rhine Westphalia, NRW), where the local *Ar-Rahmah* mosque became the foothold of the newly registered association. There, he renamed the congregation '*Millatu Ibrahim e.V.*'. Its existence was very short: The association was banned by the German Federal Ministry of the Interior on 14 June 2012, as was its successor organisation, *Tauhid Germany*, in March 2015.

The organisation was modelled after *Islam4UK*, one of the successor organisations to *al-Muhajiroun*, which operated in the UK between 2008 and 2010 under Anjem Choudary's leadership (Abou Taam et al., 2016, p. 16). During its short lifespan, MI was active in NRW (Solingen, Bonn, Dortmund, Cologne), Berlin, and had a small following in Austria, Mahmoud's birthplace. The organisation's leadership remained active well beyond June 2012 and its official ban as an association, regularly communicating from exile in Turkey and Syria with its German-speaking following via social media (at least until January 2014).

MI's leadership revolved mainly around the complementary figures of Denis Cuspert and Mohamed Mahmoud. Before Mahmoud and Cuspert met in October 2011, Mahmoud had been a long-time activist and fancied himself an Islamic scholar, while Cuspert was a newly converted ex-rapper who had entered DWR circles only a year before. After both went into exile around May/June 2012, Hasan Keskin (aka Abu Ibrahim), the local leader who was so far in charge of the NRW region, became the organisation's reference point in Germany, until he fled abroad in October 2015 to avoid a two-and-a-half year prison sentence (Diehl, 2015).

Mohamed Mahmoud, known in MI circles under the name 'Abu Usama al-Gharib', had formed in 2006 the association *Islamische Jugend*

Österreichs ('Islamic Youth of Austria'), through which he spread the belief that the world was participating in a 'crusade against the Muslims'.[20] He compiled and translated works by some of the key references in al-Qaeda circles. Shortly after, Mahmoud became the mouthpiece of the German-speaking branch of the *Global Islamic Media Front*[21] (GIMF), translating and propagating al-Qaeda material in the German language. Charged with 'participation in a terrorist association', Mahmoud was sentenced in 2007 to four years in prison, and his wife to twenty-two months (Baehr, 2011, p. 19). He was released in September 2011, one month before meeting with Denis Cuspert in Berlin.

Denis Cuspert, known as Deso Dogg during his career as a rapper, re-converted to Islam in early 2010 after meeting with Pierre Vogel, and took up the Arabic name 'Abu Maleeq'. He once stated that he had already experienced the German Islamist scene in the 2000s, coming in contact with Metin Kaplan's organisation *Kalifatsstaat* ('caliphate state') and Hizb ut-Tahrir circles in Berlin,[22] respectively banned in December 2001 and January 2003 by German authorities. As Abu Maleeq, Cuspert was invited by DWR leaders on several occasions to give talks at seminars, where he also sang *anasheed* (traditional chants sung acapella) and some of his crea-tions praising jihad. When Cuspert founded MI with Mahmoud, he changed his name again and became 'Abu Talha al-Almani', the battle name of a German-Moroccan militant, Bekkay Harrach, who was said to have stormed on a US military base in Afghanistan in 2010 and died as a 'martyr' (Abou Taam et al., 2016, p. 24). Cuspert became the organisation's char-ismatic poster-boy, a born-again Muslim embracing Salafism as true Islam.

There is not much data available about the size of MI's following. While the official members of the registered association *Millatu Ibrahim e.V.* numbered around fifty, it was not representative of MI's much larger fol-lowing (Schneiders, 2014, p. 20). MI's capacity to mobilise around 200 youths from all over Germany for the demonstrations in Bonn in May 2012 (Möller, 2016, p. 44), just six months after the organisation was created, shows its rapid growth within the German Salafi scene. There is even less data on how MI financed its activities. The contributions to the mosque in Solingen must have accounted for a large part of the organisation's budget. The invitations to talk at seminars might have brought in small honorari-ums and donations. The rest of its activities, such as distributing Qurans at *LIES!* stands, rested on volunteering.

From the start, MI made no secret of supporting the transnational politi-cal and military struggle of al-Qaeda and affiliated organisations. MI's main ideological reference was Abu Muhammad al-Maqdisi, whose book, *Millatu Ibrahim*, inspired MI's very name (Heinke & Raudszus, 2015, p. 18). Al-Maqdisi's texts enjoyed an important reception in MI circles thanks to Mahmoud's translations from Arabic into German. Al-Maqdisi is best known as the spiritual mentor of Abu Musab al-Zarqawi, the initial leader of al-Qaeda in Iraq, and has been a key reference in al-Qaeda circles until today (Wagemakers, 2012). He remained a role model for MI followers until 2014. MI leaders later distanced themselves from Al-Maqdisi, when he condemned the ISIS organisation in June 2014 and called on his supporters to join the *al-Nusra Front* instead (still affiliated to al-Qaeda at the time). MI's references further drew upon key leaders of al-Qaeda's transnational network: Ayman al-Zawahiri, who became leader of al-Qaeda in May 2011 following the death of bin Laden, Anwar al-Awlaki, the American-Yemeni imam, who became a central al-Qaeda recruiter in the 2000s, Ahmed Ashush, the leader of the Egyptian Salafi jihadi group *Ansar al-Sharia*, and Abu Yahya al-Libi, a Libyan high-ranking al-Qaeda official.

The activity of MI centred around public lectures and talks, most often published online afterwards. Its website – www.millatu-ibrahim.de – went online in November 2011 and could be retrieved until June 2012. It was used to disseminate the works of the afore-mentioned Salafi jihadi ideologues and Mahmoud's texts, written during his time in prison and which glorified armed struggle. Additionally, the group maintained YouTube channels and Facebook profiles with more accessible and attractive content. The investment in new social media was actively pursued. For instance, the group did not diffuse its videos on 'restricted forums only known to jihad-savvy users, but on the world-leading and almost completely public video hosting website YouTube' (Möller, 2016, p. 39). MI played an instrumental role in the development of a 'pop-jihadi youth scene active throughout Germany and primarily connected through the Internet' (Abou Taam et al., 2016, p. 16). With its own pop-cultural products, such as jihad-themed streetwear and authorised music (*anasheed*), MI contributed to setting a new trend towards mainstreaming jihad as a sub-culture and a recurring topic of discussion among wider Salafi circles.

Offline, MI was active in the *LIES!* campaign started by the DWR network, participating in the distribution of free Qurans in the public arena and proselytising a Salafi creed. Cuspert, especially, was regularly invited to *LIES!* stands and talked as a guest speaker at DWR seminars. MI also participated in the *Ansarul Aseer* initiative for Muslim prisoners, created in summer 2011 by Bernhard Falk (also known as Muntasir bi-llah). Parts of the initiative's personnel indeed overlapped with MI's following. Through the delivery of letters from fellow Salafi activists, the *Ansarul* network hoped to maintain imprisoned activists in close contact with the Salafi scene and present them as righteous models to follow (Abou Taam et al., 2016, pp. 27–28).

The May 2012 riots ultimately brought large public attention to MI's activities. In early May, ProNWR, a right-wing populist and xenophobic party, organised demonstrations in Solingen (1 May) and Bonn (5 May). Both times, ProNRW supporters carried large posters with caricatures of the Prophet Muhammad to provoke a reaction, amongst others, from Salafi communities. In Solingen, they did so in front of the Salafi mosque serving as MI's stronghold, and in Bonn, in front of the *König-Fahd-Akademie*, an Islamic school financed by the Saudi government. Both events represented an opportunity for MI to present itself as the true and only defender of Muslims living in Germany. In Solingen, Hasan Keskin led the counter-demonstrators against the ProNRW supporters. In Bonn, Ibrahim Belkaid (DWR) and Denis Cuspert (MI) were seen leading over 500 Salafi counter-demonstrators.[23] The rioting became especially heavy there, with supporters from both sides fighting each other and the police with stones, sticks, and kitchen knives (Möller, 2016). Five weeks later, on 14 June 2012, the organisation *Millatu Ibrahim* was banned by the Minister of the Interior because 'it promoted and accepted [...] the use of violence as a means to fight against the existing constitutional order'. Its mosque in Solingen and its website were simultaneously closed down.

Cuspert and Mahmoud went into exile after the May 2012 riots, first to Egypt, then to Turkey, and later to Syria. In this context, MI's internet presence became even more central to the continuation of the group's activities. MI's publications became less video- and more text-based. Its WordPress blog was active until February 2013, and, after its deletion, Cuspert and Mahmoud's text and video materials were relayed on Facebook, YouTube, and, less systematically, on obscure internet forums. Hasan Keskin further relayed their video messages under the name *Tauhid Germany*, the apparent successor to MI, which officially supported the ISIL (Islamic State of Iraq and the Levant) and later IS organisation.

In contrast to the other organisations presented so far, MI's relationship to political violence appears much clearer, even more so once its leaders were in exile. In winter 2012, Cuspert and Mahmoud called for attacks in Germany. Later, both participated in terrorist activity in Syria and Iraq. After a failed attempt at the Turkish border in early 2013, Mahmoud later managed to enter Syria and join the Islamic State (IS) as a foreign fighter and propagandist. In October 2014, he reportedly married Ahlam al-Nasr, 'the poetess of the Islamic State', in Raqqa, Syria (Creswell & Haykel, 2015). Cuspert joined the *al-Nusra Front* (al-Qaeda in the Levant) as a foreign fighter in February 2013, before joining ISIL in 2014 and eventually pledging allegiance to the Islamic State. He was filmed committing serious crimes such as participating in massacres and beheadings[24] and was reported leading a brigade called *Millatu Ibrahim* in what has become known as the Fall of Mosul to IS insurgents in August 2014.

Part of MI's following emulated Mahmoud's and Cuspert's example. Some consider that former MI activists 'formed the nucleus of German foreign fighter activists in Syria' (Heinke & Raudszus, 2015, p.18; see also Steinberg 2014, p. 361; and Said, 2014, p. 144). A significant number of German foreign fighters who travelled to Syria and Iraq to fight for the IS organisation (and a few to fight for its Salafi jihadi competitors) appear to have been active or former MI members. Several elements lend credit to the assessment that MI contributed to terrorism abroad. For example, Cuspert became a central spokesperson for IS outward communication in the German language. In a video released April 2014, Cuspert is seen reciting a *nasheed* addressed to Chancellor Angela Merkel, accompanied by twelve masked and armed German-speaking men singing the chorus.[25] Similarly, journalistic accounts indicate that by 2014 German foreign fighters in Syria had created their own brigade within the IS organisation and entitled it 'Millatu Ibrahim'.[26]

Muslim Association of Britain *(UK)*

The last organisation to be introduced is the *Muslim Association of Britain* (MAB). Founded in 1997 by Kamal el-Helbawy and Anas Altikriti, it has headquarters in London and 11 local branches across Britain. In the early 2000s, MAB's leading figures were Anas Altikriti and Dr Azzam Tamimi (Perry, 2018). Altikriti was born in Iraq and came to the UK as an infant when his family fled because his father was a renowned Islamist opposition figure to Saddam Hussein's Baath regime. Altikriti became a political activist, first in MAB and later by joining George Galloway's party 'Respect – The Unity Coalition', for which he stood as the leading candidate in Yorkshire and Humberside for the 2004 European Parliamentary elections. Tamimi is a British Palestinian political activist. He moved to London in the 1970s to attend college. He obtained a PhD in Political Theory from the University of Westminster in 1998 for a thesis entitled 'Islam and Transition to Democracy in the Middle East: Prospects and Obstacles'. He often spoke in an official capacity for MAB in the early 2000s and became prominent in MAB's takeover of the controversial Finsbury Park Mosque[27] in 2005.

The organisation maintains a website – www.mabonline.net – in English. Up to 2001, the organisation had a few hundred followers. This changed when MAB started campaigning in late 2002 and early 2003 against the invasion of Iraq. As Gilliat-Ray shows, MAB was 'elevated from a relatively obscure group to national prominence' due to its association with the 'Stop the War Coalition', and 'membership grew from about 400 to 1000 during this period' (Gilliat-Ray, 2010, p. 76). MAB funds itself through donations. On its website, the organisation has stated that its 'members are responsible for the upkeep, maintenance, and management of a few mosques through-out the UK' and that it 'works closely with other mosques or trusts that manage mosques'.

MAB depicts itself as an independent non-profit organisation operating for British society. In its political agenda, the organisation puts forward a set of values and ideas to bring prosperity and justice to the world, values which the Muslim Brotherhood largely inspires. In its own words: 'MAB shares some of the main principles that the Muslim Brotherhood stands for; like upholding democracy, freedom of the individual, social justice and the creation of a civil society' (MAB's official website). It shares the religious thought of international Islamic scholar Yusuf al-Qaradawi,[28] the controversial spiritual guide of the Muslim Brotherhood worldwide. MAB does not advocate the implementation of sharia law in the UK but believes that, in Muslim majority countries, 'it is the right of the masses to choose Shariah if they wish; and their democratic decision should be respected' (MAB's official website). In this regard, MAB can be characterised as an Islamist organisation, although it has rejected the terminology, arguing that Islam as a faith and an organising principle for society cannot be separated. It states on its website: 'the notion that there is a "political Islam" and a "non-political Islam" is fundamentally refuted by MAB'. Recognising the 'democratic principle of universal suffrage', MAB has relentlessly encouraged its members to vote for UK and EU elections. Altikriti himself ran for the 2004 election to the European Parliament.

MAB's activities in the British public sphere ranged from community events, talks, and lectures to engagement with local politicians and advocacy against Islamophobia (Altikriti, 2004). Its political activism increased between 2002 and 2005, starting with the mounting invasion of Iraq. MAB co-organised events with the 'Stop the War Coalition' led by Lindsey German, a left-wing British activist. In April 2002, they co-convened a 200,000-strong demonstration against the massacre of Palestinian refugees by Israeli forces in Jenin and the mounting invasion of Iraq (under the dual slogans of 'Freedom for Palestine' and 'Don't attack Iraq'). On this and further occasions, MAB mobilised 'thousands of Muslims' (Phillips, 2008, p. 105) and gained increasing visibility among British Muslim communities. In 2004, together with the Muslim Women Society, it established the organisation PRO-HIJAB in response to the veil ban in France. In 2005, according to Tamimi, MAB was 'approached by a combination of people – the old [mosque] trustees, the police, the Home Office, MPs' and asked to try and turn around the Finsbury Park Mosque (Casciani & Sakr, 2006). The takeover of the mosque, in collaboration with the public authorities, was completed at the end of 2005 and presented as a success story to 'counter more radical Islamist groups' (Gilliat-Ray, 2010, p. 77).

The organisation's leadership fragmented in early 2006. After the July 2005 London bombings, MAB members wanted a retreat from activism, including the involvement in the Stop the War Coalition, in favour of educational and community development programmes. Gilliat-Ray points out: 'By December of that year, the most prominent activists, Anas Altikriti and Azzam Tamimi, had effectively lost control of the movement at a meeting which saw a new executive board elected' (2010, p. 76). Both left the organisation (temporarily) to create the competing *British Muslim Initiative*. Up until then, MAB under Altikriti and Tamimi worked with very diverse political actors: British public authorities, the Stop the War Coalition, the Muslim Council of Britain (an umbrella organisation for more than 500 British mosques), and with Muslim Brotherhood-inspired organisations in Europe. MAB has been criticised for being too close to the Muslim Brotherhood, as well as for some of the views held by its leaders. In the early 2000s, Tamimi repeatedly made references to its support of Hamas. Some show that MAB's discourse on antisemitism has been ambiguous at times (Ismail, 2007). The organisation is active to this day, and Altikriti was elected again as President in February 2018 for a four-year term.

Similarities and differences between the organisations

Several insights emerge from the overview of the five organisations so far. A major difference is that the organisations based in Germany were created much later than those in the UK. AM and MAB were created in the 1990s, HTB already existed in the 1980s, whereas DWR appeared around 2005 and MI in 2011. The earlier development of an Islamist scene in the UK is connected *inter alia* to the UK's asylum policies of the 1990s towards persecuted Islamists from the Mediterranean and the Gulf. The German Islamist scene developed much later. The 1990s had seen the creation of a few Islamist organisations which did not last long, such as Metin Kaplan's *Kalifatsstaat* ('caliphate state'), banned in 2001 and Hizb ut-Tahrir, banned in 2003, but no Salafi organisation. As Schneiders points out, while the Salafi movement probably arrived in Germany in the mid-1990s, the first political activists appeared around 2004–2005 (2014, pp. 13, 180). However, despite the time lag, the UK and the German organisations presented here display many commonalities.

The groups' structures are closer than at first glance. All five groups have mostly the characteristics of an organisation and some of a network. They are registered associations with a name, official members, contact details, internet presences, logos, and more. Even DWR, which Wiedl qualifies as a 'network of preachers' (2014a, pp. 48–49), displays the characteristics of an organisation. At least publicly, it has appeared as an organised collective, with the same key leaders over the years, at rallies, at *LIES!* stands, and vis-à-vis media inquiries. Conversely, some of the other organisations occasionally acted as support networks, for instance when a fellow group or befriended individual was attacked in media or political discourses, or was considered persecuted by public authorities and security agencies. For example, MI defended Abou Nagie (DWR) when he was questioned in 2012 by judicial authorities regarding the *LIES!* stands. Similarly, AM supported Abu Hamza – then preacher of the Finsbury Park Mosque – when he was arrested in 2003 by British authorities to be extradited to the US.

The organisations lent leaders[29] an important role (less in HTB's case). AM, DWR, and MI's respective leaders were (self-styled) Salafi preachers first and activists second, while HTB's and MAB's see themselves as intellectuals and political activists. The figure of the Salafi preacher goes further than that of the activist insofar as it impersonates religious authority. The leaders of all five organisations attracted followers nationwide, thereby facilitating interactions between different parts of the Islamist scene. Because of their contacts, they fulfilled the function of nodal points between different organisational levels: the larger scene, loose networks, befriended groups, and foreign activists.

In terms of following and funding, the groups show similar patterns. They are self-funded, primarily through donations and publishing activities. They are supported by a small core of activists and backed by a lot more sympathisers. The capacity of the groups, despite their modest membership numbers, to mobilise hundreds of sympathisers for demonstrations points to the support they found in the larger Islamist scene.

The contrast group – MAB – aside, the four other organisations share the same superordinate political goal of establishing a caliphate. Other than that, they partly diverge on the way to establish it, the final scope it would have, and how inclusive it should be. From their official positions, HTB and DWR can be categorised as pan-Islamists (i.e. in favour of a caliphate in Muslim lands), while AM and MI appear closer to a globalist position (i.e. in favour of a world caliphate). In terms of politico-religious creed, HTB is Islamist but not fundamentalist; it wishes to represent Muslims of all creeds, Shia Muslims too, and irrespectively of schools of thought. AM, DWR, and MI reproduce a Salafi worldview in which only Salafi Muslims hold the right version of Islam and the true model of socio-political organisation. In contrast, MAB aims to represent British Muslims and promote their participation in political life. It shares the stance of the moderates within the Muslim Brotherhood, who hold that democracy and sharia law are compatible.

All five groups' generic activities are similar: they use both offline and online activism and diffuse their political message in the local language. Except for MAB, they insist on missionary work – HTB calls this, at times, 'intellectual work'. Between the early 2000s and early 2010s, online activism has evolved, but in important ways the UK and German organisations use it similarly: to announce coming conferences, seminars, and other get-togethers (festivals, barbecues, etc.), to take positions on local and international political events, to publish the translated works of foreign scholars – among others.

Interestingly, the overview so far also shows that HTB, AM, DWR, and MI looked at each other's practices and borrowed successful models. MI was inspired by AM's successor organisation *Islam4UK* (2008–2010). Similarly, several Islamist groups in Austria, Switzerland, and the UK tried to replicate DWR's *LIES!* campaign.[30] Further, the four organisations have been accused of purporting a dual message to fit their audiences: they would disguise their ideology and opt for a low public profile when public attention heats up. Further, they would sometimes use covert practices: giving the location of a conference venue or changing it at the last minute and organising seminars behind closed doors or in private premises.

Finally, the contextualisation of the organisations so far underlines the ambiguous relationship that HTB, AM, and DWR maintained towards violent means of action. The positions of AM and DWR seem to have fluctuated over time: they refer at times to a covenant of security with authorities ('you leave us alone, we leave you alone'), which implies a strategic rejection of violence, not an absolute one. For its part, HTB consistently denied allegations that it would legitimise violence yet permitted its members to defend themselves or the organisation in case of attack. The numbers of terrorism offences that are credited to (ex)members or sympathisers of the three organisations complicate the picture and point to a more flexible discourse on the use of violence. MI's relationship to violence is more readily interpreted: the organisation stressed from the beginning the necessity of armed jihad, and its leaders eventually went to wage jihad for the Islamic State. The contrast group's case is equally clear: MAB has consistently rejected the use of violence as a legitimate means of social and political change.

This chapter showed that while there are different sensibilities among Islamist organisations with regards to political projects and means, they also present commonalities. Further, some of the organisations appear to have experienced shifts in discourse and practice over the period. It is important, then, to analyse how these shifts are articulated in the organisations' texts, audios, and videos and reconstruct their phases of activism empirically.

Notes

1 The Muslim Brotherhood (full name, *The Society of the Muslim Brothers*) was created in 1928 in Egypt by the Islamic scholar Hassan al-Banna. A Sunni Islamist organisation, it became transnational after being persecuted in Egypt, resulting in its members seeking asylum in other parts of the Muslim world (1950–1960s). The Muslim Brothers reached Europe in the 1960s, with structures mainly in the UK and later in Germany. For a comprehensive political history of the Muslim Brotherhood, see Vidino (2010), Pargeter (2013), and Perry (2018).

2 One aspect of Mandaville's definition needs to be nuanced: Islamists do not all wish to implement sharia within the borders of states. The Eurocentric concept of nation-state, especially, is foreign to Islamist thought. Some Islamist actors have a nationalist agenda, such as Hamas in the Palestinian territories. Yet, most Islamists advocate the creation of a pan-Islamic political order to unite all Muslims, which would take the form of an Islamic caliphate.

3 The Toulouse and Montauban attacks committed by Mohammed Merah in March 2012 played a key role in the political, security, and media shifts which consecrated Salafism as the number one security threat. Other significant attacks in the early 2010s include the 2011 Frankfurt Airport shooting, the Moscow metro and airport attacks (2010–2011), and the 2013 Boston Marathon attack.

4 Hizb ut-Tahrir is not a party according to a Western understanding of a 'political party'. It does not strive to influence political processes through typical political channels (such as elections), does not aim to take office, and sees itself more as a consultative body for the establishment of a future caliphate and then one of its advisors.

5 Though HT was banned in Germany in January 2003, it has maintained a number of local cells, as well as an internet presence (www.kalifat.org; nowadays: www.imauftragdesislam.com).

6 See: House of Commons debate (1994, 31 March), *Racism and Anti-Semitism*, Column 1115–1120.

7 These include: www.hizb-ut-tahrir.org, www.hizb-ut-tahrir.info (from 2005 onwards), and www.khilafah.com, as well as its online magazine (www.new civilisation.com).

8 For example, one of HTB's Media Information Packs [accessed in 2013, published earlier] includes a letter from an HTB member to Zeyno Baran, expert at the Nixon Center, taking argument with and rebutting her report point by point.

9 In reference to the first converts to Islam, who emigrated with the Prophet Muhammad from Mecca to Medina in the year 622. The event is depicted as the *hijra* (i.e. migration).

10 During his first ten years in Britain, his associates in Saudi Arabia maintained some of AM's activities. OBM admitted in an interview that he kept AM on life-support, parallel to his work for HT: 'I kept this as a separate platform. I contacted my brothers in Saudi Arabia and instructed them to pursue their underground activities as part of the global HT network' (Abedin 2005).

11 The courses were offered via an organisation called 'Sakina Security Services', which specialised in firearms training overseas as it was not allowed in the UK. See Clément (2014), as well as *The New York Times*, 4 October 2001, 'A Nation Challenged: Suspects; Britain Tracing Trail of One More Jihad Group', and *BBC News*, 26 June 2000, 'British Muslims join "holy war"'.

12 Statement published on AM's website on 8 October 2004, under the title 'An official declaration dissolving al-Muhajiroun'.

13 Among the sister organisations, the most well-known were *Sharia4Belgium*, *Sharia4Holland*, *Call to Islam* in Denmark, and *Prophets of the Ummah* in Norway (Moghadam, 2017; Vidino, 2015).

14 By this time, Vogel had left for Egypt to avoid charges. A few months earlier, in May 2011, he had publicly called for a prayer for the dead ('Totengebet') for the recently killed Usama bin Laden. After this, most moderate Salafi preachers in Germany ceased any cooperation with him and EZP.

15 One example is a video by Mahmoud entitled 'Das Quran Projekt geht weiter!' (October 2012), in which he pledges support for the *LIES!* project and Abou Nagie, then under security authorities' increased scrutiny.

16 *Spiegel*, 12 April 2012. 'Salafisten bedrohen Journalisten die über Koranverteilung berichten.'

17 Abou-Taam et al. note, for instance, that DWR's Facebook community increased from approximately 8,000 followers in autumn 2011 to 166,000 in January 2016 (2016, pp. 20–21).

18 Abu Waleed's website www.salafimedia.com was copied faithfully into www. salafimedia.de and linked to its English model. The website does not exist under this address anymore.

19 Ibrahim (or *Abraham*) is a key figure in the Quran, depicted as the leader of the righteous. *Millatu Ibrahim* is also the title of a book by Abu Muhammad al-Maqdisi, a prominent source of reference among jihadi ideologues.

20 'Die IJÖ verurteilt das Schweigen der Welt bezüglich des israelischen Massaker im Heiligen Land!', written by Mohamed Mahmoud, *Islamische Jugend Österreichs* (IJÖ), 2006, p.1.

21 The GIMF was an al-Qaeda media agency dedicated to the online diffusion of propaganda material, from advice on key readings (such as al-Suri's *The Global Resistance Call*, 2005) to training instructions (Stenersen, 2008; Torres Soriano, 2012).

22 Cuspert confided this in an interview with DajjalTV, a Salafi online TV channel. The interview was conducted in October 2010 by Abu Ibrahim at-Turki and was entitled 'Von Deso Dogg zu Abu Maleeq.'

23 *Spiegel*, 2012. 'Radikale unter sich', May 5.

24 *Deutsche Welle*, 5 November 2014, 'Berlin rapper in "Islamic State" beheading video', and *Spiegel Online*, 4 November 2014, 'Video zeigt deutschen Dschihadisten bei IS-Gräueltaten'.

25 The video was posted under the title 'German group of fighters from ISIS together with Abu Talha al-Almani are singing a song for Angela Merkel'.

26 On 15 June 2014, the German Press Agency reported that the German federal prosecutor was conducting investigations into an IS combat unit called 'Deutsche Brigade Millatu Ibrahim', headed by none other than Denis Cuspert. This was also reported in a *Berliner Kurier* article entitled 'IS-Kämpfer aus Berlin Deso Dogg: "Wir schlachten euch alle!"', 3 September 2014.

27 The Finsbury Park Mosque was under Abu Hamza's control until January 2003, when the mosque was closed down 'amid a major al-Qaeda associated investigation'. Abu Hamza was later charged with terrorism-related offenses (Casciani & Sakr, 2006).

28 Qaradawi became particularly controversial in Europe around 2004 because of his declarations approving Palestinian martyrdom operations against Israeli civilians. Taking position on this issue, MAB states on its website: 'MAB recognises Qaradawi as a respected, knowledgeable scholar of Islam. Qaradawi has contributed positively to the modern Islamic discourse in many ways. In Islam, everyone may make sound or incorrect judgments or fatwas. [...] If a scholar makes an error in his judgment or opinion, this definitely does not mean that he/ she should be alienated or disrespected.'

29 Contrary to Neumann's argument that the time of Islamist preachers was already *passé* in the mid-2000s (2008, pp. 35–36), the German Islamist scene of the early 2010s still gives much importance to (self-styled) Islamic preachers. Even in the UK, Islamist preachers and scholars have continued to play a nodal role long after 2005.

30 See Wiedl and Becker (2014) and the following press articles: *Die Welt*, November 15, 2016. 'Das Missionierungsnetzwerk des Ibrahim Abou Nagie'; *Die Presse*, November 23, 2015. 'Wien: Koran-Verteilungen sollen verboten werden.'

2

Reconstructing phases of activism: group moderation, radicalisation, and extremism

This chapter turns to the empirical reconstruction of the five organisations' phases of activism. Since radicalisation processes are partly contradictory and non-linear, a more accurate characterisation of an organisation's evolving activism would reconstruct phases of moderation, radicalisation, and/or extremism. Contra studies too often labelling organisations 'radical' or 'extremist' without providing criteria for identifying a turn to political violence, this chapter aims to trace meaningful changes in group orientation empirically. The methodological approach presented here is interpretative (see introductory chapter). It is grounded in a discursive epistemology which regards language as the temporary stabilisation of meaning, whereby meaning is contested and changes over time. The chapter presents a framework for analysis which draws on a qualitative content analysis with a view to comparing discursive formations temporally. This framework was developed to study a large corpus of textual data, in which complex temporal relations between discursive articulations are involved, and to interpret and convey these relations in a way that makes their temporality visible.

The chapter starts by explaining the analytical framework and the concrete method used to study the organisations' changes in activism. Turning to the description and interpretation of the qualitative content analysis, I outline how MAB's moderation contrasts with the other organisations' forms of activism. Next, I discuss the latter, highlighting common patterns but also varied intensities in group radicalisation. Finally, I turn to the reconstruction of the organisations' respective phases of activism. The chapter ends with a discussion of the main insights and a visualisation of the phases further studied in the second part of the book.

Reconstructing phases of group moderation and group radicalisation

The empirical approach presented here explores temporally the two dimensions discussed in Chapter 1, namely the scope of the political project and the relationship to violent action of the five organisations. It does so at a linguistic level, exploring discursive articulations and potential transformations with regards to these two dimensions.

Islamist organisations' self-accounts can be viewed as discursive articulations. In a Western European context, the discourses that Islamist actors draw upon and re-produce constitute alternative, marginal discourses. They resist some of the dominant discourses re-produced by hegemonic actors. As I studied elsewhere, Islamist organisations in Western Europe contest two dominant discourses – the 'war on terror' and the 'benevolent world hegemony' discourse – and articulate alternative interpretations of both (Clément 2014). However, not all Islamist organisations re-produce similar counter-discourses. Some draw on a radical critique of the 'war on terror' *from within* Western hegemonic discourse; so does, for instance, MAB, as we will see below. Others re-produce the discourse of a 'war on Islam and Muslims' common to jihadi actors worldwide (Clément 2014). While the narrative underpinning of such discourses is studied in depth in the second part of the book, the focus lies, in the following, on exploring the question of changes in activism. In short, it is about analysing how each organisation re-presents over time its political project and forms of activism in language, thereby referring to larger discursive articulations.

In this chapter, the analytical framework draws on a qualitative content analysis (QCA) with a view to comparing discursive formations temporally. Much as other qualitative research methods, QCA shares 'the concern with meaning and interpretation of symbolic material, the importance of context in determining meaning, and the data-driven and partly iterative procedure' (Schreier, 2014, p. 173). It is different from quantitative content analysis in several ways; chiefly, it is not interested in testing hypotheses or pursuing 'validity', and 'whereas the focus of quantitative content analysis continues to be on manifest meaning, qualitative content analysis is also applied to latent and more context-dependent meaning' (Schreier, 2014, p. 173).

Concretely, QCA supports my interpretative approach in three ways. First, it helps with reducing the large amount of textual material by focusing on those aspects of meaning that relate to the research aim, that is, exploring stability and change in organisations' construction of a political project and relationship to violence. Second, it offers a way to study discursive change comparatively. As Hamann and Suckert note regarding discursive approaches: 'Stability and change, the two fundamental categories of any analysis sensitive to temporality, can only ever be visible in a comparative framework' (2018, p. 10). Temporality can pose a methodological challenge in discursive approaches and QCA is used here to facilitate the comparison of discursive articulations across time. Finally, QCA is flexible and allows zooming in and out of the empirical material. Because it involves moving beyond the individual units of coding and categories to the relations between them, it allows for both thick description of coded categories and their contextual interpretation, as well as looking for patterns and co-occurrences.

At a basic level, qualitative content analysis is a method for systematically describing the meaning of qualitative data (Schreier 2014, p. 170). This is done by assigning successive parts of the material to the categories of a codebook (or coding frame). It contains main categories, which are 'those aspects of the material about which the researcher would like more information' and subcategories, which 'specify what is said in the material with respect to these main categories' (Schreier 2014, p. 174). The categories developed in the present codebook are partly concept-driven, as they refer to the two dimensions developed in Chapter 1, and partly data-driven, as they were built inductively.

The codebook consists of *textual* elements, which refer, on the one hand, to discursive and action-related *radicalisation* and, on the other hand, to discourse-based and action-related *moderation*. While references to a political project and concrete forms of activism are both *discursive* insofar as discourse entertains an essential relationship to practice, I separate them analytically to explore different constellations and their stability or change over time. As noted in Chapter 1, different combinations between the scope of the political project and relationship to violence are imaginable. Hence, the codebook distinguishes between references to political beliefs and goals which themselves refer to larger discourses ('discourse-based') and references to material forms of (inter)actions in the real world ('action-based'). At a basic level, the categories of the codebook represent political ideas and options that are endorsed by different hues of Islamist groups, for example, supporting the exit from mainstream society or migrating to Muslim-majority countries (e.g. *hijra*). It thus typifies discourse-based and action-based textual references to political moderation or radicalisation into extremism. Table 2.1 presents the codebook at the level of main categories, categories, and codes (for a detailed version including examples illustrating each code, see Appendix C1). The corpus was coded manually and in context.[1]

As the codebook captures textual elements, 'action-based moderation' and 'action-based radicalisation' into extremism do not refer to potential *effects* on behaviour but mark references to and representations of actions that have happened or are currently happening in the real world. For example, calls to demonstrate against the imminent war in Iraq in early 2003 are coded 'Non-violent collective action' (*action-based moderation*).

Table 2.1 Codebook 'Group moderation and group radicalisation'

Main category (level 1)	Category (level 2)	Code (level 3)
Discourse-based radicalisation	Aim to establish a (world) Islamic caliphate	By converting the rest of the world
		By waging war against other collectives
		By revolution(s) and/or coup(s)
	Legitimisation of political violence	Praise of a person or group, who/which condone(d) political violence and/or who engage(d) in political violence
		Call to acts of violence and/or to participate in combat/war
		Legitimise violence theoretically or indirectly
	Specifications on how political violence should be conducted	Identification of targets or locations Identification of means
Action-based radicalisation	Support for international jihad	Financing activities abroad for *Dawa* work or relief aid, operated by insurgent organisations
		Joint activities with actors known to support jihad
		Organisation of local training camps or weapons seminars
		Contact with insurgent group(s) abroad and/or contact facilitation for would-be foreign fighters
	Reference to participation in violence locally	Participation in demonstrations and/or riots gone violent
	Reference to (planned) attacks by (ex) members or followers	Foiled attacks
		Successful attacks
	Participation in jihad	Participation in jihad as foreign fighter(s)
Discourse-based moderation	Participation	Participation in public debate and/or support for pluralism of opinion
		Delegitimisation of actors of political violence
		Rejection of political violence as a legitimate political means in UK or German society
	Exit	Withdrawal from public debate

Table 2.1 (continued)

Main category (level 1)	Category (level 2)	Code (level 3)
Action-based moderation	Participation 2	Non-violent collective action (participation in, organisation of)
		Reference to relations with (local) political leaders or leaders of civil society organisations
		Call to boycott
	Exit 2	No interaction with (host) society or state
		Encourage *hijra* (immigration to 'Muslim lands')

Similarly, in AM's corpus, several passages are coded 'Successful attacks' (*action-based radicalisation*) as they refer explicitly to an attack by former followers, namely the suicide attack committed in 2003 by two Britons, Asif Hanif and Omar Sharif, in Tel Aviv.

It is important to bear in mind that a textual corpus only mirrors part of the organisations' forms of activism. Such a textual approach is limited to those representations of actions in the real world that organisations committed to paper, recorded, or filmed. While there are limits to a textual inquiry, this approach makes it possible to explore the concomitant presence of 'moderation' and 'radicalisation' categories, even within a single text. In this regard, it provides a more fine-grained analysis of the turn to extremism, as organisations are unlikely to move from moderation to radicalisation without transition.

Analysing discursive articulations through this codebook fits the purpose of an interpretative approach to discourse attentive to temporality. It presents several advantages. First, the categories constructed around 'radicalisation' and 'moderation' go beyond the traditional dichotomy 'extremist vs non-violent'. As I argued in Chapter 1 against taking 'non-violent' as an opposite state to 'radicalising' or 'extremist', I believe 'moderation' fits better the *ex negativo* of radicalisation into extremism. Radicalisation is conceived as a process by which an organisation adopts extremist attitudes and/or behaviour directed against the minimal conditions for coexistence in an open society. Conversely, 'moderation' is conceived as the acceptance of minimal conditions for coexistence in an open society, despite holding starkly different political views from the rest of society. As a process, moderation allows describing not only the activism of groups that support moderate views and engage in non-violent politics but also groups which (re)turn to the acceptance of minimal conditions for coexistence in an open society and use of non-violent action only.

In this regard, it would not make much sense to define moderation too strictly. For example, were action-based moderation to be described only as the participation in democratic institutions, there would be no coded segments except for the *Muslim Association of Britain* (MAB). I understand moderation minimally as non-violent politics and maximally as active participation in public life. In the case of Islamist organisations in Western Europe, forms of *action-based moderation* range from a non-violent *exit* (i.e. minimal to no interaction with society) to the active peaceful participation in the socio-political sphere.

Second, studying the organisations' articulations through this codebook allows for comparison between organisations and over time. Comparison between organisations is important to explore similarities and differences, not least in terms of varied intensity of processes of radicalisation. Diachronic comparison is central to studying stability and change in the discursive articulations of each organisation over time. As Hamann and Suckert note, many approaches to discourse integrate elements of 'quantified visualisation' to the interpretation to 'depict change and stability in discourses', as it allows for a productive alternation 'between moving away from and towards the empirical material' (2018, p. 13). To support the interpretative endeavour and depict temporality, I draw on some quantifying-visualising elements from the qualitative data analysis software QDA Miner.

To identify relationships and temporal shifts that would have remained invisible within such a large corpus, I retrieved two types of coding results: coding frequency[2] and coding by variable. The former analyses the distribution of moderation and radicalisation codes, while the meaning of passages is interpreted in context. The latter – coding by variable – allows exploration of the relationship between codes and a given variable. I used the variable 'organisation' to analyse the distribution of moderation and radicalisation codes by organisation and compare how organisations construct meaning within similarly coded passages. I used the variable 'publication date' to arrange the texts in temporal order and analyse the distribution of codes across time. The juxtaposition of different discursive articulations, at different points in time, makes visible what has remained stable and what has shifted (Hamann and Suckert 2018, p. 16). Ultimately, the empirical reconstruction of phases of activism rests on interpreting structural changes in an organisation's discursive articulations. Such an approach conveys an understanding of the temporality of group activism not as rupture but rather as gradual change over a continuum between moderation and extremism.

Contrasting MAB's moderation

To begin with some descriptive results, 46,839 words were coded according to the codebook 'Group moderation and group radicalisation', that is 22.6% of all the words in the corpus. The number of coded segments amounts to 791 units of sense. All the documents in the corpus present at least one code of 'group moderation' or 'group radicalisation'. The coding categories are unequally represented in the overall corpus.

The large majority of coded segments pertain to the main category *discourse-based radicalisation*. Indeed, it represents 74.2% of all segments coded (i.e. 587 over 791 codes) and is present across 78.4% of the documents (i.e. 105 over 134 documents). While this result is not refined by organisation and timeframe yet, it already indicates that the large majority of documents in the corpus contain at least one discourse-based radicalisation code.

Action-based moderation is the second-largest category represented in the corpus, with 15% of all codes. While not a high frequency per se, this category is present across a large number of documents (41.8%). This is interesting insofar as the data for MAB represents only 6% of the overall corpus. It indicates that, in some phases, organisations may simultaneously articulate extreme political beliefs/goals and advocate moderate forms of actions.

Discourse-based moderation and *action-based radicalisation* are represented much less, both in the percentage of codes and documents. Such results could be expected for *action-based radicalisation*. However, the low presence of *discourse-based moderation* codes is surprising insofar as action-based moderation (15% of coded segments) could be expected to be matched by a similar frequency of discourse-based moderation codes, yet these represent only 6.7% of all coded segments.

At the level of single codes, there is greater disparity still. While some are strongly represented, others are under-represented[3] or not represented at all.[4] The codes 'Praise person or group', 'Legitimise violence theoretically/indirectly', and 'Call to violence/combat', all three from the category 'Legitimisation of political violence' (*discourse-based radicalisation*), represent almost half of the codes in the corpus. As a whole, the corpus thus draws strongly on political beliefs legitimising political violence.

Figure 2.1 illustrates the main categories' significance by organisation. Contrasting the coding results between organisations reveals that MAB's political activism differs significantly from the other organisations. MAB almost exclusively displays codes pertaining to *moderation* categories. In contrast, HTB, AM, DWR, and MI predominantly display *radicalisation* categories. The analysis so far is not temporally

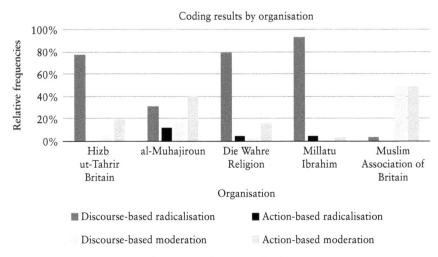

Figure 2.1 Group moderation and group radicalisation (main categories per organisation)

refined; the coding results sorted by publication date indicate different temporal trajectories.

Zooming in on MAB, Figure 2.2 displays the relative coding frequencies in its corpus. It strikingly illustrates MAB's moderation. Apart from two counts of 'Legitimisation of political violence', MAB's moderate position is firmly anchored in participation in public debate, the de-legitimisation of actors of political violence, the rejection of violence as legitimate political means, and the organisation of non-violent forms of collective action.

The two counts referring to discourse-based radicalisation are interesting as they illustrate the importance of interpreting the coding results in context. Both are found in the same document, the September 2002 issue of MAB's I.N.S.P.I.R.E. magazine.[5] The first refers to the code 'Legitimisation of violence (theoretical or indirect)', the second to 'Praise person or group'. In the first segment, MAB legitimises the 'right of the Palestinians to self-defense' with 'all the resources at their disposal', thereby legitimising political violence for a people to defend its territory. The particularities of the Israeli–Palestinian conflict and the relatively broad support for the Palestinian cause beyond the Islamist spectrum call to nuance the radical character of the segment.

The second count relates to MAB advertising an event: 'Coming Soon: MAB Winter Camp 2002 Invited Speaker: Imam Anwar Al-Awlaqi'. The reference to Anwar al-Awlaqi[6] is somewhat unexpected when one contemplates his later role as a global internet preacher with close ties to

	Count	% Codes	Cases	% Cases
Group moderation and group radicalisation				
Discourse-based radicalisation				
Establish a pan-Islamic/world Caliphate				
Legitimisation of pol violence	2	2,9%	1	12,5%
Specifications on how pol violence should be conducted				
Action-based radicalisation				
Support for transnational Jihad				
Participation in violence locally				
Reference to attacks by (ex) members				
Participation in Jihad				
Discourse-based moderation				
Participation	33	48,5%	6	75,0%
Exit				
Action-based moderation				
Participation 2	33	48,5%	7	87,5%
Exit 2				

Figure 2.2 Coding counts and relative frequencies by category (MAB only)

al-Qaeda (2007–2011). At the end of 2002, however, al-Awlaqi was an American-Yemeni imam who had just left the US after being investigated several times in the previous two years (concurrently for solicitation, possible links to Hamas, and passport fraud) without having been charged. Albeit a rather dubious character, al-Awlaqi was then an increasingly well-known imam who had conducted prayer services for the Congressional Muslim Staffer Association. He was often interviewed by the US media to answer questions about Islam and had condemned the 9/11 attacks. Hence, inviting al-Awlaqi at the time is not as problematic as it first seemed, especially given that MAB had been actively campaigning against the persecution of Muslims and especially Muslim scholars.

Overall, the stark contrast between *radicalisation* and *moderation* coding frequencies highlights MAB's singularity among the corpus. In comparison, the other organisations' discursive articulations refer little to discourse-based and action-based participation. The major difference thus lies in the almost exclusive presence of discourse-based and action-based moderation in MAB's texts, whereas the other organisations recant discourse-based moderation.

The varied intensity of group radicalisation

This section compares the coding results of each of the four organisations, which display radicalisation codes significantly. Table 2.2 displays the coding frequencies by organisation at the level of main categories. The focus

Table 2.2 Distribution of coding frequency per organisation (all except MAB)

Main categories (level 1)	Hizb ut-Tahrir Britain (%)	al-Muhajiroun (%)	Die Wahre Religion (%)	Millatu Ibrahim (%)
Discourse-based radicalisation	76.8	78.5	31.3	92.7
Action-based radicalisation	0.0	4.3	11.9	4.5
Discourse-based moderation	4.5	2.2	16.4	0.0
Action-based moderation	18.8	15.1	40.3	2.8

lies on the distribution of codes within each organisation's corpus, while the next section zooms in on interpreting temporal shifts therein.

The dominant coding category in the respective corpus of HTB, AM, and MI is unequivocally *discourse-based radicalisation*. DWR presents a more complex picture: the coding results indicate that the organisation has advocated both *more extremist* and *more moderate* actions than the other three organisations put together. As shown in the next section, this seeming paradox is largely due to the ventilation of these codes across the period 2007–2013, with DWR moving from a moderate phase to a phase of radicalisation into extremism.

Looking at the coding results in more detail, with a focus on 'group radicalisation' categories, 'Legitimisation of political violence' represents the most recurrent category in all four organisations' discursive articulations (see table 2.3).

Conversely, *action-based radicalisation* categories are substantially less frequent (and inexistent in HTB's case) compared to *discourse-based radicalisation*. This discrepancy is not surprising in the context of a move away from moderation: organisations have little interest in being too explicit about actions for which members could be convicted and the organisation banned.

Beyond these similarities, the four organisations lay partly different foci with regards to the scope of the political project and relationship to violence. A closer look at the empirical results indicates that some patterns are shared among organisations, chiefly the strong legitimisation of political violence, while others are particular to an organisation. Strikingly, HTB thematises the establishment of a pan-Islamic caliphate much more significantly than the other organisations; indeed, it is HTB's second most frequent category (see Table 2.3). In AM's and MI's corpus, it is 'Specifications on how political violence should be conducted', a category referring to the identification

Table 2.3 Discourse-based and action-based radicalisation (frequency per organisation)

Categories referring to radicalisation	*Hizb ut-Tahrir Britain* (%)	*al-Muhajiroun* (%)	*Die Wahre Religion* (%)	*Millatu Ibrahim* (%)
Establish a pan-Islamic/world caliphate	24.1	7.0	1.5	2.8
Legitimisation of political violence	45.5	47.3	28.4	60.1
Specifications on how political violence should be conducted	7.1	24.2	1.5	29.9
Support for international jihad	0	3.2	3.0	0.8
Participation in violence locally	0	0	9.0	1.1
Reference to attacks by (ex) members	0	1.1	0	0.3
Participation in jihad	0	0	0	2.2

of targets/locations and means. This may indicate that HTB places greater focus on the end state to achieve (which would fit its self-perception as an intellectual organisation), whereas AM and MI attach more importance to the underlying groundwork for the political project's realisation.

To go into greater detail, the appended table 'Radicalisation and moderation by group (except MAB)' presents the ventilation of all coding frequencies per organisation, not yet broken down temporally (Appendix C2). At a descriptive level, the statistically most relevant codes are not similar across all four organisations. MI shows close to no *moderation* codes (only 3.1% of all coded segments in its corpus), and its discursive articulations are oriented towards the appropriate modalities for violent action (prominent role models, specification of means and targets). Compared to the other organisations, it articulates most clearly an extreme political project and a preference for violent means of action.

In contrast, all three other organisations have advocated non-violent collective action at some point, especially DRW. The concomitant presence of *action-based moderation* and strong *discourse-based radicalisation* can be interpreted in several ways. First, it can be linked to the alternation of group moderation and group radicalisation phases, as already supposed in DWR's case. Second, it may be a regular feature in organisations transitioning from moderation to radicalisation, since such processes are partly contradictory and not immediate. Third, it may indicate a strategic practice: organisations would put up a front of non-violent participation for public authorities, security agencies, and the wider public, while the articulation of their political project would imply very different attitudes and actions, a practice which could be subsumed under the saying 'do what I say not what I do'. A quote from DWR's corpus illustrates this well:

> Here I directly appeal to Merkel personally [*unintelligible*] and the federal Minister of the Interior: For peaceful coexistence ... here live millions of Muslims ... and German citizens live everywhere in Islamic lands. If you don't want any German to be abducted, because there are Muslims everywhere ... [*crowd cheers*] We have seen what happened after the caricatures by Kurt Westergaard ... may Allah curse him! We have seen ... we have seen that people have died on this earth.[7] (05.2012)

Abu Abdullah made this declaration at a public rally organised in Frankfurt's city centre to protest the anti-Islam cartoon contest organised by the right-wing political party ProNRW in spring 2012.[8] While the protest was held in public and there was no show of force, Abdullah's words ring like an open threat, making German citizens worldwide explicit and legitimate targets for revenge by jihadi actors.

Some political goals and forms of activism are found predominantly in one organisation. For instance, references to 'Successful attacks', 'Contact with insurgent groups abroad', and 'Joint activities with actors support-ing jihad' are found only in AM's corpus. Similarly, references to 'Foiled attacks' and 'Participation in jihad as a foreign fighter' are found only in MI's corpus. In turn, HTB is almost single-handedly responsible for the references to establishing a caliphate by revolution or coup in the overall corpus (86.4%). Finally, DWR's texts lay great emphasis on references to 'Riots or demonstrations gone violent', which refer to the group's partici-pation in the May 2012 riots against far-right activists (and the police) in Bonn and Solingen. Overall, if the four organisations have experienced group radicalisation at some point, they each articulate a specific combi-nation of discourse-based and action-based radicalisation into extremism.

Change in activism: delineating temporal phases of activism

This section explores the organisations' potential changes in activism over time. It asks in what respects their discursive articulations have changed and in what respects they have remained the same. For this diachronic compari-son, the coding results for the four main categories – discourse-based and action-based radicalisation/moderation – are distributed temporally (by 'publication date') for each organisation and visualised in a chart format. The specific combination of radicalisation categories provide insights into an organisation's changing activism. The charts display the results by quarters, making larger trends visible, whereas viewing the monthly results might have produced too many very short phases, rendering impracticable the subsequent narrative analysis (in Part II of the book). However, when phases could less readily be delineated, I viewed the coding results by month to interpret whether a new phase might be starting or whether the corpus merely presented a punctual variation. The focus thus lies on structural changes in activism and reconstructing, for each organisation, phases of group radicalisation, and/or moderation, and/or extremism (if any). While the second part of the book delves into the narratives deployed within phases of activism in great depth, this section preliminarily interprets changes in activism with regards to the organisations' political environment and contextualises each organisation's trajectory.

Hizb ut-Tahrir Britain: phases of extremism, moderation within extremism, and radicalisation

The activism of HTB over the period 2001–2008 is difficult to assess. Among the four organisations, it is the one that most consistently displays *discourse-based radicalisation*. Conversely, it shows no references to *action-based radicalisation* throughout the period. This striking separation between discourse and action is somewhat puzzling, as one would expect corresponding action recommendations to follow such consistent articulation of its political vision. It seems that HTB restrains systematically from calling explicitly for *specific* violent actions: either because its members' work should be primarily missionary (at least in the UK) or because the organisation counts on its members to draw conclusions in terms of action, for themselves.

Sequentially speaking, HTB can be characterised as in a phase of extremism at the outset of the study period (third quarter of 2001). Up until the second quarter of 2003, HTB's corpus presents only *discourse-based radicalisation* codes. Figure 2.3 visualises HTB's evolution between the third quarter of 2001 and the third quarter of 2008.

The second quarter of 2003 sees some indication of *action-based moderation*, and the organisation's corpus displays some measure of *discourse-based moderation* at the end of 2003. However, this slight moderation should not be mistaken for the beginning of a moderate phase: first, the group's discourse remains predominantly articulated in terms of *discourse-based radicalisation*; second, references to moderation are discontinuous, that is, they partly disappear from one quarter to another. The second

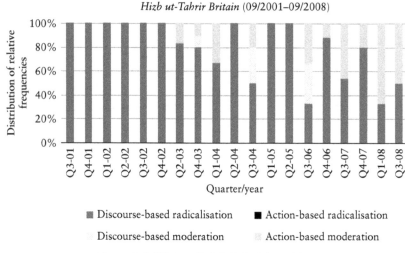

Figure 2.3 *Hizb ut-Tahrir Britain*'s activism

quarter of 2004 and the first two quarters of 2005 are good examples: in a phase which can be characterised as moderately less extremist, these quarters stand out as they display no other codes than *discourse-based radicalisation*.

In a similar vein, the period Q4-2006/Q4-2008[9] deserves close attention. At first glance, the rather large presence of *action-based moderation* gives the impression that HTB is still a phase of moderation within extremism. Yet, compared to the period Q4-2003/Q3-2006, the absence of any *discourse-based moderation* provides a different picture. Indeed, from the last quarter of 2006, the organisation recants *discourse-based moderation*. As the prior phase was one of moderation within extremism, this third phase is reconstructed analytically as a radicalisation phase. Overall, despite slight variations, HTB's activism can be broken down temporally in three phases: 1) extremism between Q3-2001/Q3-2003; 2) moderation within extremism between Q4-2003/Q3-2006, and 3) radicalisation between Q4-2006/Q3-2008. Each phase constitutes a case; all cases are summarised in Table 2.4 at the end of the chapter.

These changes in activism parallel several important events and new policies at the local and transnational levels. HTB's first phase (Q3-2001/ Q3-2003) is saturated with international events salient for a UK-based Islamist organisation. The attacks in the US in September 2001 called on Islamist organisations to take a position. At the time, HTB does not condemn the attacks, contrary to other Islamist organisations in the UK. Conversely, it explicitly condemns what it sees as the formation of an alliance between the US and most Muslim-majority countries (HTB,

18 September 2001). The swift US invasion of Afghanistan rapidly replaces its discussion of the 9/11 attacks.

During this phase, the Israeli–Palestinian conflict is an important topic as well. The second Intifada started in September 2000, and several Arab summits and negotiations with the US followed. These are highly criticised by HTB, especially the perceived subservient role of Middle Eastern heads of states. Further, the looming invasion of Iraq is breached in a long article published on 21 October 2002 in which HTB strongly denounces the joint resolution passed on 10 October by the US congress 'permitting the use of military force against Iraq'. Analysing the resolution, HTB states pithily:

> It intends to deceive international public opinion that strongly resisted the aggressive whim of Bush. All this appeared from the arguments that *deliberately linked the name of Iraq with terrorism*, repeating this linkage in various sentences and paragraphs, in a disgraceful attempt to exploit the hostile reaction against the Muslims following the events of September 11th 2001 (21.10.2002, emphasis added).

While this interpretation might be widely shared, HTB concludes that the 'armies of the Islamic Ummah' have the *fard* (duty) to depose 'the cowardly, treacherous and despotic rulers' of the Muslim world to protect the *ummah* (21.10.2002). The call to *coups d'état* is supported by repeated supplications and the assurance that the struggle is worth the sacrifice: 'Do not fear death, for daring does not shorten life and neither cowardice nor abstention lengthens life. Moreover, death for the sake of Allah is the greatest victory.' (21.10.2002) Overall, the strong reception of the international conflicts of the early 2000s indicates that HTB's *discourse-based radicalisation* parallels the outbreak of conflicts impacting Muslim-majority societies.

The second phase (Q4-2003/Q3-2006) is concomitant with a relatively less turbulent period of international politics, with no new international conflict outbreak of major relevance to a Western-based Islamist actor – except the war between Israel and Lebanon in the summer of 2006. At home, the suicide bomb attacks on the London transportation system in July 2005 constitute a major event. A month later, in August 2005, Tony Blair announces that he plans to ban HTB (as well as successor groups to *al-Muhajiroun*). Little data could be collected for the period July 2005–August 2006, which suggests that HTB either published and deleted its standpoints quickly and systematically over this period and/or reduced its activities to a minimum and presented a low profile. Overall, this suggests that domestic political violence by other Islamist actors and/or stronger public scrutiny led HTB to tune down its public activities and articulate some moderation in discourse and practice.

The third phase (Q4-2006/Q3-2008) is characterised locally by a relaxation of public scrutiny on HTB, as police and Home Office officials express doubts about the usefulness of a ban.[10] Both voice concern, along with several members of Parliament, that the proposed ban could be successfully countered on insufficient legal grounds, and they view a legal challenge as potentially more damaging than letting HTB be. Over this period, HTB's activism recentres on issues in the Muslim world, with a specific focus on Palestine and Pakistan. It discusses at length the 'Annapolis Conference for peace in the Middle East', convened by President Bush in November 2007 to talk about the Israeli–Palestinian peace process, and the Pakistani elections of October 2007 and ensuing declaration of the state of emergency by re-elected President Musharraf. Both Palestine and Pakistan are presented by HTB as textbook examples of the noxiousness of un-Islamic Muslim rulers (and their Western supporters) and stress the necessity of rising up and establishing a pan-Islamic caliphate. While HTB envisions the ultimate establishment of a worldwide caliphate as the product of the conversion of the world to the 'superior system' of Islam, in this third phase, the organisation does not preclude establishing it by force (19.03.2008; 29.03.2008). Conversely, HTB recants discursive articulations of moderation such as participating in public debate or delegitimising political violence in the UK.

Al-Muhajiroun: phases of radicalisation, extremism, and moderation within extremism

AM's activism between 2001 and 2004 is more readily reconstructed into sequences. Overall, AM's corpus articulates *discourse-based radicalisation* strongly, with some degree of *action-based moderation* over the period. Much as in HTB's case, the advocacy of moderate action is concurrent with extreme political positions and goals. Unlike HTB, however, AM articulates *action-based radicalisation* as well. Figure 2.4 illustrates AM's evolving activism between the third quarter of 2001 and the last quarter of 2004.

The organisation starts a phase of radicalisation at the beginning of the period of study, with the disappearance of its remaining discourse-based moderation. Indeed, whereas in September 2001 it still articulated some *discourse-based moderation*, this changes from October 2001 onwards, a structural change which maintains throughout the period. This first phase of group radicalisation goes on until the third quarter of 2002.

The organisation then enters a new phase characterised markedly by the emergence of *action-based radicalisation* codes. In this second phase (Q4-2002/Q2-2004), AM consistently articulates an extreme political project, combined with references to violent means of action. As an

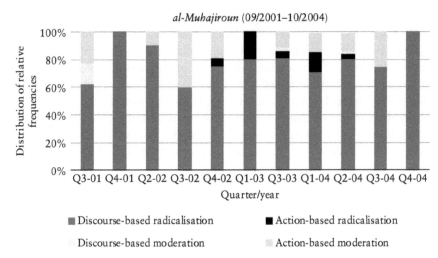

Figure 2.4 *al-Muhajiroun*'s activism

escalation of the means it advocates, this phase can be interpreted as radicalisation within extremism.

The third phase (Q3-2004/Q4-2004) is particularly interesting as it sees
the disappearance of references to violent means of action and some references to moderate forms of actions (Q3-2004) just before the group's official dissolution. This is not to say that AM is entering a moderate phase, as
its corpus still strongly articulates *discourse-based radicalisation*. However,
it is a phase in which the organisation recants from advocating violent
forms of action. Thus, it can be interpreted as a phase of moderation within
extremism. Overall, AM's evolution can be subsumed in three phases over
the period: 1) radicalisation (into extremism), over Q3-2001/Q3-2002; 2)
(radicalisation within) extremism, over Q4-2002/Q2-2004; 3) moderation
within extremism, over Q3-2004/Q4-2004.

In terms of context, AM's first phase (Q3-2001/Q3-2002) is marked,
much as in HTB's, by omnipresent references to international events.
Interestingly, AM's discursive articulations right after the 9/11 attacks
in the US are ambiguous: it condemns the attacks and asserts these were
not the work of 'pious Muslims'. Yet it welcomes their impact as they
'shake the arrogance' of the US and 'their claims to be [the] invulner-
able country in the World [sic]' (12.09.2001). Asked about his views on
the attacks, AM's leader, Omar Bakri Mohammed, states that 'it is a crime
and violation for the sanctity of Human beings [sic] which is prohibited
in Islam' and points to a US–UK conspiracy bent on blaming Muslims
(Clément, 2014, p. 433). AM argues that the US is increasingly persecut-
ing Muslims and raises concern about potential ripple effects on Muslims

in Western European societies (07.10.2001). The discussion of the 9/11 attacks is nonetheless rapidly replaced with the denunciation of the invasion of Afghanistan. AM condemns much more strongly than HTB the war against the Islamic Emirate of Afghanistan. For AM, the Emirate has special significance because it is the only regime worldwide that would come close to a true Islamic state. The organisation contends that the US is using the 9/11 attacks as a pretext to launch a long-planned war against Afghanistan (21.09.2001). On occasion, AM also thematises the Middle East conflict and what it calls 'Jewish terrorism' (24.10.2001), for instance, after the Battle of Jenin, referred to as 'the Jenin massacre' (20.04.2002).

The second phase (Q4-2002/Q2-2004) starts concurrently with the increasingly real possibility of a US-led war against Iraq. This has the effect of *a coup de grace*, less than a year after the beginning of the war in Afghanistan. From then on, AM starts calling for acts of violence more systematically and refers positively to martyrdom operations: 'If 19 Mujahideen can crash planes into the twin towers [sic] and rewrite history with their blood, we too can establish the law of Allah (swt) in this *Duniya* [world]. It requires willingness, effort, struggle and sacrifice' (03.12.2002). References to violent means of action peak in the first quarter of 2003, coinciding with the beginning of the invasion of Iraq in March 2003.

In this phase, AM also refers more often to UK politics towards the Muslim community in general and UK-based Islamic clerics in particular. The group condemns the arrest of Abu Qatada in October 2002 and his detention without trial under the new anti-terrorism law.[11] Similarly, it mobilises against 'Sheikh' Abdullah Faisal's conviction[12] in February 2003 and 'Sheikh' Abu Hamza's potential extradition to the US in August 2003. Interestingly, AM does not give much attention to the Madrid attacks (11 March 2004). Rather, it focuses on bin Laden's 'Message to the People of Europe', which came out a month later, analysing it paragraph by paragraph, justifying its rationale, and praising bin Laden's leadership: 'Sheikh Osama came out like the true Lion [sic] of a man that he is, to speak with calm and tranquillity, as the voice of truth, and the champion of the cause of the Muslims' (22.04.2004).

The third phase (Q3-2004/Q4-2004) is not marked by any new major conflict nor increased scrutiny in the UK compared to the previous phase. AM's discursive articulations are still reproducing a global jihadi discourse on the need for an Islamic caliphate and the legitimacy of political violence, but make no reference to violent forms of activism in the real world. Thus, its activism is still characterised by extremism, yet differently so. Also, it makes more references to exiting UK society – a form of non-violent action. For instance, the group newly encourages *hijra*, that is, the emigration to

Muslim lands (01.07.2004) to escape the 'servitude to man in Britain'[13] (26.07.2004). At the same time, AM's late publications centre around the obligation of jihad (26.07.2004) and reach a climax in the article 'Terrorism is a part of Islam', published 7 August 2004. Similarly, in the 'Official declaration dissolving al-Muhajiroun' (08.10.2004), leader Bakri argues that the group decided to dissolve for the sake of jihad, which would require all movements and groups to join forces.

Die Wahre Religion: phases of moderation and radicalisation into extremism

DWR is the organisation whose activism has comparatively changed the most over its period of study (2007–2013). Between October 2007 and June 2010, DWR articulates no references to *discourse-based* nor *action-based radicalisation* in its corpus. Over this period, DWR's activism is evidently moderate. Then, from the third quarter of 2010 onwards, the organisation's discursive articulations shift towards increasingly legitimising and calling to violence (*discourse-based radicalisation*). This structural change is later reinforced by increasing references to the group's participation in violence locally (in Q2-2012) and references to material support to international jihad (in Q2-2013). Figure 2.5 illustrates these shifts in the corpus.

Another distinctive feature of DWR's activism is the simultaneous presence of *discourse-based moderation* and *discourse-based radicalisation* over the quarters Q3-2010 and Q2-2012, sometimes even concurrently in some of the audio and video material. For instance, in a May 2012 speech

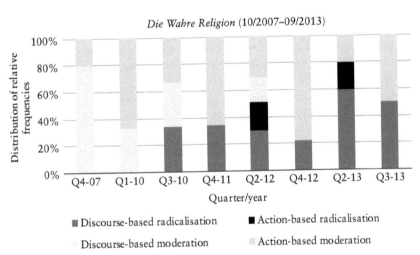

Figure 2.5 *Die Wahre Religion*'s activism

entitled 'Call to the Muslims',[14] DWR preacher Abu Abdullah calls fellow Muslims in Germany to moderation, enjoining them to show their disapproval of the caricatures of the Prophet Mohammed by demonstrating prolifically.[15] Yet towards the end of the speech, he firmly states: 'I much prefer to get there, be present, even should I get broken bones. *Wallahi* [by Allah], I much prefer to get my bones broken. I'd much rather have someone behead me than that the Prophet Mohammed a.s.s. be insulted'.[16] His expressed willingness to fight and defend the Prophet legitimises participation in (local) violence. This simultaneity hints at a slow, not unequivocal, meandering process of radicalisation over the years 2010–2013. DWR's activism can be split into two phases over the period: 1) a moderate phase between Q4-2007/Q2-2010 and 2) a phase of radicalisation over Q3-2010/Q3-2013.

In many respects, the contrast between the two phases is stark. In the first phase, DWR's discourse centres exclusively on Muslims' life in Germany, whereas, in the second phase, it increasingly focuses on international events. Also, the discourse on local politics changes dramatically. In the beginning, DWR advocates social dialogue and the necessity of reciprocal critique between Muslims and non-Muslims in Germany (Abou Nagie, 18.10.2007). Towards the end of its moderate phase, DWR sharply criticises what it views as unilateral tolerance and integration efforts on the part of the Muslim community. Accordingly, the group starts encouraging withdrawal from society ('Exit', *action-based moderation*). Abou Nagie mocks Germany's relationship to its Muslim community: 'Tolerance! We have to show the Germans that we are integrated. What does integration mean? Integration means they want you to become a *kafir*',[17] that is, someone who rejects Allah's authority (23.03.2010). To counter this, DWR recommends minimal interaction with German society. For instance, it disapproves of marriage between Muslims and non-Muslims so as to protect the faith[18] (Abou Nagie, 23.03.2010). Although these discursive articulations are still within the borders of moderation, it is noteworthy that the organisation's activism has shifted from 'Participation' to 'Exit'.

From mid-2010 onwards, DWR enters a new phase, which can be interpreted as a (slow) process of radicalisation into extremism. A few articulations crediting the group with moderation remain, such as Abu Dujana's declaration to the German TV channel ZDF that, far from trying to separate themselves from German society, 'Muslims just want to be accepted, to be recognised as they are'[19] (19.08.2010). However, the group's activism is increasingly characterised by an uncompromising position on questions of faith in society, epitomised by the May 2012 riots against the caricatures of the Prophet. Further, while DWR's *dawa* work (propagation of the faith) is interpreted as a form of non-violent collective action as it officially aims to 'bring Muslims [...] and preachers together in Germany' (Abu Dujana, 10.2012), its message towards the rest of society becomes increasingly absolutist and divisive (Abou Nagie, video 'Why do *Kuffar* hate Islam and the Muslims', 25.10.2012).

The Syrian civil war becomes the most prominent theme from June 2012 until the end of the study period. The group organises several charity events, where it appeals to followers to donate money to help the Syrian people in need and the 'brothers' who depart to Syria to help them (a reference to foreign fighters). DWR preachers start addressing participation in jihad more directly:

> To be killed is easy; why? Because the people become *shuhada* [martyrs]; what is difficult, however, is when honour and dignity are violated and sisters, honourable, covered sisters, who never did something *haram* [wrong], are raped by the *Kuffar*.[20] (Abu Abdullah, 21.04.2013)

DWR lays the blame, first, on Bashar el-Assad (and his state supporters) and, second, on the Western powers, which readily intervened in Afghanistan, Iraq, and Libya but are disinterested in the fate of the Syrian people (Abu Dujana, 28.05.2012 and 08.2013; Abu Abdullah, 21.04.2013). Participation in transnational jihad is increasingly presented as the solution to this dire situation.

Millatu Ibrahim's single phase of extremism

MI's discursive articulations over its short lifespan can be interpreted temporally as one single phase (October 2011–December 2013). The group articulates references to an extremist political project from its inception, supplemented with references to violent means of actions from December 2011 onwards. MI's corpus contains no reference to moderation in discourse and little to no moderation in practice, except in the first quarter of 2012. Figure 2.6 illustrates the stability of the group's activism.

MI's single phase of extremism is most consistent and stark: the organisation's corpus makes up more than half the references to the necessity of establishing an Islamic caliphate and the legitimisation and specification of political violence.

The first quarter of 2012 is the only quarter in which the organisation comparatively articulates *discourse-based radicalisation* less strongly but makes, for that matter, strong references to violent forms of activism. Nonetheless, the simultaneous and almost equal presence of *action-based moderation* and *action-based radicalisation* in Q1-2012 is intriguing. MI leaders tend to view moderate and violent forms of activism as complementary. In a video entitled 'Get engaged for *dawa*', spokesman Cuspert praises the merits of propagating

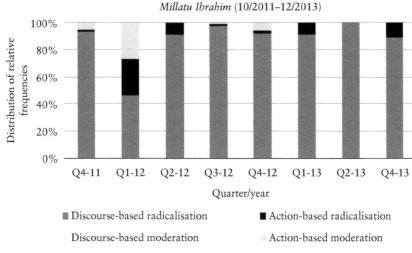

Figure 2.6 *Millatu Ibrahim*'s activism

the faith at a seminar organised by DWR's *LIES!* campaigners. In this video, Cuspert both insists on the individual obligation of doing *dawa* work (*'Non-violent collective action'*) and, a few minutes later, stresses the need for new combatants and martyrs in Syria (*'Call to violence/combat'*):

> *Subhan'allah* [all praise belongs to Allah], today we have so many *shahid* [martyr] sitting in jail. And some are killed, ha. [sic] How many *shuhada* [martyrs] were killed in the last months, *subhan'allah*, by the enemies of Allah? Yes, and we need new ones, we need reinforcements.[21] (Cuspert, 02.2012)

Depending on what helps its political aims most and where, MI recommends partly non-violent collective action to support *dawa* work, while it strongly encourages its followers to commit themselves to jihad wherever Muslims are at war.

This does not apply merely to the Syrian context. Following several controversial incidents linked to the representation of the Muslim faith, MI encourages its followers to avenge the Prophet. In an article entitled 'Settling score with Germany', Sami J. (aka Abu Assad al-Almani) announces that it is *halal* (permitted) to target the German actor who played the Prophet in the low-budget US short film 'Innocence of Muslims'. In the same vein, he states:

> The Pro-NRW, who mocked the Prophet. And those politicians who approved and allowed the caricatures to be shown. And those citizens who supported them in doing so, whomever they are. Shedding their blood, or rather, killing

them, should hold particular importance in the hearts of those eager to avenge the messenger of Allah.[22] (21.09.2012)

Defending the Prophet and, more generally, the 'sanctities of Islam' such as scholars, women, and the holy Quran justifies, according to MI, taking violent action in Germany and elsewhere.

From July 2012 onwards, the Syrian jihad takes centre stage. MI stresses the necessity of establishing a caliphate, not only to protect Muslims but, more generally, to *please* God. In comparison with AM and HT, MI does not elaborate on the particularities of a future caliphate. Conversely, it insists on the necessity of *sacrifice*, especially in the form of martyrdom. In the second half of 2012, MI leaders draw increasingly on key jihadi references – Ayman az-Zawahiri, Abu Yahya al-Libi, Ahmad Ashush. While MI leaders enjoined members early to move to Syria to help and fight, their call is heightened from the time they reach ISIS-held territory in Syria themselves (see chronology in Chapter 1). In a video in which Mahmoud burns his Austrian passport in front of the camera, he professes: 'I only accept to belong to the *ummah* of Mohammed s.a.s. [and] for it I fight, and I die. I beg Allah *azza wa-jall* [the Mighty and Sublime] to let me die as *muwahid* [true believer], as *mujahid* [combatant], and as *shahid* [martyr]'[23] (15.03.2013). In the remaining texts of the corpus, Mahmoud and Cuspert exhort MI's members to live by their example and participate in the Syrian jihad.

Muslim Association of Britain's single phase of moderate activism

MAB contrasts with the four previous organisations, as its activism is moderate throughout its period of study (Q3-2002/Q3-2004). Figure 2.7 visualises the group's moderation.

As MAB's discursive articulations were distinguished from the other organisations earlier, I now turn to characterising its moderation further. The example of the Iraq war is particularly enlightening. In early 2003, MAB is at the frontline of the pacific demonstrations against the war. While its discourse is at times vehement, it is fundamentally different from HT's or AM's over the same period. In terms of real-world actions, MAB organises many demonstrations before and after the beginning of the Iraq war, stages protests, and calls to support the boycott of US and Israeli products. Condemning the Blair government's policies as 'hypocritical, biased, and, should war break out, totally inhumane' (04.02.2003), the organisation nevertheless advocates participation in the British public debate and the importance of cooperating with non-Muslim anti-war actors. The following passage is telling:

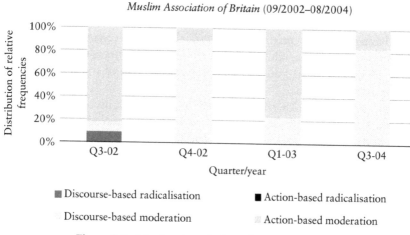

Figure 2.7 *Muslim Association of Britain*'s activism

The Muslim Association of Britain calls upon Muslims throughout Britain to pray for the Iraqi people, to remember the innocent victims of our foreign policy which wreaks [sic] of double standards in Iraq and Palestine and to announce their resolve and determination to make the 15th of February a truly historical day, by attending what promises to be the biggest ever demonstration held in Britain, under the banners 'Don't Attack Iraq' and 'Freedom For Palestine'. (04.02.2003)

Further, MAB delegitimises actors justifying political violence and those who focus their attention on them: 'Our voices are constantly being muted or ignored, especially by the majority of our media which freely devotes all Islamic news to extremists who represent no one' (13.08.2004).

Faced with attacks by Anthony Browne, a conservative UK journalist and later politician, MAB addresses in August 2004 the issue of extremism versus moderation in a vivid statement:

If we at MAB are extremists because we oppose the war on Iraq, support the rights of the Palestinians, encourage Muslims to integrate and actively participate in the political process, defend the right of our girls to cover their heads in public and join our brothers and comrades from other political and religious groups in cooperating for the benefit of our society, then who on earth does he see as deserving of the title: 'moderate'? (13.08.2004)

This is a stark contrast to the other organisations, which are not interested in being perceived as moderates, nor in fellow Muslims participating in the (local) political process. Despite this bitter statement, the group calls its members to continue participating in public debate and supporting the plurality of opinion.

Main insights and overview of the cases

The chapter set out to reconstruct empirically the five organisations' phases of activism. Several insights emerged from the interpretation of the qualitative content analysis and the temporal comparison of the organisations' discursive articulations.

First, except for MAB, the organisations have radicalised into extremism or were already in a phase of extremism during the period of study. Their texts, audios, and videos differ from MAB's corpus in that they articulate an extreme political project, reject moderate forms of participation in the public debate and tend to prefer violent means of action. Concretely, HTB, AM, MI, and (to a large extent) DWR legitimise political violence, call to acts of violence and participation in jihad abroad, and specify which locations and individuals or groups should be targeted and how. Conversely, MAB's moderation is characterised by moderation in discourse and practice. The organisation enjoins participation in the public debate, interacts with a plurality of civil society actors with whom it co-organises political events, and delegitimises actors of political violence. It is the only organisation to display consistent and constant moderation in the corpus.

Second, organisations entering a phase of radicalisation into extremism may concurrently articulate extremist political goals such as the establishment of a worldwide caliphate, justify large-scale violence, *and* participate in demonstrations against the war in Iraq or right-wing caricatures of the Prophet. HT's corpus epitomises the simultaneous articulation of extremist political goals and moderate action. In this regard, references to moderate forms of action alone do not help in distinguishing phases of activism. They are compatible with a shift in activism from moderation to radicalisation, as organisations are increasingly departing from believing in and accepting minimal conditions for coexistence in an open society and from engaging in non-violent collective action.[24] In a phase of extremism, this process is completed insofar as discursive articulations of moderation cease.

Third, if the four organisations have experienced a phase of radicalisation and/or extremism at some point, they did so in specific ways: regarding the combination of their expressed political project and preferred forms of action, how long the phase lasted, and in terms of its intensity. Noteworthy is that each organisation shares at least some of these characteristics with others. For example, while all four organisations share the strong legitimisation of political violence, further discursive emphasis differs slightly. For HTB it is the establishment of a pan-Islamic/world caliphate; for AM and MI, it is the specifications on how political violence should be conducted; and for DWR, it is the participation in violence locally. Similarly, their phases of radicalisation vary in length. AM exemplifies a short process of radicalisation into extremism (one-year phase), whereas DWR's spread over almost three years. Finally, some have experienced shifts in intensity within extremism (moderation within, radicalisation within). For example, both HTB and AM have known a phase of moderation *within* extremism, characterised respectively by reintroducing some moderation in discourse or recanting violent forms of activism.

While the reconstruction of phases of activism is an interpretive exercise, the attention to stability and structural changes over a continuum between moderation and extremism offer a more authentic and dynamic account. The organisations' phases of activism are summarised in table 2.4. Each phase constitutes a *case*, which becomes the unit of analysis in Part II of the book. The ten cases – 1-HTB, 2-HTB, 3-HTB, 4-AM, 5-AM, 6-AM, 7-DWR, 8-DWR, 9-MI, 10-MAB – are analysed in Part II of the book, which centres on exploring organisations' narrative deployments and performance of emotions in their respective phases of activism.

Several important themes have emerged from the contextualisation of the respective political environments in which the organisations entered new phases of activism. Transnational politics and conflicts in Muslim-majority

Table 2.4 Summary of the cases

Organisation	Timeframe	Phase	Case
Hizb ut-Tahrir Britain	Q3-2001–Q3-2003	extremism	1-HTB
	Q4-2003–Q3-2006	moderation within extremism	2-HTB
	Q4-2006–Q4-2008	radicalisation	3-HTB
al-Muhajiroun	Q3-2001–Q3-2002	radicalisation into extremism	4-AM
	Q4-2002–Q2-2004	extremism (radicalisation *within*)	5-AM
	Q3-2004–Q4-2004	moderation within extremism	6-AM
Die Wahre Religion	Q4-2007–Q2-2010	moderate	7-DWR
	Q3-2010–Q3-2013	radicalisation into extremism	8-DWR
Millatu Ibrahim	Q4-2011–Q4-2013	extremism	9-MI
Muslim Association of Britain	Q3-2002–Q3-2004	moderate	10-MAB

countries appear particularly prominent. All organisations react and take a position towards both local (British/German) and transnational conflictual events (concerning Muslims worldwide), although the latter tends to be given more significance. Local events are thematised in moderate phases (e.g. DWR's first phase) and in phases of radicalisation (e.g. DWR, AM, and MI), and focus around the perception of local leaders being persecuted by authorities or out-group insults of Islamic beliefs. International events, such as armed conflicts in Muslim lands, find extensive reception in phases of radicalisation. More pointedly, both the start of a phase of radicalisation into extremism and the intensification of a phase of extremism tend to coincide with the outbreak of such events. DWR might be the exception: the organisation starts a phase of radicalisation parallel to the increasingly felt persecution of Muslims in Europe, even though it intensified with the beginning of the Syrian civil war.

While some conflicts are shared thematically by several organisations, they impact their respective discursive articulations with varyingly lasting effects. For instance, HTB and AM share a common focus on Afghanistan, Palestine, and Iraq; yet the intensity with which they discuss these conflicts varies considerably. HTB focuses on Palestine more than AM does. Conversely, Afghanistan and Iraq are of greater importance to AM. Temporally speaking, while the Iraq war impacts AM's discourse up to mid-2004, HTB already enters a phase of moderation within extremism from the last quarter of 2003. Certainly, the reception of transnational political events and conflicts impacts group radicalisation processes; however, such effects are not *im*-mediate, nor of similar duration. Key events and conflicts are *mediated* by narrative(s) whose qualities lend them more or less power, over more or less time. The second part of the book addresses such powerful processes of mediation.

Notes

1 Coding manually means weighing for each unit of sense which code is more appropriate and whether more than one code might be applicable. When a given unit of sense potentially referred to two codes pertaining to the same category, the author chose between the prevalent meaning in context.

2 A coding frequency is the percentage of a code or a group of codes in the overall corpus. The chapter displays the coding results at an aggregated level to ease the visualisation.

3 Several codes are under-represented, mostly in the categories 'Exit', which suggests that none of the five organisations consider removing themselves from British or German society a desirable political option. Also little represented are the codes pertaining to the categories 'Support for international

jihad' and 'Reference to (planned) attacks by (ex)members or followers'. The very presence of such codes in parts of the corpus is noteworthy though, as they mark references to support and/or cooperation with militant organisations such as al-Qaeda or ISIS. Leaders and spokespersons were careful not to make such public statements, as these would have been enough to prosecute the organisation for terrorist offenses and crimes of incitement.

4 The codes 'Organisation of local training camps' and 'Withdrawal from public debate' are not present in the corpus.

5 MAB's I.N.S.P.I.R.E. magazine should not be confused with the English-speaking magazine created later by al-Qaeda in the Arabian Peninsula and whose first issue was released in June 2010.

6 The American-Yemeni Anwar al-Awlaqi emigrated from the US to the UK in late 2002. He moved to Yemen in early 2004. He is said to have ultimately radicalised during his imprisonment in Yemen (2006–2007) where he delved into the works of Sayyid Qutb (Shane & Mekhennet, 2010). He later provided al-Qaeda members in Yemen the protection of his tribe and is regarded as the most prominent al-Qaeda preacher of the late 2000s (Conway, 2012). His audio and video sermons have been circulated broadly in the Middle East, the US, and Western Europe to this day (Gendron, 2016).

7 Original quote in Appendix B1, quote n°1.

8 ProNRW had launched a cartoon contest with the stated goal of finding the most provocative critique of Islam possible. The top prize for the best cartoon was named after Kurt Westergaard, the Danish cartoonist who authored the Muhammad caricatures in 2005. The cartoons which emerged from the contest were seen as inacceptable offenses to Muslims' faith by part of the German Muslim community. See *Spiegel Online*, 1 June 2012. 'Islamophobes Launched a National Debate'.

9 The period of study for HTB runs from September 2001 to October 2008. As there is only one document in the fourth quarter of 2008 (on October 10th), a chart bar for Q4-2008 is not included so as not to overrate the coding results of one document.

10 BBC News, 19 November 2006, 'Blair bid to ban group "opposed"'.

11 Reference to the 2001 Anti-Terrorism, Crime and Security Act.

12 Abdullah Faisal was sentenced in February 2003 to nine years in prison for inciting hatred and soliciting the murder of Jews, Americans, Hindus, and Christians. It was the first trial of a Muslim cleric in the UK. See the *Guardian*, 24 February 2003, 'Muslim cleric guilty of soliciting murder'.

13 This is a reference to the oppression of (democratic) 'man-made' laws in contrast to Islam's divine laws.

14 German original: 'Aufruf an die Muslime'.

15 Translated, the passage reads as follows: 'Be patient and steadfast, and I ask you, dear brothers and sisters, I ask all brothers and sisters … here in Germany, I ask you, … in the coming days, to participate [...] you know, these ProNRW activists plan demonstrations and rallies, in which they want to insult Allah's emissary. Eh they want to catch more votes' (original quote in Appendix B1, quote n°2).

16 Original quote in Appendix B1, quote n°3.

17 Original quote: 'Toleranz! Wir müssen die Deutschen [sic] zeigen, dass wir integriert sind. Was bedeutet Integration? Integration bedeutet die wollen, dass du kafir wirst.'

18 The passage reads: 'If your faith is not strong enough, your children will go to church and pray to the cross, whether you want it or not. Your children will eat pork meat. Your children will be baptized. *Wallahi* [by Allah] this is the bitter truth. And so many people have witnessed this ... here in Germany.' Original quote in Appendix B1, quote n°4.

19 Original quote: 'die meisten Muslime ... wollen einfach akzeptiert werden, anerkannt werden so wie sie sind'.

20 Original quote: 'Getötet zu werden ist einfach, warum? Weil diese Leute sind *shuhada*, aber was schwer ist, ist, wenn die Ehre, die Würde verletzt wird und Schwestern, ehrenhafte, bedeckte Schwestern, die niemals haram gemacht haben, dass diese vergewaltigt werden von *kuffar*.'

21 Original quote: '*Subhan'allah*, heute wir haben so viele *shahid*, die sitzen im Gefängnis. Und die werden getötet, ha. Wie viele *shuhada* wurden die letzten Monate [sic] getötet, *subhan'allah*, durch die Feinde Allahs? Ja, und wir brauchen Neue, wir brauchen Nachschub.'

22 Original quote in Appendix B1, quote n°5.

23 Original quote: 'Ich akzeptiere nur die Zugehörigkeit zu der *Ummah* von Mohamed s.a.s., dafür kämpfe ich und dafür sterbe ich. Ich bitte *Allah azza wa-jall* mich als *muwahid* und als *mujahid*, als *shahid* sterben zu lassen.'

24 Conversely, the mere return of references to moderate forms of action does not signify a change from extremism to moderation, but it may point to a phase of moderation within extremism, as in *al-Muhajiroun*'s third phase.

Part II

Exploring the performance of collective
emotions

3

A theory of emotionalisation in narrative form

Approaching the turn from non-violent politics to militancy as a collective endeavour, in which an organisation hopes that members and sympathisers move as one collective, means exploring how it mediates change to group members and sympathisers. This chapter discusses how change in activism is mediated by group narratives which perform collective emotions. It argues that a specific, emotionalised narrative would accompany group radicalisation and extremism and incentivise decisive collective action. The theoretical focus lies on the social contextualisation of emotions and the politics of their representation in language. It is embedded in a constructivist understanding of politics in which social reality is constituted, re-produced, and changed through social actors' discursive practices. The theoretical framework presented here underpins the subsequent analysis of Islamist organisations' narrative activity (Chapter 4) and the exploration of processes of emotionalisation therein (Chapter 5).

The chapter develops the theoretical framework in three stages. The first section conceptualises emotions and their relationship with knowledge and power dynamics. It discusses emotion and affect in social scientific research and then conceptualises *collective* emotions. Building on the social functions of collective emotions, it elaborates on how collectives engage in the politics of emotion. The second section centres on the representation of emotions in language and, more specifically, in narrative form. It argues in favour of approaching collective emotions via their performance *in* and *through* narrative. The section then delves into narrative characteristics and functions. Focusing specifically on romantic narratives, it shows that a narrative creates meanings about one's collective in a political context; it orders and (de)legitimises certain social actors and provides collective and individual orientation for political action. Finally, building on the theoretical developments on collective emotions and narrative, the last section introduces the original concept of *narrative emotionalisation*. The central argument is that romantic narratives not only establish expectations towards collective action; through gradual emotionalisation, they *demand* decisive action. The chapter concludes by presenting the four sub-processes that constitute *narrative emotionalisation* and how their combined effects shape group knowledge and orient collective action.

Emotions, knowledge, and action

This section conceptualises emotions, collective emotions, and the relationship between (collective) emotions and knowledge/power dynamics. Thus, it addresses ontological questions about what emotions are and what they do politically.

Emotions

Emotions shape our individual and social lives in profound ways. They have physiological, cognitive, behavioural, and intersubjective dimensions. Most social scientists view emotions as the outward communication of feelings. Unlike feelings, emotions are 'corporeally mediated' (Ross, 2006, p. 216) and made accessible to the outside world. One of the most fundamental characteristics of emotions is their necessary communication to others, which means *inter alia* that they have to be put in a language that others may understand. Fierke points out that 'the experience of emotion may be individual, but emotions have meaning within a social world and, if expressed, they are expressed in relation to others, and in a language understandable to them, particularly if an experience is shared' (2015, p. 46). Contra an overly cognitive perspective, which holds that bodily manifestations would only derive from cognitive beliefs, I support the ontological position that views emotions as both 'biological impulses of the body' and 'cognitive constructions of the mind' (Ross, 2006, p. 199). Indeed, if emotions were pure cognitions, that is, merely evaluative, computers could have emotions too. The embodied dimension of emotions is that which moves individuals to react.

Building on this, I conceptualise emotions as the *physiological, evaluative, intersubjective judgements that emerge in reaction to an event or object (past or present, real or imagined) and are articulated in attitudes and behaviour.* This definition is both specific and inclusive. It has the merit of taking several important dimensions into account, which are discussed in the following.

First, instead of endorsing one way to define the extraordinary variety of emotional phenomena, it integrates elements found in both social-scientific affect theories and emotion research. Emotions and affects have been the objects of very different categorisations spawning extensive ontological debates within and across disciplines. In the social sciences, affect is commonly defined as the diffuse embodied experiences that are pre-conscious or beyond consciousness (Ross, 2006; Bleiker & Hutchison, 2008). Affect is not bound to a subject: it lies in the transition between embodied states, comes to be between bodies, and may diffuse across groups. Many affect theorists contest the representability of affective phenomena as it overemphasises meaning produced cognitively and the textual over the embodied. A 'more-than-representational' perspective (Lorimer, 2005) on the affective would instead focus on the politics of everyday life (i.e. the micro-political, the mundane) and the diversity of lived experience. However, some argue that a clear separation between representation and affect is misleading (Anderson, 2014, p. 59).

Notwithstanding the ontological distinction between affect and emotions, a more integrative approach would account for the great variety of emotional phenomena that play into political discourses and collective action (Clément, 2021). Further, considering how intrinsically linked affects and emotions are in social interactions, it seems somewhat artificial to study them separately (Van Rythoven & Solomon, 2019). Ultimately, in most accounts, emotions and affect display four commonalities:

- they are bodily phenomena;[1]
- they are forms of evaluation and knowledge, be they depicted as attachment patterns, forms of investments, judgements, or beliefs;
- they emerge in/through interaction;
- they have (ambivalent) effects on attitudes and behaviour.

All four commonalities are integrated in the proposed definition.

This definition emphasises the intersubjective, social character of emotions. Emotions are intersubjective judgements in at least four respects. First, we express emotions for others to perceive them – therefore, we have to make them interpersonally or discursively understandable. Second, when we express emotions, we receive negative or positive feedback, which constitutes important information about our relationship with others and how they perceive us. Third, throughout our life, we learn from significant others and social institutions, within a specific socio-cultural context, about the appropriate ways to experience and express emotions, and most of the time, we conform to them. Fourth, how we experience and express emotions is ultimately impacted by the nature of power relations, which confer us different social statuses and roles (Meur, 2013; Koschut, 2016). Thus, emotions are profoundly socially constructed. To take Sartre's example in *Being and Nothingness* (1956), shame is not a feeling a subject could elicit on its own. It presupposes the intervention of an Other, not only because the Other is the one before whom the subject is ashamed, but also because it is through the Other's look that the subject becomes aware that it exists – not only for itself but for Others – and that it is an object too. Emotions play a key role in structuring social interactions because they allow individuals to adapt to their environment and manifest their social identities and aspirations.

The proposed definition stresses the dynamic character of emotional phenomena. As processes, emotions emerge at a specific moment and are subject to change. They might transform, be intermittent, or discontinue. Emotions' different temporalities are particularly difficult to characterise. Some argue, therefore, that researchers should instead talk about 'emotion episodes' (Meur, 2013, pp. 4–7), whereby an episode means an emotional state before it changes into something else (another emotional phenomenon) or dies down. However, emotions' dynamic character does not mean that they would be necessarily short-lived. Emotions are sequences or episodes which can endure in time (Frijda et al., 1991). Interdisciplinary research points increasingly to the endurance of complex emotions. The literature on resentment shows, for instance, how specific emotions, such as envy and anger, can accumulate over time and crystallise into resentment (Petersen, 2002; Wolf, 2015, 2018). In another vein, studies on collective trauma show that emotions experienced during wars or natural catastrophes are not only intense and relatively long-lived, they are also easily reactivated[2] and at times are even more intense in the present because of the felt repetition (Bell, 2006; Brounéus, 2008; Hutchison, 2010, 2016; Resende & Budryte, 2014). Similarly, recent research on cooperation between states shows that friendship is a long-term, complex emotion (Eznack, 2012; Berenskoetter, 2013; Koschut & Oelsner, 2014). Not only do some emotions endure through time, but the memory of them can be recalled and can inform further judgements and decisions. Thus, both the endurance and the transformation of emotions over time may bear effects on individual and collective experience.

Emotions are articulated in attitudes and behaviour. They affect how we interpret new information about an event or object and, ultimately, how we decide to respond to it (Forgas, 2001). In short, they function as affective feedback loops: discarding irrelevant or unwanted information, bringing to our attention, and passing affective judgement on, relevant information. Interestingly, if emotions emerge in reaction to events or objects, the latter need not be *real*, as the proposed definition underlines. Mercer points to a practical example: 'even in cases where an illusion causes pain (as in phantom limb syndrome), the experience of pain is real' (2014, p. 519). Similarly, the experience of emotion can be linked to expectations and perceptions that do not exist in the *present* but merely in the *future*, either as a potentiality (fear of a potential threat or joy at possible happiness, etc.) or an impossibility (resentment or humiliation at the perception of a stolen future; see Murphy, 2011). In this regard, emotions can also be evaluative judgements about *imagined* events and objects. As forms of evaluation, emotions constitute modes of knowledge: they tell us something about how we perceive the world. Further, emotions impact behaviour. They prepare us to respond to the new situation arising in the interaction with an object or from an event. Unlike other forms of cognition, they 'entail an action tendency' (Wolf, 2018, p. 231). Emotions motivate (political) action, yet they have ambivalent effects on behaviour.

Social-psychological research on how specific emotions impact attitudes and behaviour argues that specific emotions are linked to specific (in)action tendencies (Pearlman, 2013). Several 'discrete emotions' (joy, fear, anger, etc.) can be found across cultures and determine emotional reactions. For instance, anger tends to be linked to aggressive action tendencies, increased risk-taking, and shorter decision-making (Rydell et al., 2008). However, these effects are not unequivocal. Reactions vary according to personality. Drawing on the example above, individuals who have a low threshold for the perception of slights tend to feel angry more often and more intensely.

Further, reactions depend on the interaction with the object. If the object of the emotion is linked to a significant other, the reaction may be influenced by other emotions and affects (love (mis)trust, enmity, etc.). When the interaction produces 'mixed emotions', effects on action tendencies are ambiguous. When the subjective experience is one of anger and fear, flight may be perceived as preferable to attack. Alternatively, when the subjective experience is one of anger and shame, aggressive tendencies may be turned against the self, or it may lead to the inability to act (powerlessness), or still lead to react with even greater aggression towards the individual(s) or group(s) perceived as responsible for this new situation.

Finally, emotional reactions are closely tied to individuals' social context (status, group membership, etc.) and the perception of their environment, as both affect their capacity to act. In the experience of anger at a slight or aggression, the perceived capability to punish the aggressor is key to act upon anger and reciprocate (Aristotle, 1954, II 2). In this vein, Lebow argues that 'anger is a luxury that can only be felt by those in a position to seek revenge' (2010, p. 74). Group membership plays an important role in this regard as individuals perceiving their in-group as strong (morally if not in terms of force) tend to experience more anger towards out-groups and be more supportive of offensive action against them (Mackie et al., 2000). Conversely, those who are not in a capacity to respond to a slight or aggression would not merely feel angry; they would experience anger mixed potentially with feelings of sadness, shame, and/or guilt. Individuals – and collectives – lacking the resources required for effective punitive action 'or seeing themselves as "weak" tend to reduce or even suppress anger' (Clément et al., 2017, p. 994).

Collective emotions

Emotions are not only socially constructed; they can at times be shared. Collective emotions can be defined as

> *Evaluative judgements widely shared within a collective (be it a small or a larger group), which emerge in reaction to an event or object (past or present, real or imagined) affecting the collective as a whole or some of its members, and which are felt by group members and articulated in group attitudes and behaviour.*

Two characteristics are thus added to the definition of emotions presented previously. Collective emotions can be shared within a group, regardless of its size, and the object or event does not need to affect a group member *personally* for them to experience a collective emotion.

Research in social psychology and political science shows indeed that collectives, even large ones such as states, can experience collective emotions (Smith et al., 2007; Sasley, 2011; Mercer, 2014), perceive even the emotions of out-groups (Seger et al., 2009; Hall, 2011), and build more or less enduring affective communities (Koschut, 2014; Hutchison, 2016). The subjective experience of collective emotions presupposes that their group identity is important to the individual. Group identity consists of self-definitional meanings, common values, beliefs and goals, and specific practices, symbols, myths, and past experiences. The more an individual considers a group membership important, the more they identify with the group. An individual's sense of self-worth draws on their group identities' relative stability and desirability, giving them a sense of significance, purpose, and self-unity over time. When their group identity is affected positively or negatively, an individual's attachment to this identity causes them to experience certain emotions; for instance, anger at an out-group in a conflict situation (Mackie et al., 2000; Rydell et al., 2008) or group pride at the extraordinary achievement of a group member (Smith et al., 2007).

Further, a group member does not need to be personally affected – positively or negatively – to feel the emotion(s) of affected group members. For example, when a group member is being discriminated against, threatened, or attacked because of their identity, other group members *feel* affected negatively and discriminated against, threatened, or attacked. Such emotional experience is not necessarily vicarious but can be felt like 'the real thing'. According to Mercer, not only can group-level emotions be felt by group members much as individual emotions, they 'can be more powerful than the individual experience of emotion because one experiences it as objectively true and externally driven, rather than as subjective and individually constructed' (2014, p. 526). Individuals feel confirmed in their emotions because of the group's 'emotional consensus', whereby their group identity provides their emotional reality (Mercer, 2014, p. 527). When a group reacts emotionally to an event or object, typical group members feel similar emotions, sometimes even more intensely than they would for themselves.

However, not all groups produce such emotional consensus to the same extent. Some collectives provide more conducive contexts for the emergence of collective emotions than others (Reus-Smit, 2014; Clément et al., 2017). This is especially the case in groups drawing on a minority identity and/or protest groups leading oppositional campaigns. At the far end of groups drawing on a minority identity, militant organisations present the strongest correspondence between individual and collective emotions. This is linked to two factors. Often organised around selective membership, militant groups vet potential members carefully, based on their adequacy to the group's values, beliefs, and objectives (Clément, 2014). Further, such collectives tend to present a hierarchical structure, in which leaders' authority is widely accepted and the emulation or mimicking of leaders' and fellow members' practices are both attractive and encouraged. In interviews with Provisional Irish Republican Army members, Smith notes that 'emotions experienced collectively or reflected in others encourage people to gravitate toward each other, developing bonds and feelings of closeness' (2017, p. 10). This, in turn, points to the social functions of collective emotions.

Centrally, collective emotions fulfil constitutive and guiding functions (drawing on Koschut, 2016). In a *constitutive* function, collective emotions sustain the (re)production of shared meanings and a common identity. In a *guiding* function, they shape collective attitudes and police behaviours. To start with the constitutive function: shared meanings and identities are in large part sustained, reproduced, or transformed through the experience of collective emotions. Focusing on group norms as a central aspect of group identity, Koschut stresses that 'emotions underpin the moral hierarchy of values and beliefs within a group by assigning emotional meaning to norms which members of the group care about' (2016, p. 6). Similarly, Ross (2014) shows that, in armed conflicts, emotions help sustain identities and norms at the international level and explain why states choose to conform to certain international norms but violate others. Collective emotions underlying beliefs, values, and norms may be institutionalised and thus endure. Indeed, as Crawford argues, the 'institutionalization of emotion is ubiquitous in world politics, not an outlier or exception' (2014, p. 537). It is the process by which collective emotions become translated into practices, procedures, and symbols to fit the 'emotional need and organizational goals' of a collective (drawing on Crawford, 2014, p. 547).

Such institutionalisation bears on a group's future emotional responses to events/objects as it offers pathways to select and filter information in

a group-appropriate way. It allows a group to discard negative information about oneself, such as out-group critique, and, conversely, tends to
reinforce stereotypes about out-groups. In short, the institutionalisation
of collective emotions impacts group knowledge and, ultimately, collective
attitudes and behaviour.

Collective emotions participate in guiding social interactions by shaping
attitudes and policing behaviour. It is important to emphasise that all collectives socialise their members into appropriate emotional performance.
They do so by setting up 'feeling rules' and expecting 'emotion work' from
individuals (Hochschild, 1979, 2016). Regarding the former, collectives
establish implicit and explicit rules concerning legitimate and illegitimate
expressions of emotions. Members are expected to display emotional reactions deemed appropriate within the collective and suppress others through
emotion work. Events, rites, and symbols play a key role therein: they
sustain collective emotional reactions and reinforce group cohesion. Much
as emotions prepare individuals to respond to a new situation, collective
emotions prepare group members to react to events and objects affecting the
group. Collective emotions bear on a group's capacity to act as a collective.

Specifically, emotions that sustain loyalty and solidarity within a group
and a sense of obligation towards its members play a central role in policing group behaviour. Especially when strategies for action involve violence,
feelings of attachment and pride towards one's collective appear to be
a powerful motive. In his anthropological research with militants often
depicted as terrorists, Sluka recounts: 'Looked at from their perspective [...]
they are primarily motivated by "love" in the sense of patriotism and/or
selfless commitment to the people and/or cause they believe they represent,
and their actions are frequently extraordinarily – even suicidally – altruistic,
brave, and objectively "heroic"' (2009, p. 149; see also Mahmood, 2010).
Powerful feelings of attachment sustain identification with members of the
group and its cause.

Collective feelings of compassion and anger further ground a sense of
obligation towards the group and its members. Drawing on James M. Jasper
(2006) and Nussbaum (1996), Clément et al. (2017) show how both need
to be performed conjointly for a group to interfere in favour of perceived
victims. They are directed at separate subjects: compassion is directed at
(in-group) victims, whereas anger is directed exclusively at the Other, often
a combination of out-group(s) and those who cannot be considered part of
the collective anymore (for example, political traitors, cowardly elites, or
apathetic moderates). In a sense, both compassion for victims and anger at
the Other are self-righteous emotions; they refer to a group's self-image as
a moral, honourable collective. Compassion as a collective emotion bears
ambivalent effects. Welland argues that as much as compassion serves to

'invoke a shared sense of suffering and hardship' and, hence, a common affective experience, 'borrow[ing] another's suffering in order to make sense of your own can have other effects' (2015, p. 123). Sometimes, compassionate actors turn out to be 'scavengers' of suffering, feeding on it to 'garner concern only for themselves' (Spelman, 2001, p. 10, in Welland 2015, p. 123). The experience of compassion delivers a double incentive: to alleviate the victim's suffering and redress one's own suffered slights.

Suffering is not in itself enough to bring about collective action. For one thing, it is the perception of injustice that transforms suffering into something intolerable (Thompson, 2006). Sufferers must be perceived as innocent of the misery that has befallen them. For another, collective anger can be experienced only when a group perceives itself as 'strong' and/or capable to act upon anger and retaliate.[3] The history of collective struggles shows that 'strong' does not necessarily mean powerful in the sense of access to political or military power. Collectives that might be considered quite powerless in material terms have perceived themselves as strong enough to wage war against powerful neighbours, overturn regimes, or fight foreign invasions. Collectives powerless in a classical sense may perceive themselves as holding enough moral high ground to spur collective action.

The politics of collective emotions

Saying that collective emotions participate in shaping collective attitudes and policing behaviours means that emotions *do things* politically. In social science, researchers have developed several concepts[4] to account for the processes through which (collective) emotions become relevant to political agency and practice. With partly different foci, they call our attention to the considerable power with which a wide range of political actors may invest emotions. Such politics of emotion refers to 'the political effects of emotion practices, no matter how such emotional practices are defined', that is, both the 'representations of feelings' understood as emotions and the 'bodily movements often identified as affect' (Åhäll 2018, p. 38). Such emotion practices range from political actors 'working to configure [diffuse] affects into narrower forms of emotion' to support a given political project, to situations in which emotions that seemed well established as a collective judgement about a political situation start to 'break down into more ambivalent affects' (Van Rythoven & Solomon 2019, pp. 139–140). In other words, studying the politics of emotion allows attending to the (changing) political effects of state and non-state attempts to normalise certain emotions over others and align affective investments. This section conceptualises non-state actors' attempts at managing emotions. Thereby, it discusses the extent to which activist and militant organisations may yield such power.

While all organisations have implicit emotion rules[5] aiming towards the appropriate performance of emotions to strengthen group cohesion and capacity for action, the more tight-knit and hierarchised an organisation, the stronger it can enforce emotion rules. Further, organisations drawing on a minority identity set up emotion rules more explicitly, as legitimate and illegitimate expressions of emotions tend to depart from majority emotion rules. Events, rites, and symbols sustaining collective performances of emotions are reactivated periodically to remind of the organisation's emotion rules. Symbolic and, sometimes, material sanctions are foreseen in case of incorrect individual performance of emotions. Closely integrated and/or hierarchical organisations allow for a large degree of emotion management from above. Leaders of activist and militant organisations set emotion rules more easily and might change them incrementally to adapt to a new political situation and orient the organisation towards (partly) new collective aims and forms of action.

Such organisations also expect a greater amount of emotion work from their members. 'Emotion work' refers to the process by which individuals try to conform to a group's emotion rules (Hochschild, 1979, 2016; von Scheve, 2012). While initially focusing on how individuals actively work to induce or suppress emotions to conform to expectations in social interactions, the concept of 'emotion work' can be extended to collectives. Drawing on comparative case studies of civil rights movements in the US and East Germany, Goodwin and Pfaff show that such work 'may also occur at a collective or group-level' (2001, p. 284). Within this literature, others have also stressed the active work that protest groups and movements put in to 'arouse', 'alter', and 'manage' emotions (Jasper, 1998; Traïni, 2009). Collectives engaging in activism require a great deal of emotion work to sustain themselves, especially when the social-political environment in which they operate changes. Studies of activist movements show that organisations may reshape collective emotions to some extent: how feminist movements transformed fear into anger to mobilise for feminist activism (Ost, 2004) and how fear and shame were reshaped into 'rage' and 'pride' in the case of AIDS activism (Gould, 2004). Movements and organisations engage in rhetorical work to normalise certain emotions over others, to colour representations of their surrounding environment emotionally, and to stage emotions in group activities and day-to-day practices.

However, such emotion management cannot be reduced to mere rhetorical work. For one thing, emotion management as a practice does not need to be intended. Rightly, Goodwin and Pfaff argue that 'the management [of emotions] is not simply a self-conscious and instrumental effort by actors, individual or collective, but may also be the unintended result of social interactions or beliefs that have other manifest purposes' (2001, p. 284).

This relaxes the purposive character of the concept and allows less visible forms of emotion work to be taken into account.

Further, even when emotion management is conscious, collective emotions cannot be reduced to mere strategic instruments. As discussed above, the political effects of collective emotions are not straightforward. While leaders of organisations may work to configure collective moods and affects into actionable forms of emotions, collective emotions are not *objects*. They are modes of sensation, perception, and knowledge infused in manifold discourses and practices. Taken in webs of meaning and practice, they are performed in ways that go beyond the intentions of specific social actors. Much as narratives, they have a life of their own and partly escape attempts by actors to produce specific political effects. The next section discusses in depth how (collective) emotions are performed narratively and thereby inform knowledge production and collective action.

The narrative performance of emotions

The representation of emotions in language as performance

As emotions are fundamentally social and necessarily communicated to others, one way to approach their constitution is through linguistic practices. This section discusses what it means to access emotional experience via representations in language and, more specifically, in narrative as a specific form of discourse.

As discussed previously, the experience of emotion is expressed in relation to others, communicated or, more appropriately, represented in a language that others can understand (Searle, 1992; Fattah & Fierke, 2009; Fierke, 2012; Lindemann, 2014). This language, which allows the mediation of emotions, includes language, strictly speaking, images, and further aesthetic and embodied practices (Hutchison & Bleiker, 2014; Bleiker & Hutchison, 2018). They allow actors to access the intersubjective expression of emotions within social spheres. Their representations in language are the first attempts by social actors to articulate what they feel 'inside' and produce effects on their social reality. Or, formulated in a Wittgensteinian perspective, focusing on language:

> We do not know our own emotions and feelings in a natural way or by observation. We produce spontaneous linguistic articulations of our feelings and impressions of the world. We express descriptive states of our affects. (Belli & Harré, 2010, p. 252, drawing on Wittgenstein, 1958)

The representation in language and (simultaneous or subsequent) meaning-making of our emotions is a powerful social practice (Schlag, 2018). It forms an intersubjective reality in which certain practices prevail over others.

Exploring representations means focusing 'on the site[s] or force[s] through which the emotional experience become[s] known' (Bially Mattern, 2011, p. 66). Social researchers study emotions, much as they would norms or ideas, by reconstructing the shared understandings that emerge around the meaning of objects, events, and practices. Reflexive reconstructions of social actors' representations of emotional experiences encompass asking how language (and aesthetic practices) represent collective emotions and how collectives make sense of emotions put into language in their specific socio-historical context.

However, it cannot be stressed enough that the expression of emotions in language is not merely a description of what social actors feel. Much like novelists try to 'put emotions in words' or, conversely to 'construct emotions through the use of words', social actors use certain words and construct certain contexts to recreate the experience of emotion (Belli & Harré, 2010, pp. 254–255, drawing on Butler 1993; see also Austin 1975). Thereby they create a performance, producing real emotions in intersubjective interactions.

While performances engender emotions, they do not always bring about political effects. According to Butler, researchers may be too quick to assume the spoken words' impacts on political realities. While performances often produce knowledge effects, they are not necessarily followed by actions or 'socially binding consequences' in Butler's terminology. Utterances[6] still have to be 'set in motion' to transform realities (Butler, 2010, p. 150). Therefore, 'fallibility is built into the account of performativity' (Butler, 2010, p. 151). Performative operations need constant reiteration to avoid 'performative breakdown' when the effects of a performative operation cease to work (Butler, 2010, pp. 152–153). In sum, the (temporary) success of attempts at managing emotions rests on the constant reiteration of the performance of emotions in language. This is an important theoretical element for the conceptualisation of *narrative emotionalisation* later in the chapter.

Adding the social context of actors to language, we can research the role of emotions in 'discursive agency'; that is, how emotions work powerfully in discursive performances 'by slowly entrenching – or gradually challenging – how we feel, view, think of the socio-political world around us' (Bleiker & Hutchison, 2018, p. 333). When we understand discourse as 'language plus sociality' (Van Rythoven, 2015), the interplay between emotions and discourse is fundamental in reproducing or contesting dominant interpretations of the socio-political world.

Of all discursive forms, narrative provides the performance of emotions par excellence. A common way to delineate narrative from discourse is to define narrative 'provisionally as discourses with a clear sequential order that connect events in a meaningful way for a definite audience and thus offer insights about the world and/or people's experiences of it' (Hinchman & Hinchman, 1997, p. xvi). However, narratives cannot be reduced to 'discourses *plus* temporal sequencing'. Because they organise events so that each event is understood through its relation to the whole story, narratives are both 'sequence and consequence' (Riessman, 2008).

Hence, in a Foucauldian approach to narrative, it is argued that 'rather than being considered as representing reality/ies, narratives should be seen as productive: narratives do things, they constitute realities, shaping the social rather than being determined by it' (Andrews et al., 2013, p. 15). Through the inscription within a spatial-temporal context and the alleged revelation of parts of the psyche and behaviour of its characters, a narrative gives the illusion of disclosing hidden truths about social actors and their relationships. In sum, if a narrative can refer to one or several discourse(s), it is not a mere vignette that would serve to illustrate said discourse(s); it *re-presents* and constitutes reality, and shapes and orients action. Circling back to the idea of emotions being performed in language, whereby representations in language recreate the experience of emotion, narratives appear to provide the performance of emotions par excellence.

Narrative characteristics, resonance, and constraints

Narrating is a fundamental human activity, so much so that some draw on the concept of 'homo narrans' to suggest that human beings' primary feature is to tell, interpret, and trade stories (Fisher, 1984; Rabatel, 2008). Narratives come in many forms: they are more or less comprehensive and diversely successful, lasting, and dominant. However, as Barthes puts it, as a form, 'narrative is international, transhistorical, transcultural: It is simply there, like life itself' (1977, p. 79). As a practice, narrative is shared by all humanity. Hardy's enumeration of all that we do in narrative form stresses how intimately intertwined emotions and narratives are: 'We dream in narrative, daydream in narrative, remember, anticipate, hope, despair, believe, doubt, plan, revise, criticize, construct, gossip, learn, hate and love by narrative' (Hardy, 1987, p. 1). This perspective is shared by narratologists (Greimas, 1966; Lukács, 1971; White, 1987; Bal, 2009; Fludernik, 2009) and largely by cultural, social, discursive, and political psychology.

Taking literary studies as a starting point, a minimal definition refers to narrative as the 'representation of at least two real or fictive events or situations in time sequence' (Prince, 1982, p. 4). Texts lacking this basic feature cannot be considered narrative texts. Non-narrative texts may draw on a 'logico-scientific' system of description instead, which is epitomised in formal mathematical language (Bruner, 1986, p. 12). The difference between narrative and non-narrative texts is thus the presence or absence of a story (Franzosi, 1998). To this temporal dimension, scholars add further criteria because narratives presenting no other features (such as a fixed group of characters) would only be very 'loosely cohesive' (Shenhav, 2006, p. 247).

Cohesive narratives would possess further structural components, such as a setting, plot, and characters (Kruck & Spencer, 2014; Spencer, 2016). Several characteristics appear central across narrative theories:

1. A narrative involves at least one disruptive event, a break from what is seen as normal and to be expected or else there would be no need to recount events in the first place (Franzosi, 1998; Kruck & Spencer, 2014). Disruptive events may be positive (a good fortune), but they tend to be negative and relate to a reversal of fortune or the further deterioration of an unenviable situation (Chatman, 1980; Ricoeur, 1984; Propp, 2010). This event indicates whether the environment is favourable or dangerous.

2. A narrative always contains a series of events, organised through time and, often indirectly, space. The temporal sequencing may be arranged in chronological order – be organised according to the historical order of events – but not necessarily (Clément et al., 2017). A narrative may relate the most current events first, be interrupted by flashbacks on older events, or be re-arranged according to fictive events. Spatial information on the location of events may be provided to the audience, but the specific vicinity of the narrated events often remains rather abstract. This is not to say that narrative unfolds in a void but rather that the story's spatial boundaries are implied in the choice of characters and timeframe and partly left to the audience's previous knowledge and imagination.

3. Events are linked to each other in a more or less causal way within a narrative. As Franzosi points out, 'the events in the sequence must be bound by some principles of logical coherence' (1998, p. 520), which is not to say that it has to be logical *outside* of the narrative's story or in a scientific sense. A narrative lets causal connections appear between specific events while hiding other events and their potential relationships. In this regard, it reduces the complexity of events to a manageable few that are brought into perspective.

4. A narrative displays a set of characters – human or 'human-like' protagonists (Kruck & Spencer, 2014, p. 148), whose characteristics are in

part elaborated within the narrative and in part by the audience, which is called to complete their characterisation. The narrative attributes, more or less explicitly, specific moral traits, motives, and behaviour to characters, which, in turn, impact how the audience perceives them. It keeps descriptive aspects to a minimum because its elements are bent towards the narration of *action*. When information is missing, for instance, about the train of thoughts of certain protagonists leading to a decision, the audience adds to the picture based on stereotypes, personal experiences in similar situations, etc. This is one of the smartest features of narrative: it constrains the reception by the audience as much as it opens it up. 'Mature narratives present not only "what happened" but further engage the listener in giving a perspective on the motivations and consequences of the events related' (Pearson & de Villiers, 2005, p. 695). Characters are key to the audience's interpretation of what is at stake in the narrative and what ought to be thought and done.

5. Finally, a narrative draws on symbols, past experiences, collective memories, cultural scripts, and complementary narratives, among others (Hammack & Pilecki, 2012; Sakwa, 2012). In short, it pulls all imaginable socio-cultural resources together, which might fit in the stories it tells. A narrative often draws on former narratives and the interpretations they were subjected to, thereby reproducing or transforming them (Toolan, 2001).

These characteristics structure all proper narratives. Beyond that, the structure of a narrative interacts with the context of its production (by whom and where), narration (told, written, visual), and reception (by whom and where). Llanque (2014) argues in this regard that the relevance of a narrative is equal part composition (or structure) and equal part context.

Narratives are widespread in political discourse because they fit in well 'with the political logic of trying to shape the present in light of lessons learned from the past' (Shenhav, 2006, p. 246). This holds not only for formal political narratives produced by institutional actors but also for stories produced by other organised actors and large sections of society, which routinely co-produce, reproduce, and contest narratives. A political narrative can be defined as 'the sensible organization of thought through language, internalized or externalized,[7] which serves to create a sense of personal coherence and collective solidarity and to legitimize collective beliefs, emotions, and actions' (Hammack & Pilecki, 2012, p. 78). Simply put, a narrative consists of beliefs and perceptions, put in story form, about one's collective and the world, which become thereby ordered and legitimised.

It is through political narratives that individuals relate to political contexts. Notions such as 'crisis' or 'security' come to exist in the first place through narrative: 'although events are unquestionably real, their social import is not determined by any of their objective features' (Krebs, 2015, p. 825). Hence, events do not prove narratives right or wrong; they *depend* on narratives to make sense in the first place. Narratives may have, but do not necessarily need, 'a material or institutional basis'; they draw much more 'on cultural presuppositions of the societies in which they originate' (Ringmar, 2006, p. 411). Narratives resonate strongly when they possess a cultural appeal and are deployed in a politically favourable context. Both culture and context impact the reception of narratives, especially minority narratives such as those (re)produced by activist and militant organisations.

Concerning context, for the narratives of activist and militant organisations to stand a chance at a large reception, the current dominant narrative has to be so contested that political elites cannot sideline contesting narratives anymore. According to Krebs, this happens around events that later come to constitute turning points and initiate policy changes (2015, p. 826). Such nodal events, and the narrative adjustments that political elites may need to undertake, can empower contesting narratives because they bring the political actors supporting the dominant narrative to the contestants' narrative terrain (Passy & Giugni, 2005; Krebs, 2015).

Concerning cultural appeal, narratives interweave linguistic and figurative elements, symbols, memories, myths, other narratives, collective experiences, that is, everything culturally familiar that might resonate with an audience. Narratives are 'emplotted in a predictable fashion', according to a narrative genre (Ringmar, 2006, p. 404). For example, the US narrative around the war in Iraq in 2003 fits in with the romantic genre (also called *romance*). This specific body of stories draws on other narratives anchored in US culture, from the struggle of the initial settlers to the fight against the Englishmen, all the way to the Cold War and, more recently, the fight against international terrorism. These cultural references are mirrored in popular culture and so familiar that their presence in the latest narrative – here, about the Iraq war – seems just *right*. This familiarity normalises events and objects and appeals affectively and aesthetically.

This appeal is perhaps most visible in the construction of culturally situated characters. Narratives stage different social identities and how they interact with one another, thereby affecting the audience emotionally. Ringmar explains that in order 'to be convincing, the story must address their [audiences'] preconceptions, hopes and fears' (2006, p. 410). Culturally appealing narratives let the audience assume what protagonists think and feel and *why* they do what they are doing or failing to do.

Culturally specific metaphors and figures of speech, literary and religious references, and scapegoat and enemy images participate in the characterisation of the story's protagonists, which allows the audience to identify with some of the characters and reject the others. What becomes important to a receptive audience is not so much what happens in the story in general but what happens to the protagonists with whom it identifies. The audience is moved by and feels with these characters.

The fact that narratives draw on culturally specific elements signals that they cannot be completely freely chosen. Political actors are constrained by the narrative references, preferences, and expectations of the audience(s) they address. While transforming elements of a narrative is possible, it is much more difficult than reproducing past narrative occurrences. New narrative deployments may fail to resonate aesthetically and affectively with audiences. Further, while political leaders tell, write, and picture the stories that eventually become part of a narrative, a narrative that endures over time cannot be reduced to their strategies alone (Krebs, 2015, p. 826). Sure, leaders have an interest in specific stories gaining traction and replacing others among their audience(s). Yet because narratives rely so much on the known and familiar and transcend time and place, they can go beyond the purpose of their creation. To some extent, established narratives have a 'life of their own', and their effects unfold in partly incalculable ways. Not only can narrative text patterns (e.g. metaphors) be effective regardless of authors' intentions (Llanque, 2014, p. 8), a narrative can also become partly independent of its creators when relayed, reinterpreted, and transformed by other political actors and/or audiences.

However, not all political actors have the same capacity to reshape narratives. Narrative's intrinsic dialogical character – both internally, in the articulation of diverse characters in dialogue and, externally, in the interplay between the telling and the reception – must be nuanced in the case of minority narratives. Because they purport minority identities, activist and militant organisations are less constrained than institutional political actors; they can afford (gradual) narrative transformation to a larger extent.

Also, while a narrative does not need to be *factually* true, it is stronger when internally coherent. Glazzard, drawing on Fisher (1987), contends that 'by satisfying an internal logic while remaining apparently true to the real world [...] narratives can appear to be more profoundly true than other, more factual forms' (2017, p. 15). In this cognitive perspective, a narrative that stays coherent and 'true to itself' increases its chances of being accepted. Thus, while political actors have some leeway in re-inventing the stories they tell, they are nonetheless bound by their former narrative deployments. Especially small, hierarchised collectives can maintain a high degree of control on narrative production and, hence, on coherence across narrative deployments. This is an important aspect for the discussion of *narrative emotionalisation* further down.

Narrative genres and the possibilities of knowledge and action

As argued above, narratives should be seen as productive: they re-present and constitute reality, and shape and orient action. Accounts from literary studies, sociology, and political science have affirmed the intimate link between interpreting narrative and committing to action (Passy & Giugni, 2005; Polletta, 2006; Cobb, 2013). Lyotard's theory of knowledge (1984) contends that narratives define the possibilities of knowledge and, hence, action in a given society. Earlier, Wittgenstein (1958) similarly argued that narration and action share the same space and are constrained by the same boundaries. In this sense, narration restricts the number of imaginable actions for individuals and groups.

Scholars in political science make similar arguments. Krebs stresses that a narrative 'defines the range of sustainable policy options' (2015, p. 811). In the same vein, Ringmar contends that 'stories present different agendas for action and thereby different moral choices' (2006, p. 404). It seems a consensus that narrative makes action *possible* in the first place. If we circle back to the argument that both narratives *and* emotions are potent forms of knowledge, emotions performed in and through narrative have a tremendous impact not only on what we 'know' happened (and why it did) but also on what we perceive as moral or immoral and what we consider right/ legitimate or wrong/illegitimate.

However, while all narratives can be said to perform emotions, some do so more than others. Ringmar formulates differences across narratives as follows: 'Taking their departure from the same basic facts, the interpretations they reach often vary and the conclusions differ' (2006, p. 404). In-between interpretation and conclusion, political narratives aim to determine commitment (Llanque, 2014, p. 8), that is, who is responsible for the political issues at stake in the narrative. Competing narratives legitimise different collective perceptions and interpretations of political problems, arrive at distinct diagnoses (e.g. blame or exoneration), and imagine different courses of action, strategies to attain collective political goals, and different futures.

Such differences can be tied to the variety of narrative *genres*. The competing narratives that came to the fore before the Iraq war in 2003 illustrate this argument well. In his study of the four narrative genres – romance, tragedy, comedy, and satire – which were used by decision-makers at the international level prior to and in the wake of the invasion of Iraq, Ringmar states: 'They told different stories about the intentions of Saddam Hussein, about the position of their own country, about the nature of world politics, and about the likely outcomes of the various actions they were contemplating' (2006, p. 403). Ringmar characterises *romance* as the preferred mode of idealists, who strive (often by fighting) to change the world; *tragedy* as the mode of pessimists, who hold that there is no escape from the laws of nature and insecurity; *comedy* as the mode of liberal 'institution-builders', who engage in conversations to win others to their views; and, finally, *satire* as the mode of distanced anti-war critics (2006, pp. 404–407). If we compare romance and satire, the interpretation of political problems and the diagnoses they arrive at are radically different.

Romance carries a black-and-white view of problems and responsibilities and considers that the world can become a better place only when wrong-doers are defeated, whereas satire depicts problems precisely as caused by hegemonic and warlike attitudes. Romance and satire support entirely different courses of action, strategies, and outcomes. While romantic narrators call to embark on a quest and prepare to fight for their conception of 'a better place', satirical narrators aim to deconstruct other narratives and, ultimately, open spaces for critique and alternative interpretations of the social world. These two narrative genres create starkly different expectations and fulfil reverse legitimation purposes.

Contrasting romance and satire not only highlights how narratives constrain the range of imaginable, desirable actions, it also stresses that some narratives rely more on emotional meanings than others. Romance is the genre that is most visibly emotional and that 'takes itself most seriously' (Ringmar, 2006, p. 406). Further, it is the only genre in which violence is presented positively, both the violent action itself and its outcome in the form of a better future.

Political actors calling for profound political transformation and/or radical action (use of force, armed resistance, etc.) tend to draw on romantic narratives. Therefore, romance is the genre that organisations radicalising into extremism would choose. Indeed, Ringmar states that 'romance seems to be for the powerful, the powerless, but not for states in between' (2006, p. 411). Both powerful and powerless collectives recur to narratives performing compassion and anger when their members see themselves as superior, either militarily, politically, or morally. In such cases, collectives cannot imagine showing indifference or cowardice, 'they cannot simply ignore a narrative of suffering that contains identifiable victims and perpetrators' (Clément et al., 2017, p. 994, drawing on Boltanski, 1999). When imagined courses of action and specific strategies imply the use of violence, romantic narrators present violence as morally desirable. Romantic narratives *create* the need to take decisive collective action. They do so by weaving cognition and emotion tightly together: the belief that something is not as it should be, yet can be reversed, gains motivational force only through emotions (Hammack & Pilecki, 2012; Koschut, 2016; Clément et al., 2017). Emotions give this belief subjects to identify with and objects to reject, motivation to assist the former and punish the latter, and present collective action as desirable, making it *feel* right.

Emotionalisation in romantic narratives

While romantic narratives are most visibly emotional compared to other narrative genres, how can we conceptualise differences in intensity among romantic narratives? In other words, if some romantic narratives perform emotions particularly intensely, how can we recognise them? Building on the theoretical developments so far, this last section introduces the original concept of *narrative emotionalisation* to grasp the process by which a romantic narrative becomes *increasingly* emotionalised. I contend that romantic narratives not only establish expectations towards collective action: through gradual emotionalisation, they *demand* decisive action. After defining what I mean by narrative emotionalisation, I present the four sub-processes constitutive thereof and how their combined effects shape group knowledge and orient collective action.

I define narrative emotionalisation as *the gradual process by which the texts and visuals pertaining to a narrative increasingly perform strong, non-conflicting, collective emotions towards distinct narrative objects and events, according to strict emotion rules*. Full narrative emotionalisation would amount to all objects and events of the narrative, in all its occurrences, being systematically and consistently wrapped in emotional meanings.[8] In other words, it corresponds to a (temporary) performative success. This overall process can be divided into sub-processes, which build on the relationships between emotions/narratives and knowledge/action problematised throughout the chapter. These four sub-processes are condensed as:

1. Emotional meanings become the only legitimate form of knowledge.
2. Conflicting emotional meanings gradually disappear, and a distinctive emotional tone crystallises.
3. Strict emotion rules are established and enforced with sanctions.
4. The performance of emotions is consistent across narrative occurrences.

The first sub-process of narrative emotionalisation refers to emotional meanings progressively becoming the only legitimate form of knowledge within the narrative. Knowledge can be individual (known by one person) or collective (regarded as general). Most scholars consider that there are four basic sources of knowledge: perception, consciousness, reason, and memory (Audi, 2009) – most of which draw on a mix of affective-cognitive processes (Bless, 2000). A piece of knowledge can be defined as the understanding of a subject or a situation through experience or study. Knowledge thus takes a great many forms: it can but need not be factual, conceptual, procedural, or moral, and so on. Depending on the collective, some forms of knowledge are valued more than others. This first sub-process focuses on knowledge rooted in collective emotional experience or, more precisely, what an organisation constructs as collective emotional experience. This sub-process implies that knowledge rooted in emotional experience becomes valued above all else, so much so that other forms of knowledge are increasingly perceived as illegitimate and discarded as ways of making sense of the social world.

Second, narrative emotionalisation is characterised by the gradual reduction of emotion expressions' variety and complexity. In this second sub-process, conflicting emotional meanings tend to disappear and a recognisable emotional tone crystallises within the narrative. Nuanced emotion expressions, such as 'we are angry, although we partly understand why they did what they did', are silenced. Mixed emotions, such as 'we were angry and worried about this new situation', are also suppressed. In this process, any asperity is erased from the performance of emotions. The events of the narrative become wrapped in clear-cut, unambiguous emotional meanings. By restricting potentially conflicting emotional meanings, this sub-process reduces narrative's dialogic character and thereby confines the possibilities of interpretation. This most coherent performance of emotions endows the narrative with a distinctive emotional tone.

The third sub-process of narrative emotionalisation refers to the emotion rules which a group expects all those who see themselves as part of the in-group to follow. This process is about the management of collective emotion – the clearer and stricter the emotion rules, the more collective the performance of emotion. Exclusive emotion rules and sanctions for deviance are being increasingly enforced. Further, members of the in-group are expected to work on their emotions to conform to this performance. Throughout this process, the multiple identities of the self are downplayed, as are the common qualities and imperfections shared with out-group(s). Overall, nuance and differentiation in the presentation of others and the self are erased – in a much more reifying way than in processes of othering.[9] In an advanced form, the emotions enforced within the in-group are distinct from those attributed to out-group(s), said to *feel differently*. At its fullest, this sub-process contributes to collectivise (and reify) the emotions felt by out-groups towards the in-group and, conversely, the emotions felt by the in-group towards out-groups. This restricts the behaviour that may be expected of out-groups and the attitudes and actions that may be considered appropriate for group members. The stronger the collective emotions of love, compassion, and anger are performed, the stronger the push for decisive collective action.

Finally, the fourth sub-process of narrative emotionalisation refers to the consistent repetition of the performance of emotions across narrative occurrences (the various texts and visuals pertaining to a given narrative). A narrative is a body of stories found in texts and visuals, which follow one another temporally.[10] Each occurrence of the narrative adds to the others and has the potential to reiterate the performance of emotions. Through consistent repetition, the emotional meanings and expressions constructed in previously heard, read, and seen occurrences are validated. Overall, it calls to view narrative emotionalisation as a continued process – instead of an instantaneous one – which builds on intertextuality.

Understood here as encompassing verbal and visual texts, intertextuality is the character of a text of being surrounded by 'the web of meaning' created by other texts (Kristeva, 1980; Fairclough, 1992, 2013). A narrative occurrence creates intertextuality either by referring explicitly to another occurrence (i.e. 'as leader XY said in his speech when we started this campaign') or when the same emotional meanings are re-articulated across narrative occurrences (i.e. 'this is a war against Islam'). By becoming increasingly intertextual, the performance of collective emotions is validated, normalised. In sum, the emotional meanings constituted through the other three sub-processes become all the more potent when political actors tell, write, and picture a given narrative in a similar way. Such consistent repetition and circulation ties past, present, and future emotional experiences together and presents the political issues addressed in each specific narrative occurrence as urgent and of existential importance.

In summary, narrative emotionalisation reduces narrative's multi-voiced, dialogic character. It mutes the plurality of points of view, thereby restricting the possibilities of interpretation of the issues at stake in the narrative. It motivates those who recognise themselves in the narrative to take decisive action under the range of legitimate options that it has circumscribed. Narrative emotionalisation thus *facilitates* or is *bent* on raising and maintaining collective action.

The combined effects of narrative emotionalisation and the specific organisational dynamics of activist and militant groups are far-reaching. As argued above, groups organised around selective memberships and/or presenting a hierarchical structure allow for a large degree of emotion management from above, are less bound by narrative constraints than institutional actors, and can maintain a higher degree of control over narrative production. Groups attempting to mobilise for political violence will tend to draw extensively on narrative emotionalisation (consciously or unconsciously). Narrative emotionalisation impacts, in turn, the attitudes and behaviour of an accepting audience in profound ways. Perhaps most evidently, it legitimises a collective orientation towards specific political goals and strategies, restricts the range of desirable moral options, and makes decisive action feel right.

Notes

1 Not all emotional experiences implicate a visceral reaction in the sense of perspiring, getting red, and so on. Emotions can be felt without such manifestations, so Damasio argues, because the brain has developed a mechanism simulating bodily responses to activate the mind (Damasio, 2004, 2006; cited in Ross, 2006, pp. 202–203).

2 This fits in with research in neuroscience, for instance Damasio et al.'s theory of the 'somatic markers' (1996), which claims that emotional states leave markers which can be reactivated at a later time for subsequent decisions; see also Vohs et al. (2007).

3 The perceived capability to punish an aggressor is a precondition for the successful mobilisation of anger. Actors who can exact revenge – even in a limited way, e.g. through asymmetrical violence – may indeed recur to narratives performing compassion and anger to mobilise.

4 Prominent concepts in this regard include: the 'institutionalisation of emotions' in world politics (Marlier and Crawford, 2013; Crawford, 2014); the 'public orchestration of feelings' (Berlant, 2005), and public governance of emotions (Shoshan, 2016); the constitution of emotional/affective communities (Koschut, 2014; Hutchison, 2016); the governance of emotions beyond the state (Eken, 2019; Eroukhmanoff, 2019); and the management of emotions by non-state actors (Goodwin and Pfaff, 2001; Traïni, 2009; Rodgers, 2010; Clément, 2019).

5 Hochschild's terminology refers to the shared norms and rules about appropriate feelings as 'feeling rules', which I call 'emotion rules' throughout the rest of the book.

6 Note that, for Butler, there need not be an actively speaking subject nor a discrete act of enunciation.

7 In this context, 'internalised' refers to sense-making *within* the mind (as a mental act), whereas 'externalised' refers to sense-making in the material world (as embodied in cultural practices).

8 It is important to stress that narrative emotionalisation does not amount to an intensification of emotion words in a quantitative sense. Emotions are not merely, or even primarily, made accessible to an audience because they are directly named as such ('we are angry') but rather because the meanings of objects and events become systematically linked to strong emotional meanings. Consider the sentence 'There is no doubt that the perpetrators of what happened in New York must be punished' – is it a lesser expression of anger than 'we are

angry' simply because 'anger' is not explicitly named? Strong performances of emotions do not build on the precision of a statement either, but rather on what is implied and 'is not straightforwardly said or written and what cannot even be brought into it [the narrative]' (Andrews et al., 2013, p. 11). What is missing or has been suppressed may play as much of a role in the overall performance.

9 This sub-process is not identical to 'Othering', i.e. the antagonistic identity construction of *other* subjects. While the third sub-process surely implies that out-groups are constructed as dissimilar to the in-group, it goes much further. First, it digs deeper than the identity politics implied in 'Othering': the collectivisation of emotions means that all group members have to *feel* the same way – a particularly illiberal practice targeted at the *in-group*. Second, this process implies that out-groups are constructed as homogeneous collectives also regarding how they *feel*, i.e. they are objectified based on their (alleged) collective emotions. The collectivisation of emotions goes both ways and is a more fundamentally reifying practice.

10 Be it in the sense of their chronological enunciation (or representation) or in the sense of their reception by a specific audience (texts and visuals might not be received in the same chronological order as they were produced).

4

The romantic narrative of Western Islamist organisations

This chapter addresses the narrative activity of HTB, AM, DWR, MI, and MAB in their respective phases of activism, reconstructed in Chapter 2. Drawing on the previous theoretical elaborations on romance, it explores the extent to which the organisations reproduce a romantic narrative in phases of group moderation, radicalisation, and extremism.

The chapter starts by explaining the methodology and introduces the narrative codebook elaborated to support the narrative approach. It then turns to the description and interpretation of the coding results, contrasting the cases corresponding to phases of moderation with the cases corresponding to phases of radicalisation and extremism. The chapter then offers an in-depth interpretation of the meanings attributed by organisations to the categories of the narrative and highlights differences and similarities across organisations. While these meanings point to partly different creedal beliefs and hierarchies of political goals, organisations are, narratively speaking, identical in phases of radicalisation and extremism. The chapter concludes with a summary of the narrative changes accompanying an organisation's move away from moderate politics and discusses subtle differences in narrative emphasis between the phases of radicalisation and phases of extremism.

Narrative approach

In the humanities and social sciences, narrative analyses come in many stripes, from the tradition of Russian formalists (Propp, 1984; Tomashevsky, 2002), to the French structuralists (Barthes, 1966; Genette, 1980 [1972], 1983), and the more recent body of work in narratology (Toolan, 2001; Bal, 2009; Fludernik, 2009). I conceive narrative analysis as the study of the specificities of a body of stories, its relation to larger narrative disputes and effects. This book aims to understand contesting narratives – those less evident bodies of stories than dominant narratives about 'security', 'terrorism', or the 'international order'. All narratives have the tendency to 'generalize, universalize and decontextualize the particular' (Wibben, 2011, p. 37) and contesting narratives are no exception. Approaching the five organisations' texts, audios, and videos through a narrative lens allows us to reconstruct the identities and roles that they attribute to members and their in-group at large, where they situate the *ummah* in relation to the international order and dominant security narratives, and what means they use to establish the parameters of collective and individual action.

Ultimately, it is about reconstructing whether and how certain stories fit in with others over time and build a narrative. Approaching the textual data narratively can be regarded as an extension of the reconstruction of phases of moderation and radicalisation. Attention to narrative shifts helps to characterise how organisations mediate changes in activism. Further, exploring differences and similarities among the cases contributes to a better understanding of the narrative underpinning of group radicalisation into extremism, while at the same time appreciating organisation-specific stories about (in)security and political violence.

As discussed in Chapter 3, narratives display what most authors call *content* (themes, metaphors, etc.) and *structure* (characters, plot, setting). However, the textual composition does not say much in itself, while content alone is undirected; Llanque underlines that it is the interaction between form and meaning that should matter to narrative researchers (2014, p. 12). The relationship between content and structure is thus key to understanding narratives. Further, *context* and *culture* are of much analytical relevance. The former refers to the larger context of production and reception of a body of stories. Concretely, it means taking into account the context of repression by security authorities and the growing concurrence between Islamist organisations. The latter refers to collectives' manifold cultural references, past and present, which infuse narratives. This means that a body of stories is shaped by many cultural narratives (Passy & Giugni, 2005). The organisations studied here do not merely draw on Islamic cultural references. Among others, their stories are embedded in Western cultural schemes and address Western/Westernised audiences. Hence, they draw on and (re)produce potentially conflicting cultural narratives.

With the aim of reconstructing these complex meanings, I developed a narrative codebook that typifies an Islamist romantic narrative in a Western European context. Narrative approaches based on codebooks are increasingly common, especially with regard to security discourses. They offer the possibility of articulating complex and potentially antagonistic stories about (in)security, as in Kreb's analysis of newspaper editorials on foreign affairs in the context of the Cold War (2015) or in Clément et al.'s analysis of political speeches justifying the use of force (2017). A narrative codebook is particularly useful to explore narrative meanings across a large corpus and to structure the comparison between cases. As a codebook's advantages for interpretative work have been discussed at length in Chapter 2, I describe the concrete approach here only briefly.

The textual data was coded manually and in context. Exploring such data allows zooming in and out of the empirical material. Throughout the chapter, I zoom in to provide a thick description and interpretation of the meaning of narrative categories and zoom out to interpret the relationships between narrative codes. As in Chapter 2, I use some quantifying-visualising elements to support the interpretative endeavour, especially to make complex narrative relationships visible. I draw on coding frequencies and the results of a co-occurrence analysis. The former analyses the distribution of narratives codes, while the meaning of the passages is interpreted in context. The co-occurrence analysis assesses the proximity and/or overlap of codes. In other words, it tells us something about whether and how strongly the elements constituting the narrative are connected to one another.

Building on the theoretical developments in Chapter 3, the narrative codebook captures the central elements of *romance* as a narrative genre and formalises them into narrative categories and codes. The *main categories* draw on narratology's three narrative characteristics: characters, setting, and plot. The *categories* are inspired by Ringmar's (2006) elaborations on romance as a narrative genre with specific values, moral choices, and agenda for action, as well as Clément and colleagues's on narrative structures and characters (Clément et al., 2017; Sangar et al., 2018). The individual *codes* have been specified inductively based on the organisations' identities, values, and choices. In a nutshell, the codebook adapts an ideal-typical romantic narrative to a Western Islamist political agenda and context of production and reception. Shortened to 'Romantic Narrative', the codebook is summarised in Table 4.1 (detailed version, with full category headings, in Appendix C3).

The main category of *Characters* refers to the identities and roles that an organisation attributes to the relevant actors populating its social world. The *Character* categories 'In-group identities' and 'Out-group identities' correspond to the dominant identities (and roles) attributed respectively to an organisation's in-group(s) and out-group(s). The three 'In-group identities' codes refer to subjects to identify with, whereas the three 'Out-group identities' codes refer to subjects to reject. These codes were attributed irrespective of whether the subjects were individuals or collectives, as long as they were clearly identifiable.

Setting encompasses the environments in which an organisation and/or its in-group(s) operate and that structure their relationships with other relevant actors. The *Setting* categories, 'Local horizon of experience' and 'Transnational horizon of experience', refer to how an organisation

Table 4.1 Codebook 'Romantic Narrative' at the levels of main category, category, and code

Main category (level 1)	Category (level 2)	Code (level 3)
Characters	In-group identities	Muslim victims
		Muslim role models
		True believers
	Out-group identities	Political enemies
		The Muslim Other
		The (non-)religious Other
Setting	Local horizon of experience	Immoral, depraved, hypocritical
		Islamophobic, repressive, harassing
	Transnational horizon of experience	Double-standard, immoral, hypocritical
		Hostile, dangerous, exploiting
Plot	Muslims and their 'way of life' are under threat	Muslims worldwide are prevented from living according to their faith
		Muslims worldwide are physically/ militarily attacked
		This is not the first time in history/ Repeated attacks
		The political leaders of the Muslim world are not protecting Muslims
	Muslims need to rise up	Resist and fight back
		The current (world) order will be replaced by an Islamic caliphate
		Obligation to help fellow Muslims/ establish the caliphate
		Muslims will be rewarded for rising up

experiences the context of its activism at different socio-political levels. 'Local horizon of experience' may refer to communal experiences (local base of the organisation, community relationships, etc.) as well as experiences of domestic UK, German, or EU policies, which would form the horizon of experience of an organisation in its daily activism. 'Transnational horizon of experience' refers to how the organisation sees itself and its in-group(s) impacted by transnational politics and dominant discourses about international (in)security. The codes pertaining to these categories point to negative horizons of experience which crystallise around either (predominantly) moral or (predominantly) political issues.

Plot refers to the identification by an organisation of great dangers to its in-group(s)' security and way of life, and what needs to be done to remedy these dangers. The *Plot* category 'Muslims and their "way of life" are under threat' captures the significant threats to the in-group(s)' security, attributes clear responsibilities, and puts these into historical perspective. The *Plot* category 'Muslims need to rise up' presents the necessity to change these circumstances as an urgent duty and sets parameters for collective and individual action.

Overall, the Romantic Narrative typified in the codebook carries, concurrently, a sombre diagnostic for an organisation's in-group(s) at present and in the future *and* the belief that the world can be made safer for them only if wrong-doers are defeated; hence decisive action is urgently needed. The following analyses the extent to which organisations draw on this narrative in their respective phases of activism. It zooms in on similarities and differences emerging from the comparison between the cases. This allows me to further characterise how organisations perform this romantic narrative in phases of radicalisation and extremism.

The Romantic Narrative across cases

This section presents the big picture. It starts with an overview of the coding results, which highlight the key differences between the cases of moderation and the other cases. In phases of radicalisation and extremism, organisations strongly draw on the romantic narrative, whereas in moderate phases, they reproduce only partial elements of the narrative. Discussing the latter cases in greater detail, I characterise organisations' respective form of moderate political activism.

Contrasting the cases of moderation with the other cases

The depiction of the coding results by case allows comparison of the relative presence of narrative categories among the cases (Table 4.2). The cases corresponding to phases of radicalisation or extremism all present the categories of the Romantic Narrative in a significant way. The same cannot be said about the moderate cases, 7-DWR and 10-MAB. Indeed, in this phase, DWR's corpus does not display any *Plot* categories and only one category with a significant frequency: 'Local horizon of experience' (*Setting*). MAB's corpus presents significant relative frequencies in the 'Out-group' category

Table 4.2 Code frequency by row at the level of categories (moderate cases highlighted)

Main category	Category	1-HTB (%)	2-HTB (%)	3-HTB (%)	4-AM (%)	5-AM (%)	6-AM (%)	7-DWR (%)	8-DWR (%)	9-MI (%)	10-MAB (%)
Characters	In-group	10.1	8.5	11.8	5.1	17.9	2.4	0.5	8.2	33.6	1.9
	Out-group	16.7	11.0	13.9	7.4	16.4	2.6	1.0	6.0	22.5	2.4
Setting	Local	2.9	2.2	10.1	3.6	21.0	2.2	2.9	21.7	26.1	7.2
	Transnational	12.3	12.8	6.6	6.6	25.6	2.4	0.5	6.2	15.2	11.8
Plot	Muslims and their 'way of life' are under threat	23.8	13.4	16.5	8.5	15.8	2.6	0.0	5.9	12.3	1.2
	Muslims must rise up	13.2	7.4	10.4	4.6	16.9	4.4	0.0	7.2	35.6	0.2

(*Character*) and in both 'Local' and 'Transnational horizon of experience' (*Setting*). However, similarly to DWR, it does not present any significant *Plot* categories.

Upon further observation, the coding frequencies in 7-DWR and 10-MAB are much lower in every main category than in the other cases, with the exception of *Setting*. For instance, both 7-DWR and 10-MAB present slightly higher frequencies in the category 'Local horizon of experience' than 2-HTB and 6-AM, two cases of moderation within extremism. Also, 10-MAB presents a higher frequency in the category 'Transnational horizon of experience' than four of the cases of radicalisation (3-HTB, 4-AM, 6-AM, and 8-DWR). Although *Setting* is overall much more significant in the cases of extremism than in the two moderate cases, it points to a potentially common interpretation of the local and transnational environment and its impact on Muslim communities. This is discussed further on when characterising DWR's and MAB's moderation.

Not only are narrative codes scarcely present within the moderate cases' corpus, they also remain largely unconnected. The narrative discrepancy between the moderate and other cases is illustrated exemplarily in Figures 4.1 and 4.2, which visualise, respectively, the narrative co-occurrences of the moderate cases, 7-DWR and 10-MAB, and a case of radicalisation (4-AM).[1]

The stark contrast between the moderate cases and 4-AM compellingly illustrates the unequal strength of narrative links in phases of moderation compared to phases of radicalisation. In both moderate cases, only four categories are significant. In contrast, narrative codes are strongly linked in case 4-AM, which speaks to the cohesiveness of the romantic narrative in this phase.

In case 7-DWR, only three characters – 'True believers', 'the Muslim Other', 'the (non-)religious Other' – and a (transnational) 'Hostile, dangerous, exploiting' setting – are connected. It might be interpreted as an embryo of a romantic narrative, as the few narrative codes appear consistently linked to each other. However, with no *Plot* codes at all, it misses action and intentionality. This incomplete story provides context but no direction. It is descriptive, static, presenting *Characters* without any indication of past, present, or future motives or actions. Comparably, MAB's embryonic narrative is erratic: there is a (local) context of hostility, attacks on Muslims, the idea of fighting back, but close to no *Characters* linked to the few *Setting* and *Plot* elements. 'The (non-)religious Other' is the only *Character* code linked narratively. Its relationship to the (local) *Setting* code 'Islamophobic, repressive, harassing' appears meaningful: it is the (non-)religious Other who creates this hostile environment.

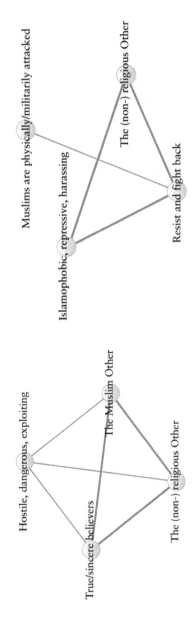

Figure 4.1 Co-occurrence analysis of the cases 7-DWR (left) and 10-MAB (right)

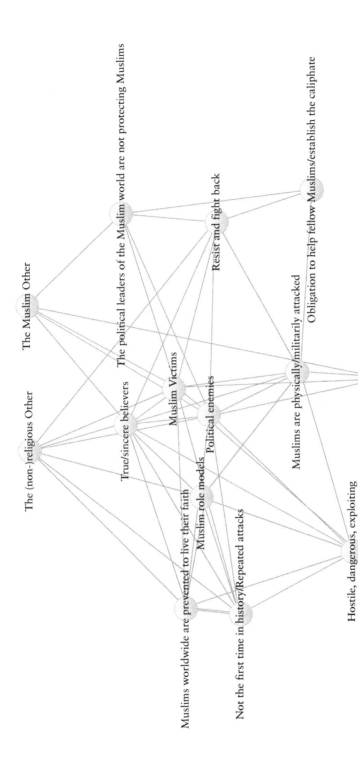

Figure 4.2 Co-occurrence analysis of the case 4-AM

In contrast, case 4-AM, corresponding to a phase of radicalisation, shows complex inter-relationships between codes: some codes are strongly linked to almost all others (e.g. *Characters* codes), while others are strongly linked only to certain codes, which in turn points to specific understandings within the narrative. For example, the code 'Obligation to help fellow Muslims/ establish the caliphate' appears strongly linked to three codes: 'Resist and fight back', 'Muslims are physically/militarily attacked', and 'The political leaders of the Muslim world are not protecting Muslims'. Co-occurring as they are, they convey an interpretation of the social world – a dire diagnostic for the in-group 'Muslims' – and consequences in terms of action for those belonging to this group. It reads almost like a formula: 'Muslims are attacked', they need to 'Fight back', yet 'The political leaders of the Muslim world are not protecting Muslims', so it becomes a collective/individual 'Obligation to help fellow Muslims/establish the caliphate'. Switching the order of the passages – for instance: 'The political leaders are not protecting Muslims', thereby 'Muslims are attacked' – still leads to a similar diagnostic in terms of action: the 'Obligation to help fellow Muslims/establish the caliphate', as will be discussed in more detail further on.

Overall, the coding results point to the relative (10-MAB) or absolute (7-DWR) absence of *Plot* codes in moderate cases and the very limited narrative relationships between the few codes present in 7-DWR's and 10-MAB's corpus. These characteristics demarcate the moderate cases from the cases of radicalisation and extremism.

Cases of moderation: embryonic narrative?

In the moderate cases, the meanings attributed in coded passages are *qualitatively* different from the cases of radicalisation. The moderate cases constitute political issues and subjects in a different way. For instance, both moderate cases give little importance to the category 'In-group identities' (*Characters*). 7-DWR presents not a single instance of 'Muslim victims' or 'Role models', and only a few instances of 'True believers'. In coded passages, the characterisation proves rather generic: for example, 'True believers' in 7-DWR's case refer to 'brothers and sisters in Islam' and, in 10-MAB's case, to 'the Muslim peoples', 'the *Ummah*', 'Muslims around the world', and a few times to 'MAB members'. In DWR's case, the generic characterisation maintains ambiguity: 'brothers and sisters in Islam' might refer to *all* believing Muslims or merely to *Salafi* Muslims as *true* Muslims. These mostly broad constructs are also found in the characterisation of 'Out-group identities'. 7-DWR presents a vague image of 'the Muslim Other', at times encompassing all Muslims who try to integrate into German society and, other times, all non-practicing Muslims and Muslims who do not behave in an Islamic way. Albeit fluctuating, these qualifiers appear exclusive and fit a Salafi worldview. This contrasts sharply with 10-MAB, in which 'the Muslim Other' refers to 'extremists who represent no one' and 'small bands of fanatics' (13.11.2002).

The characterisation of 'Political enemies' in 10-MAB's case – absent in 7-DWR – represents an exception to the construction of broad, unspecific identities. It is a significant feature of MAB's discourse and is articulated in reference to three specific groups: 'the US-led West' (28.09.2002, 13.02.2003), 'the Israeli aggressor/occupier' (04.02.2003, 13.11.2002), and 'the British Zionist movement', also termed the 'right-wing pro-Zionist lobby in the UK' (13.08.2004). The first group is perceived as dominated by the US and, to a certain extent, by the UK, which is said to emulate US war-mongering (13.02.2003, 04.02.2003). Both are characterised as capricious, arrogant, on the brink of imposing another war on their population and putting the world at large in danger (28.09.2002). The second group refers to the state of Israel, characterised as pursuing a criminal foreign policy and not shying away from 'the repeated massacre of Palestinian civilians' (28.09.2002). The last group corresponds to a *local* political enemy: the (perceived) collusion of the right-wing movement and the Zionist movement in the UK, which are said to target Muslim associations, in general, and MAB, in particular, to suppress any criticism of Islamophobic measures in the UK and inhumane foreign policies towards the Middle East (13.08.2004).

The characterisation of the three 'Political enemies' groups ranges from a sharp critique to a strongly negative image, leaving no doubt about MAB's rejection of their political aims and strategies. However, MAB does not qualify these political enemies as natural enemies or as morally 'evil', nor does it see their course of action as irreversible. Furthermore, it does not cast their political decisions as completely exogenous from the Self. Indeed, while it sharply criticises the foreign policy of the UK government, MAB sees itself as part of UK society, much like the anti-war movement. Exemplarily, MAB writes in the context of an imminent war against Iraq:

> This demonstration [...] will send a clear and unequivocal message to our Government; that the British public will not tolerate double-standards, hypocrisy or injustice, nor will it stand impassively whilst our Government claims the right to interfere in the affairs of other nations. (06.08.2002)

Not only does MAB stress belonging to UK society, but it also shares with the rest of 'the British public' the responsibility to hold the UK government accountable for its foreign policy. In the same vein, the organisation differentiates most of the time between what it calls 'the Zionist entity' (coded

'Political enemies'), whose political aims and strategies it rejects, and 'the Jews' (coded 'the (non-)religious Other'), towards whom it holds no hostility as 'Islam does recognise Judaism as a legitimate religion and accords its adherents with respect and protection' (13.08.2004).

Next, the analysis of the few instances referring to *Setting* and *Plot* codes indicates that the local horizon of experience has some relevance in both moderate cases. Therein, the organisations diagnose increasing Islamophobia: the multiplication of enemy images against Muslims in the UK/German media, the growing public tolerance towards right-wing discourses, and the attempted repression of Muslim voices within UK/German society (10-MAB, 13.08.2004; 7-DWR, 18.10.2007). A *transnational* horizon of experience only echoes in 10-MAB. The organisation stresses the hypocrisy of the US and UK governments regarding who qualifies as a terrorist and who does not, arguing that according to common definitions, Israel's Prime Minister Sharon would qualify as a terrorist (28.09.2002). Similarly, it emphasises double-standards regarding the protection of human rights worldwide, exemplified by the minimal effort the UK government would put in to stand up for human rights in Palestine (06.08.2002). However, and this is crucial, the victims of this immoral and dangerous transnational *Setting* are not characterised as *Muslim* but as human beings suffering a grave injustice. It is a major difference between 10-MAB and the cases of radicalisation.

In terms of *Plot*, 10-MAB presents a few instances of the codes 'Muslims are prevented from living according to their faith' and 'Muslims are attacked', while 7-DWR presents none. The former relate to verbal attacks by media outlets and conservative politicians, who attempt to 'tarnish the image and reputation' of Islamic scholars and 'vilify Islam and the Muslims in Britain' (10-MAB, 13.08.2004). The latter refers to the approaching war against Iraq at the turn of the year 2002/2003. In one instance, it is characterised as 'an illegitimate war not only against Iraq but against the entire Muslim world' (13.02.2003). This contrasts sharply with the organisation's discourse in prior and later occurrences, which do not emphasise victims' Muslimness. Thus, it represents a marginal moment in MAB's discourse over the period.

The absence of most categories pertaining to the Romantic Narrative and the meaning of coded passages provides valuable insights into what distinguishes cases of moderation in narrative terms. Further, contrasting the two cases reveals large differences in political activism. While they share similarities, 7-DWR's and 10-MAB's respective moderation is qualitatively different. It is particularly visible in how they respectively perceive and construct the social world in which they evolve. DWR's political discourse at the time is only just emerging. The organisation sketches a vaguely hostile context for 'truly' practicing Muslims – read *Salafi* Muslims – in Germany and Western countries in general, rooted mainly in media prejudices. When combining insights from the analysis of both codebooks – 'Romantic Narrative' and 'Group moderation and group radicalisation' – a more complete picture emerges: in an immediate environment perceived as increasingly harassing, DWR's discourse oscillates between advocating distance (code 'Minimal interactions with the rest of society') and wanting the expression of (Salafi) Muslims' difference accepted in the public space (code 'Participation in the public debate'). This hesitation between exit, on one side, and participation, on the other, characterises DWR's emerging activism.

In comparison, MAB's political discourse is elaborate and coherent. Together, the narrative elements articulated in 10-MAB paint a local context increasingly experienced as Islamophobic, making the work of an organisation defending Muslim rights in the UK difficult and a transnational context dominated by a hypocritical and hot-headed hegemon. While these broad propositions echo representations found in the cases of radicalisation, they differ significantly from them in important ways. MAB's discourse on domestic politics is characterised by the specification of political opponents without dehumanisation, the distinction made between UK government policies and UK public opinion, and its self-identification as part of British society. Further, MAB's discourse on transnational politics revolves around the argument that US-led wars increase insecurity around the world and, more generally, that *states* undermine world peace (i.e. through forced regime change) much more than any 'individuals, factions, or small bands of fanatics' ever could (13.11.2002). MAB blames the logic behind the US-led 'war on terror' for carrying 'little insight into the root causes of today's chaos' and thus missing the mark (13.11.2002).

These insights, combined with the interpretation of MAB's moderation in Chapter 2, characterise MAB's political activism as an explicit, lucid commitment to participation, despite an increasingly bleak local and transnational context, in which critique by Islamic actors is more readily suspect. Sometimes cynical about the hypocrisy of the contemporary international order, MAB's discourse remains hopeful. It believes, for instance, that a strong anti-war movement within the British public could bring the government in the long-term to adopt a more ethical foreign policy (28.09.2002; 13.11.2002). In this regard, MAB and its followers participate in the public debate and engage in non-violent collective action to denounce double standards at home and abroad. The perceived growing hostility of local political enemies and bleak international political developments are not constructed as irreversible, nor are they teleological or theological. For MAB, change comes through greater activism within the present political system. This contrasts sharply with the cases of radicalisation and extremism discussed in the following. In the latter, Islamist organisations narrate a starkly different vision of the necessities of political change.

The Romantic Narrative in cases of radicalisation and extremism

This section turns to the analysis of the characteristics of the Romantic Narrative in phases of radicalisation and extremism. It starts with a brief description of coding results to sketch the big picture, then delves into the distribution of, and meaning associated with, narrative *characters*, *setting*, and *plot* among the cases. In so doing, it discusses in-depth the commonalities and differences between the eight cases, thereby highlighting the narrative underpinning of group radicalisation into extremism and, at the same time, making organisation-specific meanings visible.

The average *Romantic Narrative*

As discussed at the beginning of this chapter, the eight cases corresponding to phases of radicalisation and extremism display the full range of narrative categories significantly. Looking at the aggregated data for these cases provides further insights into the average romantic narrative. The total number of passages coded according to the Romantic Narrative codebook is displayed in Table 4.3.

The majority of the 4,698 segments coded according to the Romantic Narrative in the cases of radicalisation and extremism pertain to *Characters*. This points to the primary importance given by organisations to continuingly qualifying, delimiting, and determining narrative characters and, beyond that, social actors.

Table 4.3 Number of coded segments in cases of radicalisation vs cases of moderation (Romantic Narrative)

Narrative codebook Main category	Cases of radicalisation/extremism 1-HTB, 2-HTB, 3-HTB, 4-AM, 5-AM, 6-AM, 8-DWR, 10-MI	Cases of moderation 7-DWR, 10-MAB
Characters	3,539	106
Setting	309	40
Plot	850	6
Total number of coded segments	4,698	152

Nevertheless, the number of segments coded *Setting* and *Plot* is not to be underestimated: if these were distributed equally across the eight cases (124 documents), *Setting* codes would be found on average two to three times in each document and *Plot* codes six to seven times. Further, *Setting* and *Plot* coded segments (often a paragraph) are much longer than *Character* coded segments (often a group of words or a sentence), since the former portray environments, depict conflicts, propose explanations for current power relations and so on. If we look at the coded passages in the percentage of words (instead of counts), *Plot* is the largest category, as Table 4.4 illustrates. *Plot* codes account for 48.9% of all coded words, *Characters* for 34%, and *Setting* for 17.1%. The narration of past, present, and future actions takes centre stage in phases of radicalisation and extremism.

The aggregated results at the category level point to further features. Table 4.5 depicts the average romantic narrative, with the respective weight of narrative codes by category and the extent of their distribution. In this *average* romantic narrative, 'In-group identities' and 'Out-group identities' are characterised almost as often and represented in virtually all documents. This indicates that both characterisations are almost equally important to

Table 4.4 Relative frequencies of the main narrative categories by case (in percentage of words)

Main category	1-HTB (%)	2-HTB (%)	3-HTB (%)	4-AM (%)	5-AM (%)	6-AM (%)	8-DWR (%)	9-MI (%)	Total
Characters	2.7	3.1	3.0	3.5	4.3	7.2	5.1	5.2	34
Setting	2.8	2.0	1.6	2.6	2.8	1.5	2.5	1.3	17.1
Plot	8.5	5.6	9.0	7.4	4.7	4.4	3.8	5.5	48.9

Table 4.5 Relative frequencies of the cases of radicalisation/extremism at the category level

Main category	Category	% of narrative codes	% of documents
Characters	In-group	36.5	100
	Out-group	38.8	97.6
Setting	Local	2.6	41.1
	Transnational	3.9	60.5
Plot	Muslims and their 'way of life' are under threat	8.9	87.1
	Muslims need to rise up	9.2	80.6

the narrative. Similarly, the *Plot* categories 'Muslims and "their way of life" are under threat' and 'Muslims need to rise up' are narrated almost as frequently within the overall corpus. In narrative terms, this means that each action (threat, aggression, etc.) is met by a reaction (counter-threat, resistance, etc.).

Interestingly, *Setting* codes are found on average more frequently about a 'Transnational horizon of experience' than a 'Local horizon of experience'. This indicates that transnational events are given greater importance in the average romantic narrative than local, partly self-experienced events. Also, *Setting* codes are less widely distributed across the corpus than codes from other categories. As discussed below, the local and transnational horizons of experience are narrated more frequently in the cases of radicalisation than in the cases of extremism.

Cross-case analysis of Characters, Setting, and Plot

Turning to the results by case, this section explores the meanings attributed by organisations to narrative categories. The discussion is structured around the compared distribution of *Character*, *Setting*, and *Plot* among the cases and interpretation of their meaning in context.

Overall, subtle variations in narrative focus can be observed between cases of radicalisation and cases of extremism. While *Character* categories populate all cases immensely, there is a distinct emphasis on in-group characters in phases of extremism. *Setting* categories appear slightly more significant in radicalisation phases than in extremist phases, and most often involve transnational events affecting the *ummah*. *Plot* categories are significantly represented among all cases, with an emphasis on the denunciation of attacks against the *ummah* in phases of radicalisation and an emphasis on fighting back in phases of extremism. These insights point to subtle variations in how the romantic narrative unfolds in radicalisation phases compared with phases of extremism – these variations are further interpreted at the end of the chapter.

Characters

The compared distribution of *Characters* across the cases highlights that the cases of extremism present by far the highest frequencies regarding all six *Characters* (see Table in Appendix C4). Indeed, 9-MI, 5-AM, and 1-HTB account for about two-thirds of the 'In-group identities' characters. Similarly, regarding 'Out-group identities', the three cases account for more than half the coded passages. The cases 9-MI and 5-AM focus especially on characterising 'The Muslim Other'. Overall, the distribution indicates that the cases of extremism lay even greater emphasis on characterising the *in-group* than they do *out-groups*. In comparison, the other cases present characters less intensively, except in a few instances in 8-DWR and 3-HTB – both corresponding to phases of radicalisation.

The first character, '**Muslim victims**' (category 'In-group identities'), is narrated very extensively in the cases of extremism (1-HTB, 5-AM, 9-MI) and extensively in the cases of radicalisation (8-DWR, 4-AM). In contrast, it is represented much less in phases of moderation within extremism (2-HTB, 6-AM). Across the eight cases, 'Muslim victims' primarily refers to Muslims living outside of Europe, very often in conflict areas. In the UK cases, 'Muslim victims' encompasses Muslims in Afghanistan, Palestine, Chechnya, and from 2002 onwards, Muslims in Iraq. In the German cases, 'Muslim victims' refers to Muslims in Afghanistan, Iraq, and from 2011 onwards, Muslims in Syria. Typical, generic references to 'Muslim victims' include 'the oppressed Muslims of [country]', 'our brothers and sister in [country]', and 'the blood of the Muslims in [country]'. 'Muslim victims' refers secondarily to the *ummah* in general, that is, the (imagined) transnational community of believers. Typical expressions are 'the Islamic Ummah', 'the Muslim Ummah', 'the Ummah of Islam'. While both types of victims – Muslims abroad and the Muslim *ummah* – remain rather broad categories, they do not constitute distant victims. Rather, they are conceptualised as the suffering parts of 'one body' (1-HTB, 2-HTB, 3-HTB, 5-AM, 9-MI). 'Muslim victims' are characterised by typically gendered attributes, such as 'innocent', 'weak', 'helpless', and 'defenceless'.

Occasionally, 'Muslim victims' refers to members of the organisation or fellow organisations. HTB mentions, for instance, the recurrent persecution of Hizb ut-Tahrir members active in authoritative countries such as Libya, Iraq, Syria, Uzbekistan, Egypt (2-HTB, 26.12.2003), and Kuwait (3-HTB, 25.08.2007). For AM, Muslim scholars and clerics *in the West*, more specifically in the UK and the US, sometimes qualify as 'Muslim victims', for instance, on the occasion of raids by the British police and MI5 on AM leaders' homes (5-AM, 01.08.2003), or the arrest of scholars invited to talk at AM events, such as the Islamic scholar Abu Qatada (5-AM, 25.10.2002) and the cleric Abu Hamza (5-AM, 27.05.2004). In MI's discourse, Muslim *female* activists imprisoned in Europe are emphasised as a particularly shocking category of 'Muslim victims'. They are said to be subjected to humiliation, rape, and torture in Europe's prisons, particularly in England, Belgium, and Germany (9-MI, 16.11.2011; 20.11.2011).

'**Muslim role models**' is a very strongly represented narrative character in the cases of extremism 5-AM, 9-MI, 1-HTB, and the other HTB cases; it is less significant in the other cases. All eight cases share a common emphasis on the figure of the Islamic scholar. This figure is designated as 'the respected Ulema' (2-HTB, 5-AM), 'the Muslim scholars' (3-HTB), 'the true scholars of Islam' (4-AM, 8-DWR, 9-MI), and 'our Sheikhs' (4-AM, 9-MI). The Islamic scholar remains a rather abstract figure in all three HTB cases and 8-DWR. In contrast, in 5-AM and 9-MI, individual scholars and sheikhs are emphasised as examples to follow. In 5-AM, these are, for instance, AM's very own Omar Bakri Mohammed, elevated to the rank of 'Sheikh', as well as 'Mullah Omar' of the Taliban (16.09.2001), Abu Qatada, described as a 'well-known scholar' and 'prominent Islamic personality' (24.12.2002), and 'Sheikh Usama bin Laden', described as a 'true lion of a man' (22.04.2004). In 9-MI, al-Qaeda scholars figure prominently – Usama bin Laden, Anwar al-Awlaki, Ayman al-Zawahiri, Abu Yahya al-Libi – and earlier scholars revered by political Salafis, such as Ibn Taymiyyah (early thirteenth century).

HTB, AM, and MI share further role models: i. Islamic movements and organisations, as well as ii. the *mujahideen* (combatants for Allah's cause). The first regroup Islamic political parties and movements (in AM and HTB cases) and Salafi organisations (in AM and MI cases). In HTB cases, the *Hizb* itself and its youth ('the *Shabab* of Hizb ut-Tahrir') constitute a model among Islamic organisations. Similarly, AM praises 'the sincere Islamic groups' and, first among them, AM itself (4-AM, 05.04.2002). MI also stresses its own role and the good work done by DWR and *Ansarul Aseer*.[2] These organisations and movements are said to be working in the path of Allah, both religiously and politically. The second role model common to HTB, AM, and MI in phases of extremism is the figure of the *mujahid*. HTB praises 'the grandsons of the Mujahideen' throughout history (1-HTB, 21.10.2002), AM hails the 'Magnificent 19' of the 9/11 attacks (5-AM, 17.08.2003; 11.09.2003; 10.03.2004), and MI heralds the *mujahideen* as 'the lions of Islam' (9-MI, 20.11.2011; 03.05.2012; 21.09.2012; 31.12.2013). Overall, they are characterised as extraordinarily brave and loyal to the *ummah*.

Finally, some differences must be noted. HTB further emphasises two classical collectives: the armies of, and the economic, political, and cultural elites in, Muslim countries. In HTB cases, the first, 'the Islamic armies of the Ummah' or 'armies in Muslim lands', are not always differentiated from the *mujahideen*.[3] The second – Muslim elites – are referred to as the 'people of *Nusrah*' from the Quran (3-HTB, 19.08.2007). Meaning 'people of support', this historical collective relates to the people of power who believed in Islam and gave material support to the Prophet to establish the rule of Islam in Madinah. Although these associations seem generic in a modern context, they refer to culturally meaningful roles.

Similarly, AM and MI emphasise other, smaller collectives that were at the forefront of establishing the rule of Islam at the time of the Prophet and started as minority groups. AM and MI stress the role of the *Sahaba*, the companions of the Prophet, and of the *Salaf*, the pious predecessors, corresponding to the first three generations of Muslims. These constitute typical trans-historical Salafi role models, to which AM and MI adjoin modern ones: al-Qaeda and the Taliban in AM's case, the Islamic State in Iraq and Syria, al-Shabaab (Somalia), Ansar ad-Din (Mali), the Taliban, and the Caucasus Emirate in MI's case.

The last 'In-group' character, '**True believers**', is the character most often represented within the corpus. This character populates heavily MI's corpus, which accounts for one third of all segments coded 'True believers'. This character also strongly populates the stories of the other two cases of extremism, 5-AM and 1-HTB, and the cases of radicalisation, 3-HTB and 8-DWR. It is comparatively less represented in the phases of moderation within extremism, 2-HTB and 6-AM. 'True believers' designate believers *in Islam* and the community they are imagined to form, the *ummah*. Across all cases, it is taken for granted that believers can only refer to Muslims, whereas all other forms of belief are consistently referring to 'The (non-) religious Other'. 'True believers' are qualified in general terms as honourable, sincere, strong, and speaking the (Islamic) truth whatever the costs. The fortitude to 'speak the truth[4] 'constitutes a common leitmotiv across all eight cases.[5] Finally, they show solidarity towards their brothers and sisters in faith and do good for Islam and the Muslim *ummah*.

However, not all Muslims are automatically considered 'True believers'. First, for the organisations, Muslims are 'True believers' if their faith does not wither and they obey Allah *in practice*, for instance, by helping to re-establish the caliphate. Second, they follow the 'right' or 'true' interpretation of Islam. HTB offers the least exclusive definition of 'True believers'. It also includes Shia Muslims and different schools of thought within Islam, thereby presenting itself as being above sectarian divides. AM, DWR, and MI restrict the pool of potential 'True believers' to Sunni Muslims and, more often than not, to *Salafi* Muslims. Salafi Muslims are praised as those who 'wish to go back to the example of the Messenger Muhammad and his companions' and 'who correctly state that a Muslim's only allegiance is to Allah and we are Muslims first and last' (5-AM, 27.09.2003). To these restrictions, AM and MI add further ways to recognise true believers: i. they will be in the minority until the re-establishment of the caliphate and know hardships and suffering as a test of their faith (5-AM, 14.08.2003, 09.2003; 9-MI, 16.11.2011, 01.2013); ii. they are the ones who truly practise *al-wala wal-bara*, loyalty to the Muslims and disavowal/rejection of the disbelievers (5-AM, 21.05.2004; 6-AM, 06.2004; 9-MI, 18.05.2012, 07.2012). Both features are used politically and echo the work of al-Qaeda leader al-Zawahiri[6] to identify and constitute the *ummah*'s fighting vanguard.

Turning to 'Out-group' characters, '**Political enemies**' is without a doubt the most prevalent out-group identity across cases. This character amounts to a quarter of the relative code frequencies for the entire codebook. The discourse of Islamist organisations is often embedded in so much religious terminology that it would be easy to forget that their struggle is, first and foremost, a political one. Compared across cases, 'Political enemies' populate HTB's narrative more than any other organisations'. The three HTB cases account for more than half the passages coded 'Political enemies' (see Appendix C4). The cases of extremism 5-AM and 9-MI, and AM's phase of radicalisation (4-AM) also draw strongly on the character 'Political enemies'.

Common to all organisations are several specific political enemies, presented in their order of importance: i. Western states, or just 'the West', most frequently the United States, European states, and Israel; ii. Arab regimes (Saudi Arabia, the Palestinian Authority, Kuwait) and, more generally, heads of state and government in 'Muslim lands'; iii. international organisations, especially the United Nations (UN) and the North Atlantic Treaty Organisation (NATO); and iv. specific political figures associated with a local horizon of experience (e.g. UK/German politicians).

Western states are characterised as archenemies. In the wake of the war against Afghanistan, HTB puts it pithily: 'The two mortal enemies of Islam and the Muslims, America and Britain' (1-HTB, 09.10.2001). The organisation further qualifies the US as having 'the style of an international bully', who engages in 'state terrorism', and whose leader G.W. Bush is a 'war criminal' and 'mortal enemy of the Islamic Ummah' (1-HTB, 21.10.2002). For AM, the 'US-led alliance' and the 'Pirate State of Israel' rank highest among political enemies (4-AM, 12.09.2001, 24.10.2001). AM reserves a special place for Israel, qualifying its policies towards Palestinian Muslims as 'worse than Nazi Germany and Apartheid South Africa in terms of atrocities' (4-AM. 20.04.2002). At times, the UK is perceived almost as badly, though: 'the American fascists' and 'the Blair regime' are characterised as 'sadistic' and 'barbaric' (4-AM, 07.10.2001). MI, which came into existence long after the US-led wars in Afghanistan and Iraq, sees the US as first among 'Western' enemies, leading 'the powers of arrogance and the Zionist alliance of the crusaders' (9-MI, 07.2012).

The second central political enemy – the Arab states and regimes in 'Muslim lands' – is unanimously identified as a product of 'the West'. The following denominations illustrate this: 'the traitorous agent rulers' (HTB cases), the 'corrupt regimes' and 'puppet governments' (AM cases), 'their bodyguards' and 'dummy regimes in our lands' (8-DWR), and 'puppet states' (9-MI). They are further characterised as cowardly, spineless, corrupt, unfaithful, treacherous, and tyrannical. HTB also mocks the 'comic rulers of the Gulf's petty states', whose only goal is to maintain their power and wealth in exchange for surrendering their 'statelets' to the United States (1-HTB, 21.10.2002).

The third political enemy – international organisations – is depicted as a mere extension of Western states. HTB provides the most comprehensive and systematic critique of international (and regional) institutions. Regarding the approaching war against Iraq, HTB pretends to disabuse the naïve about any intercession from the UN: 'the UN is one of America's strongest foreign policy tools!' (1-HTB, 21.10.2002). It also discusses at length the implications of UN resolutions and US plans regarding the Middle East conflict. After Bush's speech on Palestine (24 June 2002), HTB comments:

> She [America] is working under an international cover with international participation by utilizing international institutions and organisations. That is, the European Union, Arab states, others from the international community, the World Bank and the International Monetary Fund. She may resort to using the UN as she did in Afghanistan to hide her policies. (1-HTB, 07.07.2002)

For AM, DWR, and MI, one of the worst institutions is NATO, which let Serbs massacre Bosnian Muslims (4-AM, 07.10.2001), 'killed whole families in Afghanistan via air strikes' (8-DWR, 28.05.2012), and eradicated 'thousands upon thousands of Taliban', yet would not intervene against al-Assad in the Syrian civil war (9-MI, 18.05.2012).

The fourth common political enemy refers to individual leaders and political parties/movements within a local horizon of experience who would show a particularly strong hostility towards Muslims. Among them are Prime Minister Tony Blair (1–HT, 4-AM), UK Foreign Minister Straw (2-HTB), 'the Zionist lobby' in the UK (5-AM), 'the satanic Pro-NRW', a German anti-Muslim right-wing political party (8-DWR), Chancellor Angela Merkel and German Minister of the Interior Hans-Peter Friedrich (8-DWR, 9-MI). Overall, the two German-based organisations, DWR and MI, focus more intensely on local political enemies. They emphasise specific parts of the state apparatus, such as the German intelligence and security agencies, much more than HTB and AM. Conversely, the two UK-based organisations focus on international political actors more intensely. Among the *ummah*'s international enemies, they further identify Russia, India, Turkey, and the Caucasus states. HTB and AM also characterise enemy states more precisely as 'capitalist', 'imperialistic', 'fascist', and/or 'hegemonic'.

The character 'The Muslim Other' ('Out-group identities') is particularly strongly represented in 5-AM and 9-MI (both phases of extremism) and strongly in DWR's radicalisation phase (8-DWR). It is comparatively less represented in other cases, such as HTB's. Nevertheless, a general 'Muslim Other' is common to all four organisations: Muslims who neglect their duties and 'other defeated and deviant Muslims' (5-AM, 09.2003). This potentially large 'Muslim Other' character refers to partly different (social) groups for the organisations. Particularly degraded in HTB's, AM's, and MI's discourse is the figure of the Muslim leader and, by association, all those who support them. For HTB, AM, and MI, a proper leader should work for Allah's religion, thanks to their position of power, implement sharia law and strive to establish the caliphate. Yet 'apostate leaders' would not because they 'cling to the *dunya*', the material world, for egoistic goals (1-HTB, 20.04.2002). Such leaders are designated at times as *taghut* (pl. *tawaghit*), those who rebel against Islam and thereby commit a grave sin punishable by death. Beyond this Other, the organisations construct further, only partly shared, 'Muslim Others'.

A complementary figure, shared by HTB and MI, is that of the knowledgeable Muslim, typically the scholars of Islam, who know 'the truth of Islam' but do not consistently preach it or act according to it. HTB denunciates the 'government Shayukh [sheikhs] who [...] twist the texts to make them agree with the opinions of the rulers' and claim that their fatwas have no worth because they are 'on a payroll' (2-HTB, 31.12.2003). Similarly, MI fustigates the 'false satanic scholars, who try to make an Islam without the three fundamental principles of Aqidah [creed] ... palatable'[7] (9-MI, 11.10.2012). For HTB, a concrete example of Muslim Other from among the people of knowledge is Mohamed Sayed Tantawi, Sheikh of al-Azhar[8] at the time. After meeting with French officials, Tantawi declared in March 2003 that the French government is within its rights to pass a law banning Muslim schoolgirls from wearing headscarves. For HTB, Tantawi went against sharia, which determines what is permitted and what is forbidden, and committed treason (2-HTB, 31.12.2003).

The three Salafi organisations – AM, DWR, and MI – construct another 'Muslim Other': the *ordinary* deviant Muslim. Whereas HTB does not single out ordinary Muslims, for AM, DWR, and MI, the ordinary deviant Muslim can be of three kinds: i. a Muslim only in name, who is not practising, has a weak faith (*iman*), or colludes with disbelievers; ii. a Muslim who does not care (enough) for the *ummah*'s wellbeing, affairs, and/or sanctity; iii. a Muslim with multiple identities, for instance, Muslims who submit to man-made laws and integrate, those who marry non-Muslims and befriend disbelievers, or respect Islam as a religion but not as a complete system of life. Hence, secular Muslims, Muslims lacking solidarity towards fellow Muslims, and Muslims who feel they belong to more than one identity group are not considered proper Muslims by the three Salafi organisations.

Finally, the cases of extremism 5-AM and 9-MI exclude further Muslims *en masse*: first off, Shia Muslims, sometimes termed derogatorily by MI as 'Safavids'[9] and 'Rawafidh',[10] who are accused of colluding with the 'Political enemies' of the *ummah* and 'The (non-)religious Other'. At the opposite end, AM and MI brand the enemy *within*, the 'fake Salafis' who pretend to follow the path of the *salaf* but speak badly about the *mujahideen* or refuse to practise *takfir*, that is, accusing a (group of) Muslim(s) of apostasy and thereby excommunicating them. This appears to be the most extreme position across all characterisations of 'the Muslim Other'. Overall, while covering partly different realities across the four organisations, 'the Muslim Other' constitutes an extensive category, especially in 9-MI and 5-AM. It serves to *exclude* differently minded and differently practicing Muslims and contributes to further reinforcing the understanding that 'True believers' constitute an elite group.

'**The (non-)religious Other**' is a particularly strongly represented character in the cases 8-DWR and 9-MI and, to a lesser extent, in 5-AM and 6-AM. It is much less significant in HTB's phase of extremism. Nonetheless, the following religious Others are common to all eight cases: i. unbelievers, ii. disbelievers, iii. Jews and, to a lesser extent, Christians as a special kind of enemy. All three are considered 'enemies of Allah' and/or 'enemies of the Prophet'.

First, unbelievers (*kuffar*) appear prominently in the corpus, although it is at times unclear where this category starts and ends. Most of the time, 'unbelievers' refer to all individuals and collectives who do not recognise Allah's sole right to worship. Non-belief does not refer here to atheism but to non-belief *in Allah*. Hence, it encompasses the '*kafir* [non-believing] West', 'the infidels', Christians and Jews, Hindus, polytheists (*mushrikeen*), etc. Accordingly, HTB, AM, DWR, and MI stress that all non-Muslims are *kuffar*, a denomination used in the Quran. As there is only one religion – Islam – all non-Muslims are on the wrong path and, should they not adopt Islam before dying, will go to hell in the afterlife.[11]

Second, the disbelievers, also characterised in the corpus as 'apostates' and 'rebels' (*tawaghit*), refer to former Muslims who committed sins, disobeyed sharia commands, or rebelled against Allah. Such rebellion is considered worse than *kufr* (non-belief) because it roots in *treason*, whereas *kufr* may come from ignorance and faithlessness. HTB, AM, and MI go a step further and call Muslims to excommunicate sinful individuals and groups who have fallen from the realm of Islam (*takfir*). Salafism is predominantly responsible for *takfiri* practices outside of what most Muslim scholars see as a legitimate authority: the official clergy or the caliphate.[12] Interestingly, while HTB is not a Salafi organisation, it argues in favour of *takfir*, although it limits its use to branding *rulers* as apostates, not ordinary Muslim men and women. According to HTB, the severest of punishments by Allah await the apostate rulers in this life and the hereafter (1-HTB, 2-HTB, 3-HTB). Contrarily, AM and MI go as far as advocating the general practice of *takfir*: by every Muslim, against potentially every Muslim. The two organisations also extend the scope of legitimate justifications for casting out an individual or a group. For example, all Muslims who ally with the *kuffar* (non-believers) become *kuffar* themselves (5-AM, 9-MI).

Finally, Jews and, to a lesser extent, Christians hold a special place in all four groups' representation of 'the (non-)religious Other'. While both are included in the designation *kuffar*, they also come up separately from other 'unbelievers'. In such instances, they are cast as 'the enemies of Allah' par excellence. The UK organisations focus disproportionately on Jewish individuals and collectives, whereas the German organisations single out Christians as often as Jews. Overall, the 'animosity' of these two religious Others towards Muslims is presented as 'an almighty tradition which will always remain' (5-AM, 09.2003). HTB stresses that *kuffar* try to deceive Muslims and 'distance them from their Deen [faith]' (2-HTB, 08.11.2003). AM and MI both quote the Quran to support this argument: 'And they will never cease fighting you until they turn you back from your Deen (Islam) if they can' (Sura *Al-Baqarah*, 2: 217; 5-AM, 09.2003; 9-MI, 19.11.2001). All three organisations make repeated references to the time of the crusades to underpin this argument.

In sum, the four organisations specify the narrative *Character*, subdivide, and hierarchise them further. Strikingly, the cases of extremism deploy more facets for each narrative character than the cases of radicalisation. For instance, the ever-longer lists of 'Out-group identities' found in the cases of extremism 1-HTB and, above all, 5-AM and 9-MI serve to demarcate the in-group clearly, not least from enemies within. The separation of the in-group from political enemies and other-minded individuals and collectives restricts the number of those who can pretend to belong to the in-group. In the cases 5-AM and 9-MI, the out-groups are so numerous that the in-group is constituted as a strongly exclusive community.

Further, in comparison, the cases of radicalisation lay more emphasis on out-group characterisation, whereas the cases of extremism emphasise in-group identities as much, if not more, as out-group identities. This suggests that radicalising organisations are preoccupied with constituting enemy groups and, second, with building a separate in-group identity (e.g. rejection of multiple identities). Organisations in phases of extremism are concerned with further demarcating in-group identity and roles, filtering out potential out-group identities. In 1-HTB, 5-AM, and 9-MI, such sifting renders the in-group more cohesive (though smaller) and establishes (new) hierarchies within the group: the *good*, *better*, and *best* 'True believers'.

Setting

The *Setting* is portrayed extensively in the three cases of extremism (5-AM, 9-MI, 1-HTB) and the case of radicalisation, 8-DWR (see Appendix C4).

Interestingly, the *local* horizon of experience is less often articulated than the *transnational* horizon of experience. Further, the diagnosed political hostility towards Muslims takes precedence over the (alleged) immoral character of society and/or the world order. The meanings associated with these environments are discussed in the following.

The immoral character of the *local horizon of experience* is strongly articulated in the cases of extremism 5-AM and 9-MI and the cases of radicalisation 4-AM and 8-DWR. Portraying the local context as '**Immoral, depraved, hypocritical**', the organisations emphasise the discrepancy between the values that Western societies pretend to uphold and their application where Muslim citizens are concerned. For example, AM fustigates liberalism's pretence to carry universal values and argues its moral decay instead:

> A brief glimpse at any western [sic] society, like the USA and UK, [...] reveals a complete breakdown in the social and moral fabric with homosexuality, paedophilia, adultery, promiscuity, fornication, pornography and abortion rampant, [...] extreme divisions between the poor and the rich oligarchy. (5-AM, 24.10.2002)

Not only are liberalism and capitalism morally corrupt, but they also would not even benefit the majority economically. Further, the organisation deems the UK's ruling class to be intolerant to controversy and trying to 'buy the loyalties of the Muslims' into accepting 'a more "moderate" version of government-funded Islam' (5-AM, 02.06.2004).

MI depicts 'the life of ignorance' that Westerners allegedly lead under man-made laws in even cruder terms: they are 'the people of prostitution and impurity', the 'villains, who were born and raised in the bars of Europe, the children of fornication and perverse scum [of the earth]'[13] (9-MI, 07.2012). MI's rejection of everything 'Western' extends to democracy's 'corrupt laws, ideologies, constitutions, and principals', as well as its 'rotten governments, tribunals, slogans and flags' (9-MI, 03.2013). DWR depicts Germany as a society that offers no sure footing, no direction, in which politicians can lie because *they* write the laws. Receiving compliments in such a society should be treated with suspicion, and, conversely, people branded as terrorists should be seen as virtuous Muslims (8-DWR, 25.10.2012). Overall, these depictions serve to emphasise how undesirable the societies resting on profane legislation are, especially in contrast with Muslims' 'uprightness' (9-MI, 10.2002) and 'the beauty and justice of th[eir] perfect system', the caliphate and its divine law (4-AM, 23.05.2002).

The '**Islamophobic, repressive, harassing**' character of the local horizon of experience is particularly significant in 8-DWR, 9-MI, 5-AM, and 3-HTB. The local horizon of experience becomes a topic for HTB only towards the end of 2006, as the organisation diagnoses breeding 'xenophobia within Britain towards Muslims and Islam' (3-HTB, 20.10.2006). UK politicians are accused of inflaming topics such as the *niqab* (veil covering the face and body apart from the eyes), and using Muslims as scapegoats to deflect attention from 'the quagmire [in which] this government is mired down in Iraq and Afghanistan.' (3-HTB, 20.10.2006). AM makes similar arguments about the increasing persecution of Muslims in the UK; going into more specifics than HTB, it also relates the experience of harassment of its members (5-AM).

What starts in its radicalisation phase (4-AM) as a critique of the government's campaign to redefine what Islam is so that it would not conflict with what 'British' is, turns in its phase of extremism (5-AM) into a systematic portrayal of the injustices, racism, surveillance, and threats Muslims are subjected to within British society. AM's press statements regularly document the house raids by the UK police against its leaders and the arrests of fellow Islamic scholars. AM connects its experience of repression by the state narratively with the daily experiences of the larger Muslim community in the UK:

> With the worst housing, the highest unemployment, the largest number of race murders in Europe, a whole range of draconian laws tailored to intimidate the Muslim community, the Blair regime is today sitting on a box of dynamite and have only themselves to blame if, after attacking the Islamic Movements [sic] and the Islamic scholars, it all blows up in their face! (5-AM, 01.08.2003)

Further, the organisation is concerned about the growing activism from 'far-right factions' who threaten to attack mosques (5-AM, 20.01.2003), as well as the multiplying smear campaigns led by British media, which are 'spreading propaganda against Islam and the Muslims' (5-AM, 19.04.2004).

Years later, DWR and MI portray Germany's strikingly similar socio-political context. Media are said to cast Islam in a bad light, internet forums call to destroy mosques and expel Muslims, and right-wing movements are left to roam free by a German state, which would show complicity and engage in intimidation manoeuvres via its security agencies (8-DWR, 25.10.2012; 9-MI, 05.2012, 03.05.2012, 07.2012). MI argues that, with so much open hostility, it is increasingly difficult to live in Germany and, more generally, in Europe (9-MI, 24.04.2012). For DWR, Muslims were perceived before as *different,* but now they are perceived as *dangerous*: 'your neighbour looks at you as if you were a potential member of a sleeper cell' (8-DWR, 19.08.2010). The organisation explains that such growing 'oppression and humiliation' come from Westerners' hate for and envy towards Muslims because of the success of Islam as the fastest-growing religion and, ultimately, their *fear* that Islam becomes stronger (8-DWR, 25.10.2012,

01.09.2013; see also 9-MI, 11.10.2012, 03.05.2012). According to MI and DWR, this is the reason why Muslims are cast in categories such as 'Wahhabis', 'Salafis', 'radicals', and 'fundamentalists'. Western societies are said to 'sort out' the good (integrated) Muslims from the bad (practicing) Muslims (9-MI, 11.2011; 8-DWR, 12.2011). Overall, the spirit of the times is towards the intensification of an anti-Muslim agenda in Western societies. The organisations depict a dark future: life in Western countries is deteriorating for *all* Muslims, and it is only going to get worse (3-HTB, 5-AM, 8-DWR, 9-MI).

The transnational context's **'Double-standard, immoral, hypocritical'** character is strongly portrayed in the cases of extremism (1-HTB, 5-AM, 9-MI) and cases of radicalisation (4-AM, 8-DWR). Therein, four main arguments are made regarding the immorality of the transnational political environment: i. at a basic level, it is characterised by disinformation, fabricated accusations, conspiracies, and media blockades; ii. Western powers propagate hypocritical conceptions of terrorism and jihad; iii. they purport 'liberal' values to cover their true political goals; iv. double-standards prevail, transnationally, where Muslim lives and rights are concerned.

Starting with disinformation, the four organisations argue that fabricated claims are commonly practised by Western powers and their 'agents' in Muslim lands. For example, HTB relates that, in the wake of the 'war on terror', it has been accused of recommending the 'use of flying objects against Western targets' to its members prior to 9/11 and compares this to the Iraqi government being accused of harbouring 'weapons of mass destruction' (2-HTB, 08.11.2003, 29.07.2004). Similarly, AM denounces that the US 'rush[ed] quickly to accuse their victims, i.e. Islam and Muslims', after the 9/11 attacks (4-AM, 12.09.2001). Western media are said to play a big part in disinformation. DWR alleges that the German press, reporting on the Syrian civil war, chooses to focus on burned-down churches to stress the persecution of Christians in Syria instead of reporting on how al-Assad continues to massacre his population (8-DWR, 08.2013). The scale of this 'manipulation of the people in general and Muslims in particular' is subsumed by MI as 'psychological warfare'[14] (9-MI, 24.04.2012).

Second, Western powers are said to try to impose their definition of terrorism on the rest of the world. Of all four organisations, AM and HTB argue most adamantly that terrorism as a concept has become less and less contentious in the 'war on terror' context, and both contest its increasingly hegemonic meaning. AM refers recurrently to the general hypocrisy regarding *what* qualifies as terrorism and *who* should be considered a terrorist: while the US and UK announce 'to the world that they are fighting

"Terrorism" [sic] the same regimes continue to either remain silent or give tacit approval to the massacre of Muslims at the hands of Jewish Terrorists [sic]' (4-AM, 16.09.2001). Further, AM stresses the cynicism of phrasings such as 'we don't deal with terrorists', pointing to the fact that 'yet they deal with Gaddafi, [...] the Arab dictators, and even with Iran and Pakistan' (5-AM, 22.04.2004). Similarly, neither Western states nor the UN would condemn 'the Russians who massacre Muslims in Chechnya [...] or the Hindus who gang-rape Muslim women in Kashmir' (5-AM, 24.08.2003).

Conversely, HTB and AM point out that the same powers condemn the Palestinian armed struggle and deny it the status of 'resistance against occupation' (5-AM, 09.2003). AM concludes that states and international institutions believe that terrorism can be perpetrated only by Muslims against non-Muslims. Similarly, HTB takes offence that the Islamic concept of jihad is distorted by Western commentators as 'acts of random violence' and by the Pope as 'violence, blood and terrorism' (2-HTB, 29.07.2004, 17.09.2006). AM's and HTB's struggle over the definition of terrorism and meaning of jihad serve to expose the double-standards coursing through international politics.

Third, the promotion of liberal values and democracy in Muslim lands is used by Western powers and their agents to cover their true political goals. For HTB, these consist of securing America's economic and political interests to 'expand control and hegemony' over the whole world (2-HTB, 09.06.2005). In this regard, America would merely pretend to want democratic states in the Muslim world since, for HTB, truly democratic states would mean that Muslims would be able to free themselves 'from the shackles of Western hegemony' and establish the caliphate (2-HTB, 09.06.2005). For AM, the West's ultimate political goal is 'ensuring that the rising threat of "political Islam" is controlled' and, ultimately, to 'secularis[e] Islam' (4-AM, 04.05.2002). For DWR, Western states do not care much about liberal values or else the UN would do more than just condemn and look on as Bashar al-Assad kills his population[15] (8-DWR, 28.05.2012). In the same vein, NATO's only preoccupation would be to 'educate' and 'civilise' Muslims as if they were 'animals'.[16] For MI, Westerners pretend to hold individual freedoms high, but when their 'soldiers burn up the Quran'[17] and desecrate 'martyrs', human rights activists are nowhere to be seen[18] (9-MI, 10.2012).

Finally, all four organisations contend that Muslim lives are worth less than others in international politics. DWR and MI support this argument by showing that Western interventionism is inconsistent. They argue that if Western states were truly troubled by mass atrocities against civilians, they would have intervened in Bosnia (sooner), in Chechnya, in

Kashmir, and would presently intervene in Syria (8-DWR, 08.2013; 9-MI, 18.05.2012). HTB argues that Western states preach human rights but do not practise them, as they 'proved to the world in the prison of Abu Ghuraib [sic]' (2-HTB, 09.06.2005). Alleging that, in conflicts worldwide, *Muslims* are killed, DWR concludes that 'the blood of the Muslims has no worth nowadays'[19] (8-DWR, 28.05.2012). Ten years earlier, AM made similar arguments (5-AM, 24.08.2003, 22.04.2004, 21.04.2004).

Lastly, the transnational horizon of experience characterised as '**Hostile, dangerous, exploiting**' is narrated in much detail across the cases, with the exception of 8-DWR, which focuses more on the local context. HTB, AM, and MI paint current dangers meticulously, as well as the memory of past collective hardships and the possibilities of an even darker future. The organisations interpret the transnational political setting's *hostile* and *dangerous* character in a similar way. MI is less specific about the exploitative character of the international system than HTB and AM, which develop an anti-capitalist critique.

A key element of this setting, particularly in HTB and AM cases, draws on the understanding that the current international system was conceived for the interests of the Western few and cannot be reformed. The US, especially, comes into critique: 'America uses the United Nations and the international organisations to achieve its special interests' (1-HTB, 10.12.2001), 'the US today represents the bastion of Capitalism [sic] exploiting more countries and peoples than any other nation in the history of mankind' (4-AM, 07.10.2001), and 'it is inevitable that the present system will always secure the interests of the colonialists' (3-HTB, 17.09.2007). International organisations play a key role therein, especially the UN:

> The United Nations has demonstrated that it is nothing more than an organisation used and abused by the gangsters of this world. They have nothing to bring out peace in the world (i.e. Somalia,[20] Srebrenica, Palestine, Kashmir), as they really do not have any powers other than what their slave master [the] USA gives them. (5-AM, 22.04.2004)

The conflict examples serve to insinuate that the UN does not concern itself with the loss of Muslim lives and is merely a tool in the hands of the US and its allies.

According to AM and HTB, the grievances they voice on behalf of the *ummah* cannot be heard in the international arena because the current international system is beyond reform. The *ummah*'s affliction, hardships, needs, and interests would never be able to find an outlet in this system, and so the system would need to be replaced altogether. Interestingly, HTB and AM make a case that this would be doing the entire world a favour, not just the *ummah*:

> The whole of mankind is suffering the horrors of modern-day colonialism, the barbarity of military adventurism, the racism of colonial elitism and the travesties of economic liberalism. The horrors, however, are not limited to the political or the economic, but extends [sic] to the deeply personal – the corruption of the individual, the family and the community. (3-HTB, 01.04.2008; see also 4-AM, 26.12.2002)

While MI does not argue the benefits for non-Muslims of changing the world order, it shares AM's and HTB's diagnosis and casts the international arena as a ring in which every ideology would struggle *against* Islam. Sometimes presented as 'religions', these ideologies are identified as capitalism, liberalism, democracy, and communism, each envisioned as worse than the other (9-MI, 11.2012).

MI provides historical contextualisation for what it sees as a grave state of affairs. While 'the West always has tried to oppress and subjugate Muslims',[21] oppression came into full force after the fall of the Islamic caliphate (9-MI, 03.05.2012, 07.2012). It refers hereby to the demise of the Ottoman caliphate, brought about by an 'agent of the West', Mustafa Kemal, in 1924 (a reference also found in 1-HTB and 4-AM). MI asserts that, nowadays, Western states seek to prevent the revival of the *ummah* and, ultimately, the re-establishment of a caliphate at all costs. This assumption culminates in the idea of a worldwide conspiracy against Muslim countries: 'the conspiracies of the Kuffar, from the Christians of the West and Jews' (1-HTB, 20.04.2002), the 'US conspiracy on the greater Muslim world' (5-AM, 22.04.2004), 'the complot of the *Kuffar*' (9-MI, 24.04.2012).

This conspiracy is not only directed at Muslim *countries*; it stretches allegedly to Muslims *everywhere*: practicing Muslims and Muslim scholars in the West, Islamic political parties active in authoritarian Muslim states, and Muslims resisting occupation, among others. For instance, HTB accuses the occupying forces in Iraq of being behind the burnings of mosques and assassinations of Islamic scholars (February–March 2004), which fueled the sectarian fighting between Shias and Sunnis. HTB qualifies these events as a 'trap of the enemies' to bring Iraqi Muslims to 'target the arrows at the hearts of the Muslims instead of the hearts of the occupying Kuffar' (2-HTB, 03.02.2004). In another vein, AM and HTB argue that Western governments used the 9/11 attacks and the alleged 'war on terror' to crack down on local Islamic movements and organisations (4-AM, 5-AM, 3-HTB). Western states expect 'their agents in the Muslim world' to silence Muslim activists, going as far as setting up government-funded Islamic movements, which concern themselves with 'aspects such as prayer, fasting, hajj and morals [but] remain silent towards the injustices [sic]' (4-AM, 05.04.2002; see also 2-HTB, 24.02.2005). Similarly, in a long piece entitled 'The modern strategies of the unbelievers and apostates to combat Islam from within',[22] MI explains that Western governments try to co-opt those they call 'non-violent Salafi leaders' into bringing 'Muslims to reject any forms of armed resistance' (9-MI, 24.04.2012).

Overall, the idea that this conspiracy stretches to almost all political arenas, and may reach Muslims everywhere, constitutes a central narrative thread. It allows HTB, AM, and MI to bridge the international setting with the local setting and vice versa. AM summarises the scope of the issues: it is both 'a domestic and international crusade' (5-AM, 27.09.2003). The dysfunctionalities and injustice of the domestic and transnational political settings serve to underline, as a counterpoint, how much better a (world) Islamic political order would be.

Plot

The compared distribution of *Plot* among the cases points to two interesting features. First, *Plot* is most prominently represented in the cases of extremism (1-HTB, 5-AM, 9-MI) and the case of radicalisation 3-HTB (see Appendix C4). Second, organisations tend to prioritise different aspects of the plot depending on whether they are in a phase of radicalisation or extremism. In phases of radicalisation, organisations focus comparatively more on the first part of *Plot* – 'Muslims and their "way of life" are under threat' – whereas, in phases of extremism, they lay stronger emphasis on the second part of *Plot* – 'Muslims need to rise up'. In other words, radicalising organisations tend to focus on the narrative construction of existential threats across space and time, whereas, in phases of extremism, organisations shift the narrative focus to incentives for action.

To begin with *Muslims and their 'way of life' are under threat*, the first plot element – '**Muslims are prevented from living according to their faith**' – unfolds in phases of radicalisation and extremism along two main arguments: i. Western states are trying to prevent Muslims from living under sharia law *in Muslim countries*; ii. Western states are trying to prevent Muslims from living their faith and calling to Islam *in Western countries*. HTB and AM make the first argument in great detail. The *kuffar* would aim to bring Muslims to compromise their beliefs, change their *deen* (creed), and reduce Islam to mere worship (4-AM, 04.04.2002; 2-HTB, 29.07.2004). Correspondingly, Western states attack Muslim countries to change Muslims' 'understanding of the meaning of life and even our identity', assisted therein by Muslim governments pursuing nationalist agendas (5-AM, 21.05.2004). The rejection of Islam as a model of organisation for society and politics is said to be the reason why 'Western governments will never stop interfering into [sic] Muslim affairs or stop humiliating the Muslims' (5-AM, 22.04.2004).

HTB sharpens this argument further, focusing on concrete examples. It points out that in Afghanistan, the US government was given the power to 'impose its governance model' on the occupied Afghani people (1-HTB, 10.12.2001). Commenting on the Bonn agreement[23] provision by provision, HTB contends that the US is empowered to draw a constitution, change the legal system, administration, financial institutions, and more into a secular system (1-HTB, 10.12.2001). HTB argues that the 'same style' is adopted in dealings with the Palestinian Authority. Quoting Bush's speech on 24 June 2002, HTB highlights:

> And *when* the Palestinian people have new leaders, new institutions and new security arrangements with their neighbors, the United States of America will support the creation of a Palestinian state [...] If Palestinians embrace democracy, confront corruption and firmly reject terror, they can count on American support for the creation of a provisional state of Palestine. (1-HTB, 07.07.2002)

The organisation considers that, in calling for a 'new Palestinian leadership', the US president delivers an ultimatum. It concludes that justice in the present international system is conditional on regime change towards democracy. HTB asserts that, ultimately, such interventions in Muslim public affairs 'will give the Kuffar authority over the Muslims' (1-HTB, 07.07.2002).

Western interventionism in 'Muslim' public affairs is further exemplified, according to HTB, by the US hypocritical support for democratic elections in October 2007 in Pakistan, a regime which is oppressing its people (3-HTB, 19.08.2007). If Pakistani Muslims could vote democratically, they would elect true Islamic parties, HTB argues, quoting a survey conducted by the University of Maryland which showed that 'the majority of Muslims in Pakistan held the goal "to unify all Islamic countries into a single Islamic state or Caliphate"' (3-HTB, 01.01.2008). However, the US does not wish such 'blessings for the Muslims', aiming instead to stop Islamic parties and movements from re-establishing the caliphate (3-HTB, 01.01.2008; also 9-MI, Autumn 2011). In the same vein, AM judges that 'the kuffar are coming [to Muslim countries] to destroy what was remaining from the Islamic call [...] and they wish to force their ideology on us' (6-AM, 01.07.2004).

At home, Western states are said to prevent Muslims from living their faith and calling to Islam (*dawa*). All four organisations imply that Western governments and the media aim to redefine the borders of Islam and its meaning for believers. HTB shows that 'government backing, financial and otherwise, has been given for the creation of a "British Islam", as opposed to an "Egyptian Islam" or a "Saudi Islam"' (3-HTB, 16.08.2008). Such a '"nationalised" Islam' is said to be alien to Muslims and would only serve the purpose of dividing them (3-HTB, 16.08.2008). In the same vein, MI and DWR argue that Western politicians and media 'categorise Muslims' to bring disunity and divide Muslims into two groups: integrated Muslims, who hold the true version of Islam, and radicals, who disfigure Islam (9-MI, 11.2011; 8-DWR, 12.2011). MI asks pointedly, 'Who are the *kuffar* that they tell us how we should live, dear brothers and sisters in Islam? Who do these people think they are? A non-believer tells me how I should live my Islam?'[24] (9-MI, 11.2011).

Further, all four organisations assert that Muslims are constantly humiliated in Western societies. Their faith is insulted, presented as backward by politicians and media alike. In the UK, Labour politicians would insult Muslims, accusing them of wanting to go back to 'a medieval version of Islam' (5-AM, 27.09.2003). HTB takes offence that Islam's political ideas are presented as '"extremist" beliefs' (3-HTB, 06.07.2006), especially the establishment of a caliphate, which President Bush described as a 'radical Islamic empire' (3-HTB, 19.08.2007, speech dated 6 October 2005). Islamic beliefs are said to be regularly attacked in Western media and pop-cultural products too. For instance, MI denunciates how Westerners, especially Germans, ridicule the Prophet without consequences: 'Merkel the criminal' 'honoured' the Danish caricaturist; the ProNRW party was not condemned for insulting the Prophet; a German actor played the main role in a US short movie degrading the Prophet as a child abuser, and so forth (9-MI, 20.11.2011, 11.2012, 03.05.2012, 21.09.2012). DWR notes that, in a perverse twist, *Muslims* are then cast as 'hate preachers' (8-DWR, 19.08.2010, 24.05.2012).

Finally, Muslims in the West would be increasingly criminalised for their Islamic beliefs. HTB is concerned that a prospective 'ban on the Quran in the name of the defence of "freedom"' in the Netherlands spills over across Europe (3-HTB, 29.03.2008). AM is adamant that, under the UK's 'new anti-terrorist and race hate laws', quoting the Quran has become 'an offense', in a play to ban 'the true form of Islam' (4-AM, 04.04.2002). Ten years later, DWR makes the same argument: Muslims are labelled as extremists when they say that believers will go to heaven in the afterlife, while unbelievers will go to hell, yet they would merely tell 'what stands in the Quran' (8-DWR, 12.2011; see also 9-MI, 11.2012, 01.2003). As such, Muslims are prevented from fulfilling their commitment to carry Allah's message (8-DWR, 21.04.2013). Non-Muslim governments would not hesitate to forcefully prevent *dawa* work (5-AM, 24.05.04) and 'suppress the call for al-Khilafah [the caliphate]' by arresting Muslim scholars (1-HTB, 14.06.2003; also in 4-AM, 5-AM; 9-MI).

Overall, Muslims are said to be prevented by Western governments from living according to their faith, both in Western countries and in

Muslim-majority countries. Western governments and their agents would overtly preach their attachment to democracy but, covertly, aim to intimidate Muslims, make them doubt and compromise their beliefs, and, ultimately, change 'the Ummah's culture and identity' (6-AM, 08.10.2004). HTB talks of an 'intellectual and creedal reshaping' (2-HTB, 08.11.2003) and MI of an 'ideological offensive' (9-MI, 24.04.2012).

The *Plot* category '**Muslims worldwide are physically/militarily attacked**' is narrated extensively in 1-HTB and 5-AM, followed by 9-MI, 4-AM, and 8-DWR, that is, all phases of extremism and radicalisation. Overall, the organisations make two broad arguments. First, the wars launched by the US and its allies against Afghanistan and later Iraq are unjust, preventive attacks against Muslims. Second, the 'war on terror' is an ideological campaign used by the US and its allies as a foreign policy tool to support authoritarian, un-Islamic regimes that oppress and kill Muslims.

Both active in the early 2000s, AM and HTB draw on the wars in Afghanistan and Iraq to exemplify the first argument and refer from time to time to former conflicts in 'Muslim lands' such as Bosnia and Sudan. The invasion of the Islamic Emirate of Afghanistan is depicted as 'an unjust war against the poor and defenceless Afghan Muslims' against whom the US declared a war 'even though their government had not declared a war against them and nor did it commit aggression against them' (1-HTB, 09/21.10.2001). HTB talks of an American 'desire' to take revenge for the 9/11 attacks on US soil (1-HTB, 18.09.2001, 09.10.2001). For AM, the way the US administration directed the blame immediately at Afghanistan can only be construed as premeditated (4-AM, 21.09.2001). AM explains that the US wants to 'ensure that the Taleban [sic] do not succeed to establish the Khilafah' (4-AM, 16.09.2001, 07.10.2001). Beyond this short-term goal, the US is said to attempt more generally to 'create Islam as an opponent to the Western civilisation so that the followers of this (Islamic) civilisation stay in a constant state of fear' in order for the US to strengthen 'her hold over the world, especially the Islamic world' (1-HTB, 18.09.2001). HTB and AM thus portray 'Muslims are attacked' in the exact same way.

The invasion of Iraq in early 2003, only 17 months after Afghanistan, strengthens the argument of a Western 'war against Islam and the Muslims'. HTB talks of a 'war of aggression' which culminated in 'undiscriminating violence' (2-HTB, 07.04.2004). With the new war in Iraq, the idea that 'every crisis and calamity befall[s] Muslims' gains new momentum (1-HTB, 21.10.2002). For AM, while the 'continued war against Islam and Muslims' started much earlier (4-AM, 24.10.2001), after the invasion of Iraq 'the hidden agenda of the US government and its alliance has become clear for all ... [it] is the destruction of Islam' (5-AM, 09.2003, 22.04.2004). In this respect, HTB writes that the rise of a caliphate would be so unacceptable for the West that it engages *preventively* in a 'comprehensive war against the Muslim countries' (2-HTB, 08.11.2003).

Ten years later, DWR and MI offer strikingly similar interpretations: it is always *Muslims* who are being attacked, and it can happen anywhere, even to Muslims living in the West (8-DWR, 19.08.2010, 05.2012). This would be exemplified, according to MI, by the 'abuse and humiliation of our women, mothers, and sisters [...] in the prisons of the crusaders in Europe'[25] (9-MI, 16/19/20.11.2011). According to DWR, this global 'war against Islam has been going on for years'[26] (8-DWR, 08.2013). The European and US populations should also be considered at war with Muslims, according to MI, insofar as their governments kill Muslims (9-MI, Autumn 2011, 10.2012, 01.2013). The latest chapter in this comprehensive war is said to be Syria, where innocents are killed, and Muslim women raped simply because they are believers (8-DWR, 21.04.2013).

While DWR and MI identify Bashar al-Assad as the primary evil behind the Syrian civil war, both make broad statements to attribute responsibility further. DWR implies that NATO is about as bad as al-Assad (8-DWR, 28.05.2012) and MI accuses Western states, which are otherwise always so ready to intervene or use 'coward drones', of doing nothing to put an end to al-Assad's regime (9-MI, 11.09.2012, 18.05.2012). In one instance, DWR states more explicitly:

> We see, dear brothers and sisters, that the whole world fights against Islam in *al-Sham* [Syria]. It is not only a combat against Bashar, 12.000 Shia accursed *Kuffar* from Lebanon and Iran combat the *Muslimin* [Muslims] over there. Israel combats the *Muslimin* over there, America combats the *Muslimin* over there, the whole of humanity and Europe combat the *Muslimin* over there. (21.04.2013, original in Appendix B2, quote n°2)

DWR further explains why 'the whole world' is fighting in Syria: 'It is not a war like any other' because 'if Islam is victorious there' it will have a domino effect in neighbouring Muslim countries[27] (21.04.2013). Here again is the idea that the rest of the world tries to prevent the rise of Islamic rule and, eventually, a transnational caliphate.

Further, HTB, AM, and, to a lesser extent, DWR argue that the 'war on terror' has been used by the US and its allies as a foreign policy tool to support authoritarian regimes that oppress and kill Muslims. For HTB, the US policy change regarding the Middle East issue demonstrates best the murderous impact of the 'war on terror'. While the US previously acknowledged to some extent that the Palestinian insurgency was fighting an asymmetrical war against Israeli occupation, 'the US *now* considers armed actions by Palestinians as "acts of terrorism"' (1-HTB, 20.04.2002). This change of perception implies the illegitimacy of Palestinian armed groups and, according to HTB, the necessity to punish Palestinian society for providing sanctuary. As a result, the US would not only tolerate Sharon's plans to 'crush'[28] the Palestinian people; in fact, it would have given him 'its blessing' (1-HTB, 20.04.2002; see also 07.07.2002).

HTB, AM, and DWR also emphasise that Western states demand that their agents crack down on Islamic movements which try to 'expose their conspiracies'. For instance, security agencies in Kuwait would aim to suppress Hizb ut-Tahrir at the US' bidding (3-HTB, 25.08.2007). For DWR, this extends to the Middle East at large, where 'so many scholars have died, been killed, tortured, and are still sitting in prisons'[29] (8-DWR, 08.2013). HTB talks of an 'indirect' US war against Islamic movements, insofar as it is 'providing assistance to states which are fighting them', such as Uzbekistan (1-HTB, 20.04.2002). Both the far and near enemies of the Muslims are thus said to fight united under US leadership.

The plot element, '**Not the first time in history/Repeated attacks**', refers to all historical analogies, as well as utterances concerning parallel or consecutive attacks on Muslims. It is strongly represented in all three HTB cases, in 4-AM, 5-AM, and in 9-MI. The development below centres on past attacks kept in the organisations' collective memory as particularly traumatic. The massacres of Bosnian Muslims in Srebrenica by the Bosnian Serb army, Chechen Muslims in Grozny by the Russian army, and Kashmiri Muslims by the Indian army come up often in HTB and AM cases. Through these references, the two organisations argue that the international community under Western leadership did not care *then* and still does not care *now*, be it in the context of Afghanistan, Iraq, or Palestine (4-AM, 21.09.2001, 07.10.2001; 1-HTB, 20.04.2002, 13.04.2003).

Palestinian Muslims are presented as living proof, they who have endured a 'long line of massacres' committed by 'the Jewish entity' (4-AM, 24.10.2001), from 'Sabra and Shatila' in 1982 to the latest massacre in Jenin (1-HTB, 20.04.2002; 4-AM, 08.05.2002). Going back further in time, HTB and AM pinpoint an enabling factor in the multiplication of atrocities against Muslims worldwide: the destruction of the caliphate in 1924 (4-AM, 04.04.2002). Since then, 'even the political influence of the Vatican … is greater than the influence of Muslims' (1-HTB, 21.10.2002). The year 1924 is identified as the end of Muslims' 'well-being', and 'awe and prestige', being since then 'at the mercy of other nations' (3-HTB, 12.09.2007).

The repetitive character of aggression against Muslims is further highlighted via parallels across *space*, regardless of whether the aggressions mentioned were committed by/or with the help of *Western* governments. DWR provides a typical example for connecting political conflicts of different kinds (civil war, revolution, war of aggression, international intervention) and implying they have the same cause:

Rivers of blood, this mass of corpses, they have been witnessing this for years, we have been witnessing this for years in *Falastin* [Palestine]. In Afghanistan, weren't they slaughtered and killed? In Iraq, weren't they slaughtered and killed? In *Sumal* [Somalia] … in *Shishan* [Chechnya] … On every corner of this earth where you point your finger, our brothers and sisters are being slaughtered. Syria is not new, dear brothers and sisters, Egypt is not new. (8-DWR, 08.2013; original in Appendix B2, quote n°4)

While this passage does not provide specific perpetrators, it strongly implies that these conflicts are just one and the same. Not only because the victims are characterised (exclusively) as *Muslims*, but because Western states either commit the aggression or do not act to prevent it (see also 9-MI, 11.2012). AM is also particularly adept with spatio-temporal parallels: it argues that the current raids against Muslim scholars in the UK constitute a *repeated* attack – in the context of the war in Iraq – and should remind Muslims of the 'habit of non-Muslims of violating their sanctity when they have authority over them', as the Quran already proclaimed hundreds of years ago (5-AM, 01.08.2003).

Finally, the repetitive character of 'Western' aggression against Muslims worldwide is substantiated by the comprehensiveness of the attack: both on military and ideological fronts (9-MI, 24.04.2012). MI claims that this current war is only partly waged with firearms and explosives; much more importantly, it is waged with ideas 'which ought to shape people's heads and hearts'[30] (9-MI, 24.04.2012). Modern-day enemies are said to fight much as the early day Christians and Jews (allegedly) had. Nowadays, though, they would also try to 'bring their Muslim prisoners (and scholars and preachers) to declare publicly that they renounce jihad'[31] so that fellow Muslims stop resisting (9-MI, 24.04.2012).

The last element of the first plot *The West threatens Muslims and their 'way of life'* is 'The political leaders of the Muslim world are not protecting Muslims'. So far, the meanings associated with the other plot elements clearly highlight that for HTB, AM, DWR, and MI, Western states decide what happens transnationally. While Muslim leaders are considered mere agents of the Western states, the specific motives attributed to them give further credence to the argument that the West can *control* them. These meanings are particularly articulated by HTB and AM. Muslim leaders correspond alternatively to the characters 'The Muslim Other' and 'Political enemies'. While the former is depicted as cowardly, treacherous, and unfaithful, the latter is led by materialistic and political self-interests.

Muslim leaders are accused of wanting to stay in power *at all costs*. This single preoccupation is said to have led them to betray their constituents (read: *Muslims*) in multiple ways. First, they would accept being puppet governments, like Arafat and the Palestinian Authority (4-AM, 20.04.2002,

08.05.2002), or Musharraf who 'surrendered [Pakistan's] sovereignty to a foreign power [the US]' (3-HTB, 26.01.2008, see also 21.11.2007). Second, they allowed the West to set up military bases on the Gulf's 'sacred lands' and even pay for their maintenance (1-HTB, 21.10.2002). Similarly, MI claims that they enable Western states to 'steal the natural resources of the Muslim lands'[32] (9-MI, 02.2012). As Islam does not allow the secession of Muslim lands to unbelievers, AM states that 'the leaders have sold their *Deen* [belief] and become apostate' (5-AM, 03.10.2002). Third, the three organisations consider that even those who pretend to rule by Islam do not, as the sharia obliges them to liberate Muslim lands under occupation (3-HTB; 4-AM; 9-MI). For HTB, the 'Arab Initiative' of Saudi King Abdullah to solve the Middle East issue displays this 'collective betrayal' anew: 'they reward the Jews by granting them more land', much as they did at former Arab summits, and thus are actually 'protect[ing] the Jewish entity' and 'surrender[ing] Palestine' (1-HTB, 20.03.2002, 20.04.2002, 07.07.2002). MI explains their behaviour by their selfishness and greed[33] (9-MI, 01.2013).

Fourth, when 'the West forced them to promote secularism in Islam', Muslim leaders started to fund meek Islamic movements, only interested in theological issues, to 'neutralize the call for the re-establishment of the Khilafah' (4-AM, 05.04.2002). Much as the West, they are said to *fear* an Islamic caliphate, which would dissolve 'the present nationalistic borders that were originally carved by the colonialists' and render the current leaders obsolete (4-AM, 05.04.2002). For AM and HTB, this further explains why the rulers are inclined to collaborate with the West in its conspiracy to suppress Islamic movements (1-HTB, 09.10.2001; 5-AM, 14.08.2003). Under the banner of the 'war on terror', the Kuwaiti, Egyptian, and Uzbek governments would, for instance, persecute HT members known to call for a caliphate (1-HTB, 3-HTB).

For HTB, AM, DWR, and MI, most of these leaders[34] are not intrinsically worse than the US and its Western allies, but their political choices have led them to commit treason against the *ummah*, a great sin in Islam. Ultimately, the four organisations argue that the present leaders are not protecting the Muslims and are thus unfit to rule. Neither do they *care* about the *ummah*, nor about Islam and its Prophet – as will be detailed in the next chapter. As evidence, AM stresses that 'they remain silent' at the crimes committed against Muslims worldwide (4-AM, 08.10.2001) and refuse, for instance, to make the Israeli–Palestinian conflict 'an Islamic issue' (5-AM, 21.05.2004; also in 1-HTB). They would disregard the 'opinion of the Muslims' who do not accept occupation and want to help fellow believers (2-HTB, 08.11.2003). Even when Islam is attacked, 'as is happening in Germany, with clear insults against the Prophet Muhammad (a.s.s.) and a reiterated mockery in all European cities',[35] Muslim state leaders are said to do nothing when they could at least condemn those responsible and close embassies (9-MI, 07.2012, 09.2012). Pithily, HTB summarises the extent to which Muslim leaders have contributed to the West's (alleged) plan to destroy Islam and the Muslims: 'the strength of your enemies is due to the betrayal of your rulers' (3-HTB, 04.11.2006).

The second *Plot* category, *Muslims need to rise up*, portrays the necessity to change the *ummah*'s circumstances as an urgent duty and orients towards specific forms of collective and individual action. It consists of four plot elements: 'Resist and fight back' is the most extensively represented in the corpus, followed by the 'Obligation to help fellow Muslims/establish the caliphate', then the 'Current world order will be replaced by an Islamic caliphate', and 'Muslims will be rewarded for rising up'. The reasons for fighting back ensue from the knowledge gained from the first part of *Plot*, namely, in a condensed fashion: *The West threatens Muslims and their way of life, it has happened before, but this time it is much worse; the West will not stop because its power is uncontested, and the leaders supposed to protect Muslims are not, they even help the enemy.* In the second part of *Plot, Muslims need to rise up*, the organisations thus offer a way out of this dire situation.

Why should Muslims 'Resist and fight back'? According to AM and HTB, it would be naïve to think that diplomatic talks could achieve something amid such a comprehensive war (4-AM, 1-HTB). Peace is not an option because such a 'crusade' will not stop until something opposes it (see also 6-AM, 9-MI). The *ummah* cannot wait in vain for anything good to happen; it must take the matter into its own hands (2-HTB, 8-DWR, 9-MI). Defeat without a fight is not an option, according to HTB and MI, for the *ummah* has a long history of fighting against all odds (1-HTB, 20.04.2002) and descends from 'great warriors' (1-HTB, 9-MI). Furthermore, prevailing against the West is not impossible, as the example of the *sahaba* – companions of the Prophet – is said to show: they did not hesitate to go into battle, even when they were grossly outnumbered, and prevailed (9-MI, 5-AM, 2-HTB).

In all four organisations' corpuses, fighting back involves two courses of action: fostering unity and offering resistance. To this common basis, HTB adds more specifically the removal of the leaders in power in Muslim lands to pave the way for the re-establishment of the caliphate – a strategy found to some extent in 4-AM and 9-MI. Further forms of fighting back are narrated in certain cases, such as revenge (3-HTB and 9-MI) and martyrdom (5-AM; 9-MI). Finally, while all stress that fighting back cannot just be about 'killing *kuffar*', collective victory is envisioned differently by AM and MI, on one side, and HTB, on the other, while DWR remains vague on what would qualify as a victory.

To start with, Muslims worldwide are called to stand together because united, they are strong. All four organisations assert that the enemy is not all-powerful, and the *ummah* has more resources than it thinks. HTB has no doubt about it. 'If the Ummah was united under one banner, the kufr states wouldn't dare attack it', as 'the Islamic army cannot be subdued' (1-HTB, 18.09.2001, 3-HTB, 13.09.2008; also in 9-MI, 21.09.2012). According to DWR, if Muslims 'hold together', they will 'stay on course, be steadfast, and remain strong against everything and everyone'[36] (8-DWR, 08.05.2012). Ultimately, the fight will not be decided by economic or military strength: 'the enemies are not afraid of our military strength. But they are afraid of what stands in our chests… *Iman* [faith]!'[37] (8-DWR, 01.09.2013). Similarly, HTB reminds Muslims that their 'enemy is not all powerful, as the Coran testifies' (2-HTB, 04.11.2006), highlighting again the Quran's supposed validity in all times and places.

Islam itself is said to have the answer for how to fight: 'Islam is a religion of peace for those who want peace but it is also a religion of war, in the name of Allah (swt), i.e. Jihad, for those who want war with Muslims!' (4-AM, 25.10.2002). The four organisations often reference Allah's commands in the Quran to substantiate further the importance of Muslims' unity in fighting back. *All* believers should be concerned, not just the wealthy or powerful, and not just those living in Muslim or occupied lands. HTB reminds its followers of the words of the Prophet consigned in the treaty of Madinah – 'The war of the Muslims is one and their peace is one' – concluding that to attack one Muslim land is to attack the entire *ummah* (1-HTB, 09.10.2001). In its phase of extremism, AM states openly: 'the battlefield must not have any borders or nationality. The enemy is all over the world so we need to fight them wherever we meet them' (5-AM, 21.05.2004). Faced with what is perceived as comprehensive aggression, only a comprehensive reaction is deemed appropriate.

On several occasions, believers are explicitly called to join organisations and movements and contribute to unity in a practical way: 'HT calls you to mobilize, rally and support it in its work' (2-HTB, 09.06.2005). Similarly, MI calls sympathisers to 'team up and work together',[38] especially addressing 'the Muslim youth of Europe'[39] (9-MI, 18/21.09.2012). Further, in the cases of extremism 5-AM and 9-MI, the solution to unify all Muslims is to 'revive the meaning of Tawheed [monotheism in Islam] and Al-Wala wal Bara [sic], to hate the disbelievers and fight against them' (5-AM, 21.05.2004; also in 9-MI, 18.05.2012; on the construction of *al-wala wal-bara* as an emotion rule, see Chapter 5).

Parallel to unity, resistance is presented as not only legitimate but required by Islam. For HTB, AM, and later DWR and MI, resistance encompasses both resisting foreign invasion (e.g. US-led invasion of the

Islamic Emirate of Afghanistan) and liberating occupied Muslim lands (e.g. the Palestinian territories).

It is expected of Muslims faced with an invasion that they offer resistance: 'Afghani Muslims have to oppose America by force' (1-HTB, 10.12.2001), 'Muslims in Chechnya must fight back to defend their lives, honour and property according to Shari'ah' against Russian forces (5-AM, 25.10.2002), and 'today the people of Iraq show us the example of the early Sahaba in their heroism [...] fighting the biggest army in the world' (2-HTB, 07.04.2004). Further, Muslims *abroad* are called to support the resistance of their fellow Muslims: 'if the US launches an attack against [the] Taleban [sic]', the verdict is that 'they must be fought against' by Muslims wherever they are (4-AM, 16.09.2001). MI calls to Muslim men: 'brother, go help your brothers and sisters [in Syria]. Brother, support your brothers and sisters who want to go help the brothers and sisters'[40] (9-MI, 02.2012). HTB calls the professional soldiers in Muslim-majority countries to commit to battle alongside their fellow Muslims: 'it's time for the armies of the Islamic Ummah to defend the domains of the Muslims [...] and rush forward to the battlefields' (1-HTB, 09.10.2001). Resistance, in all the forms it may take, is justified insofar as 'Muslims don't kill for the sake of it, they retaliate only because they were invaded' – as a reaction to injustice, armed resistance is presented as always legitimate (5-AM, 22.04.2004).

Liberating Muslim lands is considered the concern of all Muslims. For AM, Palestine is 'an Islamic problem', 'not a Middle-East conflict', nor an 'Arab problem', and 'Muslims the world over are willing to sacrifice [...] their lives' for it (5-AM, 08.05.2002; see also 12.07.2002 for a similar argument on Kashmir). HTB stresses that liberating occupied lands is a divine command: 'Sharia enjoins us to liberate the entire Palestine' (3-HTB, 25.11.2007; also in 9-MI, 07.2012). Here again, HTB calls Muslim soldiers to defend the people in need instead of following the orders of the rulers who gave Palestine up: 'It is time that Muslim soldiers in Egypt, Jordan, Syria, Lebanon [...] help the Muslims of Palestine [...] and stand up against the rulers' evil' (3-HTB, 04.11.2006). Muslims in countries that are ruled by 'puppet governments' are also called to 'liberate themselves' because they are considered under colonial rule (3-HTB, 17.09.2007, 29.11.2007). MI appeals to sheikhs and Muslim scholars to strive and liberate Muslim prisoners and especially to 'end the captivity of the sisters'[41] in Europe (9-MI, 20.11.2011).

Overall, both resisting invasion and liberating Muslim lands are understood under the practice of *defensive* jihad. For AM, they 'require a solution from Islam, and the ONLY solution Islam has for the occupation of Muslim land is JIHAD' (5-AM, 20.02.2002; block letters in the original). While the four organisations have partly differing visions of what it entails, they all agree upon the necessity of jihad to fight Western aggression. Further, they consider uniformly that jihad must not be declared by a central authority in the absence of proper Islamic rule.[42] Indeed, the call to jihad is undertaken by the organisations themselves. AM thanks the *mujahideen* for 'hav[ing] revitalized the Passion [sic] for Jihad' and stresses that they should be emulated, stating, 'We must revive the mentality of jihad and the mentality to fight against the enemy' (5-AM, 22.04.2004, 21.05.2004). Similarly, MI considers that fighting must be 'carried out following the example of our noble predecessors, the *Salaf*, and ... this is done with the sword'[43] (9-MI, 24.04.2012). Even HTB, which lays the emphasis on the long-term work to re-establish the caliphate as a much more efficient way to fight Western imperialism, salutes the 'resistance by individuals and small groups from amongst the Muslim' in Afghanistan and Iraq (3-HTB, 13.09.2008).

The call to fight back under the practice of defensive jihad is completed by teleological assurances about the imminence of the Islamic caliphate. While all four groups carry the message that '**The current (world) order will be replaced by an Islamic caliphate**', it is particularly strong and detailed in HTB cases, especially 3-HTB. The re-establishment of the caliphate, sometime after its demise, would have been promised by Allah as reported by the Prophet in several Hadiths (2-HTB, 5-AM, 9-MI). Hence, AM asserts that it is the 'fundamental belief of every Muslim' that the rise of the caliphate is 'just a matter of time' (6-AM, 26.07.2004). HTB and AM argue that the UK and the US well know the caliphate will rise again, and it is precisely why they are trying their best to slow it down (3-HTB, 19.08.2007, 13.09.2008; 5-AM, 10.03.2004). What differs across organisations is the political makeup of this coming caliphate and its attitude towards the rest of humanity. Is it to be established to protect the *ummah* and fight aggressors (defensive jihad) or conquer the rest of the world (offensive jihad) as well?

For HTB, it is (mostly) the first: the coming caliphate will unite the Islamic lands and protect them, 'stand[ing] in the way of the haughtiness, aggression and arrogance of kufr' (1-HTB, 20.04.2002). For the organisation, it will be able to do so because it will bring together all Muslims in 'one immense and respected state that is feared under the banner of one Khaleefah [caliph]' (1-HTB, 10.12.2001). HTB counts on this future caliphate's sheer breadth and huge population to deter potential aggressions and reassert the *ummah*'s status. Thanks to its 'international presence [...] nobody will dare confront it' and 'the big powers of today will tremble' (3-HTB, 16.08.2008, 13.09.2008). The caliph will also 'punish the traitorous rulers for their oppression of the Muslims' (2-HTB, 26.12.2003) and, contrary to them, he will put 'the interests of the Muslims first' and honour their obligations towards one another such as liberating Muslim lands (2-HTB, 19.08.2007). HTB sees itself at the forefront of this revolution, leading the believers to the promised caliphate and presenting '[its] constitutional ideas to the future Caliph' (2-HTB, 29.07.2004, 3-HTB, 25.08.2007).

For HTB and AM, the coming caliphate would eventually benefit the whole world. It would save all nations 'from injustice, tyranny and the bullying of America in the 21st century', first because the US would not be the sole big power in the world anymore and, second, because it would propose an alternative model to inspire other nations (1-HTB, 24.05.03). The Islamic model is regarded as the 'antidote to the poison that is Western ideology' (3-HTB, 01.04.2008). Its sharia can bring people 'dignity', 'prosperity', and 'security' (3-HTB, 07.10.2008). HTB argues at great length that 'the capitalist economy is suicidal' and has only led to 'colonialist exploitation' and 'economic crises'. Conversely, the Islamic model is portrayed as providing 'a blessed, safe and secure life' for all (3-HTB, 07.10.2008). AM makes similar arguments, at least up until the beginning of the war in Iraq, stating that the caliphate would 'liberate the whole world from the shackles of Man-Made [sic] law in order for the justice of Islam to prevail' (5-AM, 16.02.2003).

AM's position changes with the war in Iraq. Much as DWR and MI nine years later, AM hopes the caliphate will conquer the rest of the world. Both AM and DWR use half-veiled statements about the hegemonic goals that the future caliphate should pursue: the 'Khilafah will carry the message [of Islam] to the world', it will be 'embraced by all the people on the earth' and 'ultimately dominate it' (5-AM, 14.08.2003, 6-AM, 26.07.2004). In DWR's words, the Quran will become 'law for the whole of mankind and the whole earth'[44] (8-DWR, 25.10.2012). Further statements show that this will not happen merely thanks to the strength of the divine message. AM hopes that the future caliphate 'striv[es] for Izhar ud-Deen, i.e. the total domination of the world by Islam', presaged in the scriptures, 'through its divine foreign policy of Jihad' (5-AM, 24.08.2003).

MI is without a doubt the organisation most explicit about the coming caliphate's use of force to submit all non-Muslims to Islamic rule. The organisation is adamant: the *mujahideen* will march and take country after country until 'the black flag blows over the White House and the Vatican', until 'they rise to the leadership of this mortal world', and 'until the whole world is ruled by the book of Allah'.[45] These hegemonic aims are clearly associated with offensive jihad, the forced conversion of the rest of humanity,[46] and the imposition of the caliphate's conception of beneficial socio-political world order. The meanings associated with a coming Islamic caliphate show, especially in AM's and MI's phases of extremism, that the category 'Muslims need to rise up' is not limited to the notions of armed resistance and liberation by a long way.

The '**Obligation to help fellow Muslims/establish the caliphate**' plays a central role in this broader call to rise up. The four organisations envision such an obligation as extensive, albeit with variations in scope and regarding the boundaries between collective and individual responsibilities. While defensive jihad is a clear *fard* (duty) towards the *ummah* in times of conflict, they differ as to whether it should be considered the primary obligation or if others come first. According to HTB, Muslims are 'one hand against the rest'; they are a brotherhood; when one is attacked, all others 'must pledge protection', and it is 'incumbent upon them' to provide immediate support to the believers (1-HTB, 18.09.2001; 2-HTB, 09.06.2005). However, HTB makes clear, throughout its phases of activism, that the return of the caliphate is 'the crown of all obligations', 'the mother of all obligations', for the *ummah* (1-HTB, 13.04.2003, 2-HTB, 31.12.2003, 3-HTB, 25.08.2007).

For AM, DWR, and MI, defensive jihad is, without doubt, the primary *fard* in times of war. According to AM, Muslims are obligated to actively support the Taliban, fight the enemy in Palestine, and assist the Kashmiri armed groups and the Chechnyan *mujahideen* in removing the occupying forces (4-AM, 5-AM). In its phase of extremism, AM declares 'the fard to fight the enemies' comparable to the 'fard of fasting', thereby equating the command to fast during Ramadan with the duty to commit to armed struggle (5-AM, 14.08.2003). In a similar fashion, MI contends that the three most important precepts of Islamic doctrine are: '*Kufr bit-Taghut, al Wala wal Bara and Jihad fisabilillah*', that is, exposing falseness and rejecting apostasy in all its forms, loyalty to the Muslims and rejection of the disbelievers, and waging jihad following the example of the Prophet (9-MI, 11.10.2012). For MI, armed struggle is hereby presented as an inescapable duty for *all* Muslims (9-MI, 24.04.12, 18.05.2012).

In its phase of radicalisation, DWR adorns the duty of jihad with a qualitative criterion. 'It is an obligation, a fard, and this obligation will ... stop only when the goal is fulfilled. When our brothers and sisters worldwide are not suffering anymore'[47] (8-DWR, 28.05.2012). The obligation to participate in the armed struggle would end when a minimum of wellbeing is achieved for all Muslims. While they conceive jihad as the primary obligation, AM and MI stress that Muslims are not exempt from their other obligations, such as establishing the caliphate, taking care of Muslims imprisoned in the West, and so forth: 'there is no excuse for neglecting any of your duties towards Allah' (5-AM, 21.05.2004; also in 9-MI).

While the way the organisations hierarchise Muslims' duties in times of war differs partly, HTB has much in common with AM, DWR, and MI, despite not sharing the latter's Salafi creed. All four see Muslims' various duties as *individual obligations*, not merely collective ones. For HTB, while the responsibility to 'depose the tyrant rulers' falls mostly on the armies of the Muslim world, the mandatory work to re-establish the caliphate rests on every single Muslim. This 'individual obligation' must be fulfilled by 'every believer [...] each in his individual capacity' (3-HTB, 13.09.2008). Similarly, AM, DWR, and MI see the contribution to jihad as an individual obligation. In its extremist phase, AM declares jihad explicitly *'fardul Ayn'*, that is, an individual responsibility (5-AM, 21.05.2004). DWR and MI stress the weight of such responsibility: 'Allah s.w.t. will ask every one of us present here *yawm al-qiyamah* [on Judgement Day]. What your responsibilities were and what you did to fulfil them. Allah s.w.t. will hold every one of us here accountable *yawm al-qiyamah*'[48] (8-DWR, 28.05.2012; also in 9-MI, 18.05.2012). On a few occasions, both Muslim men *and* women are said to share this burden. 'It is fard upon every Muslim, male or female, each one according to their circumstances, abilities and capabilities' (5-AM, 14.08.2003; also in 8-DWR, 21.04.2013).

What does participation in jihad concretely entail? The most frequent formulation reads: each Muslim must contribute 'verbally, physically, financially or militarily'[49] to jihad. Exemplarily, MI demands from its followers and sympathisers that they defend the *mujahideen* verbally (whether one agrees with all their methods or not), spend generously for the families of the German *mujahideen*, and prepare to join them in Syria as, ultimately, 'true sacrifice can only happen in jihad'[50] (9-MI, 11.10.2012). This hierarchy of sacrifice is matched with different rewards.

HTB, DWR, and MI provide further incentives to engage in political violence – AM only marginally. While the plot element '**Muslims will be rewarded for rising up**' might seem at odds with fulfilling one's obligations, the rewards in question are of a mostly immaterial kind. The organisations offer projections into the future and snippets of the afterlife awaiting Muslims who do good deeds. They also picture as a counterpoint what awaits Muslims who do not honour their duties. Both positive and negative, earthly and spiritual incentives echo the *collective* and *individual* sacrifices that are expected from 'True believers'.

Earthly rewards await Muslims, as a collective, when honouring their duties. Allah would be pleased with them, which should fulfil them with joy (6-AM, 07.08.2004; 9-MI, 14.06.2012; 8-DWR, 08.05.2012). Further, the defeat of their enemy would 'heal their hearts' (1-HTB, 13.04.2003). For HTB, Muslims would be satisfied with the punishments that the former tyrants would suffer at the hands of the new caliph (2-HTB, 26.12.2003). When they fight hard, Muslims will prevail over their enemies, and Allah will grant them 'victory', 'honour and dignity', as well as 'succession in the earth'[51] and power over all of mankind (1-HTB, 13.04.2003; 3-HTB, 01.01.2008; see also 9-MI, Autumn 2011, 16.11.2011). However, only those who sacrificed and worked to re-establish the caliphate would be able to partake because 'going through divine trials' is necessary to 'attain glory' (3-HTB, 25.11.2007; 9-MI, 19.2011).

In the hereafter, *individual* rewards await those who sacrificed for the 'common good of Muslims'[52] (9-MI, 05.2013). In the wake of jihad, martyred Muslims would go automatically to Paradise (5-AM, 02.07.2003, 22.04.2004), and this is why, ultimately, they are said to be 'war's winners' (8-DWR, 12.2011, 08.05.2012, 21.04.2013). Conversely, non-Muslims are expected to suffer in the hereafter and 'the believers will laugh at them'[53] (8-DWR, 25.10.2012). DWR argues that 'at the end, each Muslim will be a winner when entering Paradise because this is true success', as one becomes 'alive for the first time'[54] (01.09.2013; 21.04.2013). There would await the 'excellent company' of the Prophet and his *Sahaba* (companions), enjoyment much superior to life on earth, and 'everlasting bliss' (1-HTB, 20.04.2002, 21.10.2002, 29.04.2003; 2-HTB, 19.10.2003). Even regarding the hereafter, the four organisations introduce a hierarchy among Muslims. Those who have sacrificed most – respectively the *mujahideen* and those at the forefront of the caliphate – would attain 'the highest levels in the Firdaws al-A'la' [gardens of Eden]', considered a 'supreme success' (2-HTB, 31.12.2003; 3-HTB, 29.11.2007; 9-MI, 11.10.2012, 15.03.2013). Thereby, the organisations set alternative criteria for measuring collective and personal success to those prevalent in contemporary Western societies.[55]

Conclusion: the Islamist romantic narrative, from diagnosis to action

In summary, the interpretation of the Romantic Narrative among the cases highlights that organisations in phases of radicalisation or extremism draw on a similar Islamist romantic narrative, whereas they do not in phases of moderation. This points to the narrative exceptionalism of phases of radicalisation and extremism. In such phases of activism, organisations justify and incentivise political violence to bring socio-political change for the *ummah* through this romantic narrative.

As the interpretation showed, its narration produces strong causal relationships between the elements of *Plot*, *Setting*, and *Characters*. Retrieving narrative co-occurrences[56] highlights this in abridged form. Across the eight cases, the strongest narrative co-occurrences centre around the following three nodes:

1. 'Muslims are attacked', 'Repeated attacks', and 'Muslims are prevented from living according to their faith' strongly co-occur with 'Muslim victims' and, secondarily, 'True believers'.
2. 'Resist and fight back' strongly co-occurs with 'Muslim role models' and 'True believers'.
3. 'Obligation to help fellow Muslims/establish the caliphate' strongly co-occurs with 'Muslim role models' and 'True believers'.

It stresses again that 'In-group' characters overlap seamlessly with the *Plot* categories that they are expected to populate. Consequently, some of the narrative characters are being *acted upon* as they are supposed to (i.e. 'Muslim victims' and part of the 'True believers'), while others *act* the way they are supposed to (i.e. 'Muslim role models'). Thus performed, the Romantic Narrative assigns fixed roles and unequivocal responsibilities to the in-group and out-groups.

The interpretation and comparison of the narrative performance in HTB, AM, DWR, and MI cases also highlights subtle differences that demarcate the cases of extremism from the cases of radicalisation. Regarding *Characters*, the cases of radicalisation tend to focus on 'Out-group' identities (except in 8-DWR), whereas the cases of extremism tend to lay even greater emphasis on 'In-group identities' (except in 1-HTB). This points to the idea that, in phases of radicalisation, organisations are more concerned with differentiating in-group and out-group identities and constructing clearly separated out-group identities to reject. In phases of extremism, organisations further build the in-group's unidimensional identity, thereby sifting the in-group, establishing new hierarchies (*good, better,* and *best* Muslims), and praising those who take decisive action ('Muslim role models').

As regards *Setting*, the *local* horizon of experience appears to be narratively less significant than the *transnational* horizon of experience, except in DWR's phase of radicalisation (8-DWR). Further, the diagnosed transnational hostility towards Muslims is more decisive than the immoral character of the current world order. Common to all eight cases, this feature points to the primary importance of perceptions of insecurity and exploitation over perceptions of immorality and injustice. Hence, in phases of radicalisation, as in phases of extremism, political issues have primacy over moral issues.

Regarding *Plot*, the analysis reveals that organisations in phases of radicalisation focus extensively on narrating the comprehensive, repeated attacks perpetrated by out-groups (Plot part 1). In phases of extremism, organisations tend to insist comparatively more on what fellow Muslims *must* do to save the in-group (Plot part 2). Combined, these insights point towards a shift in narrative focus: from the denunciation of out-group violence and justification for armed resistance (phases of radicalisation) to spelling out the modalities of collective and individual action and incentivising group members to participate in political violence (phases of extremism).

Overall, the romantic narrative substantiates and makes a system out of the various normative, strategic, and tactical arguments made by the organisations. Each organisation then gives the individual elements of the narrative its own flavour, fitting its understanding of Islam, its horizon of experience, and subordinary political and organisational aims. Group radicalisation and extremism are thus firmly inscribed and legitimised narratively.

Notes

1 The diagrams depict the relationships between codes with a frequency index of 0.375 or stronger (Jaccard's coefficient).
2 *Ansarul Aseer* is a German-based organisation providing spiritual and material support to Salafi prisoners convicted on terrorism charges (see Chapter 1).
3 This ambiguity echoes the practices of early Islamic rule, when the soldiers of the caliph were simultaneously considered *mujahideen* because their missions were both political and divine.
4 In the German texts, this concept is found under the Arabic term: '*Haq* sprechen', i.e. 'to speak the truth'.
5 For instance in 1-HTB, 21.10.2002, 2-HTB, 26.12.2003, 09.06.2005; 4-AM, 25.10.2002, 5-AM, 27.09.2003; 8-DWR, 08.05.2012, 28.05.2012, 10.2012; 9-MI, 02.2012, 03.05.2012, 10.2012, 01.2013.
6 Al-Zawahiri published a treatise in December 2002 entitled *al-Walā' wa-l-barā': A Traditional Commitment and a Lost Reality*, in which he explains that 'the sharia forbids us [Salafi Muslims] to help the kuffar against the Muslims' (Wagemakers, 2012, p. 181).
7 German original: 'satanischer Gelehrte, die der Ummah einen "Islam" ohne die 3 wichtigen fundamentalen Aqidah-Grundsätze: Kufr biṭ-Ṭaghūt, Al Walā wal Barā und Ǧihād fīsabilillāh schmackhaft zu machen versucht [sic].'
8 A prestigious Sunni title and theological function with seat in Cairo, Egypt.
9 It refers to the Safavid dynasty, founded by Ismail I at the beginning of the fourteenth century, after he conquered Iran, established Shiism as the state religion, and ordered the conversion of its Sunni population.
10 Derogatory term used by Sunni Muslims, especially of Salafi obedience, to refer to Shias as those who reject the early Caliphs as legitimate successors to the Prophet and rulers.
11 Exemplarily, in a press statement advertising for an event about 9/11, AM declares: 'The conference will also contain a public invitation to all non-muslims [sic] to embrace Islam so that they will be safe, and to warn every Muslim and

non-muslim not to die without to submit to Islam [sic], otherwise they will face a raging fire' (5-AM, 11.09.2003).

12 Political and jihadi Salafis break this institutional framework and contend that it is the responsibility of all Muslims to practise *takfir* of an individual or a collective when they see sufficient evidence. While takfirism is part of the Salafi self-image, Salafis hold different views as to what constitute apostasy and on what grounds individuals, collectives, and even states can be excommunicated (Nedza, 2014, 2015; Pfahl-Traughber, 2015).

13 German original: 'Die Leute der Zuhälterei und Unreinheit. Diese Schurken, welche in den Alkoholbars von Europa geboren und aufgewachsen sind, Kinder der Unzucht und perverser Abschaum [der Welt].'

14 German original: 'die Manipulation der Menschheit im Allgemeinen und der Muslime im Speziellen'; 'psychologische Kriegsführung'.

15 Full quote: 'People have been slaughtered and killed for over a year! And they watch on and then come out, what's their name ... Kofi Annan and Pan Ki Moon [sic] come out and say, "we condemn [this]."' German original: 'Über ein Jahr werden Menschen abgeschlachtet und getötet! Und man guckt zu und dann kommt dem hier raus, wie sie alle heißen ... Kofi Annan und Pan Ki Moon [sic] kommen raus und "wir verurteilen [es]."'

16 German original: 'NATO! Das sind diejenigen, die uns *yani* ... wir sind hängen geblieben ... die wollen uns erziehen [...] Wir sind Tiere, wir haben keine Ahnung. Wir wissen nicht, wie wir leben können. Also kommen die in unseren Ländern und wollen uns ja zivilisieren.'

17 MI refers here to the incidents of February 2012 in Bagram, Afghanistan, when coalition soldiers burned Quran exemplars, which unleashed mass protests across Muslim countries and in Europe.

18 Full quote: 'Before that ... they burned a Quran. [...] They desecrate our dead, our *shuhada* [martyrs], they pee on our martyrs, brother. Where are you? Where are the human rights activists, huh?' German original: 'Davor ist ... wurde ein Koran verbrannt. [...] Ja, sie schänden unsere Toten, unsere *shuhada*, sie pinkeln auf unseren *shuhada*, Bruder. Wo seid ihr? Wo seid ihr Menschenrechtlern, hä?'

19 Full quote: 'We see what's happening in the world, what's happening to the Muslims in the world, everywhere in the world, where ... where blood is shed. [...] Look at Africa, it is the blood of the Muslims, look at Asia, it is the blood of the Muslims, everywhere you look, the blood of the Muslims has no worth and *wallahi* nowadays people are worried to hurt a fly, but they don't worry about Muslims.' German original in Appendix B2, quote n°1.

20 The mention of Somalia is interesting because the Somali conflict cannot be seen as an *inter-religious* conflict (Somalis are 98% of Muslim confession). Either AM might have welcomed humanitarian military interventions (if used *consistently* for the protection of civilian populations) or mentioning Somalia abstractly in a list of conflicts is used to strengthen the point with seemingly numerous examples.

21 German original: 'Das sind Beispiele dafür, dass der Westen andauernd die Muslime versucht zu unterdrücken, zu unterjochen'.

22 Original title: 'Die modernen Strategien der Kuffār und Murtaddīn zur Bekämpfung des Islām von innen'.
23 The Bonn agreement is the sum of initial agreements passed on 5 December 2001 under UN auspices and intended to re-create the State of Afghanistan. It laid the groundwork for the US and NATO-backed state-building plans for Afghanistan.
24 German original: 'Wer sind die Kuffar, dass sie uns sagen, wie wir leben sollen, liebe Geschwister im Islam? Wer sind diese Leute, ha? Ein Ungläubiger sagt mir, wie ich mein Islam zu leben habe?'
25 German original: 'das Missbrauchen und Erniedrigen unserer Frauen, Mütter und Schwestern [...] in den Gefängnissen des Kreuzes in Europa'.
26 German original: 'Dieser Krieg gegen Islam, den gibt es ... der wird schon seit Jahren geführt.'
27 German original in Appendix B2, quote n°3.
28 Original quote: 'he [Sharon] and Bush ... [are] getting ready to bring the Palestinian people to submission ... by crushing them and destroying them by force, murder, torture, deprivation and starvation.'
29 German original: 'wofür so viele wahrhaftige Gelehrten gestorben sind, getötet wurden, gefoltert wurden, immer noch in Gefängnissen sitzen'.
30 German original: 'welche die Köpfe und Herzen der Menschen beeinflusst werden [sic] sollen'.
31 German original: 'ihrer muslimischen Gefangenen (und Gelehrten und Prediger) ... dazu bringen können, dass sie sich öffentlich vom *jihad* lossagen'.
32 German original: 'damit sie unsere Bodenschätze klauen können'.
33 MI states: 'Not one of the kings and presidents (which are apostates) [would] ever allow jihad for the sake of Allah. The only type of war they care for is one that benefits them and protects their power.' German original in Appendix B2, quote n°5.
34 To the exclusion of Bashar al-Assad, dehumanised by DWR on one occasion: 'it would be an insult to animals to call him animal names' (28.05.2012).
35 Reference to ProNRW's caricature campaign mentioned previously. German original: 'was in Deutschland geschieht an klaren Beleidigungen des Propheten Muhammad (a.s.s.) und eine wiederholte Verhöhnung in allen europäischen Städten'.
36 German original: 'Einheit ist Stärke. [...] Deswegen ist es für uns sehr sehr wichtig, dass wir zusammenhalten. [...] Bleibt auf diesem Weg, seid standhaft, seid stark gegen alles und gegen jeden.'
37 German original: 'die Feinde haben nicht Angst vor unserer militärischen Stärke. Aber sie haben Angst vor dem, was in unseren Brüsten ist ... *Iman!*'
38 German original: 'Tut euch in Gruppen zusammen'.
39 German original: 'die Jugend der Muslime in Europa'.
40 German original: 'Bruder, geh deinen Geschwistern helfen. Bruder, unterstütz deine Geschwister, die rausgehen wollen, die Geschwister unterstützen wollen und helfen wollen.'
41 German original: 'die Gefangenschaft unserer Schwester aufzuheben'.

42 As there is no caliph nowadays and the current rulers are seen as apostates.

43 German original: '[Kämpfen] muss so erfolgen, wie es unsere edlen Vorfahren, die *Salaf*, vorgelebt haben und ... dies geschieht durch das Schwert'.

44 German original: 'Gesetz für die gesamte Menschheit und für die gesamte Erde'.

45 German original: 'bis auf dem Weiße Haus und auf dem Vatikan *bismillah azza wa-jall* die schwarzen Flaggen gehoben [werden]' (18.05.2012); 'die Führerschaft [...] dieser sterblichen Welt zu erlangen' (07.2012), 'bis die gesamte Erde mit dem Buche Allahs regiert wird' (11.10.2012).

46 MI claims that 'the Prophet s.a.s. announced: "You will conquer Constantinople and Rom"' and rejoices in the prospect that Rom's main square 'will *inshallah* [God willing] become the square of conversion' (9-MI, 13.10.2012). German original in Appendix B2, quote n°6.

47 German original: 'Es ist eine Pflicht, ein *fard* und diese Pflicht wird ... dann erst aufhören, wenn der Zweck erfüllt ist. Wenn unsere Geschwister überall auf der Welt nicht mehr leiden.'

48 German original: 'Allah s.w.t. [wird] jeden Einzelnen von uns hier *yawm al-qiyamah* fragen. Nach seiner Verantwortung und nach das was er gemacht hat. Allah s.w.t. wird jeden hier *yawm al-qiyamah* zu Rechenschaft ziehen'.

49 Referenced, for example, in 4-AM, 20.04.2002; 5-AM, 25.10.2002; 05.05.2004; 8-DWR, 10.2012; 9-MI, 31.12.3013.

50 German original: 'die wahre Aufopferung kann nur im *jihad* ... stattfinden'.

51 Reference to Surah *An-Nur* 24:55, which begins as follows: 'Allah has promised those who have believed among you and done righteous deeds that He will surely grant them succession upon the earth'.

52 German original: 'Allgemeinwohl der Muslime'.

53 German original: 'die Gläubigen [werden] über die *Kuffar* lachen'.

54 German original: 'Jeder Muslim ... wird am Ende ein Sieger sein. Weil er wird ein Paradiesbewohner und das ist der wahre Erfolg'; 'ab diesem Augenblick wirst du leben'.

55 In contemporary Western societies, success at the individual level is measured in terms of wealth/capital, social status, and/or fame in one's lifetime, while success at the collective level is measured by the extent of the economic, social, and cultural progress of a society and its status on the international scene.

56 The co-occurrence analysis was conducted at the level of text segments and measured in degrees of distance or similarity.

5

Narrative emotionalisation and extremism

While organisations articulate a similar romantic narrative in phases of radicalisation and extremism, the previous chapter has already outlined some preliminary differences in narrative emphasis. This chapter explores these further by contrasting the organisations' respective performance of emotions in their phases of activism. As I argued before, some performances of romance are more intensely emotional than others. Such variations can be studied by drawing on the concept of narrative emotionalisation (Chapter 3). As dicussed, this refers to *the gradual process by which the texts and visuals pertaining to a narrative increasingly perform strong, non-conflicting, collective emotions towards distinct narrative objects and events, according to strict emotion rules.*

Narrative emotionalisation is particularly strong when the performance of emotions is consistent across narrative occurrences, that is, across an organisation's texts, audios, and visuals. It is a complex process that builds up through repetition rather than an outcome at a specific time. Chapter 3 specified four sub-processes conjointly participating in this overall process to study narrative emotionalisation empirically:

1. emotional meanings become the only legitimate form of knowledge;
2. conflicting emotional meanings (gradually) disappear, and a distinctive emotional tone crystallises;
3. strict emotion rules are established and enforced with sanctions;
4. the performance of emotions is consistent across narrative occurrences.

The sub-processes are not hierarchised; none is *a priori* more important than the other. The presence of only some of the four sub-processes is referred to as partial emotionalisation, whereas full narrative emotionalisation requires all four sub-processes. Full narrative emotionalisation represents a (temporary) performative success.

The following section explains the hermeneutic approach developed to study narrative emotionalisation in the empirical cases. The chapter then turns to the four sub-processes successively and offers an interpretation of how they unfold within the cases. The focus lies on contrasting the phases of extremism (1-HTB, 5-AM, 9-MI) with the phases of radicalisation (3-HTB, 4-AM, 8-DWR). The chapter ends with a discussion of the main differences in narrative emotionalisation between these phases. In addition, it highlights some important differences in the performance of emotions of HTB, AM, and MI in their respective phase of extremism.

Hermeneutic approach

No study has addressed emotionalisation in such a comprehensive way so far. I develop a hermeneutic approach which specifies the interpretative process for each of the four sub-processes. In general terms, this approach foregrounds the importance of tracing how these processes unfold, thereby making apparent the knowledges and practices that organisations' performances invisibilise or, conversely, normalise and lend power to. The concrete analytical steps are detailed below. The comparison within and across the cases lends further nuance to the interpretation of a partial or full emotionalisation of the narrative performances.

The first sub-process – *emotional meanings increasingly become the only legitimate form of knowledge* – means that other forms of knowledge are (gradually) perceived as illegitimate. As argued in Chapter 3, knowledge can be individual or collective. It draws upon perception, consciousness, reason, and/or memory, that is, upon a mix of affective-cognitive processes (Bless, 2000; Audi, 2009). In short, a piece of knowledge can be defined as the understanding of a subject or a situation through experience or study. To trace this first sub-process, I characterise the importance given by organisations to knowledge rooted in collective emotional experience compared to other forms (and sources) of knowledge. More specifically, I explore the (potential) increasing legitimacy of emotion-based knowledge (and, conversely, the delegitimisation of other forms of knowledge) from three angles. First, I question whether an organisation holds emotion-based knowledge as a superior form of knowledge, which might indicate that other forms are increasingly discarded. A typical indication would be, for instance, claims to the superiority of 'feeling' over 'thinking'. Second, I search for explicit attempts at delegitimising other forms of knowledge and analyse the arguments on which delegitimisation rests. Third, I trace whether certain forms of knowledge disappear (i.e. are not articulated *anymore*) from a phase of activism to the next. I then compare insights between the cases and interpret the centrality of knowledge rooted in collective emotional experience.

The second sub-process – *conflicting emotional meanings (gradually) disappear, and a distinctive emotional tone crystallises* – implies that the variety and complexity of emotional expressions are suppressed. The subjects and events of the narrative become wrapped in clear-cut, unequivocal emotional meanings. The narrative thereby presents ever-fewer nuances and eschews mixed emotions. This lends an un-complicated, unequivocal emotional tone to the organisation's narrative. While political science research on emotions in language often focuses on emotional expressions or emotion-signifying words, the interpretative process proposed here goes beyond studying emotion words. Exploring which emotional meanings become dominant and how – and whether an emotional tone crystallises – calls for tracing whether potentially conflicting emotional meanings tend to disappear from an organisation's narrative deployments. It means studying complex emotions and their interactions. I trace continuities and discontinuities in the performance of conflicting emotional meanings and hence the evolution of mixed emotions[1] across phases of activism.

The third sub-process – *strict emotion rules are established and enforced with sanctions* – refers to organisations' expectations of a collective performance of emotions towards specific in- and out-groups. The higher the expectation of a collective performance of emotions, the stronger the imperative to feel in a certain way towards in-groups and out-groups. Tracing this sub-process calls, first, for analysing the implementation of emotion rules. Organisations need to specify such rules when they convey minority ideologies as they depart from 'dominant feeling rules' (Hochschild, 1979; Traïni, 2009). Spelling out emotion rules gains even more importance when organisations introduce changes in orientation, as emotion rules may need to be adapted. To study specific rules, I reconstruct what ought to be felt, not to be felt, and under what circumstances (von Scheve, 2012) according to each organisation. Reconstructing such rules allows interpreting what each considers appropriate in terms of emotions' intensity, direction, and duration in a given situation (Thoits, 2004).

Second, I zoom in on the emotion rules that aim at the suppression of certain emotion expressions. Organisations expect emotions considered illegitimate to be suppressed through *emotion work*. Drawing on Goodwin and Pfaff's (2001) conception, I further argue that when expectations towards members' emotional performance change (due to new political goals, strategies, etc.), organisations need to modify or set new emotion rules. When emotion expressions that were acceptable before become illegitimate, organisations call their members to work on suppressing them and cultivating others and may warn of the consequences of emotional deviance.

Third, I question the anticipated effects of the implementation of group-specific emotion rules. As argued in Chapter 3, the group-appropriate performance of emotions not only serves to strengthen group cohesion (socialising newcomers, making sense of the social effects of expressing emotions, fostering belonging), it engenders individual and collective action. This calls for making apparent the anticipated effects of emotion rules on action. Together, the three analytical steps help in interpreting the extent to which emotion expressions are collectivised – and to which effects – in the different phases of activism.

The last sub-process – *narrative emotionalisation builds up through repetition* – hinges on the *consistency* of the performance of emotions: the more consistent the performance of emotion within a case, the stronger the emotionalising effects of the narrative. Here, the interpretative process centres on characterising whether the performance of collective emotions is re-actualised across an organisation's narrative occurrences.[2] The performance would be less consistent, for instance, if the leaders of an organisation were to perform *dissimilar* emotions towards the same objects. This might seem evident, but the successful invocation, transmission, and cultivation of group-appropriate emotions hinge upon the consistency of the performance. This is not to say that strong emotionalisation depends on the absolute precision of the performance of collective emotions but rather on its re-actualisation across narrative occurrences. For example, the absence of one of the emotion rules in a text or visual does not necessarily make the whole performance inconsistent. However, if one leader systematically performs an emotion rule and, in a similar situation, another does not, it might be inconsistent. What would also threaten the performance's overall consistency would be the introduction of a contradictory emotion rule. For example, performing compassion towards European non-Muslims, while the emotion rule on compassion otherwise states that it is not allowed to feel compassion for *anyone* outside of the *ummah*, would qualify as an inconsistent performance.

Differences in style are not considered of importance to the consistency of the performance. The level of language or speech speed are not significant either. What matters is whether an organisation's emotion rules have become so established that even if the performance, for example, of 'unconditional love towards true believers' is missing in a narrative occurrence, readers or listeners can complete the performance themselves. There are at least three ways the audience would know the rest of the performance in this example: i. 'unconditional love' fits in with the rest of the narrative told in that specific text, audio, or video – it is internally logical, coherent; ii. the other narrative occurrences produced by the organisation always performed 'unconditional love' in combination with the other emotion rules that are performed in this specific text, audio, or video; iii. in other texts, audios, or videos, by Islamist organisations conveying a similar narrative, 'unconditional love' is systematically performed. The first way has been detailed at length in the previous chapter: the romantic narrative attributes fixed roles and clear responsibilities to characters, thereby informing the audience how to feel about them. Its internal coherence helps the audience to fill in the gaps. Such gaps would not happen too often, or else 'unconditional love' would not be an established emotion rule. The second and third ways in which the audience would complete the performance draw on intertextuality.

As discussed in Chapter 3, by becoming increasingly intertextual, the performance of emotions is validated, normalised. The second way – other narrative occurrences by the organisation performed these emotion rules in combination – can be explored by tracing inconsistencies in an organisation's performance of emotions within each phase of activism. Conversely, exploring the third way would be unrealistic. If the audience manages to fill in the blanks because it recognises the performance from other known texts and/or visuals, the possibilities are close to infinite. For example, it might resonate with decontextualised passages of the Quran, with articles by another German or UK group, or an al-Qaeda video watched previously. Showing positively the presence of such extensive intertextuality would be a daunting task methodologically. Hence, the interpretative focus lies here on tracing inconsistencies within an organisation's narrative occurrences. As consistency is a highly qualitative feature, I discuss the cases comparatively and interpret the performances of emotions from most consistent to merely partly consistent.

The primacy of emotion-based knowledge

In the first sub-process of narrative emotionalisation, emotional meanings would gradually become the only legitimate source of knowledge. A first analytical insight is that organisations draw heavily on emotion-based evaluations to make sense of local and international events. Regarding Western foreign policies in the Middle East and the Far East, for instance, the meaning of new events is constructed around how out-groups *feel* towards Muslims and the *ummah*. This is a cross-case feature insofar as it applies to the three phases of HTB's activism (1-HTB, 2-HTB, 3-HTB), the first two phases of AM's (4-AM, 5-AM), DWR's phase of radicalisation into extremism (8-DWR), and MI's phase of extremism (9-MI).

If we take the example of the wars in Afghanistan and Iraq, HTB and AM both attribute specific emotional motives to out-groups. The US-led alliances are said to show no mercy towards innocent Muslims during their invasions and occupation of Muslim lands (1-HTB, 10.12.2001) because the West *hates* Muslims and Islam (1-HTB; 5-AM). Similarly, MI argues that Germany *hates* Muslims, which is why they are persecuted and their

Prophet attacked (9-MI, 24.04.2012, 21.09.2012, 11.10.2012). In the cases of radicalisation, the West's main motive is its hostility towards Islam and Muslims (3-HTB; 4-AM; 8-DWR). Further emotion-based motives refer to the West's desire to humiliate Muslims (1-HTB; 5-AM; 8-DWR) and its *fear* of the re-establishment of an Islamic caliphate (2-HTB; 3-HTB; 5-AM).

Similarly, HTB and AM make sense of the (alleged) minimal reaction by international organisations, media, and human rights organisations to the killing of Muslims in emotional terms as well. Both explain that a Western-dominated international order sees Muslims as second-class human beings whose blood would be worth *less*.[3] Western governments are said not to hear the concerns and opposition of local Muslim communities to their foreign policies in the Middle East and Far East because they would feel nothing but contempt for them. Talking about the UK context, HTB contends that:

> Islam, in particular its political ideas such as Shariah, Khilafah and Jihad [sic], are today attacked under the guise of attacking 'Islamism'. 'Islamism' was a term created to label those Muslims who stand up to colonialism, speak out against dictators, and desire the return of Islam to state and society in the Muslim world. (3-HTB, 06.07.2006)

For HTB, those who try to oppose the colonialist endeavours of the UK and other Western governments are branded contemptuously as 'Islamists' with 'backward ideas' (3-HTB, 06.07.2006; see also 5-AM, 24.10.2002).

In the same vein, MI explains that the Muslim rulers do not feel shame at the invasion of Muslim lands because they disregard their subjects and do not care enough about Islam (9-MI, 11.2011, 07.2012, 18.09.2012). HTB also is adamant: 'These are your rulers [...] They hand over her [the *ummah*] issues to the Kafir colonialists, with submission and disgrace. They feel no shame from Allah and the servants of Allah [sic]' (2-HTB, 19.10.2003, also 09.06.2005). Further, the (perceived) lack of solidarity from parts of the Muslim *ummah* is interpreted based on emotion evaluations: attacked on all sides, Muslims are at risk of becoming deaf to the complaints of victims. For AM, the issue of compassion fatigue[4] is central:

> The media show the killings in Palestine, in Iraq etc. ... every day, after a while, you will begin to become immune to it all. [...] The numbers have begun to mean nothing, and Muslims have become used to it. The feelings and emotions will become dead after a while. (5-AM, 21.05.2004)

In AM's interpretation, Muslims worldwide are at risk of becoming uncaring, much as the Muslim rulers, and eventually falling into the category 'Muslim Other'.

Overall, the events of the narrative plot, '*Muslims and their way of life are under threat*' – detailed in Chapter 4, are wrapped in interpretations drawing on the emotions allegedly felt by out-groups. Especially in their phases of extremism, HT, AM, and MI make sense of out-group (in)actions based on what out-groups are said to *feel* towards Muslims.

In this process, other explanations for out-group (in)actions tend to disappear and/or become explicitly disqualified. For AM and DWR, the feelings of the West and their agents towards the Muslim *ummah* appear to constitute the sole explanation for worldwide attacks on Muslims. Both consider economic exploitation and the domination of the international order as consequences – not motives – of Western invasions and occupation of Muslim lands. This largely applies to MI's perspective as well. Only twice does the organisation, in the voice of Denis Cuspert, mention in passing that economic exploitation might constitute another motive and not merely a consequence of Western aggression: 'Look at all these regimes, they are all puppets of... the West. Nicely put in place, implanted, so that they can steal our natural resources'[5] (9-MI, 02.2012; see also 03.05.2012).

In HTB cases, however, a secondary explanation for Western threats to Muslims and their 'way of life' is put forward at times: big power competition. For example, HTB argues that, following Bush's call for new leaders to replace Arafat at the head of the Palestinian Authority (24 June 2002), Europe tried to position itself by disagreeing with the US president 'under the pretext that it [...] goes against the basic norms of international law' (1-HTB, 07.07.2002). The reference to a 'pretext' implies that HTB does not believe European governments voiced such opposition out of normative concerns but rather strategically. HTB further decodes Europe's dissident position as follows:

> The American government wants a Palestinian 'Hamid Karzai' of her own making and not of Europe making [sic]. [...] The European reaction was swift and blunt. The reaction took the guise of a protest against the prospect of removing Arafat [...] However, the issue is much more far-reaching than that. [...] Especially now that Europe, more than at any other time, wants greater influence and real participation in making the decisions which effect [sic] international politics. (1-HTB, 07.07.2002; also in 2-HTB, 24.02.2005)

HTB paints a picture of Europe as a strategic player trying to wrestle some influence on international politics away from the US after years of unilateralism. For HTB, this explanation in terms of big power competition complements the explanation based on the feelings the West holds towards Muslims. While the West's hostility towards Muslims and fear of a coming caliphate are seen by HTB as *primary* motives, the US's wish to maintain unilateral power and, conversely, Europe's struggle to regain some, complete the picture.

In the same vein, while security and economic motives might play a role, they are placed much lower in the hierarchy of motives attributed by HTB to enemies:

> These statements [of the Hizb] have exposed that the US uses Kuwait as a launching point for its economic, military, and political agenda in the region: [...] the security arrangements between America and Kuwait, protecting American military bases in Kuwait, the treaties by virtue of which the US continues to plunder oil resources of the region, and *above all*, the hate that the Kuffar occupiers led by America harbour for those who work for the Khilafah [...] (3-HTB, 25.08.2007, emphasis added)

Thus, even for HTB, which at times expands the pool of potential explanations for understanding Western aggressions against the *ummah*, emotion evaluations dominate.

A second central insight is that emotion-based evaluations replace, little by little, other modes of experience and, ultimately, knowledge. Other ways of experiencing and knowing are increasingly portrayed as wrong or illegitimate. The four organisations often depart from *factual* knowledge, especially when they lay the blame on political enemies for the sufferings of the *ummah*. The following quote is a particularly vivid example of arguments presented as knowledge, despite being factually unsound. Writing about sectarian violence in Iraq in spring 2004, HTB contends:

> The Kafir occupiers under the leadership of America in Iraq, and in any country they occupy with their army or influence, are the ones who have an interest in Muslims killing themselves [...] Otherwise, is it an accident that we have seen in the last few weeks a string of assassinations of 'Ulama (scholars) of Muslims in Iraq, both Sunni and Shi'i [...]? And all of this took place in front of the occupying forces, which control the country [...] The enormity of the incident does not require more explanation and clarification. However, we would like to warn the Muslims not to fall prey to the plans of the enemy by engaging in (sectarian) fighting. It will realise the hopes of the occupying Kuffar [...] and fill with delight those who hate Islam and the Muslims. (2-HTB, 02.03.2004)

Declarations such as HTB's above do not need to be corroborated by facts from local accounts, testimonies, or strategy documents. To give the appearance of knowledge, they rely on emotional experience and the overall strength of the narrative (among others, the causal links it establishes).

In the same vein, the claim of a conspiracy against 'Islam and the Muslims', expressed extensively in all three cases of extremism (1-HTB, 5-AM, and 9-MI), draws on emotional knowledge insofar as it feels *true* for individuals who have experienced (real or alleged) persecution based on their beliefs or practices, as is the case for the organisations' leaders and at least part of their members and followers. In phases of extremism, emotional experience appears to be the preferred mode of knowledge.

It is sometimes unclear with which *other* forms of knowledge the organisations compare emotion-based knowledge. The in-group's emotional knowledge is often contrasted with the 'false' knowledge produced by hegemonic media and/or political actors. Talking about media reporting, AM states that it is 'a duty for Muslims to doubt anything that the Kuffar say', as 'the Qur'an is clear that they are in fact, in origin, a bunch of liars' (5-AM, 09.2003). Deception as an allegedly unchanging, natural trait of non-Muslims is documented in almost all of the cases.[6] For instance, HTB denounces how 'the Pope' and the European states propagate 'lies upon Islam' and enjoins Muslims to 'reflect, so that the falsehood may be made clear from the truth and the lies from the reality' (2-HTB, 17.09.2006). On the opposite, Islam is compared to 'the truth, which lies in the hearts and minds of the Islamic Ummah' (2-HTB, 08.11.2003). Under such conditions, all that conforms to the opinions carried by hegemonic media and political actors become suspicious.

One might argue that it is not so much a specific *form* of knowledge that is rejected but rather those who produce it. However, several observations indicate that it goes beyond the identity of the knowledge producer and has to do with the acceptance of other sources of knowledge. The German-based organisations enjoin fellow Muslims, on occasion, to 'reverse' their emotional experience to understand a situation or a subject. Much as one would reverse a stigma by infusing it with positive meaning, fellow Muslims are called to transform negative emotional experiences into pieces of knowledge. As an example, DWR tells Muslims who 'feel as foreigners' in Germany that they should rejoice because it means they are on the right path:

> Don't pay attention to RTL and the BILD newspaper and these losers, these *kuffar*, ok? What they tell people, this is not our yardstick. When they speak ill of a Moslem, that is a good Moslem. When they say that a Moslem is a terrorist, then this is a God-fearing Moslem. Always the contrary of what they claim, ok? When they praise you as a Moslem, then you should be afraid. (8-DWR, 25.10.2012; original in Appendix B3, quote n°1)

Experiencing rejection, and being conscious of it, should ultimately inform Muslims about their situation in Germany, that is, foster (emotion-based) knowledge. This transformation of 'feeling rejected' into knowledge can be found in MI's corpus as well (9-MI, 19.11.2011). Against the background of *false* knowledge, the organisations' own knowledge – emotional or based on their interpretations of Islamic texts – is presented as *true* knowledge.

Furthermore, some forms of knowledge are re-defined as emotion-based knowledge. For instance, on one occasion, MI states emphatically that even religious knowledge is rooted in emotion. This is surprising insofar as most Islamist organisations emphasise at length how *rational* the Islamic system is and how *objective* and just its laws are. However, for leader Mahmoud, truly living Islam means sacrificing oneself in the hope that it is of use:

> That is knowledge, brother, that is knowledge. Not 1 plus 1 equals 2; *wallahi* religion was never about logic. Religion – knowledge – does not follow logic. [...] Religion is never about opinion and never about logic, yes? *Wallahi*, when you see that there is a benefit for Islam ... and you know well that when you do this or that action, you will go to prison or be killed, and you do it anyway, you will attain the highest ranks of the *mujahideen* and *shuhada*!! That is Islam. (9-MI, 05.2013; original in Appendix B3 quote n°2)

In other words, for MI, activism is not based on a rational-choice calculus; it rests on faith, hope, and self-sacrifice, that is, acting despite knowing it will cost much (prison), if not everything (death). In that sense, truly living Islam is not 'logical' or 'reasonable'.

Even HTB, which emphasises time and again the rationality of Islamic law and its advantages over all other political systems, ultimately grounds the motivation to re-establish the caliphate on *love*: 'Whoever truly loves RasulAllah (saw) [Allah's Messenger] and the Quran al-Kareem should stand up and work sincerely to re-establish the Khilafah' (3-HTB, 29.03.2008). The re-establishment of the caliphate is posited as a collective duty, but the strength of individual commitment would vary with the depth of each Muslim's emotional experience.

Overall, emotional experience tends to be the primary source of legitimate knowledge. The organisations dismiss other forms of knowledge as false and other sources of knowledge as illegitimate. Especially in phases of extremism (5-AM; 9-MI; 1-HTB) and to a certain extent in phases of radicalisation (8-DWR; 3-HTB; 4-AM), organisations assert the primacy of emotion-based knowledge.

Emotional tone: suffering and the promises of jihad

The second sub-process identified as part of narrative emotionalisation refers to the gradual disappearance of conflicting emotional meanings, resulting in a distinctive emotional tone. The stronger this process, the fewer nuances and mixed emotions should be found. The analysis thus centres on the evolution of mixed emotional meanings across an organisation's phases of activism. The HTB and AM cases lend themselves well to interpretation because potentially conflicting emotional meanings can be traced throughout their respective phases of activism. The presence of mixed emotions about events and actions would interfere with (or 'muddle') the emotional tone of the narrative.

The meanings created by AM around 9/11 provide an example of an initially conflicting interpretation. In 4-AM (radicalisation phase), the organisation ascribes mixed emotional meanings to the attacks. In the very same document, dated 12 September 2001, AM displays a whole range of (partly) conflicting emotions and interpretations regarding the attacks. It considers the attacks as a sin in Islam:

> [The] US Government and its Military [sic] forces are a legitimate target as far as Islam is concerned, however, it is not a justification to attack American People [sic] [...] Islamically speaking, the whole recent attack against the civilians in the USA is prohibited and a crime as far as Islam is concerned. (4-AM, 12.09.2001)

Further, AM stresses that 'there is no proof that Muslims are behind the attacks'.[7] It argues that the accusation that *Islamist* terrorists were behind the attacks proves again 'how they rush quickly to accuse their victims, i.e. Islam and Muslims'. However, in the next paragraph, AM writes that one of the lessons to take from the attacks is that it has 'shake[n] the arrogance of the Western Government[s] ... and show[s] that there is no defen[ce] system [that] could stand in the way of the determination of a person who wants to become a Martyr' (4-AM, 12.09.2001), whereby the organisation concedes that the perpetrators might have had Islamist motives after all.

In the following weeks, in the wake of the invasion of Afghanistan, AM's representation of the events becomes increasingly negative. The 9/11 attacks are constructed as bearing overwhelmingly *negative* consequences for Muslims, both those living in the US and Western countries, who are bound to be subjected to a 'witch-hunt' (4-AM, 07.10.2001), as well as those living in Muslim-majority countries, especially Afghanistan, which the US 'intended to invade anyway' (4-AM, 21.09.2001). The interpretation that now dominates is that Western governments are exploiting the 9/11 attacks to violate the sovereignty of the Islamic Emirate of Afghanistan (4-AM, 16.09.2001, 07.10.2001).

However, in its phase of extremism (5-AM), the organisation departs from this conflicting interpretation and re-ascribes a strictly *positive* meaning to the 9/11 attacks. Indeed, a year after, AM calls Muslims in the UK to celebrate 'A towering day in History' in reference to the destruction of the World Trade Center. The actions of the 19 hijackers are exalted: 'If 19 Mujahideen can crash planes into the twin towers [sic] and rewrite history with their blood, we too can establish the law of Allah (swt) in this Dunya [world]' (5-AM, 03.12.2002). Similarly, on the two-year 'anniversary' of the attacks, AM praises 'the Magnificent 19',[8] dedicating a conference in Birmingham to them, with the stated goal beinng to 'discuss the lives, motives, and reasons' behind their actions (5-AM, 11.09.2003). Before the events, the organisation rejoices at the thought that 'Blair and Bush are still choking on the smoke from the fall out of September the 11th' and announces: 'on September the 11th 2003, Muslims worldwide will again be watching replays of the collapse of the Twin Towers, praying to Allah (SWT) to grant those magnificent 19, Paradise [sic]' (5-AM, 17.08.2003). In the transition from 4-AM to 5-AM, the 9/11 attacks have been re-presented as unequivocally positive for the Muslim *ummah* and negative for its (alleged) enemies.

Similar processes of ascribing unambiguous, uniform meanings to events and actions unfold in 9-MI, 1-HTB, and to some extent in 8-DWR. In these cases, particularly impermeable emotional meanings are performed. It points to an important finding: conflicting emotional meanings disappear when an organisation enters a phase of extremism. This is not all too surprising considering that the cases of extremism strongly exhibit the romantic narrative, as discussed in Chapter 4. The denunciation of wrongdoings and the necessity to redress injustices imply strongly negative emotion evaluations towards wrongdoers and strongly positive emotion evaluations towards righters of wrong. While conflicting meanings may disappear in phases of radicalisation as well, as 8-DWR shows, it is not necessarily the case. Indeed, emotional meanings are less clear-cut in AM's and HT's phases of radicalisation.

In the cases of extremism (1-HTB, 5-AM, 9-MI) and (minimally) in 8-DWR, this process culminates in the performance of highly negative emotions and highly positive emotions towards *strictly separate* events and objects. Nuance and complexity are hereby erased. The organisations perform highly negative emotions towards (what is perceived as) the international order under Western domination and its wars of aggression against the Muslim *ummah*. Conversely, they perform highly positive emotions towards resistance, jihad, and a future caliphate. While these objects and events were characterised in detail in the previous chapter, the focus below is on illustrating and interpreting this separation.

The elimination of nuance is particularly striking around the bold comparisons made by the three organisations with regards to Western governments' actions. In its phase of extremism, AM compares the UK's new anti-terror and extraditions laws to the practices of the Nazi regime: 'one would be excused for thinking that this is Britain in the new millennium as opposed to Hitler's Germany during the second world war [sic]' (5-AM, 24.12.2002). AM makes further historical analogies regarding the 'war on terror': 'With 1000's of innocent Muslims still in captivity under barbaric conditions in Guantanamo bay [sic], the US inquisition against Islam and Muslims shows no signs of subsiding' (5-AM, 17.08.2003).[9]

In their phases of extremism, HTB and AM make comparisons between the time of the crusades and ongoing conflicts: the war in Afghanistan, the US support for Israel against Palestinian Muslims, the US support for India against Kashmiri Muslims, and the war in Iraq.[10] Besides its frequent references to 'the crusading, Zionist alliance', MI specifically equates the mass violence perpetrated against Muslim women during the Christian crusades (eleventh to thirteenth centuries) to the purported imprisonment and rape of Muslim women in Europe by modern-day crusaders (9-MI, 16/19/20.11.2011, 21.09.2012). DWR equates NATO's actions in Muslim lands, as well as Western humanitarianism in Africa, with colonialism's civilising intent (8-DWR, 28.05.2012, 21.04.2013).

Conversely, the organisations perform highly positive emotions towards resistance, jihad, and a future caliphate, especially in 5-AM and 9-MI, and to some extent in 1-HTB. AM looks 'forward to the day the Islamic State (Al-Khilafah) returns to bring mankind out of its current injustices and darkness in the justice and beauty of Islam' (5-AM, 21.01.2003). MI praises the 'sweetness of the Islamic caliphate' (9-MI, 07.2012). For HTB, only the Islamic state can bring victory and joy to the Muslim *ummah*, as the Quran would attest:

> So capture your own affairs, O Muslims, and help the cause of your Lord, by establishing the righteous Khilafah, then He will help you and heal your hearts with the defeat of your enemy: 'And on that Day, the believers (Muslims) will rejoice (at the victory of Allah)' [TMQ 30:4]. (1-HTB, 13.04.2003)

The coming caliphate is exalted, and so is armed resistance: 'Jihad in Islam is the effusion of life in the souls, the rays of justice and light (shining) through the oppression and darkness of the world; all of this is palpable and noticeable in the lands which Islam entered in the days of the Islamic conquests' (2-HTB, 17.09.2006). For the three organisations, resistance through armed action is not only the *right* thing to do; it is also a completely new experience – full of life, and beautiful – that one should not miss out on.

Conversely, this is not the case in 8-DWR: resistance and jihad are primarily seen as duties. Highly positive emotional meanings revolve almost exclusively around the *rewards* one can hope for in the *hereafter*. DWR only performs strong positive emotions a few times with regards to the battlefield (8-DWR, 21.04.2013).

The most glaring examples of a highly positive representation of jihad are found in MI's performance. The paragraph below, from the document entitled 'Freedom in Jihad'[11], paints in great detail the many graces that fighters have the chance to experience in jihad:

> When you start jihad on the path of Allah, you enter a completely new world. [...] For where is it possible to better learn and bring into your life *tawhid* [the Oneness of God] than on the battlefield?

- Where is one more conscious about death than on the battlefield?
- Where is the love to the creator bigger than on the battlefield because you realise that any benefit and harm happens not without the permission of your lord?
- Where do you have more longing to encounter your lord than on the battlefield?
- Where do you feel more aversion against the *dunya* [mortal world] **than on the battlefield?**
- Where do you feel more affection for the *akhira* [hereafter] **than on the battlefield?**
- Where is life freer than the life of a *mujahid* **on the battlefield?**
- Where is living up to the *Quran* **and** *Sunnah* **more intense than on the battlefield?**
- Where is the eagerness for the religion of Allah **bigger than on the battlefield?**
- Where is concern for the *ummah* **bigger than on the battlefield, where you see the children of the ummah die in your arms?**
- Where is your sacrifice for Islam or the *ummah* **bigger than on the battlefield?**
- Where do you feel more honour, dignity and pride, but also tranquillity, virtue and humility, if not on the battlefield?
- Where is one closer to devotion to the Almighty than on the battlefield?
- And where is one closer to the delight of the Sublime, the Creator of heaven and earth, than on the battlefield?

(9-MI, 11.10.2012, layout, bold and italic in the original; original in Appendix B3, quote n°3)

In this passage, everything about waging jihad is moral and religious elevation, grace, beauty, and exaltation. It conveys the idea that the path itself is rewarding, not only the goal of liberating the *ummah*. This representation becomes ever more pervasive from the time when MI leaders (all except Keskin) leave Germany and go into exile (spring/summer 2012).

In comparison, HTB does not always perform strictly separate positive and negative emotional meanings. For instance, it stresses much more often the hardships linked to the re-establishment of the caliphate. HTB does not minimise the dark sides of such a struggle. In an article denunciating the new campaign of arrests of fellow Hizb members in Egypt, the organisation writes:

> The strong campaign against Hizb ut-Tahrir has been continuing for years, and many have been martyred in the prisons of Libya, Iraq, Syria and Uzbekistan. And now we see Egypt pursuing the Shabab[12] with such vigour, with one case after another. [...] This has happened in other areas of Central Asia as well. Also, we see the prisons of Syria full of the Shabab, a number of whom have served their sentences but are still not released; this is leaving aside all those hidden in the corridors of the security services without knowing what their fate will be. There is hardly a prison belonging to the tyrant rulers that does not contain the Shabab of the Hizb. (2-HTB, 26.12.2003)

It is dangerous activism, especially in autocratic regimes, and although HTB encourages (potential) followers, it does not trivialise its dangers. In stark contrast, MI often mocks Muslims living in Germany who are afraid to go to prison (and thus are not as active as others), for it is actually 'not bad' since one can use the time to 'learn the Quran by heart' and 'do a bit of training' (9-MI, 02.2012, 10.2012).

Furthermore, HTB expresses mixed emotions about the 9/11 attacks in its phase of extremism and throughout its other phases. For the organisation, they do not *only* represent a positive event. First, HTB states adamantly that such attacks are not the correct method to fight America's 'dominance over the world' – the re-establishment of the caliphate is. However, HTB also expresses understanding for these forms of action and declares:

> How can America demand that the Muslims join their ranks while their president announces without shame that he will wage a crusade on all Muslims who do not bow before America, and not only on Bin Ladin [sic] and Afghanistan. [...] this haughtiness and arrogance is what gave rise to the hatred for America in the hearts of people and made them sacrifice their lives in order to harm America and seek revenge on her. America is reaping what she has sown. (1-HTB, 18.09.2001)

Thus, it also expresses satisfaction at the US being punished for its 'arrogance'. However, HTB fears the consequences for the Muslim *ummah* more than it is ecstatic about 9/11. It leans thereby towards a negative construction of the meaning of 9/11.

Later, HTB leader Patel would summarise the ambiguity of this event, for the organisation (and the *ummah*), in the following terms:

> The consequences of 9/11, in particular the invasions and occupations of Afghanistan and Iraq, have harmed Muslims and led to the brutal death of thousands. But it has also raised the levels of concern and awareness of Muslims regarding the true nature of America and her allies [sic]. (2-HTB, 29.07.2004)

For HTB, the events of 9/11 eventually brought Muslims together but at a very high price. HTB thus performs emotionally more nuanced interpretations, even in its phase of extremism, than AM and MI.

Overall, contrasted with the other cases, 5-AM and 9-MI perform the narrative with a distinctive emotional tone, extremely negative around the parts of the narrative concerning the international order and the wars against the *ummah* and extremely positive around the parts concerning resistance, jihad, and a future caliphate. This emotional tone conveys absolute clarity about the depth of the dangers the collective is facing and, conversely, the height of the path towards its liberation.

The imperative to *feel* and monopoly on compassion, anger, and love

The third sub-process refers to the emotion rules that the organisations expect members and supporters to follow. The clearer and stricter the emotion rules, the more *collective* the performance of emotion. This section reconstructs the main emotion rules, how these are said to differ from those of the out-groups, and the social effects that a group-appropriate performance is expected to have on collective action.

The organisations' expectation of a collective emotion performance centres around: i. the imperative to *feel* deeply with and for the *ummah*; ii. ascribing radically different emotions to out-groups; iii. asserting a monopoly on compassion, rightful anger, and unconditional love. Further, this section discusses how hatred towards out-groups is performed in some cases and not in others. Noteworthy is that DWR does not perform as many emotion rules as the other three organisations, and when it does, it is not as systematically as HTB, AM, and MI. As such, DWR does not establish emotion rules to the point that they would be truly collectivised. The following developments thus emphasise HTB's, AM's, and MI's phases of activism.

(i.) While the romantic narrative creates expectations towards the performance of collective emotions, in phases of extremism, these expectations turn to commands. Indeed, in the cases 1-HTB, 5-AM, and 9-MI, feeling intensely with and on behalf of the *ummah* is an imperative. It serves to collectivise the emotions of the in-group and eliminate those who do not feel the exact same way. These enemies within are identified either by their complete lack of emotion or their merely hypocritical performance of collective emotions.

The political leaders of Muslim-majority countries are the first targets. HTB, AM, and MI apply themselves to demystify their performance.

Writing about the absence of progress on 'Muslims' issues' at the Islamic summit conference in Malaysia, HTB states: 'They meet and disperse without doing anything good for you. [...] They hand over her [*ummah*] issues to the Kafir colonialists, with submission and disgrace. They feel no shame from Allah and the servants of Allah' (1-HTB, 19.10.2003). Similarly, when the countries of the G8 make 'projects for the Middle East' without consulting with the rulers of the region, HTB is indignant that the latter 'don't feel ashamed nor are they concerned that they will be ruined and their resources plundered' (2-HTB, 09.06.2005). The absence of feelings of shame on the part of Muslim leaders is a recurrent theme in 5-AM and 9-MI as well.

AM claims that the political leaders in Muslim-majority countries are not interested in the feelings of their constituents. In an article dedicated to Palestine, in which the organisation argues that this enduring conflict is an *Islamic* issue, for which the *ummah* has to stand united, AM contends: 'Their real feelings were exposed when Saddam Hussain's intelligence intercepted a conversation between the leaders of Saudi Arabia and Kuwait who were heard saying that Palestine has nothing to do with them' (5-AM, 21.05.2004). The leaders are accused of pretending to feel with the Muslims; their feelings are false, inauthentic. The Muslim leader's performance is judged insincere compared to those who care about the *ummah*'s problems.

HT describes what a *sincere* performance of collective emotions should look like:

> The sincere intellectuals and politicians among the Ummah's sons are asking about the path of liberation, with every crisis or calamity befalling Muslims. They are asking because they deeply feel the pain, distress, and sadness for the state of this good Ummah, the best Ummah, the Ummah of Muhammad. (1-HTB, 21.10.2002)

Since the leaders do not feel – truly and deeply – for, and with, the rest of the *ummah*, they should not be considered part of it any longer. For HTB, the only emotion which Muslim leaders perform authentically is 'false pride'. They have an exaggeratedly high opinion of themselves, which is not based on any real achievements for their Muslim subjects (1-HTB, 26.12.2003). Worse, they look for 'recognition, honour, and pride' from the Western powers (3-HTB, 13.09.2008).

Similarly, MI explains that the rulers in the Muslim world perform only *false* feelings: they prize themselves more highly than they prize the Prophet – an extreme form of vanity – thereby being untruthful about their faith (9-MI, 07.2012). Denouncing an absence of reaction from the rulers of Muslim countries to the caricatures of the Prophet in Europe, MI accuses them of 'disrespect for the emotions of their Muslim subjects and peoples, who are suffering at the pain caused to the Prophet – goodness and peace be upon him' (9-MI, 07.2012). This view is largely shared by AM and HTB. In its phase of extremism, HTB characterises such betrayals[13] as revealing the *hatred* of the Muslim rulers for the *ummah*. Referring to the cooperation of most Muslim countries with the US-led alliance in providing support for attacking Afghanistan, HTB decries:

> The last few days have shown the extent the ruling clans in the Islamic world, including the Arab world, have reached in serving the Kafir and being faithful to him, and the extent of the hatred of these clans for the sons of the Islamic Ummah. (1-HTB, 09.10.2001)

In this, the feelings of the rulers in the Muslim world are equated with those of the Western governments; together, they share a common hatred for the *ummah*.

The three organisations draw similar consequences from this demystification: true believers must practise *takfir* against Muslim rulers because they have become disbelievers (*kuffar*): 'The ruler who does not rule by what has been revealed by Allah and rejects Islam, has been described in the Qur'an as being a kafir' (3-HTB, 13.09.2008). AM and MI expand the practice of *takfir* much further. For AM, it extends to Muslims who support said rulers, Muslims who befriend enemies of the *ummah*, Muslims who deny that the command to 'terrify the enemy of Allah' is part of Islam, and so forth (6-AM, 07.08.2004). Further, practising *takfir* is presented as an obligation upon *all Muslims* as proof of worship to Allah (5-AM, 09.2003; 9-MI, 28.10.2001, 18.05.2012, 11.10.2012).

While HTB does not explicitly mention the concept of *takfir*, the organisation is utterly clear about the fact that the rulers should not be considered part of the *ummah* any longer. In an article dated April 2004, HTB accuses the 'men who have power over the Muslims' of 'sit[ting] as spectators' during the 'brutal aggression' of Iraq (2-HTB, 07.04.2004). Significantly, HTB attributes this passivity to their incapacity to *feel*:

> If it was said that these rulers are dead and there is no life in those whom you call to, then we say the Sharee'ah verdict regarding the dead person is that they should be buried without delay. So who will hasten to bury these rulers, O Muslims, so that your Lord will be pleased with you, your Deen will be honoured, and your enemies humiliated? (2-HTB, 07.04.2004)

The metaphor of leaders being 'dead inside', incapable of feelings, is also found in MI's case. For MI, this danger potentially extends to all believers:[14] the 'death of the hearts' is said to be the 'greatest disease' that might 'ravage someone' (9-MI, 16.11.2011, 01.2013).

Al-Muhajiroun also multiplies the warnings for those who hesitate to practise *takfir*. If a Muslim man or women refuses, they risk being excommunicated too:

> To say the rulers of Muslim countries are not kafir has serious implications. It means that any person can change their deen, kill Muslims, ridicule Allah, his Messenger, the Muslims, the Ulema, the Mujaahideen [sic] and still remain Muslim [...] In order to purify our 'Aqeedah and Tawheed and most importantly: to remain Muslim, we must declare them Kafir, or we too may fall under the banner of kufr. (5-AM, 09.2003)

To remain part of the *ummah*, fellow Muslims have to tread carefully. Both organisations issue reminders of the costs of becoming 'defeated, deviant Muslims' (5-AM, 09.2003; 9-MI, 18.09.2012). From sicknesses and calamities in this world to Allah's discontent and punishments in the hereafter, emotional deviance is interpreted as a form of disbelief.

Cautioning 'ungrateful' Muslims who do not show enough support for the *mujahideen* in Syria, MI leader Mahmoud similarly warns those who feel unconcerned:

> And then some Muslims come and say, aye *ari* [brother] we are in Europe here, why should we care for the other [Muslims]? The one who says that, by Allah, he is not far away from *kufr*! If he is not already a *kafir*.[15] (9-MI, 18.05.2012)

The suspicion of disbelief thus hangs over all who do not perform compassion appropriately. Caring deeply for the *ummah*, that is, performing compassion properly according to the organisations' standards, is not optional; it is imperative so as to remain a Muslim. At stake is the (successful) collectivisation of emotions within each organisation and, beyond that, within the *ummah*.[16] It enables the organisations to sort out the emotionally deviant and 'purify' the group. It also provides a way to fight compassion fatigue and re-actualise the collective emotions which keep extremist activism going.

(ii.) Another striking feature is only present in the cases of extremism: Western political enemies and religious Others are ascribed radically different emotions from those of the Muslim *ummah*. In the organisations' phases of extremism, 'the West' seems to have a limited emotional life.

HTB, AM, and MI often imply that Western states and Westerners feel other emotions than the *ummah*. By that, I do not mean the same emotions in a different way but *strictly separate emotions*. For instance, as opposed to Muslims, Western states and their peoples are said to be incapable of feelings of compassion. While they praise universal human rights and the superiority of international conventions, their actions are said to point to the contrary. For instance, the United States' conduct of the war in Afghanistan is depicted as the 'deliberate' and 'wilful' killing of innocent civilians (1-HTB, 10.12.2001). DWR partakes in this attribution of heartlessness, claiming that Western states and media are unmoved by the massacres of civilians in Syria (8-DWR, 28.05.2012, 08.2013). AM and MI both thematise the US torture of Muslim prisoners, in contempt of the Geneva conventions (5-AM, 11.05.2004; 9-MI, 13.10.2012). MI further depicts Germany – and Europe at large – in an analogous way: 'their soldiers are sent to our lands to torture, rape and slaughter mercilessly our brothers and sisters'[17] (9-MI, 21.09.2012). At home, the German state and its prison guards are said to act ruthlessly against 'innocent Muslim brothers and sisters', 'torturing them on a daily basis'[18] (9-MI, 16.09.2011; 21.09.2012).

In addition, AM and MI deny 'the West' any right to the emotion of *anger*. HTB concedes this emotion to its enemies only a few times – when referring to 'the US anger' at the Muslim world leaders for not cracking down enough on the Hizb (2-HTB, 19.10.2003, 3-HTB, 25.08.2007) – but not once in its phase of extremism.

One of the emotions that the three organisations do ascribe to their enemies is *fear*. As discussed in Chapter 4, Muslim leaders and Western leaders are both said to fear the rise of an Islamic caliphate because it would respectively destroy claims to power over Muslim countries and challenge the current international order. According to HTB, AM, and MI, their fear reveals their weakness. The US, especially, is painted as a colossus with feet of clay. HTB underlines that the alleged military and strategic strength of the US did not prevent it from falling into a 'quagmire' in Afghanistan and Iraq, where US soldiers encountered 'a fierce fighting resistance from the Muslims' which led them ultimately to ask 'their allies for support' (2-HTB, 24.02.2005, 09.06.2005, 20.10.2006).

Similarly, AM points out that 'the USA [is] shaking and [is] terrified by a tiny portion of the Muslims who live in caves and fear none but Allah' (5-AM, 14.08.2003). Western states are losing their battles because they fear Islam and Allah's soldiers. MI draws identical conclusions regarding the success of the Quran distribution campaign in German cities. The German state is said to crack down on the *LIES!* campaign because it *fears* the strength of the Quranic message: 'Germany belongs to the strongest countries militarily and economically. And what shook it, what made it tremble?!! [...] A Quran, *allahu akbar* [Allah is greatest], a Quran, a book'[19] (9-MI, 10/11.2012). In short, the emotions of the enemies are collectivised as well, and they are cast as radically different from the emotions of the Muslim *ummah*.

(iii.) Conversely, true Muslims embody the very emotions 'the West' is denied or incapable of. Especially in phases of extremism, the *ummah*'s emotional life is presented by HTB, AM, and MI as diametrically opposite to the West's. True Muslims are said to show unlimited compassion for other Muslims, perform rightful anger at the enemies, and not know fear except in relation to Allah.

First, for the three organisations, compassion is measured by how much one empathises with suffering Muslims worldwide – and with them only. Their pain must be felt deeply, continuously, despite the distance, because all belong to the same *ummah*. HTB talks about the 'love, concern, and brotherhood that exist amongst Muslims for one another' and their refusal to abandon their fellow Muslims (3-HTB, 16.08.2008; also in 8-DWR[20]). As MI puts it, 'the pain of any Muslim at the end of China pains his brother in the vast Maghreb!'[21] (9-MI, 19.11.2011). According to the organisation, 'the affection, or compassion, for the believers must be in all concerns'[22] (9-MI, 10.2012).

For HTB, AM, and MI, compassion for, and love towards, the believers are one and the same thing. In its phase of extremism, AM makes references to Quranic passages to that effect:

> The prophet Muhammad said:
> 'My Ummah is like a body, if one part of it aches and shivers in pain, the rest of the body aches and shivers in pain' [...]
> We the Muslims feel the pain and the anguish of the Muslims who are suffering by the hands of the very regimes which you and I reside under, like Britain. (5-AM, 03.12.2002; layout in the original)

And here again:

> 'The example of the believers in the way that they look after each other is as one body – if one part of it suffers then all of it suffers' ... And the most important part of the body is the heart. (5-AM, 21.05.2004)

The body metaphor is narrated in several variations. MI recounts the sayings of the Prophet as follows:

> One of you is not devout until he loves for his brother what he loves for himself. And he said: 'The love, compassion, and solidarity for one another is like one body, if any part of it suffers, the rest of the body follows it with fever and sleeplessness'.[23] (9-MI, 16.11.2011; also in 18.05.2012; and 5-AM, 14.08.2003, 21.05.2004)

What would be a more extreme form of empathy – putting oneself in the position of the other and feeling his/her emotions – than falling ill with the sick? Both organisations push compassion so far that it becomes boundless empathy and one's physical body disappears before the collective body. Boundless empathy becomes the basis for sacrifice.

The choice of the body metaphor by AM and MI, compared to HTB and DWR,[24] is interesting in further respects. The characterisation of the *ummah* as a (female) body couples loyalty to a transnational community of Muslims with gendered constructions of masculinity and femininity, in which women reproduce the nation and men protect and avenge it. AM and MI often address Muslims *men* in particular. References to the *ummah* – meaning 'nation' in Arabic – as a body naturalise such constructions, a practice well documented in nationalism and gender studies (Connor, 1993; Peterson, 1994; Pettman, 1996; Najmabadi, 1997; Eriksen, 2004; Safran, 2008; Juergensmeyer, 2010; Mostov, 2012). However, compared to most nationalist performances of emotion, AM and MI expect Muslim *men* to feel boundless empathy with, and love towards, all other Muslims, not just towards 'the motherland'. Further, they expect Muslim *men* to feel empathy and love in a way that would be stereotyped as *female* in most Western societies, such as crying or singing one's pain out. In linking masculinity with the performance of compassion for other Muslims, AM and MI construct meanings around the protection of the *ummah* in a partly different way from traditional nationalist discourses.

Boundless empathy towards true believers is parochial, though, as all other human beings are excluded from it. AM is most explicit about the boundaries of empathy:

> It is well known that it is not allowed to feel any sympathy for the kuffar [...] Not only is it obligatory to fight them, it is haram[25] to feel sorry for them when they are killed. It is haram for us to feel sorry for them when Allah sends on them [sic] natural disasters, let alone when they are killed deliberately for the sake of Allah [i.e. in jihad]. Moreover, Allah (swt) says.
>
> 'Fight them, Allah will punish them with your hands, and humiliate them and support you against them and cure the hearts of the believers ...' [EMQ 9: 14]
>
> Allah made it clear for us that any calamity that occurs to them will make us satisfied in our hearts (6-AM, 07.08.2004, layout in the original).

The words chosen are significant: Not only is it prohibited to *display* sympathy for political enemies and (non-)religious others, but Muslims are also not allowed to *feel* sympathy or *feel* sorry for them. AM expects fellow Muslims not just to perform appropriately but to actively work on suppressing illegitimate emotions towards non-Muslim Others. MI similarly expects followers to suppress such feelings towards out-groups (9-MI, 10.2012).

Second, contrarily to their enemies, true believers have an exclusive right to anger. The organisations perform *anger at* enemies in several ways: for themselves, for fellow Muslims worldwide, and/or for Allah and his Prophet. The very words 'anger' and 'rage' appear almost exclusively in 9-MI, with only a few instances in 5-AM and 1-HTB. However, the emotions themselves are omnipresent in the cases of extremism and, to a large extent, in the cases of radicalisation. In HTB, anger is first displayed at the leaders of the Muslim world: 'Hizb ut-Tahrir warns the traitorous rulers of the wrath of Allah and the anger of Allah's servants' (2-HTB, 26.12.2003; see also 20.03.2002). The US and its allies are a close second, with HTB performing strong anger at the West for their 'war on Islam and the Muslims'. AM's anger is primarily targeted at the US and the UK, especially after the revelations about Abu Ghraib and Guantanamo Bay (5-AM, 11.05.2004, 27.05.2004). Anger at political and/or religious leaders is less frequently displayed by AM and MI (5-AM, 03.12.2002; 9-MI, 09.2012).

Often, MI shows anger at enemies *for Allah*. Not on behalf of, but as a proof of love for and loyalty to Allah and the Prophet Muhammad. Quoting the Imam Ibn Al-Qayyim, MI states authoritatively: 'The more the heart is alive, the stronger is its anger for Allah and His Messenger, and the more absolute is its support for the religion!'[26] (9-MI, 16.11.2011). In short, those who do not perform strong anger *for* Allah are 'less alive' and maybe do not love Allah as much as they claim. Further, MI hints at the attitudinal impact of rightful anger: the experience of (collective) rightful anger precludes the possibility of doubt. Rightful anger at an Other attributes clear responsibility to him/her and dismisses one's own, as well as other (potential) parties to blame. In the absence of doubt, support for the cause of Allah becomes absolute.

Third, true believers are *alien* to feelings of fear, except in their reverence for Allah. For all four organisations, Muslims are necessarily God-fearing.[27] The question is whether they fear God *enough*. MI is at the forefront of emotion work in this regard. The organisation admonishes members and followers who hesitate to help their fellow Muslims and urges them to fear Allah *more* (9-MI, 16.11.2011, 02.2012; also in 8-DWR, 21.04.2013, 05.2012). Further, it warns its members – and true believers at large – that Allah will replace the Muslim *ummah* if Muslims do not follow his commands. Quoting the Quran, MI threatens: 'And if you refuse, Allah will replace you with another people and you do not harm him in any way' (9-MI, 16.11.2012). Conversely, those who fear Allah appropriately and show *trust* in him, even through adversity and trials, are part of the chosen, the vanguard. Writing an article about an imprisoned 'Muslim sister', MI leader Mahmoud is adamant:

> The test must come so that Allah purifies the ranks and purges out those with weak hearts, and then will Allah's victory come! [...] So, thank Allah, O sister, for having chosen you from the millions [of Muslims] to carry His religion and to be tested on His path because, I swear, this is a great honour, that no one receives, except the one Allah has chosen! (9-MI, 19.11.2011; original in Appendix B3, quote n°5)

Such trials are deemed necessary to sort out those who are afraid of suffering for Islam. Further, trials should be viewed positively because good deeds bring rewards from God. Accepting sufferings and trials is conceived as a necessary proof of faith – which ultimately constitutes the basic tenet of martyrdom.

Except for Allah, true believers would fear nothing and no one. They would show great courage in battles, even when the odds are against them, and not fear the consequences.[28] HTB depicts the soldiers of Islam as the opposite of Western soldiers: 'The tyrant forces have begun to retreat [...] even though they have much by way of weaponry they lack men of courage and resolve to face the armies of Islam' (2-HTB, 24.02.2005). MI makes references to the bravery of the *mujahideen* worldwide. In a very long text (4,400 words), published for the beginning of Ramadan in July 2012, MI portrays the recent battles won by the *mujahideen* globally. With much pathos, it depicts the *mujahideen* as 'heroes' and congratulates them for their sacrifice:

> You are the ones, with your fragrant blood, who water the tree of life of the Islamic ummah, under whose shades the Muslims can enjoy the protection of the Islamic shari'ah state. [...] They [*mujahideen*] refuse to live, except under the shades and the dominance of the Islamic shari'ah. They take no path but the short path, which is the path of jihad, to restore the ummah's honour, pride, and awe. (9-MI, 07.2012; original in Appendix B3, quote n°6)

Sacrifice is also writ large in AM and HTB. AM does not root sacrifice in *bravery* like MI or HTB, though. For AM, all true believers, not just Muslim soldiers or the *mujahideen*, are fearless.[29]

In a piece dedicated to bin Laden's audiotape 'Message to Europe' (15 April 2004), AM explains:

> Even Jack Straw[30] came out and said, 'These are people (i.e. Al Qaeda, etc.) who do not fear death'. Muslims do not fear death as we know those killed in the struggle to make Islam the highest are in Jannah (Paradise), whilst the disbelievers (kuffar) are in the Naar (hellfire), hence [this is] why Sheikh Osama says later in his letter *'For those who reject reconciliation and want war, we are ready'*. (5-AM, 22.04.2004; emphasis in the original).

AM believes that this world is merely transitory and the hereafter is what matters; as such, death *in this world* does not constitute an object of fear but rather a necessary transition. In this view, nothing is easier than sacrifice for Allah. While fearlessness is a practical impossibility, AM establishes it nonetheless as the gold standard for all Muslims.

Finally, what about feelings of hate? Is hatred not potentially an emotion shared by both in- and out-groups in their relation to each other? For HTB and DWR, hatred is an emotion only attributed to political enemies and (non-)religious Others – true believers do not *hate* others. Reversing the stigma attributed to Muslim minorities, HTB interprets the Muhammad caricatures as an example of European countries' 'historic persecution of minorities' and stresses:

> Muslims are often told that our responses are too emotional, but their attacks on Islam are little more than vitriolic hatred. When it comes to Islam, they make emotional rants and spread lies. (3-HTB, 29.03.2008)

Similar arguments are made by DWR a few years later during Germany's very own caricature controversy (8-DWR, 03.05.2012). Responding to those who have labelled him a 'hate preacher' because of how his organisation propagates Islam, DWR leader Abou Nagie claims that he warns non-Muslims (that they will go to hell if they don't convert to Islam) not out of hatred but 'out of gratitude towards his fellow humans' (8-DWR, 24.05.2012). In HTB and DWR cases, hatred is not part of the in-group's performance of emotions.[31] 'True believers' are above feelings of hatred, which remain an exclusive attribute of out-groups. This sharp distinction allows the organisations to claim the moral high ground.

In their respective phase of extremism, MI and AM diverge from HTB and DWR on this account. MI and AM urge their followers to revive *al-wala wal-bara*, that is, loyalty to the Muslims and disavowal and rejection of the disbelievers. With this, they draw on Wahhabi and Salafi doctrine and emphasise two passages of the Quran (sura 60 'al-Mumtahanah'). AM and MI translate this precept into emotional terms for their members (and Muslims at large) to follow, that is, into an emotion rule. Exemplarily, AM reframes the Quranic passages as follows: 'O Believers in Allah and the Final Abode, Allah (swt) has ordained for you to hate, distance, and reject the Kuffar and Love, Support and ally with the Believers' (5-AM, 06.2004;[32] capitals in the original). Rejecting disbelievers is hereby equated with *hating* them, whereas proving support to the believers is equated with *loving* them. *Al-wala wal-bara* is transformed into an emotion rule.

It is safe to assume that HTB and DWR know the sura 'al-Mumtahanah' as well, yet the two organisations do not mention it in the corpus. It may be because they interpret it differently – which is most probably HTB's case, as it does not subscribe to a Salafi interpretation – or choose not to use it for strategic reasons – which is probably DWR's case, as it would attract the unwanted attention of security agencies. So why would AM and MI establish it as an emotion rule when it could be detrimental to claiming the moral high ground? A potential interpretation is that the performance of boundless empathy towards the *ummah* lowers the threshold for feelings of hatred. If both organisations perform such an extreme form of empathy (encouraging the negation of one's own body), they are more likely to perform other 'extreme' emotions. When one is ready to sacrifice the self completely, what is hatred against the enemy?

A closer look at what *al-wala wal-bara* would entail as an emotion rule opens further interpretations. First, love for the believers goes beyond the performance of compassion discussed previously. AM and MI conceive of love as affection *and* unconditional support for fellow Muslims. It is a demanding conception, for it means that 'a Muslim must always stand side by side with his fellow Muslim' (5-AM, 09.2003), 'even if you disapprove of the actions of said Muslim' (9-MI, 16.11.2011[33]). Criticism is not allowed. For instance, speaking ill about the *ummah*'s *mujahideen* is unacceptable, as each Muslim should be grateful that 'they defend *their* honour and pride' (9-MI, 01.2013, emphasis added; also in 10.2012). MI's articles by Sami J. (aka Abu Assad al-Almani) take clear paternalistic overtones regarding love:

> Our life before your life and thus our blood before your blood. [...] Our bodies ache from overcoming the obstacles that you put in our path. Yet we accept all this sorrow and all these tortures on the path to satisfy the Glorified.[34] (9-MI, 12.01.2013, 07.2012)

Even when some Muslims don't reciprocate their affection or deny them recognition (or when their help is unsolicited!), the *mujahideen* would still fight to protect Muslims because they would love unconditionally and know best what the *ummah* needs.

Showing hatred towards disbelievers has to be unconditional as well, insofar as it is *prescribed* by Allah (5-AM, 09.2003, 21.05.2004; 9-MI, 10.2011). This is not a choice – the organisations deflect thereby any blame – but a command. Interestingly though, AM differentiates between *hatred* and *injustice* towards disbelievers:

> As for the feelings that we must have towards non-Muslims, the Messenger Muhammad (saw) was once asked by a Jew: 'Do you like me?' To which he replied: 'No, I hate you, but I will never be unjust towards you.' i.e. that he would treat them in accordance with the divine justice of Islam although he (saw) had no love whatsoever in his heart towards the Jew. (5-AM, 09.2003)

For the organisation, hating the (non-)religious Other – who often overlap with political enemies in AM's case – would not be incompatible with showing fairness in the application of sharia law.[35]

AM's and MI's respective understanding of hatred differs somewhat. For the former, 'Muslims hate the USA' primarily because of its current actions against the *ummah* and, secondarily, because of its disbelief (6-AM, 07.08.2004). In contrast, the latter argues that Muslims ought to fight against Western countries because they must fight disbelief wherever it is and even more so when disbelievers happen to be at war with the *ummah* (9-MI, 10.2011, 16.11.2012, 15.03.2013). Thus, for MI, the Other must be hated primarily because of its nature. On two occasions, this rule draws on the evident dehumanisation of disbelievers (9-MI, 21.09.2012, 11.10.2012). Both times it happens right after events seen by the organisa- tion as deeply humiliating for the *ummah*: the caricature contest organised by the right-wing party ProNRW and the release of the US short film depict- ing the Prophet's life, with a German actor playing the Prophet.

At any rate, by their logic, AM and MI would *share* feelings of hatred with their enemies: they would hate 'the West' and 'disbelievers' as much as those would hate the Muslims and the *ummah*. In turn, this weakens the idea that the *ummah* leads a completely different emotional life from that of its enemies. This performance of hatred towards political enemies may be conceived as a reaction to the (alleged) trans-historical hatred of the West for the Muslim *ummah*, in the sense of 'our enemies started it'. This argument makes Western states and their allies responsible for the *ummah*'s feelings of hatred against them, whereby the organisations may still claim some moral high ground. Some evidence points to this interpreta- tion. AM and MI consider that Muslims must *practise* hatred (on behalf of Allah and the *ummah*) to differentiate clearly friends from foes and be able to act upon it. The repetition of the necessity to *practise* hatred implies that fellow Muslims would not be used to performing this emotion. It provides a way to exculpate the collective: Muslims would hate *for Allah*, not for themselves.

Finally, hatred and love are perceived as necessary to fight enemies. Indeed, AM and MI establish a causal relationship between hating for Allah and showing the enemies hostility *in action* by fighting. Talking about the leaders of the 'traitorous kingdom' of Saudi Arabia, MI leader Cuspert claims: 'I hate them for Allah, and I am ready to fight against them at all costs'[36] (9-MI, 11.2011; see also 18.05.2012, 10.2012). Interestingly, love is as much actionable as hatred, maybe even more so. While jihad is presented first and foremost as a duty, MI claims that fighting is supposed to come naturally to true believers, 'out of love for the *ummah*' (9-MI, 11.10.2012, 01.03.2013). AM also sees the clear 'distinction in our [i.e. Muslims'] feelings' towards believers on one side and disbelievers on the other as expedient for collective and individual action (5-AM, 09.2003). In any case, MI and AM successfully impose 'hating and loving for Allah' as an emotion rule.

Beyond this specificity, HTB, AM, and MI establish similar and par- ticularly strict emotion rules for their members and fellow Muslims to follow. DWR performs (limitedly) part of them. In phases of extremism (1-HTB, 5-AM, 9-MI), organisations collectivise *both* the emotions of the out-groups and those of the in-group. Muslims who do not feel the way HTB, AM, and MI posit as appropriate incur the risk of being rejected, not only by the organisation but also by the *ummah*. They successfully establish clear and strict emotion rules bent on incentivising members and followers to take collective and individual action.

Consistent performances of emotions?

The fourth and last sub-process of narrative emotionalisation refers to the repetitive character of the performance of emotion within an organisation's narrative. The more consistently the performance of emotions is re-actualised, the more intensity it gains. Studying this process means assessing the extent to which collective emotions are performed in a similar way across narrative occurrences. While the temporal character of narrative emotionalisation was implicit in the first three sub-processes, here it is addressed more directly. I lay the emphasis on the consistency of emotion rules through time and, when applicable, across leaders. In practical terms, I trace *inconsistencies* in the performance of emotions across narrative occurrences. For the German cases, as the data is mainly composed of audios and videos with clear authorship, I further explore whether potential inconsistencies can be linked back to the different leaders.

The cases corresponding to AM's phases of activism can be interpreted in comparison as partly consistent (4-AM) to very consistent (5-AM and 6-AM). While mixed emotions towards certain events were performed in its phase of radicalisation into extremism (4-AM), these were suppressed in the transition to its phase of extremism (5-AM). Also, the emotion rules established by the organisation are consistent within its respective phases of activism. While the specific authorship of each text composing the data is not known – as they are uniformly signed with the organisation's logo, '*Al-Muhajiroun. The voice, the eyes & the ears of the Muslims*' – they appear extraordinarily similar. There is only one exception in the corpus: a statement written by Abu Muhammad (a member of the evasive 'Muslim Youth Forum') in conjunction with AM. In this text, the author does not perform dissimilar emotions towards narrative events or objects, nor does he introduce a new and contradictory emotion rule. Whether AM leader Omar Bakri Mohammed authored all other texts, or whether top members Anjem Choudary and Hassan Butt reproduced his prose becomes irrelevant; the overall performance of emotions is repeated most consistently.

Next, the cases corresponding to HTB's phases of activism can be interpreted as very consistent (1-HTB) to only partly consistent (2-HTB, 3-HTB). First, there is no dissimilarity in the performance of emotions in the texts written by HTB compared to the few texts written by HT Pakistan and published on HTB's website. While HT Pakistan focuses on Pakistani issues to exemplify the dangers of a Western-dominated international order, how emotions are performed is amazingly similar to HTB's texts. Second, regarding the first and second sub-process, the analysis showed that in its phase of moderation within extremism (2-HTB) and radicalisation (3-HTB), the organisation provides, at times, explanations for out-group action which deviate from emotion-based knowledge and that mixed emotions sometimes endured, notably regarding 9/11.

Regarding the third sub-process, in its phase of extremism (1-HTB) and moderation within extremism (2-HTB), there is no departure from the established emotion rules (feeling deeply, compassionately with the *ummah*, being angry at the Muslim rulers and their allies, and rejecting fear except in reference to Allah). In its phase of radicalisation (3-HTB), however, while the organisation continues to perform love, compassion, and anger, it also performs *disappointment in* and *anger at* the *ummah* in several narrative occurrences. For instance, in an article dated 25 November 2007, HTB denounces how the 'agent rulers betray[ed]' Muslims once more, this time at a summit organised by Bush in Annapolis, and 'surrendered Palestine',[37] and blames therein the *ummah* for its lack of reaction:

> But the most strange thing is that the great Ummah of Islam is silent over their treacherous deeds while they are bent upon destroying the lands and people consistently. [...] Why will the bloods [sic] of this Ummah which overpowered the Tatars, the Crusaders, and captured Constantinople, not curdle in its veins? How can it remain a silent spectator while Bush and his European allies and Jews buy and sell its lands? How?? (3-HTB, 25.11.2007)

Similar instances of disappointment in, and anger at, fellow Muslims are found, for instance, towards Pakistani Muslims who are said to have accepted Musharraf's betrayals for too long (3-HTB, 17.09.2007, 29.11.2007, 26.01.2008). The organisation thus departs several times from performing according to the rule 'unambiguous love and compassion towards the *ummah*'. In-between, HTB publishes other texts in which the performance of emotions corresponds again to the emotion rules previously established. Overall, the performance of emotions in its phase of radicalisation is much less consistent than in the organisation's phase of extremism.

In DWR's phase of radicalisation (8-DWR), the performance of emotions is not always consistent across *leaders*. DWR's three leading figures – Abou Nagie, el Emrani (aka Abu Dujana), and Belkaid (aka Abu Abdullah) – do implement the following emotion rules jointly: fear of Allah, compassion for the believers (not boundless though), and anger at out-groups. However, they sometimes perform emotions outside of these rules and not always uniformly (across leaders). The overall performance of emotions is less recognisable than in the phases of radicalisation of HTB and AM and appears at times dissonant.

Leader Abou Nagie performs *pride* on many occasions. For him, Muslims ought to be proud of their religion and each other (8-DWR, 19.08.2010, 12.2011, 25.10.2012) and proud to live like the *salaf*, the pious predecessors (8-DWR, 24.05.2012). While this performance is not contradictory to the emotion rules established by the group, it is not performed by the other two leaders.[38] Pride is not successfully established as an emotion rule. Further, Abou Nagie performs *love* towards 'non-Muslims' and 'all humans' several times (8-DWR, 24.05.2012, 25.10.2012), which represents a clear departure from the exclusive rule 'compassion and love for the believers'.

El Emrani's performance of emotions derogates on occasion from emotion rules otherwise established during DWR's phase of radicalisation. In a video, he vents *anger* at Muslims living in Western countries. Further, he performs *hatred* towards Muslim rulers and their Western allies several times. Anger at the in-group is interesting insofar as it diverges from the rest of his videos;[39] it might represent a minor inconsistency if it was not for similar evidence in Belkaid's performance (see below). *Hatred* towards out-groups is more problematic. In videos in which he talks about the Syrian civil war, el Emrani goes beyond the group-appropriate performance of *anger* at Syria's president and performs hatred. Characterising el-Assad and his soldiers, he states: 'Women are being raped, dear brothers and sisters, *wallahi* [by Allah], our sisters are being raped by these animals ... May Allah punish them!'[40] (8-DWR, 28.05.2012). Similarly, anger at Western state leaders and the UN Secretary-General is mixed with hatred: 'Do not be fooled, dear brothers and sisters, when one of these dogs comes out and says, "we condemn this" [...] What condemnation?! For over a year, people are being slaughtered and killed!'[41] (8-DWR, 28.05.2012; see also 08.2013). The reference to animality is a typical expression of hatred, which diverges from the performances by Abou Nagie and Belkaid, who maintain the distinction of the in- and out-groups' emotional lives (e.g. Muslims do not hate / the enemies of the *ummah* hate Muslims).

The third leader, Belkaid, performs anger at *the believers* powerfully on one occasion, tainting anger with sadness, disappointment, and shame:

> Allah's Messenger said: If Syria is lost, if you lose Syria, *al-Sham*, then there is nothing good in you, nothing good in you, dear brothers and sisters. Nothing good in you, [*voice shaking and crying*] nothing good in you at all, if Syria is lost.[42] (8-DWR, 21.04.2013)

With guilt-laden efficacy, Belkaid establishes that Syrian Muslims and German Muslims have a common destiny – if Muslims worldwide do not help in Syria, they will be lost as well – and tries to shame German Muslim men specifically[43] into taking decisive action.

Overall, while the performance of positive emotions towards the believers remains dominant, el Emrani's and Belkaid's performing anger at German Muslims reads as an incongruity. Combined, it signals an inconsistent performance of the emotion rule 'compassion and love for the *ummah*' and clashes with Abou Nagie's lone performance of 'pride'. DWR performs emotions repeatedly in a dissonant way across its phase of radicalisation. The consistency of its performance is much weaker compared to the other organisations so far.

In MI's case (9-MI), the key figures of the organisation uniformly establish the following rules: compassion for the believers, no fear (bravery), anger at the outgroups, and loving and hating for Allah. These four rules are consistently re-actualised across all texts and visuals. The performance of these emotions appears truly collectivised.

However, what demarcates MI's performance from the other organisations is the conjunct performance of *pride* by its leaders and top members. Mahmoud, Cuspert, Keskin, and Sami J. alternate the positive and negative performance of pride. They provide, in turn, positive examples for being proud group members *and* negative examples of fellow Muslims not behaving as they ought to and lessening thereby pride in the collective.

An example of the positive performance of *pride* is the following declaration by Cuspert in a video entitled 'Where are your honour and your pride?'[44]

> Only Allah s.w.t. could give me pride and honour, true pride and honour, and *wallahi* he gave them to me. *Alhamdulillah,* I am proud to be a Muslim. [...] *Alhamdulillah,* I am proud that I have met the brother Abu Usama al-Gharib. *Alhamdulillah* here is a brother, from whom I can say, he is a brother with honour, and I am honoured to have a brother like him. (11.2011, see also 03.05.2012; original in Appendix B3, quote n°7)

In this passage, Cuspert makes clear that the honour and pride of fellow group members impact one's honour and pride – here in relation to co-leader Mahmoud (aka Abu Usama al-Gharib). In a similar vein, Mahmoud reverses the stigmata against the Quran and performs pride instead:

> Yes, dear brothers and sisters, the word 'kill' occurs about 128 times in the Quran, of which 27 times in the imperative. They thought they would provoke us with this, that we would be ashamed of Islam. Well, 'kill' occurs 128 times in the Quran, of which 27 times in the imperative, if this *kafir* counted correctly, and we are proud of it. We are proud of it! (11.2012; original in Appendix B3, quote n°8)

The criteria for pride are to be found within the *ummah*, not outside of it and not according to criteria made by out-groups.

In case positive performances of why fellow Muslims should feel proud and live a life of honour (by engaging in violent activism) are not enough, MI leaders also provide negative incentives. In a video entitled 'How long should this life of humiliation go on?',[45] Keskin attacks followers' feelings of pride to spur collective action:

> Alone the pictures from Syria! Hm, from Afghanistan! From Iraq! From Chechnya! From Somalia ... should be enough for you! It should be enough for anyone who has a portion of honour or a portion of pride!! Because the heart should be burning, the heart should be burning! We should be crying! [...] Return [to Islam], before it is too late, for this *ummah* needs lions, needs soldiers who work for Allah the Mighty and Sublime! (01.2013, also in 10.2012; original in Appendix B3, quote n°9)

Keskin appears to goad his audience into feeling unworthy as long as Muslim *men* have not all committed themselves to armed struggle. Similarly, in an article denouncing new attacks on Islam's Prophet, Sami J. mocks fellow German Muslims for their attachment to the transient world:

> Due to your lack of eagerness, the German crusaders have once again managed to demonstrate their hatred of Islam; and due to your love for the *Dunya* [this world], you Muslims in Germany have once again proved that your lives matter more to you than the honour of Allah's noble Messenger a.s.s. (21.09.2012; original in Appendix B3, quote n°10)

At the end of the article, Sami J. calls *the same audience* to 'organise into groups' and 'conduct operations' to take revenge on those who 'drag the Prophet through the dirt'. Further, he contends that it is not too late to 'write your actions with your blood' and 'live in pride' as the *sahaba* did at the time of the Prophet. Hence, much like Keskin, he offers the possibility to repent, change one's ways, and do the right thing at long last, that is, sacrifice oneself.

Overall, positive and negative performances of pride alternate in much of MI's corpus. Also, the organisation's leaders are alternating roles: Cuspert and Mahmoud also shame fellow Muslims on occasion (Cuspert, 31.12.2013; Mahmoud, 18.05.2012, 16.11.2012), whereas Sami J. regularly renders ecstatic performances of honour and pride as well (11.10.2012, 12.01.2013). Compared to DWR's embryonic performance of anger at fellow Muslims, MI's performance of *pride* does not lead to the inconsistency of the group's overall performance of emotions. First, pride is not incompatible with the other rules established by the organisation. Second, while initially perplexing, the alternation of positive and negative performances of pride appears systematic: all key figures partake in it. The performance of pride can be interpreted as constituting a complementary emotion rule.

Turning now to the comparison between cases, AM's performance of emotions appears very consistent in 5-AM and 6-AM, respectively, and less consistent in 4-AM (radicalisation phase). HTB's is consistent in its phase of extremism (1-HTB) and phase of moderation within extremism (2-HTB) but less consistent in its phase of radicalisation (3-HTB). DWR's performance of emotions is repeatedly inconsistent in its radicalisation phase (8-DWR). Finally, MI's performance appears consistent (9-MI). Together, these interpretations point to a major difference between phases of radicalisation into extremism and phases of extremism. Organisations perform emotions less consistently in phases of radicalisation than in phases of moderation within extremism and phases of extremism.

The 4th sub-process unfolds fully only in the latter. In phases of extremism and moderation within extremism, the performance of emotions is consistently repeated and thereby normalised. Group-appropriate emotion rules become, for instance, truly institutionalised. The collective emotional meanings constituted through the other three sub-processes become all the more powerful. The performance's continued reactivation allows organisations to maintain a high level of commitment from members and incentivise individual and collective action.

The intensity of emotionalisation in comparison

The interpretation of the processes of emotionalisation has made apparent key differences between the cases. In comparison, all four sub-processes unfold in the cases of extremism, whereas they only partially unfold in the cases of radicalisation and of moderation within extremism. Thus, in phases of extremism, the full emotionalisation of organisations' narrative can be interpreted as a (temporary) performative success.

First, organisations establish the primacy of emotion-based knowledge in phases of extremism, as well as in the cases 3-HTB and 8-DWR corresponding to phases of radicalisation. They dismiss other forms of knowledge as false or ignorant. Further, the feelings of out-groups towards Muslims explain why out-groups would act or not act. Other explanations for out-group (in)action disappear, especially in 1-HTB, 5-AM, and 9-MI, the cases of extremism. Finally, the organisations encourage members to work on their emotions, not only by suppressing or amplifying certain emotions (i.e. the third sub-process) but also by transforming negative emotional experiences into pieces of knowledge about the dangers faced by the in-group.

In the cases of extremism, emotion-based experience emerges as an actionable form of knowledge.

Second, emotional meanings are less nuanced, less mixed, in the cases of extremism and, to some extent, in the cases of radicalisation. Organisations in phases of extremism – and DWR in its phase of radicalisation – have largely eliminated conflicting emotional meanings. Especially in 5-AM and 9-MI, and to a large extent in 1-HTB, organisations perform highly negative emotions and highly positive emotions towards *strictly separate* objects and actions: on one side, the international order and the wars of aggression against the *ummah*, and, on the other side, towards a future caliphate, resistance, and jihad. As a result, a distinctive emotional tone emerges, which conveys absolute clarity about the depth of the dangers the collective is facing and, conversely, the height of the path towards its liberation.

Third, the organisations establish and enforce emotion rules to diverse degrees. While the imperative to feel deeply with and on behalf of the *ummah* is performed both in phases of radicalisation and phases of extremism, it is much more pronounced in the latter. The organisations ascribe *distinct* emotions to Other(s) only in phases of extremism. In 5-AM, 9-MI, and 1-HTB, the organisations attribute a reduced emotional life to Western countries and Muslim rulers, whereas true Muslims embody the very emotions that these Others are denied. The emotional rules set by the three organisations are rigorous, the performance is collectivised, and the costs of non-performance are very high. AM and MI perform additionally 'unconditional love and hate' in phases of extremism, sealing thereby even more tightly the boundaries of their emotional community.

Fourth, tracing the consistency of the performance of emotions highlighted that AM cases, HTB cases (except 3-HTB), and MI's case are the most consistent. DWR's performance of emotions is less collectivised, less systematic, and at times discontinued. Similarly, in its phase of re-radicalisation (3-HTB), HTB articulates conflicting emotional meanings and its performance of emotions deviates in some texts from the emotion rules previously established, which weakens the consistency of its performance. In MI's case, the alternate performance of *pride* by the four leading figures appears systematic enough not to be detrimental to the organisation's overall performance. Thus consistently repeated, such performances tie past, present, and future emotional experiences together and present the political issues addressed in each narrative occurrence as of existential importance.

In summary, the cases of radicalisation – 3-HTB, 4-AM, and 8-DWR – only partially display the four sub-processes characteristic of narrative emotionalisation. Conversely, in the phases of extremism, the four sub-processes unfold strongly (1-HTB) to very strongly (5-AM and 9-MI) in the organisations' narrative performance. In such phases, the romantic narrative is intensely emotionalised; it pushes for decisive collective and individual action.

Among the three cases of extremism, subtle differences can nonetheless be noted. The analysis highlighted the strong similarity between 5-AM and 9-MI, especially in how the first three sub-processes of narrative emotionalisation unfold. Conversely, in its phase of extremism, HTB brings more nuance into the narrative by, at times, attributing diverse motives to enemies (even though the primary ones are emotional), providing a more complex interpretation of events and not concealing the hardships of resistance and jihad. Aside from this, HTB establishes emotion rules strikingly similar to AM's and MI's and, as well, enforces them as strictly, even though AM and MI are often blunter about it.[46] Furthermore, its performance in this phase is most consistent, same as AM and MI.

The absence of hatred towards enemies most strikingly distinguishes HTB's performance of emotions from the other two. Throughout the organisation's narrative, hatred is performed only *by enemies* against Muslims. Contrarily, in their phases of extremism, AM and MI address at length Muslims' necessary hatred for disbelievers. This is particularly interesting, as it indicates that not only is hatred not performed by organisations in phases of radicalisation into extremism (as 3-HTB, 4-AM, and 8-DWR show), *nor* is it necessarily performed in phases of extremism (as 1-HTB shows). This suggests that group hatred for out-groups would not play a role in radicalisation into extremism and not necessarily play one in phases of extremism either.

Lastly, there are subtle differences in the degree of emotionalisation between AM and MI. For instance, MI performs rightful anger, unconditional love for Allah and the believers, and hatred towards disbelievers even more absolutely. For one thing, it performs anger against all *'kuffar'* equally: the organisation makes no difference between the US and European countries in terms of wrongdoings. Also, the organisation is more exhaustive in its rejection of *kufr*, just like *al-Qaeda*, it hates the US and European states as well as their *populations* (9-MI, 10.2011, 01.2013, 10.2012). Finally, MI stresses virile masculinity much more than any other organisation as part of its performance of pride, multiplying misanthropic statements about gender.[47]

Beyond these group-specific variations, the romantic narrative is fully emotionalised in the three cases representing phases of extremism. The primacy of emotion-based knowledge discards other ways to experience and know; it binds individual and collective experience together and confounds them. The organisation's emotional knowledge becomes the only source of knowledge. The organisation *knows* that armed resistance and the re-establishment of the caliphate are the only legitimate courses of action. The emotional tone is bleak, heavy with suffering – the *ummah* is in grave danger – but there is hope, because fellow Muslims are awakening and rising to their duties. The tone is urgent, pressing; everything can still happen, decisive action is needed. The emotion rules set respectively by the organisations are strict, exacting. They demand clear, continuous commitment, exclusive emotional bonds and allegiances, unconditional support for the collective, also when it implies resorting to extreme means. Every new text, audio, and video is received through the lens of the texts, audios, and videos that came before. Such repetition amplifies the emotionalising effects of the narrative. It reinforces the feeling that action is needed *now*. Collective and individual actions must be decisive; it is right; it *feels* right. Through full narrative emotionalisation, HTB, AM, and MI push members to act according to the narrative's injunctions, to mobilise and engage collectively and individually in fighting back.

Notes

1 Mixed emotions are conceived as the interplay of several emotions, past and present, which may result in confluent or conflictive emotional meanings. Such 'mixtures' can be conscious or unconscious, potentially result in such a complete melting together that the original emotions disappear, and might merge varied emotional experiences (i.e. emotions, affect, feelings, and/or moods) together (Ross, 2014). As mixed emotions are but one dimension among several in the study of the sub-processes, I stick to a short definition.

2 By narrative occurrences, I mean the texts, audios, and visuals produced by an organisation and drawing on the romantic narrative.

3 For instance, 1-HTB, 20.04.2002, 21.10.2002, 13.04.2003; 2-HTB, 19.10.2003; 4-AM, 12.09.2001, 5-AM, 24.08.2003, 22.04.2004.

4 Often defined as a gradual lessening of compassion over time, it is a condition common among individuals who work with victims of disasters, trauma, and war. Some have argued that news and social media contribute in extending this condition more widely to society by saturating media with visual and textual depictions of suffering. For critical views on the risks of desensitisation and growing indifference to 'global suffering', see Kinnick et al. (1996), Moeller (2002), Höijer (2004).

5 German original: 'Guck mal die ganzen Regierung[en], das sind alles Marionetten von der ... von der, vom Westen, ha. Schön eingesetzt, schön reingepflanzt, damit sie unsere Bodenschätze klauen können.'

6 Among others: 1-HTB, 09.10.2001; 2-HTB, 08.11.2003, 17.09.2006; 3-HTB, 16.08.2008; 4-AM, 21.09.2001, 05.04.2002; 5-AM, 09.2003; 8-DWR, 25.10.2012; 9-MI, 07.2012.

7 Immediately after 9/11, bin Laden praises the attacks but denies responsibility for the planning. In November 2002, a letter purportedly from the al-Qaeda

leader explained the motives behind the attacks. Bin Laden would not officially take responsibility for the attacks until late October 2004, in a videotape broadcast by al-Jazeera.

8 AM refers here to a specific passage of the Quran: 'Soon will I cast him [the disbeliever] into Hell-Fire! And what will explain to you what Hell-Fire is? [...] Over it are Nineteen (Angels). And We have set none but angels as Guardians of the Fire.' AM likens the 19 hijackers of the 9/11 attacks to the 19 angels of the Quran.

9 See also 5-AM, 01.08.2003, with a reference to both the US and the UK.

10 Exemplarily in 1-HTB (18.09.2001, 09.10.2001, 20.04.2002) and 5-AM (09.03.2002, 16.02.2003, 27.09.2003).

11 Written by MI member Sami J. aka Abu Assad al-Almani.

12 Refers to 'the youth' of the Hizb, i.e. young party members.

13 Betrayal is a form of non-recognition characterised by the loss of 'trust or a sense of belonging to a family or nation' that proves 'unreliable' (Fattah & Fierke, 2009, p. 72). For the betrayed party, this is an intimate negative experience, inflicted by a party supposed to be on one's side. HTB later openly designates the ruling class in Muslim-majority countries as 'traitors' and 'treacherous rulers' (3-HTB, 25.11.2007).

14 This idea is mentioned once in DWR's phase of radicalisation, in relation to (the lack of) empathy with the (Muslim) victims of the Syrian war: 'what about your hearts, do you have hearts?! That are beating, in which there is blood?' (21.04.2013).

15 German original: 'Dann kommen manche Muslime und sagen, ja *ari* wir sind hier in Europa, was kümmern uns die anderen? Sagen wir ... eh wer das sagt, wallahi, der ist nicht weit von *kufr* entfernt! Wenn er nicht schon ein *kafir* ist.'

16 AM insists on the role of the Islamic scholars throughout the world: 'Ulema have an important role to play to motivate Muslims for Jihad. They must make the Ummah understand that Palestine is an Islamic issue. They must work to turn the hearts of the Ummah in the right direction' (5-AM, 21.05.2004).

17 German original: 'Dem Land, welches Soldaten in unsere Länder schickt, um unsere Geschwister zu foltern, vergewaltigen und erbarmungslos abzuschlachten.'

18 German original: 'Dem Land, indem unsere Geschwister unschuldig in Gefängnissen [sic] geworfen, wo sie tagtäglich gefoltert werden.'

19 German original: 'Deutschland gehört von [sic] den stärksten Ländern militärisch und wirtschaftlich und ... Und was hat Deutschland erschüttert, was [hat] Deutschland zum Zittern gebracht?!! [...] Ein Quran, *allahu akbar*, ein Quran, ein Buch.'

20 For DWR, Muslims in Germany should feel concern for fellow Muslims in need worldwide (08.05.2012, 28.05.2012, 08.2013). Interestingly, DWR continuously addresses its audience as 'liebe Geschwister' ('dear brothers and sisters'); on average, it does so five to six times in every single document, which might indicate the importance of *love* towards the *ummah*. Yet, the injunction to care about suffering Muslims worldwide is more about 'pleasing Allah' (08.05.2012) than loving fellow Muslims.

21 Note the insistence on the masculine here and in the previous quote (brotherhood, brothers). While the *ummah* is represented as a 'she' (her lands, her sons, etc.), the true believers that belong to the *ummah* are primarily conceived as *male*. German original: 'Der Schmerz von irgendeinem Muslim am Ende von China schmerzt seinen Bruder im weiten Maghrib!'

22 German original: 'die Zuneigung, beziehungsweise die Barmherzigkeit über den Gläubigen, muss in allen Belangen sein'; see also, 9-MI, 07.2012, 18.05.2012, 19.11.2011, 20.11.2011.

23 Original in Appendix B3, quote n°4.

24 DWR preacher el-Emrani (aka Abu Dujana) alludes once to 'the one body', without further elaborating on it: 'Where is this one body? Do we feel this?!' (28.05.2012). HTB also mentions the one body of the *ummah* only once (1-HTB, 18.09.2001).

25 *Haram* designates something that is forbidden by sharia.

26 German original: 'Denn je vollständiger das Leben des Herzens ist, desto stärker ist seine Wut für Allah und Seinen Gesandten und seine Unterstützung für die Religion umso vollkommener!'

27 Among others, see 1-HTB, 20.03.2002; 2-HTB, 26.12.2003; 3-HTB, 19.08.2007, 17.09.2007, 01.01.2008; 5-AM, 03.12.2002, 15.09.2003; 8-DWR, 08.05.2012, 24.05.2012, 28.05.2012, 21.04.2013; 9-MI, 16.11.2011, 15.07.2012, 11.09.2012.

28 Among others in 1-HTB, 29.04.2003; 5-AM, 14.08.2003; 6-AM, 07.08.2004; 9-MI, 11.2011, 07.2012, 11.09.2012.

29 Fearlessness can be defined as not knowing fear, whereas bravery is to experience fear but to refuse to let it control one's actions. Often used in a colloquial way, fearlessness is, however, all but impossible. Some individuals may experience fearlessness punctually, when suffering from specific mental disorders (antisocial personality disorder and bipolar disorder). Further, fearlessness as an enduring *state* exists only as a consequence of a recently discovered genetic disorder called Urbach-Wiethe disease. This disease destroys the sides of the amygdala (brain damage) and results in affected persons being incapable of experiencing fear (see Feinstein et al., 2011).

30 UK foreign secretary between 2001 and 2006.

31 Or, in DWR's case, not routinely; see the next section on the consistency of the performance of emotions.

32 Also in 5-AM, 21.05.2004, and in 9-MI, 18.05.2012, 07.2012, 01.2013.

33 Later in this text, MI talks of a 'duty towards Allah to stand by and show affection to the believers and to treat enemies with hostility.'

34 German original: 'Unser Leben vor eurem Leben und somit unser Blut vor eurem Blut. [...] Unsere Körper schmerzen beim Überwinden der Hindernisse, welche ihr uns in den Weg stellt. Doch all diesen Kummer und all diese Qualen nehmen wir in Kauf, auf dem Weg zur Zufriedenheit des Erhabenen.'

35 Also, if a (non-)religious Other converts, he or she is redeemed and becomes an integral part of the *ummah*.

36 German original: 'Und ich hasse sie für Allah und ich bin bereit gegen sie zu kämpfen mit aller Macht, die ich habe.'

37 HTB uses strong words to demystify Muslim leaders' actions: 'they persist in their deception with a sick man's wild imagination and lie to their people about wanting to save the third holiest shrine'.

38 Belkaid talks in one video of 'Ehre' (21.04.2013), which generally means 'honour' in German, but he does not talk once about 'being proud' in the corpus.

39 In the video passage, el Emrani decries Muslims who still believe Western countries might do something to help Syria's civilians: 'How long do you want to stay deluded? Has this still not become clear to you, dear brothers and sisters? [...] *alhamdulillah* [thank God] that the *ummah* of Muhammad a.s.s. slowly slowly wakes up.' German original: 'Wie lange wollt ihr noch verblendet bleiben s.w.t.? Ist es immer, ist es Euch immer noch nicht klargeworden, diese Sache, liebe Geschwister? [...] aber *alhamdulillah*, dass die *Ummah* von Mohamed a.s.s. so langsam langsam mal von ihrem Schlaf aufsteht'. (8-DWR, 08.2013).

40 German original: 'Frauen werden vergewaltigt, liebe Geschwister, *wallahi*, unsere Schwestern werden vergewaltigt und getötet von diesen Tieren ... Möge Allah sie bestrafen!'

41 German original: 'Lasst euch nicht reinlegen, liebe Geschwister, wenn irgendein Hund von denen rauskommt und sagt "ja wir verurteilen das"! [...] Was für [sic] verurteilen?! Über ein Jahr werden Menschen abgeschlachtet und getötet!'

42 German original: 'Der gesandte Allah a.s.s. sagte: Wenn Syrien verloren geht, wenn ihr Syrien, al-Sham, verliert, so ist nichts Gutes in euch, nichts Gutes in euch, liebe Geschwister. Nichts Gutes in Euch [*brüchige und weinende Stimme*], nichts Gutes überhaupt in Euch, wenn al-Sham verloren geht.'

43 He reduces, for instance, the decision to leave for Syria and help in combat to questions of manhood and trust in Allah. The passage begins as follows: 'Shame on anyone, who calls himself a man, *wallahi* shame on you! *Wallahi* nothing is easier than to help them, nothing is easier than supporting our [Syrian] brothers and sisters.' German original: 'Schande über jeden, der sich ein Mann nennt, *wallahi* Schande über euch! *Wallahi* nichts ist einfacher als sie zu unterstützen, nichts ist einfacher als unsere Geschwister [in Syrien] zu unterstützen.'

44 Original title: 'Wo sind Eure Ehre und Euer Stolz?'

45 Original title: 'Wie lange soll dieses erniedrigte Leben noch weitergehen?'

46 For instance, AM and MI address more directly than HTB the necessity to suppress feelings of compassion for the disbelievers.

47 For instance, MI believes that an 'unconcerned' Muslim man, who does not care enough for the *ummah*, is 'probably a hermaphrodite or ... a woman or something, *wallahi*, that has no sense of shame or manhood, hm' (18.05.2012; see also 01.2013). German original: '*Subhan'allah*, abgesehen davon ist er wahrscheinlich ein Zwitter oder eine... eine Frau oder irgendwas, *wallahi*, der kein... kein Schamgefühl, keine Männlichkeit besitzt, ah.'

Conclusion

This book asked how organisations legitimate the turn towards (violent) extremism and incentivise members and followers to engage in political violence. It studied comparatively the phases of activism of several Islamist organisations in the UK and Germany in the 2000s – *al-Muhajiroun, Hizb ut-Tahrir Britain,* and the *Muslim Association of Britain* – and late 2000s/ early 2010s – *Die Wahre Religion and Millatu Ibrahim.* The research presented here explored mobilisation for political violence in three successive analyses, drawing on a qualitative interpretative methodology.

The first part of the book problematised previous categorisations of Islamist activism. By highlighting its partly ephemeral character and the ambiguity maintained by most organisations towards political violence, it offered a nuanced approach to fluctuations between moderation and extremism. Studying the organisations' textual, audio, and video data demonstrated how they articulate stability and change in discourse and practice. These changes were interpreted temporally and comparatively. Attention to shifts over a continuum between moderation and extremism led to the empirical reconstruction of temporal phases of activism. These phases of moderation, radicalisation into extremism, and (moderation within) extremism constituted subsequently the cases studied in the second part of the book.

Part II of the book turned to the core argument: political violence has to feel right, as a collective, for an organisation and its followers to move from moderate activism to extremism and violent action. After laying the theoretical groundwork, the book explored organisations' narrative deployments and how collective emotions are performed in and through narrative. Specifically, it asked whether organisations reproduce a similar romantic narrative in their respective phases of activism. The thick description and comparison across cases revealed a sharp contrast between phases of moderation on one side and radicalisation and extremism on the other. The interpretation emphasised the narrative exceptionalism of group radicalisation and extremism, which are mediated and legitimised narratively. Finally, the sub-processes of *narrative emotionalisation* were explored hermeneutically. The extent to which each sub-process unfolds within the cases of radicalisation and cases of extremism was traced and interpreted. The analysis highlighted that organisations perform collective emotions much more consistently and strongly in phases of extremism than in phases of radicalisation. In phases of extremism, the emotionalisation of organisations' romantic narrative is a performative success. Narrative emotionalisation plays a key role in incentivising members and followers to engage collectively and individually in political violence.

The following recaps the main research insights regarding the book's central argument. Next, it stresses their implications for research on radicalisation and (violent) extremism, and discusses some limits and future avenues for research. The third section turns to the book's theoretical and methodological contribution to studying collective emotions in (world) politics. The chapter concludes by addressing the relevance of this research for political practice and prevention.

Main research insights

The collective turn towards (violent) extremism is couched in a romantic narrative. This narrative was commonly shared by the four organisations, which have known a phase of radicalisation into extremism and/or a phase of extremism: AM, HTB, DWR, and MI. In contrast, in the cases of moderation, organisations did not mediate worldviews, social identities, and political goals through a romantic narrative.

The interpretation of organisations' narration of romance stressed several insights. First, in phases of radicalisation and extremism, an organisation's narrative performance produces strong causal relationships between events, attributes fixed roles to social actors, and unequivocal responsibilities. Political change for the *ummah* is constructed as necessarily revolutionary: change must happen outside of what the current local and transnational political orders allow. This commonly shared romantic narrative justifies the use of political violence because of the urgency to act (e.g. 'Islam and Muslims are in great danger – therefore, armed resistance must happen now') and because it is the solution foreseen by Islam in such cases (e.g. 'Allah commands armed resistance'). Thus, the narrative as it is performed substantiates the organisations' normative, strategic, and/or tactical changes towards political violence.

The analysis also showed that each organisation gives this common Islamist romantic narrative its own flavour, for instance, regarding the priorities of collective action, the scope of individual responsibility, and the role of the in-group in the coming caliphate. Interestingly, no major narrative difference appear between the organisations based on their (main) country of activity (UK or Germany). All four organisations construe, in strikingly similar ways, the respective role of the UK and Germany in the growing hostility against local Muslim communities and these countries' respective participation in transnational conflicts involving the *ummah*. Nor are there major dissimilarities, in the performance of the romantic narrative, according to creedal variations. The Islamist organisation HTB does not perform the narrative differently from the Salafi organisations AM, DWR, and MI. If anything, HTB is often surprisingly closer to the exclusionist positions of AM and MI than its declared position, of openness 'to all schools of thought in Islam', should accommodate. At the same time, DWR's articulations are often less exclusionist than its fellow Salafi organisations'.

Finally, the temporal contexts in which the respective organisations performed the narrative do not make for blatant discrepancies. Although relevant local and transnational events had partly changed when the German organisations were founded, their respective performances of the romantic narrative are strikingly similar to those of the UK organisations. For example, AM and MI are in many ways closer to each other than MI is to its contemporary, DWR.

Further, the organisations emphasise the *transnational* horizon of experience much more than the *local* horizon of experience (except in DWR's case). The transnational setting appears thus more actionable, which, in turn, indicates that events less familiar to the audience – however fuzzy or inaccurate the depiction – fit harmoniously into the narrative. Finally, the diagnosed exploitative, hostile character of this transnational order is narratively more decisive than its immoral character. Hence, in phases of radicalisation and extremism, political issues and perceptions of insecurity have primacy over moral issues.

Lastly, the interpretation of the romantic narrative highlighted several differences between the cases of radicalisation and extremism. Organisations in phases of radicalisation tend to emphasise out-group characters and plot elements referring to attacks against the *ummah*. Conversely, organisations in phases of extremism tend to focus increasingly on in-group characters and plot elements referring to the need to fight back, thus indicating a shift in narrative focus when an organisation enters a phase of extremism.

Overall, these findings point to several central research insights into Islamist organisations' narrative activity:

- Islamist organisations – which may otherwise carry different creedal beliefs (classical Islamist/Salafi), hierarchise subordinate political goals differently, and have been active in partly different spatial-temporal

contexts (UK/Germany) – are narratively speaking identical in phases of radicalisation.
- Shifts in an organisation's political activism can be traced using the hermeneutics of the romantic narrative.
- There is no major qualitative narrative difference between organisations in phases of radicalisation (3-HTB, 4-AM, 8-DWR) and phases of extremism (1-HTB, 5-AM, 9– MI).
- There is no major qualitative narrative difference between organisations in phases of discourse-based extremism (1-HTB) and organisations in phases of both discourse-based and action-based extremism (5-AM, 9-MI).

Turning to *narrative emotionalisation*, the book argued that organisations' respective narrative performances are not equally emotionalised. Organisations incentivise members and potential followers to engage in collective and/or individual violent action by delivering a repetitive, strong performance of collective emotions. The interpretation highlighted that this performance is much stronger in the cases of extremism than in the cases of radicalisation. In the former, the comprehensive emotionalisation of an organisation's narrative thus parallels its extremist activism.

The comparison between the cases of radicalisation and the cases of extremism stressed the unequal emotionalisation of narrative performances. The four sub-processes characterising narrative emotionalisation are only partly unfolding in the phases of radicalisation of HTB, AM, and DWR. Contrarily, they unfold comprehensively in the phases of extremism. First, in such phases, AM, HT, and MI clearly establish the primacy of emotion-based knowledge, that is, the superiority of the group's emotional experience over other sources of knowledge. In this process, the organisations attribute clear-cut emotions to out-groups (hatred, fear, and no compassion) towards the *ummah*.

Second, in phases of extremism, conflicting emotional meanings disappear from narrative occurrences; highly negative and positive emotions are performed towards strictly separate narrative objects and actions, which produces a distinctive emotional tone (albeit less in HTB's case). Third, the organisations establish and enforce group-appropriate emotion rules and expect emotion work from members and followers to conform to them. While this applies to phases of radicalisation too, organisations only ascribe truly distinct emotional lives to in-group and out-groups in phases of extremism. Out-groups are said to feel radically different emotions than the *ummah*. The organisations assert for the latter a monopoly on compassion (towards Muslims), rightful anger, and unconditional love (towards Allah and the *ummah*). Fourth, only the three cases of extremism displayed a consistent performance of collective emotions across narrative deployments.

Further, the interpretation pointed to some differences between HTB's, AM's, and MI's phases of extremism regarding the *intensity* of narrative emotionalisation. HTB's emotional tone is not as unambiguously positive towards armed resistance, in its extremist phase, as it is in AM's and MI's. Another difference between the three cases regards feelings of hatred. HTB does not perform hate, an emotion it attributes, conversely, to out-groups (in their feelings about HTB and the *ummah*), whereas AM and MI do perform hate *towards* out-groups in phases of extremism. This difference is interesting in many ways. First, it implies that extremism does not necessarily require the collective performance of hate towards out-groups. Second, it shows that the absence of hatred is not merely linked to creedal differences between a Salafi minority and the larger Islamist scene as the Salafi organisation DWR does not enforce hate towards enemies as an emotion rule either. Third, insofar as it is only performed in the cases that presented both discourse-based and action-based forms of extremism, hatred as an emotion rule can be interpreted as accompanying the narrative changes involved in *violent* extremism.

These findings point to central research insights into the politics of emotions within organisations engaging into (violent) extremism:

- Changes in a group's expectations are performed emotionally: new group aims, strategies, and/or tactics are mediated through (the incremental adaptation of) an organisation's performance of emotions. Political violence has to feel right, as a collective, for an organisation and its followers to move (further) towards (violent) extremism.
- The strong incentivisation to commit violence (collectively/individually) hinges on the consistency and intensity of narrative emotionalisation.
- changes in the consistency and intensity of the performance of emotions, for instance an incremental change in emotions rules, suggest qualitative shifts within extremist activism.

The relevance of these research insights for scholarship and policy are discussed in the following.

Implications for research on radicalisation and extremism

This research is relevant for the scholarship on radicalisation, political extremism, and terrorism, as well as for the scholarship on militancy in the context of rebellions, revolutions, and civil wars, in a least three ways. First, research on radicalisation and militancy needs to systematically integrate accounts of how collective emotions are performed by groups. Second, the research insights call on scholars to minimise the importance that has been given so far to ideology. Third, research on group radicalisation gains from being grounded on methodology-driven, empirical accounts of organisations' evolving forms of political activism. These implications are discussed in greater detail below.

(1) The growing scholarship on group radicalisation and political extremism can no longer ignore emotions. The research presented in this book shows how changes in activism at the group level rely on getting collective emotions right. The major changes in normative goals, strategy, and tactics implied in the turn to political violence are justified and sustained narratively and emotionally. The immense group energy flowing into narrative activity and the systematic performance of collective emotions therein attest to this. In this regard, the specificity of extremism in discourse and action (MI and AM's phase of extremism) compared to extremism in discourse (HTB) needs to be played down. In terms of narrative and, to a large extent, emotional performance, they are very much alike. Incidentally, this finding echoes the argument found in the literature on individual trajectories into extremism – that between an individual who holds extremist beliefs and an individual who holds extremist beliefs and acts upon them through violent means, there is often no difference in commitment to the organisation's political aims, values, and means.

Further, the narrative performance of emotions by the leaders of an organisation reveals much about its relationship to the social environment. It conveys a sense of past and present interactions with other parts of society, and how these interactions were/are interpreted (tolerance, indifference, diffidence) and kept in the group's collective memory. It tells us how an organisation perceives state institutions and security authorities and the quality of their interactions; for instance, whether the state is more repressive with the organisation's in-group than with other minority groups (e.g. suspicion of leniency towards right-wing extremists). It also provides insights into a group's evolving perceptions of its immediate environment and the current political (world) order, whom it is said to benefit and in which double-standards are said to prevail. As such, an organisation's specific performance of emotions reveals how it experiences injustice. It is thus particularly relevant to the literature addressing the links between grievances and extremism and the literature on cumulative radicalisation.

Systematically integrating accounts of how collective emotions are performed would also go a long way towards better understanding why certain extremist organisations lose members, split, or disappear. Regarding the organisations studied here, those who have experienced phases of extremism did not last long as organisations, except for HTB, which is still active. MI and AM disappeared (temporarily) as organisations. It can be argued that their respective performances resonated well beyond their core membership and ultimately led to bans by public authorities.[1] Conversely, while HTB has endured over time, the organisation lost many followers to other organisations in the early 2000s – notably to AM in those days. This difference can be ascribed to the discrepancy between a remarkably systematic discourse on the necessities of fighting back and the comparatively underwhelming, concrete actions the organisation pursued in the UK.

Both examples – dissolution and membership loss – point to the limits of performative operations. In HTB's case, the performance of emotions failed to be 'set in motion' and be followed by actions, which led to a performative breakdown. Its effects ceased to work. In AM and MI's cases, conversely, the respective performance of collective emotions may have taken a life of their own, reproduced and outbid by members and followers in ways that led to counter-performatives, that is, exceeding what it was expected to produce and backfiring. Overall, there is good reason to believe that studying group performances of collective emotions over time would further inform research on group splintering, dissolution, and competition.

The analysis also revealed interesting gender dynamics[2] in the performance of collective emotions in and through the romantic narrative, especially around the topos of protection. In the processes of narrative emotionalisation, gender dynamics were less explicit and partly deviated from the expected gender rules associated with emotions. For instance, the performance of boundless compassion was expected by HTB, AM, and MI from Muslim brothers who go and 'fight in the path of Allah'. In phases of extremism, political violence is to be perpetrated by the strongly excluding community of care constituted by the organisations. Such a performance of emotions is gendered in ways that would be stereotyped as 'feminine' in Western gender hierarchies and differ from traditional gendered roles in fighting. That certain emotion rules might apply even more to male than female group members may provide further insights into differences in the uneven mobilisation of men and women in Islamist organisations. At any rate, it opens an interesting avenue of inquiry and highlights the importance of emotions considered 'positive' (love and compassion) in fostering a collective commitment to (violent) extremism.

Research on narrative emotionalisation may also prove fecund for studying the effects of counter-narratives by public institutions and non-governmental organisations working in the field of prevention. Scholars argue that counter-narratives bear low efficacy because narratives of political violence cannot be countered with better facts and arguments. As a result, interventions by scholar-practitioners and policy recommendations have increasingly advocated designing emotionally appealing alter-narratives (Aarten et al., 2018). State and non-state attempts at deploying alternative narratives can be critically explored through the prism of narrative emotionalisation. Incidentally, such an endeavour may offer insights into what democratic narratives and narratives of conflict management should *not do* to feel right for a plural society.

(2) The role of ideology in the turn to extremism should not be overestimated. The research presented in this book suggests that classical Islamist organisations and Salafi organisations have much more in common than the literature has so far let on. Sure, HTB differs from the three Salafi organisations on political priorities (i.e. the establishment of the caliphate should come first, then the liberation of Muslim lands through jihad), and it does not exclude as many 'Muslims Others' from the *ummah* as AM, DWR, and MI do. Nevertheless, the analysis showed that its characterisation of the international setting and the *ummah*'s political enemies is often closer to AM's than MI's or DWR's are. Further, in their respective phase of extremism, HTB's, AM's, and MI's performances of emotions are strikingly similar. Studying group narratives and collective emotions allows us to move beyond deceptive politico-religious differences and highlight the commonalities between organisations engaging in extremist activism.

Furthermore, 'ideology' does not appear to be what binds Islamist organisations' members with Muslims worldwide. The successful constitution of such a transnational imagined community happens in and through an (Islamist) romantic narrative. Organisations drawing on this narrative do not necessarily need a full-fledged ideological construct. MI and DWR are glaring examples. In contrast with the intellectual HTB, which developed a robust ideological framework, complete with publications and a prepared constitution for the future Islamic caliphate, MI and DWR are ideological lightweights. They transmit merely basic fragments of Jihadism to their followers, needing to do no more than this – (re)producing this romantic narrative, infusing it with their references and experiences renders it their own and binds their members to an imagined transnational, select community of activists.

The interpretation of narrative emotionalisation underscored the argument made in the introduction that ideology does not explain *how* changes in orientation happen. When an organisation radicalises into (or within) extremism, it introduces such change narratively, relying on the narrative's affective underpinning. One of the clearest examples is the consecration of emotion-based knowledge in phases of radicalisation and extremism. The analysis showed that, in such cases, emotion-based forms of experience and knowledge tend to supplant all other sources and forms of knowledge. Some forms of knowledge are also redefined as emotion-based knowledge, even religious knowledge at times. Especially in extremist phases, the primacy of knowledge rooted in collective and individual affective experience is entrenched. Members are asked to perform emotion work to transcend negative affective experiences into pieces of knowledge and, ultimately, feel positive about their difference from the rest of society. Similarly, out-groups' (in)action is explained by attributing emotional motives to other groups. Emotion-based knowledge culminates in the perception of radically distinct affective capacities: a reduced emotional life is imputed to Western enemies and Muslim rulers. Conversely, the *ummah* would feel noble emotions and intensely so.

Overestimating the role of ideology has detrimental consequences in the policy field when research transferred towards policy-makers is neglecting other dimensions. It casts the efforts necessary to 'counter' radicalisation and extremism at the level of an ideological battle instead of construing them as socio-political issues necessitating multiple socio-political answers. Thereby, it overlooks many dimensions of these phenomena that run deep into societies and communities: the memory of contested political events, particularly asymmetric power relations, unequal access to participation in the political process, among others. Such a perspective renders radicalisation and extremism ahistorical by evading key factors intimately linked to collective emotions. Overall, the research insights presented in this book offer alternative ways to represent and interpret the dynamic processes involved in group radicalisation into and within extremism.

(3) Research on group radicalisation gains from methodologically grounded, empirical accounts of organisations' evolving forms of political activism. When group radicalisation is conceived of as the product of complex, partly contradictory processes, which may stop, resume, or reverse, studying organisations' move towards and away from extremism rests on tracing shifts in political projects and preferences for action. As such, it calls for a methodology able to capture multiple political positions and choices on a continuum between political moderation and extremism in a concrete socio-political context. The research presented here sketches a way to do so at the level of language. The codebook 'Group moderation and group radicalisation', adapted to a Western European socio-political context of activism, lends itself to the interpretation of group activism over time. Instead of lending too much meaning to ephemeral changes in discourse or practice, it contributes to focusing on changes establishing themselves over time. This methodological approach also delineated phases of *moderation within extremism* and *radicalisation within extremism*.

This approach has implications beyond terminological work. Using concepts and drawing on methodologies that strongly reflect the fluidity and processual character of such group processes goes a long way towards dispelling modern myths (and a certain fascination) about radicalisation and extremism, and can impact political communication about these phenomena. Moreover, such a theoretical and methodological approach re-anchors the study of group processes into political violence firmly in a conflict theoretical perspective. Thereby it de-exceptionalises the production of knowledge about radicalisation/extremism and links up to the broader peace and conflict studies research agenda. Finally, the practice of characterising organisations as 'radical' or 'extremist' as if holding true in all time and place, instead of talking of their forms of activism, is not merely inaccurate and political. It also bars the necessity of re-evaluating such characterisations in the future and constrains forms of socio-political engagement.

Moreover, exploring *phases* of activism can further our understanding of escalation and moderation processes. Much theory-building is still needed around the concepts of 'radicalisation within extremism' and 'moderation within extremism'. For instance, theorising moderation within extremism, at the group level, away from the notions of 'de-radicalisation' and 'disengagement' would come a long way in advancing our understanding of organisations pursuing low-intensity campaigns. Bridging these concepts to the recent scholarship on the issue of restraint would be particularly welcome. While restraint has been generally conceived as the process of holding back from doing (more) violence (Busher & Bjørgo, 2020), the concept of moderation within extremism has the potential not only to shed light on processes of limiting/recanting from violence and/or using nonviolent means but also re-introducing political moderation in discourse. The research findings indicate that organisations in phases of moderation within extremism may not only circumscribe the scope of legitimate political violence or type of targets considered appropriate, but they may also reintroduce some dialogical engagement with other political positions, as seen in HTB's case, thereby mitigating anti-pluralistic beliefs. Theory-driven empirical research into collective change *within* extremism may be inspired, methodologically speaking, by the process-oriented study of moderation as discourse- and action-based phenomenon.

The research presented in this book presents several limitations. First, an approach to radicalisation based on the discursive articulations of Islamist organisations implies studying what the organisations committed to paper, recorded, or filmed – and this only. It limits the analysis of their real-world actions to those mentioned in written or (audio)visual texts. Admittedly, this is one limitation of studying group moderation and group radicalisation at the level of language.

The second limitation refers to assessing the reception of the emotionalised romantic narrative by the organisations' members and (potential) followers. While the focus was on how organisations legitimise and incentivise change while turning to (violent) extremism, it would be interesting to study resonance with members empirically, that is, whether and how the performance of collective emotions impacted their commitment and forms of (collective) action, as well as resonance within the larger followership. Interrogating the respective resonance of incomplete vs full emotionalisation with members and the larger followership seems promising. When narrative emotionalisation is particularly intense, can organisations retain control over the performance in the long run? Members might say or do things that leaders may not condone – precisely because they feel intensely. Such empirical research may question the spatial and temporal boundaries of organisations' control over the performance of emotions.

There is much evidence that the narrative deployments of the banned organisations – AM, DWR, and MI – have had a life of their own after the organisations ceased to exist. This afterlife is perhaps most evident in the case of AM. Its textual, oral, and visual materials have resonated remarkably far and across time, notably thanks to its social media channels, active well into the 2010s. For instance, on YouTube, it constituted an interlinked, coordinated network of dozens of channels, addressing audiences far beyond the UK.[3]

While I believe that many of the insights offered in this book would apply to other political actors turning to political violence, the research findings primarily extend to one political actor – as heterogeneous as it is: Islamist organisations, in the socio-political context of Western Europe in the 2000s and 2010s. The cases studied here are still relevant in today's Western European context. HTB is still active in the UK and its political message has recently gathered renewed interest in other Western European countries. Banned in 2003 in Germany, Hizb ut-Tahrir has experienced a resurgence lately, notably around the movement 'Generation Islam', whose online and offline campaigns have mobilised important followership between 2018 and 2020 (Baron, 2021).

Further, today's organisations have been shaped in many ways by the three banned organisations, not just nationally but also across borders. Successive organisations followed AM in the UK with much of the same personnel – among others: *al-Ghurabaa*, *The Saved Sect*, *Islam4UK*, *Need4Khilafah*. It was also a model for activists in other Western European countries in the 2010s, with the creation of *Sharia4Belgium*, *Sharia4Holland*, *Call to Islam* in Denmark, and *Prophets of the Ummah* in Norway. In the same vein, DWR's *LIES!* campaign was emulated a few years later in the UK, with guest appearances by Abou Nagie. The UK campaign was unabated in November 2016, when German authorities banned DWR, and most of its personnel were arrested. MI continued its online activities after it was officially banned in May 2012. A successor organisation was created a few months later under the name *Tauhid Germany*, subsequently banned in 2015. In contrast, much of the leading personnel of MI joined the armed struggle, first, of *al-Nusrah* and, later, ISIS, ultimately creating an MI brigade within the IS organisation.

Beyond organisational and personnel legacies, the groups' textual, audio, and visual materials can still be partly found on web archives, sharing platforms, and messaging services.[4] Compared to organisations operating in the 1980s or 1990s, modern information and communication technologies have enabled the groups' bodies of stories to be preserved to a large extent. As such, their narrative deployments still contribute to the intertextuality – 'the web of meaning' – of later Islamist militant texts. Narratives endure long after organisations are gone.

Further comparative research in varying spatio-temporal settings is needed to extend these insights beyond the socio-political context of Western Europe in the 2000s and the 2010s. Focusing on Islamist organisations active in other Western countries, such as North America and Australia, might highlight regional specificities in the re-production of an Islamist romantic narrative and some differences in the performance of collective emotions. If so, such research might question the idea of a uniform transnational narrative circulating between revolutionary Islamist organisations and help localise the issue and the political and social responses thereof, as discussed further on about prevention.

Future research could also explore the relevance of the findings in the case of Islamist organisations operating in less consolidated democratic systems and authoritarian contexts. The characterisation of discourse-based and action-based group radicalisation and moderation would need to be adapted to these contexts. As political extremism relates to a society's political make-up, norms, and values at a given time, the legitimisation of change and incentivisation to political violence is bound to take on other characteristics. Similarly, exploring cases less contemporary would deepen our understanding of narrative practices in militant activism. At any rate, the codebooks 'Group moderation and group radicalisation' and 'Romantic Narrative' developed to support the interpretative work can be adapted to the political goals, practices, and horizon(s) of experience of organisations across various spatio-temporal contexts.

Future research also needs to interrogate whether the insights presented here apply to other actors across the political spectrum. There is reason to believe that far-right organisations radicalising into extremism would similarly draw on a romantic narrative and perform collective emotions. There is much potential for exploring the aesthetic and affective dimensions of (militant) activism, looking at the growing strand of research studying far-right group practices (Castelli et al., 2014; Shoshan, 2016; Schedler, 2017; Bogerts & Fielitz, 2019). Moreover, the reconfigurations of far-right movements towards more digital network structures and less organisation-based forms of activism speak for the even greater centrality of narrative re-production and diffusion. In this regard, a theoretical and methodological perspective that accounts for narrative change would lend itself well to comparative research exploring Islamist and far-right mobilisations concurrently. Regarding left-wing (militant) activism, recent research suggests that anarchist and anti-fascist networks would narrate their struggle against fascism as 'self-defence' and, more recently, as a 'transnational war' (Koch, 2018; Lundberg, 2020). And yet, the use of interpersonal violence remains extremely marginal in practice; as such, large narrative differences are expected.

Implications for research on emotions in (world) politics

The research presented in this book has implications for the scholarship on emotions in (world) politics as well. First, the empirical analysis provides important insights into collective emotions in the context of political violence. Second, the book offers a methodological contribution to the transdisciplinary research agenda on emotions. Third, it adds to the growing literature on non-state agency in world politics.

The research offers important insights into the management of collective emotions by non-state actors, thereby furthering our understanding of the politics of emotions. It was argued that if emotions come to be in and through their performance, then narratives are the place to access them. Narrative distinguishes itself by its very flexible form: while a given body of stories has distinguishing features, it accommodates political actors' partly specific performances of emotions. The question then became: how can we conceptualise and study the varied intensity of social actors' narrative performances? The book showed that the organisations routinely perform collective emotions through a shared Islamist romantic narrative, legitimising political violence and the preference for violent action. The performance of collective emotions in and through this narrative *makes* action *possible*.

The book then compared organisations' respective performances of emotions through a hermeneutic approach. The comparison between the cases highlighted that the intensity of narrative emotionalisation was strongest in AM's and MI's respective phases of extremism – the two organisations from which (ex-)members ultimately planned and engaged in physical violence.[5] Through emotionalisation, an organisation's narrative performance incentivises members to violent action.

Furthermore, interpreting performances of emotions through the concept of narrative emotionalisation made apparent how the collectivisation of emotions follows from a comprehensive process. Narrative performances justifying decisive political change through violent action draw on a wide range of collective emotions. Emotions such as empathy and love played therein a central role in fostering individual and collective commitment. Further, the discussion highlighted the significance of emotion rules and emotion work within group dynamics of social control. The analysis also stressed how the narrative produces totalising meanings when primacy is given to sources and forms of knowledge based exclusively on individual and collective affective experiences. Exemplarily, the (assumed) emotions attributed to Others, in their feelings towards the in-group, are established as 'truths'. Overall, the analysis stressed how powerfully collective emotions are performed in the process of narrative emotionalisation. These findings point to the intimate relationship between collective emotions and collective action.

Approaching collective emotions via their performance in and through narrative can further our understanding of social actors' modes of relating to and producing knowledge/power effects on the social world. This is also true for further areas of research in political science and neighbouring disciplines. For instance, it can contribute to theory-building efforts in research on political leadership forms and their impact on policy, in comparative research on populism in democratic and autocratic regimes, research on democratic responses to natural catastrophes and terrorist attacks, and so on. In this regard, narrative emotionalisation as a concept and the four subprocesses identified therein represent a promising, original mode of inquiry. Future research could focus on theorising and refining it further. Theorising processes of emotionalisation in other narrative genres would be particularly fruitful. How would emotionalisation look like in tragic, satiric, and comic narratives? They might build on similar processes – refer to forms of knowledge (de)legitimisation, have a specific emotional tone, set emotion rules and demands towards emotion work, etc. – or they might build on alternative sub-processes altogether.

Conversely, exploring 'narrative de-emotionalisation' seems an important avenue for future research. Theorising de-emotionalisation and developing a hermeneutic approach to trace its processes may break new ground in research on moderation processes in the context of extremism and political violence, but not limited to it. By characterising the processes that might mitigate narratives of political violence and/or (in)security, such research would bear much potential for conflict de-escalation, engagement and mediation, and reconciliation processes.

This book proposed a comprehensive methodological approach for conceptualising and exploring collective emotions. Some aspects thereof drew on existing research. Others were novel. This research contributes to further pushing the transdisciplinary research agenda on emotions: not only is it possible to study collective emotions, but research misses a large part of socio-political life when it does not.

More specifically, this research adds to the growing literature in political science, which shows how rich political narrative activity is and how researchers can draw on narrative as an object of study and a methodological approach. Combining a literary-critical approach drawing on narrative categories with a systematic comparison within and between cases allows for a good balance between interpreting in-depth how collective emotions are performed by social actors while making apparent how their performances may intersect.

Further, by introducing the concept of 'narrative emotionalisation' and tracing its processes hermeneutically, this research provides a novel methodological approach, which allows the interpretation of the varied intensity of performances of collective emotions and what it means in terms of political action. I believe that through such an approach, we can research mediated emotions without reducing emotions' depth and intensity. The research findings show that this original approach allows both the general and the particular to be characterised: the four Islamist organisations perform collective emotions in similar ways (the four sub-processes), yet not quite in the same way (resulting in varied intensity).

While I believe that narrative emotionalisation opens up new avenues for exploring the differential emotional power of narratives, there are some limits to the proposed methodology. The hermeneutic approach developed to study narrative emotionalisation specified the interpretative process for each of the four sub-processes. It detailed the concrete analytical steps to trace how these processes unfold within the cases. The intensity of narrative emotionalisation was further characterised through the comparison between organisations' phases of activism. As such, while narrative emotionalisation can be studied on a single case, the intensity of the process is best studied in contrast, around cross-case comparison (e.g. between several political organisations) or within-case comparison (e.g. a political organisation over a longer period).

A further limit concerns its adequacy to study narratives reproduced by actors less hierarchically organised (e.g. a protest movement) or institutional actors representing much larger collectives (e.g. the European Commission). While such political actors undoubtedly reproduce narratives, their capacity to control narrative production and reception is much more limited than the organisations studied in this book. On the other hand, institutional actors would have less difficulty enforcing emotion rules: as they tend to reproduce dominant narratives, their performance of emotions draws on implicit rules often largely accepted within their audience. Exploring such differences would contribute to fine-tuning the concept and methodology.

Finally, it remains to be seen whether this methodology may be adapted to research projects exploring data characterised by very brief texts, such as social media posts. Although such 'miniature texts' undoubtedly function as a 'narrative sense-making practice' (Graef et al., 2020, p. 436), they cannot be expected to display full-fledged characters, setting, and plot elements. In a similar vein, there is much potential in exploring ways to intersect the proposed narrative approach with visual discursive methodologies for research projects drawing primarily on visual texts.

Finally, this book adds to the scholarship on non-state agency in world politics. In terms of theory-building, a research focus on collective emotions support efforts towards breaking the hierarchal view of (high) state actors and (low) non-state actors in mainstream IR theory. Analysed through the lens of affective agency, asymmetric political actors have much more in common than their disparate institutional make-ups would let on. State and non-state actors display many commonalities in terms of narrative activity and the politics of emotions – for instance, the establishment of emotion rules or demands toward collective emotion work. Such a perspective opens further ways to interrogate state/non-state interactions and re-cast the question of knowledge/power hierarchies. Future research could explore how the collectives involved in the formulation, implementation, and enforcement of security policies in the field of terrorism – e.g. 'security experts', security agencies – produce emotion-based meanings and manage emotions within their ranks, to take an example close to the book's research. Ultimately, such endeavours would foster comparative research into the politics of emotion.

Importantly, exploring collective emotions in (world) politics contributes to decentring research from a Western perspective, overly emphasising rationality. As Ross diagnosed, approaches to world politics are 'overly detached and artificially cleansed of complex motivations and commitments that make human actors behave the way they do' (2014, p. viii), inter alia emotion-based motivations and commitments. In this disciplinary context, rationality tends to be attributed to Western political actors, whereas non-Western actors tend to be more often associated with emotionality.

Pushing forward an agenda sensitive to emotional phenomena thus means decolonising the perception that collective emotions and affects would be the practice of 'backward' collectives. Emotions and affects are ubiquitous in social life and politics. They are not the purview of minorities, protest movements, or insurgent groups. To draw on the example of emotion rules and sanctions in the present research, while some may be culturally specific (e.g. ex-communication as a sanction), the suppression of fear is a gendered emotion rule routinely operating in Western and non-Western collectives. Uncovering similarities between performances of emotions by Western and non-Western political actors would bring such efforts a long way.

Relevance for political practice and prevention

The research findings are relevant to political practice and prevention. This section addresses selected, concrete insights that may inform practitioners' work and then discusses potential implications, more broadly, for public discourse, political communication, and public diplomacy.

While this book focused on group processes, it offers some insights for political education interventions and prevention work with individuals and families. First, prevention initiatives aiming to address radicalisation and (violent) extremism by fostering political participation and engagement in socio-political life may gain from a stronger focus on the *local* level. The research insights highlight that, except for DWR's, the organisations' narrative performance draws more strongly on the transnational socio-political environment than the local environment (i.e. national, communal). Events far away remain abstract and are less intimately 'known'. Organisations embed them more easily in the romantic narrative, which does not rest on 'truthfulness' or accuracy. While the local environment (e.g. the experience of anti-Muslim racism) might appear less scandalous than the transnational one (e.g. the experience of war in Muslim-majority countries), the latter can only attain emotional resonance precisely because it echoes personal and/or community experiences. All these experiences are merged narratively and *felt* by those recognising themselves in the narrative.

Re-embedding the horizon of experience in the local environment would help decouple transnational events from local issues and weaken the narrative's hold. The local level is a concrete political arena where people can experience the complexity of political positions, social needs, and processes to negotiate them. Beyond the (very real) experiences of anti-Muslim racism and discrimination, engaging individuals and minority communities at the local level means highlighting the grey areas. Projects at the local level have the advantage to show that, while building common understandings among very different people is a complex process, it is the daily activity of local institutions, and it is possible to reach community solutions. The process puts 'real people' in the picture (the potential Other becomes concrete) and encourages campaigning locally against discrimination and for equal treatment. The prevention subtext would read as: 'you do not have to go to country XY to change power relations tangibly and more durably'. When Islamist organisations tie local issues to transnational politics, prevention initiatives should re-anchor these issues and potential political and social responses to local politics.

Second, civil society prevention initiatives may develop activities to re-introduce complexity and ambiguity in individual and collective emotional experience. The research insights show that narrative emotionalisation casts in-group emotions as wholly distinct from out-group emotions and, at its fullest, as necessary collective performances. Practitioners working with individuals engaging with extremist organisations' materials and those who have disengaged (former activists) could incrementally address both aspects.

The first means de-constructing the perception of homogeneous communities of feelings, which would be hostile towards one's group, and opening up to the variety of emotions that other people may experience. This process aims at recognising that other groups can feel similar emotions as one's own, that feelings about political issues are often mixed, sometimes even contradictory. That collective emotions are constructed and not 'naturally' there. The second aspect means re-individualising affective experience. Not in the sense of 'your emotions are your own' – as most emotions are fundamentally social and not 'things' that one 'has' – but of regaining the capacity to *express* emotions. Practitioners' work with teenagers and young adults could integrate or strengthen (existing) modules for learning mechanisms to appropriate emotions and express them in a social context (contrary to emotion suppression) as well as for questioning gendered demands to perform, suppress, or transcend specific emotions, that is, injunctions to feel (collective) emotions in a certain way.

Emotion competence, much as other social competencies, may be regarded as an integral part of political education and universal prevention – and to some extent, it already is. To mention a few examples: perspective-taking role plays with youth groups; literary engagements with past conflicts from the perspective of victims; theatre and dance workshops to mix youth from different backgrounds through embodied practices. In civil society prevention work and grassroots initiative with youth, practitioners aim to complement political education, foster positive understandings about social coexistence and (reciprocal) integration, and prevent the development of misanthropic and anti-pluralistic attitudes (typically: antisemitism, Islamophobia, racism, fundamentalism, etc.).

Within such multifaceted endeavours, strengthening emotion competencies may include empowering techniques similar to those mentioned above (e.g. de-constructing gender expressions of emotions), aesthetic projects in safe spaces, and peer-to-peer mentoring programmes to open spaces outside the family circle.[6] Attention to emotional competence should not lead to (new) forms of (state) governance of emotions or the state-security-oriented production of 'resilient subjects'. Rather, it should come from critical interventions and grassroots initiatives, be conceived as a potentially eman-cipatory practice, and counter-balance modern societies' enduring rational imperative.

An epistemic shift is needed at the political level, namely the comprehen-sive acknowledgement that collective emotions are standard phenomena in the public space. They are not exceptions, as the liberal, rational imperative would have it. Emotions are commonplace in socio-political discourses and practices. The refusal to acknowledge this has been increasingly politically damaging in late-modern societies: people are expected to routinely sup-press emotions, yet large parts of society reject this increasingly and turn towards populist parties, extremist organisations, or disengage wholly from socio-political life. As mentioned in the introduction to this book, during the US presidential election in 2016, many US voters stressed how 'free' Donald Trump was and how thrilled they were about his unfiltered mood expressions.

In many different ways, the modern imperative to suppress emotions in the public space and politics is increasingly undermined. This point is not to say that democratic politics should embrace populist parties' or radicalis-ing organisations' performances of emotions. Quite the contrary, address-ing collective emotional phenomena in the public space would open up to the possibility of making them more visible (instead of relegating them to the private space). Such visibility would enable questioning their assumed 'collectiveness' and problematising unequal expectations towards emotion work in society (based on gender, class, minority status, ethnicity, etc.).

At the level of political communication, sensitivity to the various, ambivalent, and potentially conflicting emotions expressed by society's diverse publics, especially around divisive events, should foster more inte-grative performances of emotions by public authorities and policy-makers. Emotion-sensitive political communication would better reflect the plural-ist character of democratic societies. For instance, governmental reactions after terrorist attacks would, in the short run, recognise the possibility of experiencing (individually/collectively) mixed emotions about such events and their meanings, and open spaces for the (plural) perspectives of victims to be heard. Putting forward the plural character of victims represents the exact opposite of the romantic narrative's constitution of exclusively in-group victims. In the same vein, public policies, from commemoration to the allocation of funds for prevention by civil society actors, should be designed to address the needs of those affected by Islamist extremism and right-wing extremism on equal terms. As the reception of terrorist attacks goes beyond a country's borders, public reactions and longer-term soci-etal responses also impact transnational perceptions of solidarity (or lack thereof) towards minority communities.

Overall, cultivating such a political practice would run counter to the strict emotion rules practised by extremist organisations; it would foster forms of empathic engagement. At the level of international politics, public diplomacy sensitive to collective emotions would perform public emotions towards victims of political violence, whether far or near, more consistently. With time, it might contribute to decolonising pity politics, moving beyond parochial empathy towards like-people to send concrete political messages about the equal worth of all human lives.

Collective emotions are relevant for political representatives, social actors, and researchers alike: they tell us much about the state of relationships in a given society and between societies, about social needs, and what could be done to render collective performances of emotions at the local, national, and international level more integrative.

Notes

1 AM dismantled before the British government's ban passed, to avoid proscription and re-create under a new name. Its successor organisations were ultimately banned in 2006 under the Terrorism Act 2000.

2 As well as a number of intersectional dynamics, for instance, the recurring figure of the 'poor women of the Middle East' articulated in HTB's narrative or the figure of the 'poor black African Muslim who does not know how to pray' articulated in DWR's. Those representations hint at Western Islamist organisations' race, class, and gender prejudices.

3 The interlinked YouTube channels included, for instance, *Shariah4Belgium*, *Shariah4Holland*, *Shariah4AlAndalus* (Spain), *Shariah4Tunisia*, *Shariah4Egypt*, *Shariah4Pakistan*, and *Shariah4Australia* channels (Klausen et al., 2012).

4 The videos can be retrieved, for instance, on sharing platforms, providing one knows what to look for (the video title or place where/date when it was recorded). Klausen et al. have also shown that on YouTube, finding earlier videos by AM is relatively easy because AM channels have been resistant to disruption thanks to coordinated efforts; the group's video archives have been systematically transferred from a newly taken down channel to reserve channels in a matter of days (2012, pp. 48–49).

5 While members of DWR engaged in low-level violence during the demonstrations in Solingen and Bonn in 2012, such spontaneous outbreak of limited physical violence differs from the premeditated planning of suicide attacks (in some AM members' case) and preparations to join an insurgent organisation (in some AM ex-members' and several MI members' case).

6 A number of civil society projects are addressing male teenagers, particularly from honour-based cultures, which formulate strongly gendered expectations towards the expression of emotions. In Germany, 'Heroes®', managed by the association *Strohalm e.V.*, is one such project, conceived as 'feminist youth work' (www.heroes-net.de).

Appendices

Appendix A

List of primary data

A1 Primary data *Hizb ut-Tahrir Britain*

2001. 'Alliance with America is a great crime forbidden by Islam'. 18.09.2001.

2001. 'Communiqué from Hizb ut-Tahrir. America and Britain declare war against Islam and the Muslims'. 09.10.2001.

2001. 'The Bonn agreement consolidates the American control over Afghanistan and puts the basis for uprooting Islam from it'. 10.12.2001.

2002. 'The Arab summit conferences are an American political tool which must be stopped, and from whose evil the Ummah must be saved'. 20.03.2002.

2002. 'George Bush's Third Crusade against the Muslims'. 20.04.2002.

2002. 'The new style of American policy in occupied Palestine will lead to division and more spilling of the pure innocent blood of Muslims'. 07.07.2002.

2002. 'The American Government and Congress enact an aggressive resolution against the Islamic Ummah authorising President Bush to "Use military force against Iraq"'. 21.10.2002.

2003. 'A Call from Hizb ut-Tahrir. Only with the Khilafah will you be Victorious'. 13.04.2003.

2003. 'Hizb ut-Tahrir announces the death of its Ameer'. 29.04.2003.

2003. 'America's domination of the international situation is a danger to the world and only the Khilafah can save it'. 24.05.2003.

2003. 'Communiqué from Hizb ut-Tahrir'. 14.06.2003.

2003. 'The Muslims' Rulers are a harm (Darar) and reciprocation of harm (Diraar) upon the Ummah in the Summit Conference'. 19.10.2003.

2003. 'Bush's speech declares a comprehensive war against the Muslim countries. It is the beginning of the demise of the United States of America'. 08.11.2003.

2003. 'Hizb ut-Tahrir warns the traitorous rulers of the wrath of Allah and the anger of Allah's servants'. 26.12.2003.

2003. 'Call from Hizb ut-Tahrir to the Scholars of Azhar'. 31.12.2003.

2004. 'An Open letter from Hizb ut-Tahrir to President Chirac, President of the Republic of France'. 01.01.2004.

2004. 'Call from Hizb ut-Tahrir: O Muslims, beware of the (sectarian) fighting'. 02.03.2004.

2004. 'The war on Iraq is a curse on the rulers in the Muslim countries'. 07.04.2004.

2004. 'Inside Hizb ut-Tahrir: An interview with Jalaluddin Patel, Leader of Hizb ut Tahrir in the UK'. Mahan Abedin, Jamestown Foundation, 29.07.2004.

2005. 'Bush's current tour of Europe exposes the shaking of the throne of American unilateralism in international politics'. 24.02.2005.

2005. 'O Muslims! Shape the Middle East by your own hands, for you are its rightful owners'. 09.06.2005.

2006. 'Would the Pope dare to attack Islam if the Islamic State – the Khilafah Rashidah – had been established?' 17.09.2016.

2006. 'Labour attacks Muslim community to cover up leadership crisis and disaster in Iraq and Afghanistan'. 20.10.2006.

2006. 'Oh! The Muslim soldiers: Is there not a wise person amongst you, who is concerned about the condition of Islam & Muslims, their modesty and honour?' 04.11.2006.

2007. 'Hizb ut-Tahrir and the struggle for Khilafah'. 06.07.2007.

2007. 'America hopes to prevent the establishment of the Khilafah, by supporting the present corrupt system'. 19.08.2007.

2007. 'Kuwait on hunting campaign directed at the Shabab of Hizb ut-Tahrir. Accuses them of working for establishing the Islamic Khilafah!' 25.08.2007.

2007. 'This is why we call for establishing the Khilafah State!' 12.09.2007.

2007. 'Only the Khilafah will end colonialist exploitation'. 17.09.2007.

2007. 'Palestine will not be freed by the Ministers stooping at the door-steps of Bush at Annapolis; It will be liberated by armies fighting Jews at the al-Quds Walls'. 25.11.2007.

2007. 'Reject elections in this colonialist system and establish the KHILAFAH'. 29.11.2007.

2008. 'America campaigns for democracy so as to eradicate Islam'. 01.01.2008.

2008. 'To Pervez Musharraf, Dictator of Pakistan from Hizb ut-Tahrir Britain'. 26.01.2008.

2008. 'Only the return of the Khilafah will silence those who attack Islam'. 29.03.2008.

2008. 'Oh people: Your rulers are shameless!' 30.03.2008.

2008. 'Europe launches the West's new front in its war on Islam'. 01.04.2008.

2008. 'Islam demands the political unity of this Ummah'. 16.08.2008.

2008. 'A Message from the Amir of Hizb ut-Tahrir on the 87th Remembrance of the Destruction of the Khilafah'. 13.09.2008.

2008. 'The capitalist economy is suicidal just as the communist socialism was, only the Islamic model is the sure-cure and safe from economic pitfalls'. 07.10.2008.

A2 Primary data *al-Muhajiroun*

2001. 'A Muslim activist questioning Sheikh Omar regarding the recent attack on USA'. Website of Omar Bakri Mohammed (www.obm. clara.net), 12.09.2001.

2001. 'Press release. USA at war with Islam'. Website OBM, 16.09. 2001.

2001. 'Communiqué. Demonstration outside Pakistani Embassy on Friday 21st September 2001'. Website OBM, 21.09.2001.

2001. 'Press release. A war against Afghanistan is a war on Islam'. Website OBM, 07.10.2001.

2001. 'Press statement of Adeel Shahid'. Pakistan Press International, 08.10.2001.

2001. 'Jewish terrorism in Palestine'. Website OBM, 24.10.2001.

2002. 'UK judge outlaws Qu'ran and Hadith'. Website *al-Muhajiroun*, 04.04.2002.

2002. 'Secularism: A tool to silence Islam'. Website *al-Muhajiroun*, 05.04.2002.

2002. 'Fascist Jewish state will never see peace'. Website *al-Muhajiroun*, 20.04.2002.

2002. 'Islam gives full credit to Martyrdom bombings'. Website *al-Muhajiroun*, 08.05.2002.

2002. 'India prepares for "final, conclusive" battle against Islam'. Website *al-Muhajiroun*, 23.05.2002.

2002. 'A shout in the face of falsehood'. Website *al-Muhajiroun*, 12.07.2002.

2002. 'Western values are perverted values'. Website *al-Muhajiroun*, 24.10.2002.

2002. 'Moscow hostages justified'. Website *al-Muhajiroun*, 25.10.2002.

2002. 'Sanctity of Muslims in UK violated by Abu Qatada arrest'. Website *al-Muhajiroun*, 25.10.2002.

2002. 'Letter to the Ulema'. Written by The Muslim Youth Forum, in conjunction with/published on *al-Muhajiroun*'s website, 03.12.2002.

2002. 'Camp X-Ray and Muslim captives in Cuba, USA, UK, Germany, Holland, Italy etc. ...' Website *al-Muhajiroun*, 24.12.2002.

2002. 'Declaration from the conference on Muslim hostages'. Website *al-Muhajiroun*, 26.12.2002.

2003. 'Gods house has no sanctity under man made law'. Website *al-Muhajiroun*, 20.01.2003.

2003. 'Iraq – The international crusade against Islam and Muslims continues ...' Website al Muhajiroun, 16.02.2003.

2003. '"In Israel there are no civilians". Interview with Anjem Choudary, UK leader and spokesman of *Al-Muhajiroun*'. With Journalist Ori Golan, Jerusalem Post, 02.07.2003.

2003. 'A cry for the Shari'ah. Press Conference'. Website OBM, 01.08. 2003.

2003. 'Return of the Khilafah'. Website *al-Muhajiroun*, 14.08.2003.

2003. 'Bush and Blair choke on the fallout from September the 11th'. Website *al-Muhajiroun*, 17.08.2003.

2003. 'The United Nations: A legitimate target?' Website *al-Muhajiroun*, 24.08.2003.

2003. 'Introduction to the "Magnificent 19" conference'. Website *al-Muhajiroun*, 11.09.2003.

2003. 'Crusader Trevor Phillips does Blair's bidding'. Website *al-Muhajiroun*, 27.09.2003.

2003. 'Shari'ah Islamic magazine'. Website *al-Muhajiroun*, volume 1 issue 3, September 2003.

2004. 'Al-Muhajiroun in the UK: An interview with Sheikh Omar Bakri Mohammed'. With Mahan Abedin, The Jamestown Foundation, 10.03.2004.

2004. 'Sheikh Osama's message to Europe. Peace or war; the choice is yours'. Website al- Muhajiroun, 15.04.2004.

2004. 'Press release. Lies and Fabrications of Reuters exposed'. Website *al-Muhajiroun*, 19.04.2004.

2004. 'A WAR FOR PEACE. An analysis of the Message from Osama bin Laden to the people of Europe, not the POLITICIANS of the West'. Website *al-Muhajiroun*, 22.04.2004.

2004. 'Muslim demonstration shakes the heart of London'. Website *al-Muhajiroun*, 05.05.2004.

2004. 'Bush's whores practise their freedom in Iraq'. Website *al-Muhajiroun*, 11.05.2004.

2004. 'Why have Muslims turned their backs on Palestine?' Website *al-Muhajiroun*, 21.05.2004.

2004. 'An open appeal for members of al-Muhajiroun to calm and to restrain themselves against police brutality'. Website *al-Muhajiroun*, 24.05.2004.

2004. 'Which one do you prefer: Death penalty or life in prison?' Website *al-Muhajiroun*, 27.05.2004.

2004. 'Blair contests the incontestable...' Website *al-Muhajiroun*, 02.06.2004.

2004. 'David Beckham will not take you to heaven! Article by Abu Zakeeyyah'. Website *al-Muhajiroun*, June 2004.

2004. 'The difference between al salafiyyah and al salafiyyatul khalaf with regards to dar ul Islam and dar ul kufr'. Website *al-Muhajiroun*, 01.07.2004.

2004. 'Londonistan under Islam: Rally for Islam IX'. Website *al-Muhajiroun*, 26.07.2004.

2004. 'Guardian lies on behalf of MI5 serve Blair's crusade against Islam and Muslims: Media profile or media lies?' Website *al-Muhajiroun*, 04.08.2004.

2004. 'Whoever denies that terrorism is a part of Islam is Kafir'. Website *al-Muhajiroun*, 07.08.2004.

2004. 'An official declaration dissolving al-Muhajiroun'. Website *al-Muhajiroun*, 08.10.2004.

A3 Primary data *Die Wahre Religion*

2007. 'Stellung der Frau im Islam'. Blog DWR/EZP, 18.10.2007.

2010. 'Smart integration part 1 and 2: Abou Nagie'. Video, 23.03.2010.

2010. 'Das Interview mit dem DWR-Team_Abu Dujana und Abou Nagie'. Video, posted on YouTube 19.08.2010.

2011. 'Appeal to my brothers and sisters in Islam_Persecution (Abou Nagie)'. Video, December 2011.

2012. 'Abu Abdullah-Aufruf an die Muslime'. Video, May 2012 (between 1 May and 5 May).

2012. 'Abu Abdullah offene Drohungen an Deutsche und Merkel_ Escalation'. Video, 05.05.2012.

2012. 'Demo vom 08.05.2012 in Köln_Interview mit Abu Abdullah – Worte, die das Herz bewegen'. Video, 08.05.2012.

2012. 'Interview mit Ibrahim Abou Nagie'. Audio by Holger Schmidt, journalist at SWR, 24.05.2012.

2012. 'Spende für deine Geschwister in Syrien (Abu Dujana. Sheikh Abdellatif. Abu Abdullah)'. Video posted on YouTube, 28.05.2012.

2012. 'Die Ehre eines Muslims (Abu Dujana)'. Video, October 2012.

2012. 'Warum hassen die Kuffar den Islam und die Muslime'. Video, 25.10.2012.

2013. 'Benefizveranstaltung vom 21.04.2013 Hamburg – Abu Abdullah'. Video, 21.04.2013.

2013. 'Die aktuelle Lage der Umma – Abu Dujana.' Video, August 2013.

2013. 'Abu Adam (Afrika Brunnen Festival) Dortmund_only the beginning'. Video, 01.09.2013.

A4 Primary data *Millatu Ibrahim*

2011. 'Das islamische Urteil bezüglich der Verwendung des Begriffes Zivilisten'. Translation of the 4th edition of al-'Qaeda's *Inspire* magazine (winter 2010), published later by *Millatu Ibrahim*, Autumn 2011.

2011. 'Abu Talha Al-Almani: Wo sind eurer Stolz und Ehre?' Video, November 2011.

2011. 'Die Prüfungen Allahs fallen über den Kafir sowie auch über den Muslim'. Written in prison by Abu Usama al-Gharib (09.08.2011), published later on *Millatu Ibrahim*'s website, Autumn 2011.

2011. 'Sind mehrere unterschiedliche Herren besser als Allah der Eine der Allmächtige?!' Written in prison by Abu Usama al-Gharib, published later by *Millatu Ibrahim*, 28.10.2011.

2011. 'Ein Aufruf um die muslimischen Frauen in den Gefängnissen der Kreuzzügler zu unterstützen'. Written in prison by Abu Usama al-Gharib, published later by *Millatu Ibrahim*, 16.11.2011.

2011. 'Für *'Umm 'Ubaydah* aber gibt es keine Weinende'. Written in prison by Abu Usama al- Gharib, published later by *Millatu Ibrahim*, 19.11.2011.

2011. 'Wer unterstützt *'Umm Sayfillāh Al-Anŝāriyyah*?' Written in prison by Abu Usama al- Gharib, published later by *Millatu Ibrahim*, 20.11.2011.

2012. 'Abu Usama Al-Gharib: An erster Stelle steht der Tauhid (Khutbah)'. Video, January 2012.

2012. 'EX DESO DOGG_Abu Talha Al-Almani: Bewegt euch für die Dawah'. Video, February 2012.

2012. 'Die modernen Strategien der Kuffar und Murtaddin zur Bekämpfung des Islam von innen'. Written by Abu Umar al-Almani, published by *Millatu Ibrahim*, 24.04.2012.

2012. 'Abu Tahla al-Almani: Dies ist die Grenze!' Video, 03.05.2012.

2012. 'Abu Usama Al-Gharib: Wa Islamah!' Video, published on archive. org, 18.05.2012.

2012. 'Abu Usama Al-Gharib: Stellungnahme zu den Razzien'. Video posted on alghorabaa.wordpress.com, 14.06.2012.

2012. 'Ein Schrei … Unterstützend unseren Propheten (saws)'. Written by Ahmad Ashush, published by GIMF, July 2012.

2012. 'Gratulation an die muslimische Ummah für das Ankommen des Monats Ramadan'. (Author unknown), published by GIMF, July 2012.

2012. 'Stellungnahme zur Kondolenz und Gratulation an die islamische Ummah für das Märtyrertum von Sayh Abu Yahya al-Libi, Allah möge sich seiner erbarmen'. Published by GIMF, 11.09.2012.

2012. 'Abrechnung mit Deutschland'. Written by Abu Assad al-Almani, published by GIMF, 21.09.2012.

2012. 'Eine Fatwah bezüglich der Verpflichtung der Tötung des Regisseurs, Produzenten und Schauspieler des Schmäh-Videos'. Written by Ahmad Ashush, translated and published by GIMF, 18.09.2012.

2012. 'Die Freiheit im Gihad'. Written by Abu Assad al-Almani, published by GIMF, 11.10.2012.

2012. 'Unterstützung des Gesandten. Eine Botschaft von Sayh Ayman Az-Zawahiri'. Translated and published by GIMF, 13.10.2012.

2012. 'Abu Ibrahim: Liebe und Hass für Allah'. Video, October 2012.

2012. 'Abu Usama al Gharib: Das Quran Projekt geht weiter!' Video, October/November 2012.

2012. 'Abu Usama Al-Gharib: Ist es nicht Zeit! Is it not time to rise up'. Video, posted on ansaralshariah.wordpress.com, 16.11.2012.

2013. 'Abu Ibrahim: Wie lange soll dieses erniedrigte Leben noch weitergehen?', Video, January 2013.

2013. 'Anschläge auf die Bevölkerung in dar al-harb. Eine Fatwa von Shaykh Anwar al-Awlaki'. Translated in German and published by GIMF, January 2013.

2013. 'Unser Leben vor euer Leben und somit unser Blut vor eurem Blut: Ein Brief an die Ummah'. Written by Abu Assad al-Almani, published by GIMF, 12.01.2013.

2013. 'Abu Usama al-Gharib: Passverbrennung'. Video, 15.03.2013.

2013. 'Abu Usama Al-Gharib: Das Urteil über das Unterstützen der Kuffar gegen die Muslime'. May 2013.

2013. 'Abu Tahla al Almani: Warum steht ihr nicht auf'. Video, late December 2013.

A5 Primary data *Muslim Association of Britain*

2002. 'Press release: Palestine/Iraq joint demonstration 28 Sept 2002', 06.08.2002.

2002. 'Press release: The biggest demonstration for justice and peace in decade', 28.09.2002.

2002. 'Standing firm, two years on', in 'I.N.S.P.I.R.E. A special edition newspaper produced by the Muslim Association of Britain', 28.09.2002, pp. 1 and 3.

2002. 'We can make a change', in 'I.N.S.P.I.R.E.', 28.09.2002, p. 2.

2002. 'Over two years of resistance in the face of an army equipped with all the latest armoury', in 'I.N.S.P.I.R.E.', 28.09.2002, p. 3.

2002. 'About MAB: The organisation', in 'I.N.S.P.I.R.E.', 28.09.2002, p. 16.

2002. 'About MAB: MAB activities and events', in 'I.N.S.P.I.R.E.', 28.09.2002, p. 17.

2002. 'MAB & other groups react to latest UN Resolution on Iraq', 11.11.2002.

2002. 'Press release: Blair further rubbing salt into our wounds!' 13.11.2002.

2003. '11th February: A day of Eid, solidarity and resolve for Muslims in Britain', 04.02.2003.

2003. 'Muslim leaders' declaration on Iraq', 13.02.2003.

2004. 'MAB responds to vile attack', 13.08.2004.

Appendix B

Original quotes in German

B1 Original longer quotes from Chapter 2

1. DWR, 05.05.2012: 'ich ap ... appelliere hier an die Merkel persönlich [unverständlich] direkt und an den Bundesinnenministern: Für das friedliche Zusammenleben ... hier leben Millionen von Muslimen ... und es leben deutsche Bürger überall in islamischen Ländern. Wenn Sie wollen, dass kein Deutscher verschleppt wird, denn es gibt überall Muslime ... [*Publikum jubelt*] Man hat gesehen, was passiert ist, nach den Karikaturen von Kurt Westergaard ... möge Allah ihn verfluchen! Man hat ... man hat gesehen, dass Menschen gestorben sind auf diese[r] Erde.'

2. DWR, 03.05.2012: 'Seid geduldig und seid standhaft und ich bitte, liebe Geschwister, ich bitte alle Geschwister ... hier in Deutschland, ich bitte alle Geschwister, an den kommenden ... an den kommenden äh Tagen, teilzunehmen. [...] wisst ihr, dass diese ProNRW-Aktivisten, [...] Demos bzw. Kundgebungen planen, in den sie den gesandten Allah a.s.s. beleidigen wollen. Äh die wollen auf Stimm[en]fang gehen.'

3. DWR, 03.05.2012: 'mir ist es viel viel lieber, dass ich irgendwo hinkomme, Präsenz zeige und auch wenn mir alle Knochen gebrochen werden. Wallahi, mir ist es viel viel lieber, dass mir alle Knochen gebrochen werden. Mir ist es viel viel lieber, dass man mich ein Kopf kürzer macht, als dass der Prophet Mohamed a.s.s. beleidigt wird.'

4. DWR, 23.03.2010: 'Wenn deine[r] Glaube nicht stark ist, deine Kinder werden in die Kirche gehen und ein Kreuz anbeten, ob du willst oder nicht willst. Dein[e] Kinder werden Schweinefleisch essen. Dein[e] Kinder werden getauft werden. Wallahi das ist eine bittere Wahrheit. Und das bezeugen so viele Menschen ... hier in Deutschland.'

5. MI, 21.09.2012: 'Die Pro-NRW, die unseren geliebten Propheten (Allahs Friede und Segen auf ihn) in Karikaturen belustigten. Und jene Politiker, welche die Genehmigung für das zeigen dieser Karikatur guthießen und erlaubten. Und jene Mitbürger, die sie darin

unterstützen, egal wer sie sind. Ihr Blutvergießen bzw. ihre Tötung soll eine besondere Wichtigkeit in den Herzen jener haben, die darauf brennen den Gesandten Allahs (Allahs Friede und Segen auf ihn) zu rächen, und die darauf brennen nach dem Wohlgefallen ihres Herrn zu streben.'

B2 Original longer quotes from Chapter 4

1. DWR, 28.05.2012: 'Wir sehen was auf der Welt passiert, was den Muslimen auf dieser Welt passiert, überall auf dieser Welt, wo ein … wo Blut fließt. […] Schaust du nach Afrika, ist es das Blut der Muslime, schaust nach Asien, ist es das Blut der Muslime, überall wo du hinschaust, das Blut der Muslime hat keinen Wert und wallahi heutzutage machen sich die Leute … Gedanken und haben Angst, eine Fliege etwas anzutun, aber machen sich keine Gedanken über die Muslime.'
2. DWR, 21.04.2013: 'Wir sehen, liebe Geschwister, dass die gesamte Erde kämpft gegen den Islam in al-Sham. Es ist nicht nur ein Kampf gegen Baschar, dort kämpfen 12.000 schiitische verfluchte Kuffar aus dem Libanon und aus dem Iran gegen die Muslimin. Dort kämpft Israel gegen die Muslimin, dort kämpft Amerika gegen die Muslimin, dort kämpfen die gesamte Menschheit und Europa gegen die Muslimin.'
3. DWR, 21.04.2013: 'Es ist kein Krieg, wie ein anderer Krieg. […] die wissen ganz genau, wenn der Islam dort siegt, dann ist Israel nicht wie gestern Israel. […] wenn der Islam siegt, dann ist morgen Ägypten nicht mehr das Ägypten von gestern und Syrien nicht das Syrien von gestern und Irak nicht das Irak von gestern.'
4. DWR, 08.2013: 'Flüsse von Blut, diese Menge von Leichen, das ist doch, das erleben die doch seit Jahren, das erleben wir in Falastin seit Jahren. […] In Afghanistan, wurden sie nicht abgeschlachtet und getötet? In Iraq, wurden sie nicht abgeschlachtet und getötet? In Sumal … in Shishan … Überall auf jeden Fleck [sic] dieser Erde, wo du mit dem Finger zeigst, werden unsere Geschwister abgeschlachtet. Syrien ist nicht neu, liebe Geschwister, Ägypten ist nicht neu.'
5. MI, 01.2013: 'Keiner der Könige oder Präsidenten (welche Abtrünnige sind) [würde] den Ğihād auf dem Weg Allāhs erlauben. Die einzige Art des Krieges, welchen sie erlauben würden, ist ein Krieg, von dem sie selbst profitieren und der ihre Macht beschützt.'
6. MI, 13.10.2012: '[Es ist] die Verkündung des Propheten s.a.s.: "Ihr werdet Rom erobern, ihr werdet Rom erobern, ihr werdet Konstantinopel und Rom erobern" … Und dann wird auf dem Petersplatz oder wie das heißt, ja, das wird inshallah der Platz der Konvertierung sein.'

B3 Original longer quotes from Chapter 5

1. DWR, 25.10.2012: 'Achtet nicht auf RTL und BILD-Zeitung und diese Versager, diese Kuffar, ja? Was die alles erzählen, das ist nicht unser Maßstab. Wenn sie über einen Moslem schlecht reden, das ist ein guter Moslem. Wenn Sie sagen, dass ein Moslem ein Terrorist ist, dann ist es ein gottesfürchtiger Moslem. Immer das Gegenteil von dem was die Kuffar behaupten, ja? Wenn sie dich loben als Moslem, dann musst du Angst haben.'

2. MI, 05.2013: 'Schau, das ist Wissen Brüder, das ist Wissen. Nicht ah, 1 plus 1 ist 2, wallahi Religion war niemals nach Logik. [...] Religion ist niemals nach Meinung und niemals nach Logik ja? Wallahi wenn du siehst, es gibt ein Nutzen für den Islam hm ... und du weißt ganz genau, wenn du das tust, wie diese und jene Tat, wenn du das tust, kommst du ins Gefängnis oder du wirst getötet und du machst das trotzdem, wirst du in den höchsten Stufen der mujahideen und shuhada!! Das ist Islam.'

3. MI, 11.10.2012: 'Mit dem Antritt zum Ǧihād fīsabilillāh ist es als ob du eine vollkommen andere Welt betrittst. [...] Denn wo kann man den *Tauḥīd* besser lernen und in sein Leben einbringen als auf dem Schlachtfeld?

   • Wo ist man sich des Todes bewusster als auf dem Schlachtfeld?
   • Wo ist die Liebe zu deinem Schöpfer größer, als auf dem Schlachtfeld, da dir klar wird, dass jeglicher Nutzen und Schaden nicht ohne die Erlaubnis deines Herrn eintrifft?
   • Wo hast du mehr Sehnsucht darauf deinem Herrn zu begegnen als auf dem Schlachtfeld?
   • Wo empfindest du mehr Abneigung für die *Dunyā* **als auf dem Schlachtfeld?**
   • Wo empfindest du mehr Zuneigung für die *Aḫirah* **als auf dem Schlachtfeld?**
   • Wo ist das Leben freier als das eines *Muǧāhids*, **auf dem Schlachtfeld?**
   • Wo ist das Ausleben von *Qur'ān* und *Sunnah* **intensiver als auf dem Schlachtfeld?**
   • Wo ist die Eifersucht für *Allāhs* Religion **größer als auf dem Schlachtfeld?**
   • Wo ist die Sorge für die *Ummah* **größer als auf dem Schlachtfeld, wo du doch die Kinder dieser Ummah in deinen eigenen Armen liegend sterben siehst?**
   • Wo ist deine Aufopferung für den *Islām* **bzw. für die** *Ummah* **größer als auf dem Schlachtfeld?**

- Wo verspürst du mehr Ehre, Würde und Stolz, zugleich aber auch Ruhe, Tugendhaftigkeit und Demut als auf dem Schlachtfeld?
- Wo ist man der Ergebenheit zum Allmächtigen näher als auf dem Schlachtfeld?
- Und wo ist man dem Wohlgefallen des Erhabenen, dem Erschaffer der Himmel und der Erde näher als auf dem Schlachtfeld?' (Layout, italic, and bold in the original)

4. MI, 16.11.2011: 'Der eine von euch ist nicht gläubig, bis er für seinen Bruder das liebt, was er für sich selbst liebt. Und er sagte: "Ein Beispiel für die Gläubigen in ihrer Liebe, Barmherzigkeit und Solidarität zu einander ist der eine Körper, wenn ein Körperteil davon leidet, dann folgt ihm der Rest des Körpers mit Fieber und Schlaflosigkeit."'

5. MI, 19.11.2011: 'Die Prüfung muss kommen, damit Allah die Reihen läutert und daraus diejenigen die schwache[n] Herzen haben reinigt und danach kommt Allähs Sieg! [...] So danke Allah O Schwester dafür, dass Er dich von den Millionen auserwählt hat, um Seine Religion zu tragen und auf Seinen Weg geprüft zu werden, denn bei Allah, es ist eine große Ehre, die niemand erlangt, außer wen Allah dazu auserwählt!'

6. MI, 07.2012: 'So seid ihr diejenigen, mit eurem duftenden Blut, welche den Baum des Lebens der Islamische Ummah tränken, unter dessen Schatten die Muslime den Schutz des islamischen Shari'ah-Staats genießen. [...] Und sie lehnen es ab zu leben, außer unter dem Schatten und der Dominanz der Islamischen Shari'ah. Sie nehmen keinen Weg, außer den kurzen Weg, welches der Weg des Jihads ist, um die Ehre der Islamischen Ummah, dessen Stolz und Ehrfurcht wiederherzustellen.'

7. MI, 11.2011: 'Stolz und Ehre, wahrhaftig Stolz und Ehre, konnte mir nur Allah s.w.t. geben. Und *wallahi*, die hat er mir gegeben. *Alhamdulillah*, ich bin stolz, ein Muslim zu sein. [...] *Alhamdulillah* ich bin stolz, dass ich den Bruder Abu Usama al-Gharib kennen gelernt habe. *Alhamdulillah* und da ist ein Bruder, wo ich sagen kann, der ist ein Bruder mit Ehre und es ehrt mich diesen Bruder zu haben.'

8. MI, 11.2012: 'Ja, liebe Geschwister, "töten" kommt ungefähr 128-mal im Quran vor, davon 27-mal in Befehlsform. Die dachten ... sie dachten, sie werden uns damit provozieren, wir würden uns für den Islam schämen. Pff, "töten" kommt 128-mal im Quran vor, davon 27-mal in Befehlsform, wenn dieser *Kafir* richtig gezählt hat, ja, und wir sind stolz drauf. Wir sind stolz drauf!'

9. MI, 01.2013: 'Alleine die Bilder aus Syrien! Ja, aus Afghanistan! Aus Irak! Aus Tschetschenien! Aus Somalia ... muss reichen für euch! [sic] Wer ein Stückchen Ehre oder ein Stückchen Stolz hat, müsse ... muss

das reichen!! Da brauch ich nicht mehr viel zu erzählen!! Weil das Herz muss brennen, das Herz muss brennen! Wir müssen weinen! [...] *Subhan'allah ari*, Koran und Sunna ist klar [sic], Bruder, klar und offen, deswegen kehre zurück, bevor es zu spät ist, denn diese Ummah braucht Löwen, braucht Soldaten, die für Allah *azza wa-jall* arbeiten!'

10. MI, 21.09.2012: 'Die deutschen Kreuzzügler haben es wieder einmal Dank eurer Eifersuchtlosigkeit geschafft, ihr Hass gegen den Islam unter Beweis zu stellen, und ihr Muslime in Deutschland habt wieder einmal Dank eurer Liebe zur Dunya bewiesen, dass euer Leben euch lieber ist, als die Ehre des edlen Gesandten Allahs (Allahs Friede und Segen auf ihn).'

Appendix C

Codebooks and tables

C1 Codebook 'Group moderation and group radicalisation' with examples

Main category	Category	Code	Examples
Discourse-based radicalisation	Aim to establish a (world) Islamic caliphate	By converting the rest of the world	'Carrying the message of Islam to the world and striving for *izhar ud-deen* i.e. the total domination of the world by Islam'
		By waging war against other collectives (expansion)	'Jihad for the sake of Allah (swt) to defend the *deen* of Allah and the citizens of the *khilafah* (Muslim or non-Muslim) and to conquer the whole world by *dawa* and jihad, are all duties upon Muslims'
		By revolution(s) and/or coup(s)	'There is no other way to restore the pride and glory of Muslims except to overthrow the corrupt regimes, and work to establish a *khilafah* state.'
	Legitimisation of political violence	Praise of a person or group, who/ which (have) condone(d) political violence and/or who engaged in political violence	'Our Shaykh Abu Muhammad al- Maqdisi' (known supporter of waging jihad to reclaim Muslim lands)
		Call to acts of violence or to participate in combat/war	'Al-Qaeda and all its branches and organisations of the world, that is the victorious group and they have the *emir* and you are obliged to join.'

Main category	Category	Code	Examples
		Legitimise violence theoretically or indirectly	*Theoretical*: 'our main concern is to please Allah, and to die in the cause of Allah and go to *jannah* (paradise). If the U.S. continues with her policy against Islam and the Muslim world, Muslims will be more inclined to strike blows against America.' *Indirect*: 'The bombings in non-Muslim lands should not be viewed any different from what the Muslims are facing every day in Palestine, Afghanistan and Iraq.'
	Specifications on how political violence should be conducted	Identification of targets or locations	'There should be no doubt in the minds of any Muslims that the Jews and Christians are *kafir* and the enemy of Islam and Muslims.'
		Identification of means	'Muslims in the world need to participate in the struggle to liberate Muslim land physically, financially or verbally.'
	Support for international jihad	Financing activities abroad for *dawa* work or relief aid, operated by insurgent organisations	'Brother, support financially your brothers and sisters who want to go and help your brothers and sisters [in Syria].'
Action-based radicalisation		Joint activities with actors known to support jihad	'Conference with Anwar al-Awlaki' Organisation of conferences and seminars with prominent actors supporting jihad and/or heading jihadi organisations
		Organisation of local training camps or weapons seminars	Take position on 'training camp' affairs uncovered by the media
		Contact with insurgent group abroad and/or contact facilitation for would-be foreign fighters	Possess direct sources of information from/ communication with insurgent groups abroad

Main category	Category	Code	Examples
	Reference to participation in violence locally	Participation in demonstrations and/or riots gone violent	Leaders and/or members participated in riots and local violence in UK or Germany
	Reference to (planned) attacks by (ex) members or followers	Foiled attacks	Sauerland cell in Germany; Shoe bomb attack in UK; etc.
		Successful attacks	Tel Aviv suicide attack by Britons; London subway attacks; etc.
	Participation in jihad	Participation in jihad as a foreign fighter	'I am a *mujahid* [fighter performing jihad], who strives to destroy these regimes, this democracy, this laicism, these dogs.'
Discourse-based moderation	Participation	Participation in public debate and/or acceptance of pluralism of opinion	'[We] constantly called for open dialogue to be conducted with all elements of society, whether it be with the various faith communities or otherwise.'
		Delegitimisation of actors of political violence	'As far as the events are concerned, in particular the assaults on the World Trade Center and the Pentagon, we said that such attacks are not condoned by the sharia.'
		Rejection of political violence as a legitimate political means in UK or Germany	'Extremism is rejected in Islam'
	Exit	Withdrawal from public debate	Refuse any dialogue with other actors in the public sphere
Action-based moderation	Participation 2	Non-violent collective action (participation in, organisation of)	Community events, demonstrations, information stands, distribution of leaflets, etc.
		Reference to relations with political leaders or leaders of civil society organisations	'To improve the relationship between the Muslim community and the British institutions'

Main category	Category	Code	Examples
		Call to boycott	'Calling on our peoples and the free peoples of the world to boycott U.S. and Israeli products and the products of every state that declares its participation in the crime of invading Iraq.'
	Exit 2	No interaction with (host) society and/or state	'Do not pollute or even negate your *iman* [faith] by having any inclination whatsoever to other than those to whom Allah (*swt*) asks you to ally with.'
		Encourage *hijra* (immigration to Muslim lands)	'Muslims can no longer be considered to have sanctity and security here, therefore they should consider leaving this country and going back to their homelands.'

C2 Radicalisation and moderation by group (except MAB): relative code frequencies

Codes	HTB (%)	DWR (%)	AM (%)	MI (%)
By converting the rest of the world	27.3	0.0	54.5	18.2
By waging war/expansion	31.6	0.0	26.3	42.1
By revolution or coup	85.7	4.8	9.5	0.0
Praise person or group	3.3	0.6	19.9	76.2
Call to violence/combat	31.0	8.0	6.9	54.0
Legitimation of violence (theoretical or indirect)	17.1	10.5	43.8	28.6
Identification of targets or locations	2.5	1.3	29.1	67.1
Identification of means	7.3	0.0	26.8	65.9
Financing activities abroad	0.0	33.3	16.7	50.0
Joint activities with actors supporting jihad	0.0	0.0	100.0	0.0
Contact with insurgent groups abroad	0.0	0.0	100.0	0.0
Riots or demonstrations gone violent	0.0	60.0	0.0	40.0
Foiled attacks	0.0	0.0	0.0	100.0

Codes	HTB (%)	DWR (%)	AM (%)	MI (%)
Successful attacks	0.0	0.0	100.0	0.0
As foreign fighter	0.0	0.0	0.0	100.0
Participation in public debate and support for pluralism of opinion	12.5	75.0	12.5	0.0
Delegitimisation of actors of political violence	40.0	20.0	40.0	0.0
Rejection of violence as legitimate political means	28.6	57.1	14.3	0.0
Non-violent collective action	21.9	35.9	31.3	10.9
Talks and relations with (local) political leaders	100.0	0.0	0.0	0.0
Call to boycott	62.5	0.0	25.0	12.5
Minimal or no interactions with (host) society	0.0	42.9	28.6	28.6
Encourage *hijra*	0.0	20.0	80.0	0.0

Percentage of coded segments across organisations, for each code (any given row equals 100%).

C3 Codebook 'Romantic Narrative' with examples

Main category	Category	Code	Keywords and examples from the data
CHARACTERS	In-group identities	Muslim victims	*Keywords*: persecuted; discriminated, innocent, killed, tortured ... Muslims *Example*: 'the defenseless Muslims in Afghanistan'
		Muslim role models	*Keywords*: heroes; warriors (*mujahideen*); martyrs (*shuhada*); admirable Muslims; esteemed religious figures (*ulema, sheiks*); Islamic movements or groups *Example*: 'O grandsons of *mujahideen*'
		True believers (Muslims)	*Keywords*: Islamic *ummah* (community of believers); the Islamic world; sincere Muslims; authentic/ righteous/ truth-seeking/-telling/ faithful Muslims *Example*: 'the *Shabab* of the *Hizb*' (i.e. the youth of Hizb ut-Tahrir)

Main category	Category	Code	Keywords and examples from the data
	Out-group identities	Political enemies	*Keywords*: Western governments; Western-backed regimes; international institutions/organisations; political personalities (presidents, ministers); Western militaries
			Example: 'the American fascists', 'the tyrant George Bush', 'the agents of the West'
		The Muslim Other	*Keywords*: secular Muslims; apostates; nationalist Muslims; Muslims of other creeds (Shia, Sufis)
			Example: 'the fake Salafis'
		The (non-) religious Other	*Keywords*: unbelievers (*kuffar*); (groups of) people of other faiths (Jew, Christian, Buddhist, Sikh, Hindu); polytheists; atheists
			Example: 'the Jews, the enemies of Allah'
SETTING	Local horizon of experience	Immoral, depraved, hypocritical	*Keywords*: immoral; hypocritical; plotting; depraved; unprincipled
			Example: 'A brief glimpse at any western society, like the US and UK, […] will reveal a complete breakdown in the social and moral fabric with homosexuality, pedophilia, adultery, promiscuity, fornication, pornography and abortion rampant'
		Islamophobic, repressive, harassing	*Keywords*: political hostility; Islamophobic; state repression; media harassment
			Example: 'The intensification of the anti-Islamic agenda in the West serves to generate a potent atmosphere of fear, hostility and distrust against Muslim populations in the West'
	Transnational horizon of experience	Double-standard, immoral, hypocritical	*Keywords*: immoral; unjust; deceptive; double-standards; hypocritical; untruthful
			Example: 'Of course nobody cares about the untold number of Muslims slaughtered by the Americans, but when *kafirs* [unbelievers] are killed it is different.'

Main category	Category	Code	Keywords and examples from the data
PLOT		Hostile, dangerous, exploiting	*Keywords*: dangerous; exploiting; imperialistic; colonialism; under the hegemony of *Example*: 'We do see Western imperialism as the key factor in the continuing decline of the Islamic world'
	Muslims and their 'way of life' are under threat	Muslims worldwide are prevented from living according to their faith	*Keywords*: Muslims labelled extremists; allegation of 'hate crimes'; wrongly accused of terrorism; imposition of secular justice from the outside; foreign powers prevent the rule of sharia *Example*: 'Islam, in particular its political ideas such as *shariah*, *khilafah* and jihad, are today attacked under the guise of attacking "Islamism".'
		Muslims worldwide are physically/ militarily attacked	*Keywords*: war against; attack against; aggression; crusade; kill; exterminate; destroy; bomb; military action; colonise (when targeted at 'Muslim victims') *Example*: 'they are unleashing all their lethal weapons against the defenceless Muslims in Afghanistan'
		Not the first time in history/ Repeated attacks	*Keywords*: repeated attack; temporal indicators ('worst attack since …'); long history/tradition of; cosmologic references ('last battle') *Example*: 'The second crusader campaign of Bush was against the Muslim Kashmiri groups in Pakistan, when he took India's side.'
		The political leaders of the Muslim world are not protecting Muslims	*Keywords*: abandoned the *ummah*; failed their duties; do not protect Muslims, their wealth/lands; subordination; submission *Example*: 'This is the point to which the Arab rulers from the hypocrites and traitors have reached by collaborating in the conspiracy and colluding with America and the Jews in these massacres.'

Main category	Category	Code	Keywords and examples from the data
	Muslims need to rise up	Resist and fight back	*Keywords*: [with reference to in-group identities] defend; protect; liberate; refuse defeat; avenge; [with reference to out-groups] resist; punish; humiliate; prevail over; defeat the enemy
			Example: 'O Muslims, stand together and unite our *ummah* to fight against the enemies of Allah (*swt*) and his Messenger Muhammad in this time of need.'
		The current (world) order will be replaced by an Islamic caliphate	*Keywords*: caliphate (*khilafah*); caliph (*khaleefah*); the *khilafah* system; the Islamic state
			Example: 'As for the radical work which will solve the problems of the Islamic *ummah*, it is the establishment of the righteous *khilafah* which will unite the Islamic lands and peoples in one state'
		Obligation to help fellow Muslims/ establish the caliphate	*Keywords*: duty, obligation, binding, responsibility, must (go help, fight, contribute financially); are accountable, incumbent upon, required of
			Example: 'Our obligation is to confront the aggression against our brothers and sisters in Iraq by all means, whether that be verbally, physically or financially.'
		Muslims will be rewarded for rising up	*Keywords*: rewarded by Allah; sacrifice worth it; grace/blessing of God; gift/ price/recompense; granted victory; paradise; salvation
			Example: 'And know that Allah has promised that those of you who believe and do righteous deeds will be granted succession in ruling'

C4 Romantic Narrative by case: relative code frequencies

Each row adds up to 100%. Reading example: the highest relative frequency for the code 'Muslim victims' is found in case 9-MI (32.8%); 9-MI is thus responsible for almost a third of all coded segments 'Muslim victims' across all eight cases.

Main category	Category	Code	1-HTB (%)	2-HTB (%)	3-HTB (%)	4-AM (%)	5-AM (%)	6-AM (%)	8-DWR (%)	9-MI (%)
CHARACTERS	In-group identities	Muslim victims	14.8	5.9	9.9	7.9	20.2	0.5	8.1	32.8
		Muslim role models	7.1	9.5	12.1	3.6	21.7	3.4	2.6	39.9
		True believers (Muslims)	10.0	9.6	13.1	4.8	15.4	2.9	12.1	32.0
	Out-group identities	Political enemies	22.0	14.6	18.9	9.9	18.5	1.0	3.9	11.2
		The Muslim Other	2.1	7.2	7.2	5.5	18.7	6.8	11.5	40.9
		The (non-)religious Other	13.0	5.3	6.6	3.0	11.9	5.3	9.6	45.4
SETTING	Local	Immoral, depraved, hypocritical	8.0	0.0	16.0	0.0	32.0	0.0	16.0	28.0
		Islamophobic, repressive, harassing	2.0	3.0	10.1	5.1	21.2	3.0	26.3	29.3
	Transnational	Double-standard, immoral, hypocritical	10.0	11.4	0.0	8.6	41.4	1.4	17.1	10.0
		Hostile, dangerous, exploiting	16.5	16.5	12.2	7.0	21.7	3.5	0.9	21.7
PLOT	Muslims and their 'way of life' are under threat	Muslims are prevented from living according to their faith	8.8	18.6	21.6	8.8	17.6	5.9	8.8	9.8
		Muslims are physically/militarily attacked	30.7	5.5	2.4	11.0	22.0	2.4	11.0	15.0
		Not the first time in history/Repeated attacks	23.6	13.9	15.3	9.7	13.9	2.8	1.4	19.4
		The political leaders of the Muslim world are not protecting Muslims	30.5	17.8	28.8	5.1	9.3	0.0	0.8	7.6
	Muslims need to rise up	Resist and fight back	11.2	7.3	6.8	6.3	17.6	3.9	4.9	42.0
		The current (world) order will be replaced by an Islamic caliphate	18.0	12.0	28.0	2.0	16.0	10.0	2.0	12.0
		Obligation to help fellow Muslims/establish the caliphate	11.7	5.5	10.9	4.7	21.1	3.9	7.8	34.4
		Muslims will be rewarded for rising up	20.8	8.3	6.3	0.0	4.2	2.1	20.8	37.5

Appendix D

Data preparation and representation

D1 Data preparation

The primary data is partly composed of audios and videos. The German-based organisations – *Die Wahre Religion* and *Millatu Ibrahim* – relied in the early 2010s less on texts and more on audio and video messages to communicate with their followership. The selected audios and videos have been transcribed to be brought into the data management system QDA Miner (Provalis®). In the transcripts, the presence of important visual elements (e.g. another speaker or an object such as a flag, a Quran, etc.) and changes in tone (e.g. trembling voice, laughing, shouting, etc.) are indicated through notes in italics placed in square brackets.

The language of the video and audio material is German, punctuated by some Arabic words and expressions for reasons relating to target audiences and language competency. Apart from words found in the Oxford English Dictionary (e.g., 'Allah', 'Sunna', 'Koran', 'Hadith'), expressions in Arabic were transcribed in italics and translated in square brackets on the first occurrence. For example, 'Dear brothers and sisters, *barak allahu fikum* [Allah bless you], I ask you not to bring any weapons'. When coding the data, the Arabic expression and the German translation were coded as one item.

Arabic words and expressions in the corpus were transliterated for easier representation. The transliteration in English uses vocals and consonants typical for the English language; for example, the word 'combatants' is transliterated *mujahideen* in English. Further, as is common in non-specialist texts, the author transliterated without marking Arabic accents. For instance, the word 'hypocrite' was transliterated *munafiq* instead of *munāfiq*. Words and expressions spoken to the glorification of gods, prophets, and other religious figures, such as 'Mohammed *alayhi salatu wa salaam*', meaning 'Muhammad, goodness and peace be upon him', were not systematically transcribed in full but abbreviated according to convention, in the example here as 'Mohammed a.s.s.'. Note that the UK-based organisations – AM and HTB – follow these conventions in their texts too.

The data management system QDA Miner does not recognise – at the time of this research – Arabic script. On the relatively rare occasions that whole sentences were spoken in Arabic – corresponding to quotes from the Quran, which were translated thereafter in German by the speaker – they were left out of the transcript. This pragmatic choice was also made in order not to lengthen artificially the coded segments. Similarly, the author took out the passages in Arabic script (i.e. passages of Islamic scriptures) in the written texts, as they are directly followed by the organisation's own translation in English or German.

Grammar or syntax errors in the original speech were transcribed either with correction in brackets when possible (additions only) and, when not applicable, with the original error followed by '[sic]', indicating that the text was transcribed as it was spoken. Similarly, repetitions of single words or hesitations were transcribed for authenticity; the former by writing the words several times, the latter by inserting '…' or hesitation vowels such as 'ah' or 'hm'.

D2 System for representing the data

The data has not been anonymised. The texts produced by the UK organisations were published in their name, that is, without an individual author. For example, publications by *al-Muhajiroun* typically ended – to the exception of a few texts signed by leader Omar Bakri Mohammed – with the following signature:

'Al-Muhajiroun
The Voice, The Eyes & the Ears of The Muslims' [original layout]

As for the German organisations, some of the texts by *Millatu Ibrahim* were signed under the logo of the German-speaking branch of the Global Islamic Media Front (GIMF), others with the author's name.

Audios and videos displayed the speakers unambiguously as their faces are not hidden and speakers often introduced themselves by name. Further, audios and videos were designed to be spread on social media; there is hence little reason for anonymising their authors.

Most of the German organisations' leaders changed their civil names to Arabic names. In the empirical analysis, leaders are referred to by their given names, only mentioning aliases to trace the authorship of the data. In Part I of the book, quotes from the data are referenced by organisation and date. After the reconstruction of phases of moderation, radicalisation, and extremism in Chapter 2 and subsequent delineation of *cases*, quotes from the data are thereupon referenced by *case* and *date* (book Part II). Referencing quotes in this way is a pragmatic choice; it allows precise quoting while keeping the references in brackets to a reasonable length.

The publishing dates of the texts by UK-based organisations are complete. The German-based organisations present a small number of texts, audios, and videos for which the publishing *day* could not be reconstructed; they are referenced per month and year.

Short quotes are kept in the text's main body, whereas longer quotes are indented. Quotes from the data in German were translated by the author into English. Original quotes under 50 words are referenced in footnotes; longer quotes are appended by chapter (Appendices B1 to B3) and referenced with the Appendix and quote number in the text.

References

Aarten, P. G. M., Mulder, E., & Pemberton, A. (2018). The narrative of victimization and deradicalization: An expert view. *Studies in Conflict & Terrorism, 41*(7), 557–572.

Abay Gaspar, H., Daase, C., Deitelhoff, N., Junk, J., & Sold, M. (2018). Was ist Radikalisierung? Präzisierungen eines umstrittenen Begriffs. *PRIF Report 5.* Frankfurt am Main: Hessische Stiftung Friedens- und Konfliktforschung.

Abdi-Herrle, S., Nothofer, S., & Breitegger, B. (2016, November 15). Fanatiker in Deutschlands Fußgängerzonen. *Die Zeit.* Retrieved from www.zeit.de/gesellschaft/zeitgeschehen/2016-11/die-wahre-religion-islam-salafisten-faq [accessed 5 November 2017].

Abedin, M. (2004). Inside Hizb ut-Tahrir: An interview with Jalaluddin Patel, leader of Hizb ut-Tahrir in the UK. *Spotlight on Terror, 2*(8).

Abedin, M. (2005). Al-Muhajiroun in the UK: An interview with Sheikh Omar Bakri Mohammed. *Spotlight on Terror, 2*(5).

Abou Taam, M., Dantschke, C., Kreutz, M., & Sarhan, A. (2016). Kontinuierlicher Wandel: Organisation und Anwerbungspraxis der salafistischen Bewegung. PRIF Report 2. Frankfurt am Main: Hessische Stiftung Friedens- und Konfliktforschung.

Abrahms, M. (2006). Why terrorism does not work. *International Security, 31*(2), 42–78.

Abrahms, M. (2008). What terrorists really want: Terrorist motives and counterterrorism strategy. *International Security, 32*(4), 78–105.

Abrahms, M. (2012). The political effectiveness of terrorism revisited. *Comparative Political Studies, 45*(3), 366–393.

Åhäll, L. (2018). Affect as methodology: Feminism and the politics of emotion. *International Political Sociology, 12*(1), 36–52.

Åhäll, L. & Gregory, T. (eds). (2015). *Emotions, Politics and War.* London/New York: Routledge.

Ahmed, H. & Stuart, H. (2009). *Hizb ut-Tahrir: Ideology and Strategy.* London: The Centre for Social Cohesion.

Ahmed, H. & Stuart, H. (2010). Profile: Hizb ut-Tahrir in the UK. *Current Trends in Islamist Ideology, 10,* 143–172.

Alimi, E. Y., Bosi, L., & Demetriou, C. (2015). *The Dynamics of Radicalization: A Relational and Comparative Perspective.* New York: Oxford University Press.

Altikriti, A. (2004, August 5). No, we don't want to conquer the world. *Guardian.* Retrieved from www.theguardian.com/world/2004/aug/05/islam.religion [accessed 30 July 2017].

Anderson, B. (2014). *Encountering Affect: Capacities, Apparatuses, Conditions.* Farnham: Ashgate.

Andrews, M., Squire, C., & Tamboukou, M. (2013). *Doing Narrative Research* (2nd edn). London: Sage.

Aristotle. (1954). *Rhetoric* (W. R. Roberts, Trans.). New York: Modern Library.

Ashour, O. (2009). *The De-Radicalization of Jihadists: Transforming Armed Islamist Movements.* New York: Routledge.

Audi, R. (2009). The sources of knowledge. In P. K. Moser (ed.), *The Oxford Handbook of Epistemology* (pp. 71–94). Oxford: Oxford University Press.

Austin, J. L. (1975). *How To Do Things With Words.* Oxford: Oxford University Press.

Baehr, D. (2011). *Der deutsche Salafismus: Vom puristischen Denken eines Hasan Dabbaghs bis zum jihadistischen Salafismus von Eric Breininger.* München: Grin Verlag.

Bal, M. (2009). *Narratology: Introduction to the Theory of Narrative* (3rd edn). Toronto: University of Toronto Press.

Baran, Z. (2004). *Hizb ut-Tahrir: Islam's Political Insurgency.* Washington: The Nixon Center.

Baron, H. (2021). *Die Hizb ut-Tahrir in Deutschland.* Bonn: Bundeszentrale für politische Bildung.

Barthes, R. (1966). Introduction à l'analyse structurale des récits. *Communications*, 8(1), 1–27.

Barthes, R. (1977). Introduction to the structural study of narratives (S. Heath, Trans.). In *Image, Music, Text* (pp. 79–125). London: Fontana.

Bassey, A. (2001, November, 4). We expose traitor luring fellow Brits to fight for Taliban. *Sunday Mercury*.

BBC. (2003, November 6). Al-Muhajiroun leader comments on arrest of 10 'fundamentalists' in UK. *BBC Monitoring Middle East*.

Bell, D. (ed.) (2006). *Memory, Trauma and World Politics: Reflections on the Relationship Between Past and Present.* Houndmills: Palgrave Macmillan.

Belli, S. & Harré, R. (2010). What is love? Discourse about emotions in social sciences. *Human Affairs*, 20(3), 249–270.

Berenskoetter, F. (2013). *Friendship Matters.* London: Sage Publications.

Berlant, L. (2005). The epistemology of state emotion. In A. Sarat (ed.), *Dissent in Dangerous Times* (pp. 46–78). Ann Arbor: University of Michigan Press.

BfV. (2012). *Verfassungsschutzbericht 2011.* Berlin: Bundesministerium des Innern Retrieved from https://publikationen.uni-tuebingen.de/xmlui/bitstream/handle/10900/63256/vsb2011.pdf?sequence= [accessed 16 November 2017].

Bially Mattern, J. (2011). A practice theory of emotion for International Relations. In E. Adler & V. Pouliot (eds), *International Practices* (pp. 63–86). Cambridge: Cambridge University Press.

Biene, J. & Marcks, H. (2014). *From Attitude to Militancy. Challenging the Concept of Radicalization.* Paper presented at the PSA 64th Annual International Conference 'Rebels & Radicals' 14–16 April, Manchester.

Biene, J., Daase, C., Junk, J., & Müller, H. (2016). *Salafismus und Dschihadismus in Deutschland: Ursachen, Dynamiken, Handlungsempfehlungen.* Frankfurt am Main: Campus Verlag.

BKA/BfV/HKE. (2015). *Analyse der Radikalisierungshintergründe und -verläufe der Personen, die aus islamistischer Motivation aus Deutschland in Richtung Syrien oder Irak ausgereist sind.* Wiesbaden: BKA.

Bleiker, R. & Hutchison, E. (2008). Fear no more: Emotions and world politics. *Review of International Studies, 34*(S1), 115–135.

Bleiker, R. & Hutchison, E. (2018). Conclusion: Methods and methodologies for the study of emotions in world politics. In M. Clément & E. Sangar (eds), *Researching Emotions in International Relations* (pp. 325–342. London/New York: Palgrave Macmillan.

Bless, H. (2000). The interplay of affect and cognition: The mediating role of general knowledge structures. In J. P. Forgas (ed.), *Feeling and Thinking: The Role of Affect in Social Cognition* (pp. 201–222). New York: Cambridge University Press.

Bloom, M. (2005). *Dying to Kill: The Global Phenomenon of Suicide Terror*. New York: Columbia University Press.

Bogerts, L. & Fielitz, M. (2019). "Do you want meme war?" Understanding the visual memes of the German Far Right. In M. Fielitz & N. Thurston (eds), *Post-Digital Cultures of the Far Right* (pp. 137–153). Bielefeld: transcript Verlag.

Boltanski, L. (1999). *Distant Suffering: Morality, Media, and Politics*. Cambridge/New York: Cambridge University Press.

Bosi, L. (2016). Violence/militancy. In K. Fahlenbrach, M. Klimke, & J. Scharloth (eds), *Protest Cultures: A Companion* (pp. 190–197). New York/Oxford: Berghahn Books.

Bosi, L., della Porta, D., & Malthaner, S. (2019). Organizational and institutional approaches: Social movement studies perspectives on political violence. In E. Chenoweth, R. English, A. Gofas, & S. N. Kalyvas (eds), *The Oxford Handbook of Terrorism* (pp. 133–147). Oxford: Oxford University Press.

Boubekeur, A. (2007). Political Islam in Europe. In S. Amghar, A. Boubekeur, & M. Emerson (eds), *European Islam: Challenges for Public Policy and Society* (pp. 14–37). Brussels: Centre for European Policy Studies.

Brounéus, K. (2008). Truth-telling as talking cure? Insecurity and retraumatization in the Rwandan Gacaca courts. *Security Dialogue, 39*(1), 55–76.

Bruner, J. S. (1986). *Actual Minds, Possible Worlds*. Cambridge, MA: Harvard University Press.

Bryson, R. (2017). *For Caliph and Country: Exploring How British Jihadis Join a Global Movement*. London: Tony Blair Institute for Global Change.

Busher, J. & Bjørgo, T. (2020). Restraint in terrorist groups and radical milieus: Towards a research agenda. *Perspectives on Terrorism, 14*(6), 2–13.

Butler, J. (1993). *Bodies that Matter: On the Discursive Limits of 'Sex'*. London: Routledge.

Butler, J. (2010). Performative agency. *Journal of Cultural Economy, 3*(2), 147–161.

Calhoun, C. (2001). Putting emotions in their place. In J. Goodwin, J. M. Jasper, & F. Polletta (eds), *Passionate Politics: Emotions and Social Movements* (pp. 45–57). Chicago, IL: University of Chicago Press.

Casciani, D. & Sakr, S. (2006, February 7). The battle for the mosque. *BBC News*. Retrieved from http://news.bbc.co.uk/2/hi/uk_news/4639074.stm [accessed 10 July 2017].

Castelli Gattinara, P. & Froio, C. (2014). Discourse and practice of violence in the Italian extreme right: Frames, symbols, and identity-building in CasaPound Italia. *International Journal of Conflict and Violence, 8*(1), 154–170.

Chatman, S. B. (1980). *Story and Discourse: Narrative Structure in Fiction and Film*: Ithaca, NY: Cornell University Press.

Choueiri, Y. M. (1990). *Islamic Fundamentalism*. Boston, MA: Twayne Publishers.

Clément, M. (2014). Al-Muhajiroun in the United Kingdom: The role of international non-recognition in heightened radicalization dynamics. *Global Discourse, 4*(4), 428–443.

Clément, M. (2019). *Islamist Organizations in Western Europe: The Role of Collective Emotions in Group Radicalization Processes*. (PhD), Frankfurt am Main: Goethe University Frankfurt.

Clément, M. (2020). Kollektive Emotionen und politische Gewalt: Konturen eines neuen Forschungsprogramms in der Terrorismusforschung. In S. Koschut (ed.), *Emotionen in den Internationalen Beziehungen* (pp. 189–212). Baden-Baden: Nomos.

Clément, M. (2021). Emotions and affect in terrorism research: Epistemological shift and ways ahead. *Critical Studies on Terrorism, 14*(2), 247–270.

Clément, M. & Sangar, E. (2018). *Researching Emotions in International Relations. Methodological Perspectives on the Emotional Turn*. London/New York: Palgrave Macmillan.

Clément, M., Lindemann, T., & Sangar, E. (2017). The 'hero-protector narrative': manufacturing emotional consent for the use of force. *Political Psychology, 38*(6), 991–1008.

Cobb, S. B. (2013). *Speaking of Violence: The Politics and Poetics of Narrative in Conflict Resolution*. New York: Oxford University Press.

Connor, W. (1993). Beyond reason: The nature of the ethnonational bond. *Ethnic and Racial Studies, 16*(3), 373–389.

Constantinou, C. M. (2000). Poetics of security. *Alternatives, 25*(3), 287–306.

Conway, M. (2012). From al-Zarqawi to al-Awlaki: The emergence and development of an online radical milieu. *CTX: Combating Terrorism Exchange, 2*(4), 12–22.

Copeland, S. (2019). Telling stories of terrorism: A framework for applying narrative approaches to the study of militant's self-accounts. *Behavioral Sciences of Terrorism and Political Aggression, 11*(3), 232–253.

Crawford, N. C. (2014). Institutionalizing passion in world politics: Fear and empathy. *International Theory, 6*(3), 535–557.

Crenshaw, M. (1990). The logic of terrorism: Terrorist behavior as a product of strategic choice. In W. Reich (ed.), *Origins of Terrorism: Psychologies, Ideologies, Theologies, States of Mind* (pp. 7–24). New York: Cambridge University Press.

Creswell, R. & Haykel, B. (2015, 1 June). Battle lines – Want to understand the jihadis? Read their poetry. *The New Yorker*. Retrieved from www.newyorker.com/magazine/2015/06/08/battle-lines-jihad-creswell-and-haykel [accessed 30 November 2017].

Crone, M. (2016). Radicalization revisited: Violence, politics and the skills of the body. *International Affairs, 92*(3), 587–604.

Cronin, A. K. (2006). How al-Qaida ends: The decline and demise of terrorist groups. *International Security, 31*(1), 7–48.

Damasio, A. R. (2004). William James and the modern neurobiology of emotion. In D. Evans & P. Cruse (eds), *Emotion, Evolution, and Rationality* (pp. 3–12). New York: Oxford University Press.

Damasio, A. R. (2006). *Descartes' Error*. New York: Random House.

Damasio, A. R., Everitt, B. J., & Bishop, D. (1996). The somatic marker hypothesis and the possible functions of the prefrontal cortex. *Philosophical Transactions: Biological Sciences*, 1413–1420.

Dantschke, C. (2014). 'Lasst euch nicht radikalisieren!' Salafismus in Deutschland. In T. G. Schneiders (ed.), *Salafismus in Deutschland: Ursprünge und Gefahren einer islamisch-fundamentalistischen Bewegung* (pp. 171–186). Bielefeld: transcript Verlag.

Demetriou, C., Malthaner, S., & Bosi, L. (2014). *Dynamics of Political Violence: A Process-Oriented Perspective on Radicalization and the Escalation of Political Conflict*. Farnham: Ashgate.

Diehl, J. (2015, 10 October). Flucht vor Haftstrafe: Salafisten-Anführer setzt sich ins Ausland ab. *Spiegel*. Retrieved from www.spiegel.de/politik/deutschland/top-salafist-hasan-k-flieht-vor-haftstrafe-ins-ausland-a-1055726.html [accessed 5 November 2017].

Egerton, F. (2011). *Jihad in the West: The Rise of Militant Salafism*. Cambridge: Cambridge University Press.

Eken, E. M. (2019). How geopolitical becomes personal: Method acting, war films and affect. *Journal of International Political Theory*, 15(2), 210–228.

Eriksen, T. H. (2004). Place, kinship and the case for non-ethnic nations. *Nations and Nationalism*, 10(1–2), 49–62.

Eroukhmanoff, C. (2019). Responding to terrorism with peace, love and solidarity: 'Je Suis Charlie', 'Peace' and 'I Heart MCR'. *Journal of International Political Theory*, 15(2), 167–187.

Esposito, J. L. (1997). *Political Islam: Revolution, Radicalism, or Reform?* Boulder, CO: Lynne Rienner.

Eznack, L. (2012). *Crises in the Atlantic Alliance: Affect and Relations among NATO Members*. London: Palgrave.

Fairclough, N. (1992). Discourse and text: Linguistic and intertextual analysis within discourse analysis. *Discourse & Society*, 3(2), 193–217.

Fairclough, N. (2013). *Critical Discourse Analysis: The Critical Study of Language* (2nd edn). London: Routledge.

Fattah, K. & Fierke, K. M. (2009). A clash of emotions: The politics of humiliation and political violence in the Middle East. *European Journal of International Relations*, 15(1), 67–93.

Feinstein, J. S., Adolphs, R., Damasio, A., & Tranel, D. (2011). The human amygdala and the induction and experience of fear. *Current Biology*, 21(1), 34–38.

Fierke, K. M. (2012). *Political Self-Sacrifice: Agency, Body and Emotion in International Relations*. Cambridge: Cambridge University Press.

Fierke, K. M. (2015). Human dignity, basal emotion and a global emotionology. In L. Åhäll & T. Gregory (eds), *Emotions, Politics and War* (pp. 45–57). London/New York: Routledge.

Fisher, W. R. (1984). Narration as a human communication paradigm: The case of public moral argument. *Communications Monographs*, 51(1), 1–22.

Fisher, W. R. (1987). *Human Communication as Narration: Toward a Philosophy of Reason, Value, and Action*. Columbia, SC: University of South Carolina Press.

Flam, H. & King, D. (2005). *Emotions and Social Movements*. London: Routledge.

Fludernik, M. (2009). *An Introduction to Narratology*. London: Routledge.

Forgas, J. P. (2001). *Feeling and Thinking: The Role of Affect in Social Cognition*. Cambridge: Cambridge University Press.

Franzosi, R. (1998). Narrative analysis – or why (and how) sociologists should be interested in narrative. *Annual Review of Sociology*, 24(1), 517–554.

Frijda, N. H., Mesquita, B., Sonnemans, J., & van Goozen, S. (1991). The duration of affective phenomena or emotions, sentiments and passions. In K. T. Strongman (ed.), *International Review of Studies on Emotion* (Vol. 1, pp. 187–225). New York: Wiley.

Gendron, A. (2016). The call to Jihad: Charismatic preachers and the Internet. In A. Aly (ed.), *Violent Extremism Online: New Perspectives on Terrorism and the Internet* (pp. 25–44). New York: Routledge.

Genette, G. (1980 [1972]). *Narrative Discourse* (J. E. Lewin., Trans.). Oxford: Basil Blackwell.

Genette, G. (1983). *Narrative Discourse: An Essay in Method.* Ithaca, NY: Cornell University Press.

Gilliat-Ray, S. (2010). *Muslims in Britain.* Cambridge: Cambridge University Press.

Glazzard, A. (2017). Losing the plot: narrative, counter-narrative and violent extremism. *The International Centre for Counter-Terrorism Research Report,* 1–21.

Goodwin, J. & Jasper, J. M. (2004). *Rethinking Social Movements: Structure, Culture, and Emotion.* Lanham, MD: Rowman & Littlefield.

Goodwin, J. & Pfaff, S. (2001). Emotion work in high-risk social movements: Managing fear in the US and East German civil rights movements. In J. Goodwin, J. M. Jasper, & F. Polletta (eds), *Passionate Politics: Emotions and Social Movements* (pp. 282–302). Chicago, IL: University of Chicago Press.

Gould, D. B. (2004). Passionate political processes: Bringing emotions back into the study of social movements. In J. Goodwin & J. M. Jasper (eds.), *Rethinking Social Movements: Structure, Meaning, and Emotions* (pp. 155–176). Lanham, MD: Rowman & Littlefield.

Graef, J., Da Silva, R., & Lemay-Hebert, N. (2020). Narrative, political violence, and social change. *Studies in Conflict & Terrorism, 43*(6), 431–443.

Greimas, A. J. (1966). Eléments pour une théorie de l'interprétation du récit mythique. *Communications, 8*(1), 28–59.

Guardian Editorial. (2005, July 22). Background: The Guardian and Dilpazier Aslam. *Guardian.* Retrieved from www.theguardian.com/media/2005/jul/22/theguardian.pressandpublishing1 [accessed 30 July 2017].

Guibet-Lafaye, C. & Rapin, A.-J. (2017). Individualisation et dépolitisation d'une notion: Evolutions contemporaines de la sémantique de la radicalisation. *Politiques de communication, 1*(8), 127–154.

Gunning, J. (2007). A case for critical terrorism studies? *Government and Opposition, 42*(3), 363–393.

Hafez, F. (2019). Muslim civil society under attack: The European Foundation for Democracy's role in defaming and delegitimizing Muslim civil society. In J. L. Esposito & D. Iner (eds), *Islamophobia and Radicalization* (pp. 117–137). Cham: Springer.

Hall, T. H. (2011). We will not swallow this bitter fruit: Theorizing a diplomacy of anger. *Security Studies, 20*(4), 521–555.

Hamann, J. & Suckert, L. (2018). Temporality in discourse: Methodological challenges and a suggestion for a quantified qualitative approach. *Forum Qualitative Sozialforschung / Forum: Qualitative Social Research, 19*(2), 1–32.

Hamid, S. (2016). *Sufis, Salafis and Islamists: The Contested Ground of British Islamic Activism.* London: IB Tauris.

Hammack, P. L. & Pilecki, A. (2012). Narrative as a root metaphor for political psychology. *Political Psychology, 33*(1), 75–103.

Hardy, B. (1987). *The Collected Essays of Barbara Hardy*. New Jersey: Harvest Press.

Harré, R. & Gillett, G. (1994). *The Discursive Mind*. London: Sage.

Heinke, D. H. & Raudszus, J. (2015). German foreign fighters in Syria and Iraq. *CTC Sentinel, 8*(1), 18–21.

Hinchman, L. P. & Hinchman, S. (1997). *Memory, Identity, Community: The Idea of Narrative in the Human Sciences*. Albany: State University of New York Press.

Hizb ut-Tahrir. (2000). *Hizb ut-Tahrir*. London: Al-Khilafah Publications.

Hochschild, A. R. (1979). Emotion work, feeling rules, and social structure. *American Journal of Sociology, 85*(3), 551–575.

Hochschild, A. R. (1983). *The Managed Heart: Commercialization of Human Feeling*. Berkeley, CA: University of California Press.

Hochschild, A. R. (2016). *Strangers in Their Own Land: Anger and Mourning on the American Right*. New York: New Press.

Höijer, B. (2004). The discourse of global compassion: The audience and media reporting of human suffering. *Media, Culture & Society, 26*(4), 513–531.

Holbrook, D. (2020). Internal debates, doubts and discussions on the scope of Jihadi violence. *Perspectives on Terrorism, 14*(6), 77–90.

Horst, F. W. (2013). *Towards a Dynamic Analysis of Salafi Activism. Conclusions from a Dissection of Salafism in Germany*. Herzliya: International Institute for Counter-Terrorism.

House of Commons Debate. (1994, 31 March). Racism and Anti-semitism. Columns 1115–1120.

HT Britain. Media Information Pack. Retrieved from www.hizb.org.uk/hizb/images/PDFs/HT_media_pack.pdf [accessed 12 October 2017].

Hutchison, E. (2010). Trauma and the politics of emotions: Constituting identity, security and community after the Bali bombing. *International Relations, 24*(1), 65–86.

Hutchison, E. (2016). *Affective Communities in World Politics: Collective Emotions after Trauma*. Cambridge: Cambridge University Press.

Hutchison, E. & Bleiker, R. (2014). Theorizing emotions in world politics. *International Theory, 6*(3), 491–514.

Ismail, S. (2007). What is the Muslim Association of Britain? Retrieved from www.workersliberty.org/story/2007/03/15/what-muslim-association-britain [accessed 6 August 2018].

Jackson, R., Breen Smyth, M., & Gunning, J. (2009). *Critical Terrorism Studies: A New Research Agenda*. Abingdon: Routledge.

Jasper, J. M. (1998). The emotions of protest: Affective and reactive emotions in and around social movements. *Sociological Forum, 13*(3), 397–424.

Jasper, J. M. (2006). The study of emotion: An introduction. In S. Clarke, P. Hoggett, & S. Thompson (eds), *Emotion, Politics and Society* (pp. 3–30). Basingstoke / New York: Palgrave Macmillan.

Johnston, H. (2016). The mechanisms of emotion in violent protest. In C. Demetriou (ed.), *Dynamics of Political Violence* (pp. 27–50). London: Routledge.

Juergensmeyer, M. (2010). The global rise of religious nationalism. *Australian Journal of International Affairs, 64*(3), 262–273.

Karagiannis, E. & McCauley, C. (2006). Hizb ut-Tahrir al-Islami: Evaluating the threat posed by a radical Islamic group that remains nonviolent. *Terrorism and Political Violence, 18*(2), 315–334.

Kepel, G. (2000). Islamism reconsidered. *Harvard International Review, 22*(2), 22–27.

Kinnick, K. N., Krugman, D. M., & Cameron, G. T. (1996). Compassion fatigue: Communication and burnout toward social problems. *Journalism & Mass Communication Quarterly, 73*(3), 687–707.

Klandermans, B. & Mayer, N. (eds). (2006). *Extreme Right Activists in Europe: Through the Magnifying Glass.* Abingdon: Routledge.

Klausen, J., Barbieri, E. T., Reichlin-Melnick, A., & Zelin, A. Y. (2012). The YouTube Jihadists: A social network analysis of Al-Muhajiroun's propaganda campaign. *Perspectives on Terrorism, 6*(1), 36–53.

Koch, A. (2018). Trends in anti-fascist and anarchist recruitment and mobilization. *Journal for Deradicalization, 14*, 1–51.

Koehler, D. (2016). Right-wing extremism and terrorism in Europe. *Prism, 6*(2), 84–105.

Koschut, S. (2014). Emotional (security) communities: The significance of emotion norms in inter-allied conflict management. *Review of International Studies, 40*(3), 533–558.

Koschut, S. (2016). *Introduction to Edited Volume 'The Power of Emotions in World Politics'.* Paper presented at the DFG Research Network 'Constructivist Emotion Research', Berlin.

Koschut, S. & Oelsner, A. (2014). *Friendship and International Relations.* London/ New York: Palgrave.

Köttig, M., Bitzan, R., & Pető, A. (eds). (2017). *Gender and Far Right Politics in Europe.* Cham: Springer.

Krebs, R. R. (2015). How dominant narratives rise and fall: Military conflict, politics, and the Cold War consensus. *International Organization, 69*(04), 809–845.

Kristeva, J. (1980). *Desire in Language: A Semiotic Approach to Literature and Art.* New York: Columbia University Press.

Kruck, A. & Spencer, A. (2014). Vom 'Söldner' zum Samariter'? Die narrativen Grenzen strategischer Imagekonstruktion von privaten Sicherheitsdienstleistern. In W. Hofmann, J. Renner, & K. Teich (eds), *Narrative Formen der Politik* (pp. 145–167). Wiesbaden: Springer.

Kundnani, A. (2012). Radicalisation: the journey of a concept. *Race & Class, 54*(2), 3–25.

Kundnani, A. (2015). *A Decade Lost: Rethinking Radicalisation and Extremism.* London: Claystone.

Kydd, A. H. & Walter, B. F. (2006). The strategies of terrorism. *International Security, 31*(1), 49–80.

Lambert, R. (2008). Salafi and Islamist Londoners: Stigmatised minority faith communities countering al-Qaida. *Crime, Law and Social Change, 50*(1), 73–89.

Lebow, R. N. (2010). *Why Nations Fight: Past and Future Motives for War.* Cambridge: Cambridge University Press.

Lindekilde, L. (2014). A typology of backfire mechanisms. In L. Bosi, C. Demetriou, & S. Malthaner (eds), *Dynamics of political Violence: A Process-Oriented Perspective on Radicalization and the Escalation of Political Conflict* (pp. 51–69). Aldershot: Ashgate.

Lindemann, T. (2012). Vers l'identification empirique des dénis de reconnaissance dans les relations internationales. Le cas des attentats de Londres en 2005. In I. Sommier & X. Crettiez (eds), *Les dimensions émotionelles du politique* (pp. 209–224). Rennes: Presses Universitaires de Rennes.

Lindemann, T. (2014). *Towards a Synergy of Methods between International Relations and the Sociology of Mobilisations – The Study of Emotions in the London Bombings 2005*. Paper presented at the ECPR, Glasgow.

Llanque, M. (2014). Metaphern, Metanarrative und Verbindlichkeitsnarrationen: Narrative in der politischen Theorie. In W. Hofmann, J. Renner, & K. Teich (eds), *Narrative Formen der Politik* (pp. 7–29). Wiesbaden: Springer.

Lorimer, H. (2005). Cultural geography: the busyness of being 'more-than-representational'. *Progress in Human Geography, 29*(1), 83–94.

Luhmann, N. (1986). *Love as Passion: The Codification of Intimacy*. Cambridge, MA: Harvard University Press.

Lukács, G. (1971). *The Theory of the Novel: A Historico-Philosophical Essay on the Forms of Great Epic Literature*. Cambridge, MA: MIT Press.

Lundberg, V. (2020). 'The antifascist kick': A signifying cultural practice in the history of transnational antifascism? *Fascism, 9*(1–2), 272–287.

Lyotard, J.-F. (1984). *The Postmodern Condition: A Report on Knowledge*. Minneapolis, MN: University of Minnesota Press.

Mackie, D. M., Devos, T., & Smith, E. R. (2000). Intergroup emotions: Explaining offensive action tendencies in an intergroup context. *Journal of Personality and Social Psychology, 79*(4), 602–616.

Madriaza, P. & Ponsot, A.-S. (2015). *Preventing Radicalization: A Systematic Review*. Montreal: International Centre for the Prevention of Crime.

Mahmood, C. K. (2010). *Fighting for faith and nation: Dialogues with Sikh militants*. Philadelphia, PA: University of Pennsylvania Press.

Malik, S. (2004, September 13). For Allah and the caliphate. *New Statesman*. Retrieved from www.newstatesman.com/node/195114 [accessed 12 Ocotber 2017].

Malthaner, S. (2011). *Mobilizing the Faithful: Militant Islamist Groups and their Constituencies*. Frankfurt am Main: Campus Verlag.

Malthaner, S. (2014). Contextualizing radicalization: The emergence of the 'Sauerland-Group' from radical networks and the salafist movement. *Studies in Conflict & Terrorism, 37*(8), 638–653.

Malthaner, S. (2017). Radicalization: The evolution of an analytical paradigm. *European Journal of Sociology, 58*(3), 369–401.

Mandaville, P. (2007). *Global Political Islam*. London/New York: Routledge.

Marlier, G., & Crawford, N. C. (2013). Incomplete and imperfect institutionalisation of empathy and altruism in the 'responsibility to protect' doctrine. *Global Responsibility to Protect, 5*(4), 397–422.

Martin, R. & Barzegar, A. (eds). (2010). *Islamism: Contested Perspectives on Political Islam*. Stanford, CA: Stanford University Press.

Martini, A., Ford, K., & Jackson, R. (eds). (2020). *Encountering Extremism: Theoretical Issues and Local Challenges*. Manchester: Manchester University Press.

Meijer, R. (2009). *Global Salafism: Islam's New Religious Movement*. London/New York: Hurst & Co/Columbia University Press.

Mercer, J. (2014). Feeling like a state: Social emotion and identity. *International Theory, 6*(3), 515–535.

Meur, E. (2013). *Triangulation méthodologique et hybridation des techniques: Les clés du succès dans l'appréhension des épisodes émotionnels en relations internationales?* Paper presented at the 12th Congress of the French Political Science Association, Paris.

Moeller, S. D. (2002). *Compassion Fatigue: How the Media Sell Disease, Famine, War and Death.* London: Routledge.

Moghadam, A. (2017). *Nexus of Global Jihad: Understanding Cooperation among terrorist Actors.* New York: Columbia University Press.

Möller, P. (2016). Der Weg zur Generation Syrien – die Entwicklung des deutschen Dschihadismus. *Journal Exit-Deutschland. Zeitschrift für Deradikalisierung und demokratische Kultur, 3,* 34–46.

Mostov, J. (2012). Sexing the nation/desexing the body: Politics of national identity in the former Yugoslavia. In T. Mayer (ed.), *Gender Ironies of Nationalism. Sexing the Nation* (pp. 103–126). London: Routledge.

Murphy, F. (2011). Archives of sorrow: An exploration of Australia's stolen generations and their Journey into the Past. *History and Anthropology, 22*(4), 481–495.

Najmabadi, A. (1997). The erotic vaṭan [homeland] as beloved and mother: To love, to possess, and to protect. *Comparative Studies in Society and History, 39*(3), 442–467.

Nedza, J. (2014). 'Salafismus' – Überlegungen zur Schärfung einer Analysekategorie. In B. T. Said & H. Fouad (eds), *Salafismus. Auf der Suche nach dem wahren Islam* (pp. 80–105). Freiburg: Herder Verlag.

Nedza, J. (2015). The sum of its parts: The state as apostate in contemporary Saudi militant Islamism. In C. Adang, H. Ansari, M. Fierro, & S. Schmidtke (eds), *Accusations of Unbelief in Islam: A Diachronic Perspective on Takfir* (pp. 304–326). Leiden: Brill.

Neumann, P. R. (2008). *Joining al-Qaeda: Jihadist Recruitment in Europe.* London: Routledge.

Nussbaum, M. (1996). Compassion: The basic social emotion. *Social Philosophy and Policy, 13*(1), 27–58.

Ost, D. (2004). Politics as the mobilization of anger: Emotions in movements and in power. *European Journal of Social Theory, 7*(2), 229–244.

Pantucci, R. (2015). *'We Love Death As You Love Life': Britain's Suburban Terrorists.* Oxford: Oxford University Press.

Pape, R. A. (2006). *Dying to Win: The Strategic Logic of Suicide Terrorism.* New York: Random House.

Pargeter, A. (2013). *The Muslim Brotherhood: From Opposition to Power.* London: Saqi Books.

Passy, F. & Giugni, M. (2005). Récits, imaginaires collectifs et formes d'action protestataire. *Revue française de science politique, 55*(5), 889–918.

Pearlman, W. (2013). Emotions and the microfoundations of the Arab uprisings. *Perspectives on Politics, 11*(2), 387–409.

Pearson, B. Z. & de Villiers, P. A. (2005). Child language acquisition: Discourse, narrative, and pragmatics. In Keith Brown (ed.), *Encyclopedia of Language and Linguistics* (2nd edn) (pp. 686–693). Oxford: Elsevier.

Perry, D. L. (2018). *The Global Muslim Brotherhood in Britain: Non-Violent Islamist Extremism and the Battle of Ideas.* London: Routledge.

Petersen, R. D. (2002). *Understanding Ethnic Violence: Fear, Hatred, and Resentment in Twentieth-Century Eastern Europe*. Cambridge: Cambridge University Press.

Peterson, S. V. (1994). Gendered nationalism. *Peace Review, 6*(1), 77–83.

Pettman, J. J. (1996). Boundary politics: Women, nationalism and danger. In M. Maynard & J. Purvis (eds), *New Frontiers in Women's Studies: Knowledge, Identity and Nationalism* (pp. 187–202). London: Routledge.

PEW. (2005). Islamic extremism: Common concern for Muslim and Western publics. Retrieved from www.pewglobal.org/2005/07/14/islamic-extremism-common-concern-for-muslim-and-western-publics/ [accessed 1 December 2018].

PEW. (2009). Little support for terrorism among Muslim Americans. Retrieved from www.pewforum.org/2009/12/17/little-support-for-terrorism-among-mus lim-americans/ [accessed 1 December 2018].

PEW. (2011). Muslim Americans: No signs of growth in alienation or support for extremism. Retrieved from www.people-press.org/2011/08/30/muslim-amer icans-no-signs-of-growth-in-alienation-or-support-for-extremism/ [accessed 1 December 2018].

Pfahl-Traughber, A. (2015). Salafismus – was ist das überhaupt? Retrieved from www.bpb.de/politik/extremismus/radikalisierungspraevention/211830/salafis mus-was-ist-das-ueberhaupt [accessed 20 October 2015].

Pfeifer, H. & Spencer, A. (2019). Once upon a time: Western genres and narrative constructions of a romantic jihad. *Journal of Language and Politics, 18*(1), 21–39.

Phillips, R. (2008). Standing together: The Muslim Association of Britain and the anti-war movement. *Race & Class, 50*(2), 101–113.

Pisoiu, D. (2015). Subcultural theory applied to jihadi and right-wing radicalization in Germany. *Terrorism and Political Violence, 27*(1), 9–28.

Polletta, F. (2006). *It Was Like a Fever: Storytelling in Protest and Politics*. Chicago, IL: University of Chicago Press.

Prince, G. (1982). *Narratology: The Form and Functioning of Discourse*. Berlin: Mouton.

Propp, V. (1984). *Theory and History of Folklore*. Minneapolis, MN: University of Minnesota Press.

Propp, V. (2010). *Morphology of the Folktale*. Austin, TX: University of Texas Press.

Quent, M. (2016). *Rassismus, Radikalisierung, Rechtsterrorismus*. Basel: Beltz Juventa.

Rabatel, A. (2008). *Homo narrans: Pour une analyse énonciative et interactionnelle du récit*. Limoges: Éditions Lambert-Lucas.

Resende, E. S. A. & Budryte, D. (eds). (2014). *Memory and Trauma in International Relations: Theories, Cases, and Debates*. London: Routledge.

Reus-Smit, C. (2014). Emotions and the social. *International Theory, 6*(3), 568–574.

Richardson, L. (2006). *What Terrorists Want: Understanding the Enemy, Containing the Threat*. New York: Random House.

Ricoeur, P. (1984). *Time and Narrative*. Chicago, IL: University of Chicago Press.

Riessman, C. K. (2008). *Narrative Methods for the Human Sciences*. New York: Sage.

Ringmar, E. (2006). Inter-texual relations: The quarrel over the Iraq War as a conflict between narrative types. *Cooperation and Conflict, 41*(4), 403–421.

Rodgers, K. (2010). 'Anger is why we're all here': Mobilizing and managing emotions in a professional activist organization. *Social Movement Studies, 9*(3), 273–291.

Roex, I. (2014). Should we be scared of all Salafists in Europe? A Dutch case study. *Perspectives on Terrorism, 8*(3), 51–63.

Ross, A. A. G. (2014). *Mixed Emotions: Beyond Fear and Hatred in International Conflict.* Chicago, IL: University of Chicago Press.

Ross, A. A. G. (2006). Coming in from the cold: Constructivism and emotions. *European Journal of International Relations, 12*(2), 197–222.

Roy, O. (1996). *The failure of political Islam.* Cambridge, MA: Harvard University Press.

Rydell, R. J., Mackie, D. M., Maitner, A. T., Claypool, H. M., Ryan, M. J., & Smith, E. R. (2008). Arousal, processing, and risk taking: Consequences of intergroup anger. *Personality and Social Psychology Bulletin, 34*(8), 1141–1152.

Safran, W. (2008). Language, ethnicity and religion: A complex and persistent linkage. *Nations and Nationalism, 14*(1), 171–190.

Said, B. T. (2014). *Islamischer Staat: IS-Miliz, al-Qaida und die deutschen Brigaden.* München: Beck.

Said, B. T. & Fouad, H. (2014). *Salafismus: Auf der Suche nach dem wahren Islam.* Bonn: Bundeszentrale für Politische Bildung.

Sakwa, R. (2012). Conspiracy narratives as a mode of engagement in international politics: The case of the 2008 Russo-Georgian War. *The Russian Review, 71*(4), 581–609.

Sangar, E., Clément, M., & Lindemann, T. (2018). Of Heroes and cowards: A computer-based analysis of narratives justifying the use of force. In M. Clément & E. Sangar (eds), *Researching Emotions in International Relations* (pp. 179–206). London/New York: Palgrave Macmillan.

Sartre, J.-P. (1956). *Being and Nothingness* (H. E. Barnes, Trans.). New York: Philosophical Library.

Sasley, B. E. (2011). Theorizing states' emotions. *International Studies Review, 13*(3), 452–476.

Schedler, J. (2017). Die extreme Rechte als soziale Bewegung. In F. Virchow, M. Langebach, & A. Häusler (eds), *Handbuch Rechtsextremismus* (pp. 285–323). Wiesbaden: Springer.

Schiffauer, W. (2010). *Nach dem Islamismus: Eine Ethnographie der Islamischen Glaubensgemeinschaft Milli Görüş.* Frankfurt am Main: Suhrkamp.

Schlag, G. (2018). Moving images and the politics of pity: A multi-level approach to the interpretation of images and emotions. In M. Clément & E. Sangar (eds), *Researching Emotions in International Relations* (pp. 209–230). London/New York: Palgrave Macmillan.

Schmid, A. P. (2011). Glossary and acronyms on terrorism and counter-terrorism. In A. Schmid (ed.), *The Routledge Handbook of Terrorism Research* (pp. 598–706). London: Routledge.

Schmid, A. P. (2013). Radicalisation, de-radicalisation, counter-radicalisation: A conceptual discussion and literature review. *The International Centre for Counter-Terrorism Research Paper,* 1–91.

Schneiders, T. G. (ed.) (2014). *Salafismus in Deutschland: Ursprünge und Gefahren einer islamisch-fundamentalistischen Bewegung.* Bielefeld: transcript Verlag.

Schreier, M. (2014). Qualitative content analysis. In U. Flick (ed.), *The Sage Handbook of Qualitative Data Analysis* (pp. 170–183). London/Thousand Oaks: Sage.

Schuurman, B. & Taylor, M. (2018). Reconsidering radicalization: Fanaticism and the link between ideas and violence. *Perspectives on Terrorism, 12*(1), 3–22.

Searle, J. R. (1992). *The Rediscovery of the Mind*. Cambridge, MA: MIT Press.

Seger, C. R., Smith, E. R., Kinias, Z., & Mackie, D. M. (2009). Knowing how they feel: Perceiving emotions felt by outgroups. *Journal of Experimental Social Psychology, 45*(1), 80–89.

Seidensticker, T. (2014). *Islamismus: Geschichte, Vordenker, Organisationen*. München: Beck.

Shane, S. & Mekhennet, S. (2010, May 8). Imam's path from condemning terror to preaching jihad. *The New York Times*. Retrieved from www.nytimes.com/2010/05/09/world/09awlaki.html [accessed 5 December 2018].

Sheets-Johnstone, M. (1999). Emotion and movement: A beginning empirical-phenomenological analysis of their relationship. *Journal of Consciousness Studies, 6*(11–12), 259–277.

Shenhav, S. R. (2006). Political narratives and political reality. *International Political Science Review, 27*(3), 245–262.

Shoshan, N. (2016). *The Management of Hate: Nation, Affect, and the Governance of Right-Wing Extremism in Germany*. Princeton, NJ: Princeton University Press.

Simcox, R., Stuart, H., Ahmed, H., Murray, D., & Carlile, A. (2011). *Islamist Terrorism: The British Connections* (2nd edn). London: The Henry Jackson Society.

Sinclair, K. (2010). *The Caliphate as Homeland: Hizb ut-Tahrir in Denmark and Britain*. (PhD), Odense: University of Southern Denmark.

Sjoberg, L. (2009). Feminist interrogations of terrorism/terrorism studies. *International Relations, 23*(1), 69–74.

Sluka, J. A. (2009). The contribution of anthropology to critical terrorism studies. In R. Jackson, M. B. Smyth, & J. Gunning (eds), *Critical Terrorism Studies. A New Research Agenda* (pp. 138–155). London/New York: Routledge.

Smith, D. (2018). So how do you feel about that? Talking with Provos about emotion. *Studies in Conflict & Terrorism, 41*(6), 1–17.

Smith, E. R., Seger, C. R., & Mackie, D. M. (2007). Can emotions be truly group level? Evidence regarding four conceptual criteria. *Journal of Personality and Social Psychology, 93*(3), 431–446.

Spelman, E. V. (2001). *Fruits of Sorrow: Framing our Attention to Suffering*. Boston, MA: Beacon Press.

Spencer, A. (2016). *Romantic Narratives in International Politics: Pirates, Rebels and Mercenaries*. Manchester: Manchester University Press.

Sprinzak, E. (2009). Rational fanatics. *Foreign Policy*. Retrieved from https://foreignpolicy.com/2009/11/20/rational-fanatics/ [accessed 25 October 2016].

Staemmler, D. (2017). Der Wandel der extremen Rechten in Europa. *Forschungsjournal Soziale Bewegungen, 30*(2), 228–230.

Steinberg, G. (2014). *Al-Qaidas deutsche Kämpfer: Die Globalisierung des islamistischen Terrorismus*. Hamburg: edition Körber-Stiftung.

Stenersen, A. (2008). The internet: A virtual training camp? *Terrorism and Political Violence, 20*(2), 215–233.

Taji-Farouki, S. (2000). Islamists and the threat of jihad: Hizb al-Tahrir and al-Muhajiroun on Israel and the Jews. *Middle Eastern Studies, 36*(4), 21–46.

Tellidis, I. & Toros, H. (eds). (2015). *Researching Terrorism, Peace and Conflict Studies*. Abingdon: Routledge.

Thoits, P. A. (2004). Emotion norms, emotion work, and social order. In A. S. R. Manstead, N. Frijda, & A. Fischer (eds), *Feelings and Emotions: The Amsterdam Symposium* (pp. 359–378). Cambridge: Cambridge University Press.

Thompson, S. (2006). Anger and the struggle for justice. In S. Clarke, P. Hoggett & S. Thompson (eds), *Emotion, Politics and Society* (pp. 123–144). Basingstoke/New York: Palgrave Macmillan.

Tomashevsky, B. (2002). Story, plot, and motivation. In B. Richardson (ed.), *Narrative Dynamics: Essays on Time, Plot, Closure, and Frames* (pp. 164–178). Columbus, OH: The Ohio State University Press.

Toolan, M. (2001). *Narrative: A Critical Linguistic Introduction*. London: Routledge.

Torres Soriano, M. R. (2012). Between the pen and the sword: The global Islamic media front in the West. *Terrorism and Political Violence, 24*(5), 769–786.

Traïni, C. (2009). *Émotions … Mobilisation!* Paris: Les Presses de Sciences Po.

Tsintsadze-Maass, E. & Maass, R. W. (2014). Groupthink and terrorist radicalization. *Terrorism and Political Violence, 26*(5), 735–758.

Van Rythoven, E. (2015). Learning to feel, learning to fear? Emotions, imaginaries, and limits in the politics of securitization. *Security Dialogue, 46*(5), 458–475.

Van Rythoven, E. & Solomon, T. (2019). Encounters between affect and emotion: Studying order and disorder in international politics. In E. Van Rythoven & M. Sucharov (eds), *Methodology and Emotion in International Relations: Parsing the Passions* (pp. 133–151). Abingdon: Routledge.

van Stekelenburg, J. (2017). Radicalization and Violent Emotions. *PS: Political Science & Politics, 50*(4), 936–939.

Vidino, L. (2009). Homegrown jihadist terrorism in the United States: A New and Occasional Phenomenon? *Studies in Conflict & Terrorism, 32*(1), 1–17.

Vidino, L. (2010). *The New Muslim Brotherhood in the West*. New York: Columbia University Press.

Vidino, L. (2015). Sharia4: From confrontational activism to militancy. *Perspectives on Terrorism, 9*(2), 2–16.

Vohs, K. D., Baumeister, R. F., & Loewenstein, G. (eds). (2007). *Do Emotions Help or Hurt Decisionmaking? A Hedgefoxian Perspective*. New York: Russell Sage Foundation.

von Scheve, C. (2012). Emotion regulation and emotion work: Two sides of the same coin? *Frontiers in Psychology, 3*, 496, 1–10.

Wagemakers, J. (2012). *A Quietist Jihadi: The Ideology and Influence of Abu Muhammad al-Maqdisi*. Cambridge: Cambridge University Press.

Wazir, B. (2002, 24 February). Essex boys sign up for 'holy war'. *The Observer*. Retrieved from www.theguardian.com/uk/2002/feb/24/religion.september11 [accessed 3 November 2016].

Weinberg, L. & Perliger, A. (2010). How terrorist groups end. *CTC Sentinel, 3*(2), 16–17.

Welland, J. (2015). Compassionate soldiering and comfort. In L. Åhäll & T. Gregory (eds), *Emotions, Politics and War* (pp. 115–128). London: Routledge.

Wendling, M. (2001, 21 September). UK Islamic Group, banned from campus, claims misrepresentation. *CNSNews.com*. Retrieved from https://web.archive. org/web/20011122202951/www.cnsnews.com/ViewPrint.asp?Page=%5CFo reignBureaus%5Carchive%5C200109%5CFor20010921g.html [accessed 3 November 2016].

Whine, M. (2003). Al-Muhajiroun: The portal for Britian's suicide terrorists. Retrieved from https://ict.org.il/al-muhajiroun-the-portal-for-britians-suicide-terrorists/ [accessed 11 July 2017].

Whine, M. (2006a). Is Hizb ut-Tahrir changing strategy or tactics? *Center for Eurasian Policy Occasional Research Paper, I*(1), 1–11.

Whine, M. (2006b). Will the ban on Al Muhajiroun successor groups work? Retrieved from https://ict.org.il/will-the-ban-on-the-al-muhajiroun-successor-groups-work/ [accessed 11 July 2017].

White, H. (1987). *The Content of the Form: Narrative Discourse and Historical Representation*. Baltimore, MD: Johns Hopkins University Press.

Wibben, A. T. (2011). *Feminist Security Studies: A Narrative Approach*. London: Routledge.

Wiedl, N. (2014a). Außenbezüge und ihre Kontextualisierung und Funktion in Vorträgen ausgewählter salafistischer Prediger in Deutschland. In *IFSH ZEUS Working Paper 7*. Hamburg: IFSH.

Wiedl, N. (2014b). Geschichte des Salafismus in Deutschland. In B. T. Said & H. Fouad (eds), *Salafismus: Auf der Suche nach dem wahren Islam* (pp. 411–441). Bonn: bpb.

Wiedl, N. (2017). *Zeitgenössische Rufe zum Islam: Salafistische Da'wa in Deutschland 2002–2011*. Baden-Baden: Nomos.

Wiedl, N. & Becker, C. (2014). Populäre Prediger im deutschen Salafismus: Hassan Dabbagh, Pierre Vogel, Sven Lau und Ibrahim Abou Nagie. In T. G. Schneiders (ed.), *Salafismus in Deutschland. Ursprünge und Gefahren einer islamisch-fundamentalistischen Bewegung* (pp. 187–215). Bielefeld: transkript Verlag.

Wiktorowicz, Q. (2005). *Radical Islam Rising: Muslim Extremism in the West*. Lanham, MD: Rowman & Littlefield.

Wiktorowicz, Q. (2006). Anatomy of the Salafi movement. *Studies in Conflict & Terrorism, 29*(3), 207–239.

Wiktorowicz, Q. & Kaltenthaler, K. (2006). The rationality of radical Islam. *Political Science Quarterly, 121*(2), 295–319.

Wittgenstein, L. (1958). *Philosophical Investigations* (G. E. M. Anscombe, Trans.). New York: Macmillan.

Wolf, R. (2015). Emotionen in den internationalen Beziehungen: Das Beispiel Ressentiments. In K.-R. Korte (ed.), *Emotionen und Politik: Begründungen, Konzeptionen und Praxisfelder einer politikwissenschaftlichen Emotionsforschung* (pp. 187–212). Baden-Baden: Nomos.

Wolf, R. (2018). Political Emotions as Public Processes: Analyzing Transnational Ressentiments in Discourses. In M. Clément & E. Sangar (eds), *Researching Emotions in International Relations* (pp. 231–253). London/New York: Palgrave Macmillan.

Wright-Neville, D. & Smith, D. (2009). Political rage: Terrorism and the politics of emotion. *Global Change, Peace & Security, 21*(1), 85–98.

Index

Note: 'n.' after a page reference indicates the number of a note on that page

Milton Keynes UK
Ingram Content Group UK Ltd.
UKHW020634010823
426108UK00004B/42

9 781526 167699